Essays on Latin American Security

The Collected Writing of a Scholar-Implementer

By

Russell W. Ramsey, Ph.D., D.Min

for Fred Smith –

Edited by
Celeste W. Bennett

Soldier, patriot, friend and classmate USMA 1957 with highest regards

Russ Ramsey

© 2003 by Russell W. Ramsey, Ph.D. All rights reserved.

No part of this book may be reproduced, stored in a retrieval system, or transmitted by any means, electronic, mechanical, photocopying, recording, or otherwise, without written permission from the author.

ISBN: 1-4033-9894-1 (e-book)
ISBN: 1-4033-9895-X (Paperback)
ISBN: 1-4033-9896-8 (Dustjacket)

Library of Congress Control Number: 2002096825

This book is printed on acid free paper.

Printed in the United States of America
Bloomington, IN

1stBooks - rev. 01/21/03

**Dedicated to
General Alvaro Valencia Tovar
Colombian Army**

- Friend and Mentor
- the greatest soldier
Scholar of the 20th century

CONTENTS

I. Contents iii

    QUIZ ON LATIN AMERICA xiii

II. Setting 1

    "World Systems, Challenges: 1993-2025," Reserve Officers Association National Security Report, *The Officer*, April, 1993 1

    "LATIN AMERICA: The European Canon and the Black Legend," Lecture at Key Auditorium, St. Johns College, October 29, 1999. 4

    Reviews of: *The Wealth of The World and the Poverty of Nations*, by Daniel Cohen, Cambridge: M.I.T. Press, 1998; and *The Wealth and Poverty of Nations*, by David Landes, New York: Norton Publisher, 1998. Reviewed in: *Journal of Comparative Strategy*, 1999 19

    Review of: *Made by the USA: The International System*, by Alex Roberto Hybel, New York: Palgrave-St. Martin's Press, 2001. Reviewed in: *Parameters, Journal of the US Army War College*, Summer, 2002. 22

    "Strategic Reading on Latin America," Review Essay, *Parameters, Journal of the US Army War College*, Summer, 1994 24

    "Strategic Reading on Latin America: 1995 Update," *Parameters, Journal of the US Army War College*, Winter, 1995-1996 29

    "Strategic Reading on Latin America: Long on Quality, New Rumbles from the Left," *Parameters, Journal of the US Army War College*, Winter, 1996-1997 36

    "Strategic Reading on Latin America, 1998 Update," *Parameters, Journal of the US Army War College*, Spring, 1998. 43

    "Latin America: A Booming Strategic Region in Need of an Honest Introductory Textbook," *Parameters, Journal of the US Army War College*, Spring, 1999. 50

    "Strategic Reading on Latin America," Review Essay, *Parameters, Journal of the US Army War College*, Spring, 2000. 56

"Strategic Reading on Latin America," Review Essay, *Parameters, Journal of the US Army War College*, Winter, 2000-2001. 60

"War and Its Aftermath: New Writing on Latin America," *Parameters, Journal of the US Army War College*, Spring, 2002. 64

Strategic Reading on Latin America: Economic, Political, & Military.............67

III. U.S. Policy 72

"United States Security Assistance Influence in Latin America – the Unheralded Treasure," Lecture at the *Civil Society and Security Issues for the 21st Century Conference,* Western Hemisphere Institute for Security Cooperation, Ft. Benning, Georgia, November 28 – 30, 2001........................72

"US Strategy for Latin America," *Parameters, Journal of the US Army War College*, Autumn, 1994. 76

Review of: *Eisenhower: The Foreign Policy of Anti-Communism and Latin America*, by Stephen G. Rabe, Chapel Hill, N.C.: University of North Carolina Press, 1988. Reviewed in: *Military Intelligence*, April-June, 1989. 91

Reviews of: *Sharing the Secrets: Open Intelligence and the War on Drugs*, by J.F. Holden-Rhodes, Westport, CT: Praeger Publishers, 1997; and *Drugs And Security in the Caribbean: Sovereignty Under Siege*, by Ivelaw Lloyd Griffith, University Park, PA: Pennsylvania State University Press, 1997. Reviewed in: *Strategic Review*, Spring, 1998. 93

"Reading Up On the Drug War," Review Essay, *Parameters, Journal of the U.S. Army War College*, Autumn, 1995. 97

Review of: *Cocaine Politics: Drugs, Armies and the CIA in Central America,* by Peter Dale Scott and Jonathan Marshall, Berkeley, CA: The University of California Press, 1991. Reviewed in: *Military Review*, April, 1992. 102

"The U.S. Andean Counter-Narcotics Initiative," *Military Review*, Hispanic Edition, May-June, 1991. 104

IV. Caribbean and Central America 107

Review of: *Conflict, Peace, and Development In The Caribbean,* by Jorge Rodríguez Beruff, J. Peter Figueroa, and J. Edward Greene, Eds, St.

Martin's Press, New York, 1991. Reviewed in: *Marine Corps Gazette*, December, 1993.. 107

"Analysis of the US-Mexican Border: A Strategic Literature Yet to Come," *Parameters, Journal of the US Army War College*, Autumn, 1997.. 108

Reviews of: *Cien Biografías de Militares Distinguidos*, by Brig. Gen. Mario Perez Torres, Mexican Government Press, 1988; *Generals in The Palacio: The Military in Modern Mexico*, by Roderic Ai Camp, Oxford University Press, 1992; and *Cuban Leadership After Castro: Biographies of Cuba's Top Commanders*, by Rafael Fermoselle, U. of Miami North-South Centre, 1992. Reviewed in: (British) *Army Quarterly & Defence Journal*, April, 1994. 110

"The Bolivian Diary of Ernesto Che Guevara," *Hispanic American Historical Review*, November, 1996.. 111

"On Castro and Cuba: Rethinking the Three Gs," Review Essay, *Parameters, Journal of the US Army War College*, Winter, 1994-1995. 113

"Strategic Writing on Cuba," Review Essay, *Parameters, Journal of the US Army War College*, Winter, 2001-2002. 117

Review of: *Fidel Castro*, by Robert E. Quirk, New York: Norton Publisher, 1993. Reviewed in: *North-South*, February-March, 1994. 121

Review of: *Operation ANADYR: U.S. and Soviet Generals Recount the Cuban Missile Crisis*, by Gen. Anatoli I. Gribkov and Gen. William Y. Smith. Edition q, Inc., NY, 1992. Reviewed in: *Army*, September, 1994...... 122

Review of: *Eyeball to Eyeball: The Inside Story of the Cuban Missile Crisis*, by Dino A. Brugioni, New York: Random House, 1992. Reviewed in: *Army*, November, 1992.. 124

"Castro's Cuba: Insular Immutability Amid Winds of Change," *Journal of Defense and Diplomacy*, April, 1990. 126

Review of: *Cuba's Foreign Policy in The Middle East*, by Damian J. Fernández, Boulder: Westview Press, 1988. Reviewed in: *Naval War College Review*, Spring, 1990... 131

Review of: *The Secret War in Central America: Sandinista Assault on World Order*, by John Norton Moore, Frederick, MD: University

Publications of America, 1987. Reviewed in: *The Friday Review of Defense Literature*, March 11, 1988. 133

"Cuba and Mexico: Profiles in 1994," (British) *Army Quarterly & Defence Journal*, April, 1994. 136

"Invasion: A Small Step in a Long Process," *Army Times*, November 12, 1994. 140

Review of: *Learning from Conflict: The US Military in Vietnam, El Salvador, and the Drug War*, by Richard Duncan Downie, Westport, CT: Praeger Publishers, 1998. Reviewed in: *Military Review*, January, 2000. 143

Review of: *Nicaragua v. United States: A Look at the Facts*, by Robert F. Turner, McLean, VA: Pergamon-Brassey's, 1987. Reviewed in: *Naval War College Review*, Autumn, 1988. 145

"Civil-Military Relations in Guatemala: What the Literature Reveals," *Military Review (Hispanic Edition)*, March-April, 2002. 147

Review of: *We Answer Only to God: Politics and the Military in Panama, 1903-1947*, by Thomas L. Pearcy, Albuquerque, NM: Univ. of New Mexico Press, 1998. Reviewed in: *Hispanic American Historical Review*, August, 1999... 150

Review of: *Panamá and the United States: The Forced Alliance*, by Michael L. Conniff, Athens, GA: The Univ. of Georgia Press, 1992. Reviewed in: *Military Review*, March, 1993.. 152

Review of: *Operation Just Cause: The Storming of Panamá*, by Thomas Donnelly, Margaret Roth and Caleb Baker, New York: Lexington Books, 1992. Reviewed in: *Army*, July, 1992. 154

"Keeping Peace with the Panama Canal," *Journal of Defense & Diplomacy*, December, 1986... 156

"Panama Today: The West Should Help," (British) *Army Quarterly & Defence Journal*, July, 1989... 159

"The Rough Rider Legacy: SUPERCOP in Panamá," *Journal of Defense and Diplomacy*, April, 1988.. 163

V. Colombia: A Case Model.. 167

"Insecurity and Violence in Colombia," *Military Review*, July – August, 1999. 167

"U.S. Commits Money, Military to Drug War," *Columbus Ledger-Enquirer*, Sunday, November 19, 2000. 172

Review of: *Mayo del 68: Una Razon Historica*, by Jesus Antonio Rodriguez, Santafé de Bogotá: Oficina de Publicaciones Universidad Distrital, Francisco José de Caldas, 1995. Reviewed in: *Hispanic American Historical Review*, February, 1997. 176

Review of: *Testimonio de una Epoca Años Signados por el Conflicto en el que han Vivido Inmersos el Estado y la Sociedad Colombianos Bajo el Rotulo de la Violencia. [Testimony of an Epoch: Years Marked by the Conflict in Which the State and Colombian Society Have Lived Immersed under the Banner of 'The Violence']*, by General Alvaro Valencia Tovar, Bogotá: Editorial Planeta, 1992. Reviewed in: *Military Review Hispanic Edition*, November-December, 1992. 178

"US Narcotics Addiction Wrecks Colombian Democracy," (British) *Army Quarterly & Defence Journal*, January, 1990. 180

"Internal Defense in the 1980s: The Colombian Model," *Journal of Comparative Strategy*, Winter, 1984. 185

James D. Henderson's Review of: *Zarpazo de Bandit: Memoirs of an Undercover Agent of the Colombian Army*, by Evelio Buitrago Salazar, University of Alabama Press, 1977. Reviewed in: *Hispanic American Historical Review*, November, 1978. 198

"The Colombian Battalion in Korea and Suez," *Journal of Inter-American Studies*, October, 1967. 199

VI. European Influence... 220

"The Spanish Military Orders," (British) *Army Quarterly & Defence Journal*, July 1983. 220

"The Defeat of Admiral Vernon at Cartagena in 1741," *The Southern Quarterly*, July, 1963 223

"German Espionage in South America, 1939-45," (British) *Army Quarterly & Defence Journal*, January, 1988. 240

"The Third Reich's Third Front," *Military Review*, December, 1987. 244

VII. Revolution and Guerrilla Warfare 250

    Review of: *Guerrillas and Revolution in Latin America,* by Timothy P. Wickham-Crowley, Princeton, New Jersey: Princeton University Press, 1992. Reviewed in: (British) Army *Quarterly & Defence Journal*, July, 1994. 250

    Review of: *Latin American Revolutionaries: Groups, Goals, Methods*, by Michale Radu and Vladimir Tismaneau, a Foreign Policy Institute Book, Washington D.C.: Pergamon-Brassey, 1990. Reviewed in: *Military Intelligence*, April-June, 1991. 252

    Review of: *Will It Liberate? Questions About Liberation Theology*, by Michael Novak, New York, NY: Paulist Press, 1986. Reviewed in: *Journal of InterAmerican Studies and World Affairs*, Winter, 1987-1988 253

    Review of: *Guerrillas: The Men and Women Fighting Today's Wars*, by Jon Lee Anderson, Times Books, 1993. Reviewed in: *Army*, August, 1993 255

    "Neo-Marxism Rides the Black Legend," *Journal of Low Intensity Conflict & Law Enforcement,* Winter, 1997 256

VIII. US - Latin American Military Relations 263

    "The Role of Latin American Armed Forces in the 1990s," *Strategic Review*, Fall, 1992. 263

    "US Military Courses for Latin Americans are a Low-Budget Strategic Success," *North-South*, February-March, 1993 274

    "A Military Turn of Mind: Educating Latin American Officers," *Military Review*, August, 1993 278

    Review of: *Hemispheric and U.S. Policy in Latin America*, Edited by August Varas, Boulder, Colorado: Westview Press, 1989. Reviewed in: *International Freedom Review*, Summer, 1990. 288

    "Training Latin American Forces," *Journal of Defense and Diplomacy*, April, 1988. 292

    "World Needs School of the Americas," *The Albany Herald*, March 20, 1995 302

"Human Rights Instruction at the US Army School of the Americas," *Human Rights Review,* April-June, 2001.* 305

"Military Leaders and the Warrior's Code," *Military Review (Hispanic Edition),* May – June, 1994 327

"Assembly's Call to Close School of the Americas Challenged," *The Presbyterian Layman*, September-October, 1994 332

"The US Army School of the Americas & the Presbyterian Church," 1st Presbyterian Church, Americus, Georgia, Wednesday Night Supper, September 29, 1999. 335

"Affective Education and Values Transference, the US Army School of the Americas," *Journal of Resources Management,* Spring, 1997. 337

"Military & Police Roles in Latin American Sustainable Development," *Dialogo, The Forum of the Americas*, April-June, 1999. 341

"The Democratic Sustainment Course at the US Army School of the Americas," *Dialogo, The Forum of the Americas,* Fall, 2000. 344

Review of: *Security Cooperation in the Western Hemisphere: Resolving the Ecuador-Peru Conflict*, by Gabriel Marcella and Richard Downes, Boulder, CO: Lynne Rienner, 1999. Reviewed in: Parameters, *Journal of the US Army War College,* Winter, 1999-2000. 349

About the Author 351

QUIZ ON LATIN AMERICA*

(answers on p. xiv)

1. From 1830 until 1935, how many wars occurred between the countries of Latin America?

    a. 21
    b. 14
    c. 2
    d. 9

2. In which Western Hemisphere country is this the box score on Presidents?

    10% murdered while in office
    12% survived an assassination attempt
    25% failed to complete elected term
    25% first became important as a general

    a. Argentina
    b. Mexico
    c. United States of America
    d. El Salvador

3. Since 1830, which of the following world regions has had the lowest percentage of its males serving in the armed forces and/or police?

    a. Eastern Europe/Russia
    b. Sub-Saharan Africa
    c. Latin America
    d. Middle East.

4. During the Cold War, the United States provided military assistance programs to foreign countries, and also engaged in the sale of weapons to foreign countries. Which of the following pairs of numbers expresses the correct percentage of military assistance and weapons sales that went from the U.S.A. to Latin America?

    a. 48% of all military assistance, 34% of arms sales
    b. 19% of all military assistance, 23% of arms sales
    c. 2% of all military assistance, 4% of arms sales
    d. 11% of all military assistance, 10% of arms sales

5. Which pair of Latin American regimes had armed forces ranked in the Top 25 of the world by percent of males in uniform?

xiii

    a. Batista's regime in Cuba/Somoza's regime in Nicaragua
    b. Perón's regime Argentina/Varga's regime in Brazil
    ✓c. Castro's regime in Cuba/Ortega's regime in Nicaragua
    d. Noriega's regime in Panama/Rojas Pinilla's regime in Colombia

6. Which famous political philosopher wrote publicly that Simón Bolívar, the Liberator of Andean America, was a buffoon?

    a. Adam Smith
    b. Alexis de Tocqueville
    ✓c. Karl Marx
    d. Thomas Jefferson

7. Which of the following countries had the largest number of armed forces personnel operating outside its own national boundaries and within sub-Saharan Africa: 1981-1989?

    a. Republic of South Africa
    b. United States of America
    ✓c. Cuba
    d. Union of Social Socialist Republics

8. Which famous political figure expressed strong hope that the United States would quickly defeat Mexico in late 1846, then annex Mexico and Central America right on down to the Isthmus of Panama?

    ✓a. William Gladstone
    b. Napoleon III
    ⓒ Karl Marx
    d. Charles Darwin

9. Who invaded Mexico in 1864 and imposed an Austrian Archduke as Emperor?

    a. United States of America
    b. Prussia
    d c. France
    d. Great Britain

10. How many wars have been fought between the countries of Latin America since 1935?

    a. 14
    b. 11
    ⓒ 1
    ✓d. 9

xiv

i* The correct answer to all 10 questions is "c."

SETTING

"World Systems, Challenges: 1993-2025," Reserve Officers Association National Security Report, *The Officer*, April, 1993.

"What national security strategy now should the West pursue?" is the question being asked. Everything from "keep the big stick" to "pass out the peace dividend" is being offered by politicians, intellectuals, and columnists.

National security professionals must begin the "what policy/strategy now?" exercise by examining a paradigmatic array of likely world systems, and next by determining a logical spectrum of challenges, threats, and destabilizers. Policy and strategy options can then flow logically with coherence.

The Tri-Polar Economic World replaced the Bi-Polar Political World in 1989, and it will define power well into the 21st century. Its components are, in descending order, the North American Free Trade Alliance (NAFTA); the European Community (EC '92); and the Pacific Rim Constellation. Their respective power components, until 2025, may be ranked.

Power	Economic	Political	Military
NAFTA	1	1(tie)	1
EC '92	2	1(tie)	2
PAC RIM	3	3	3

Each giant in the triad has sub-constellations, some of these shared. For example, South America links to NAFTA, EC '92, and PAC RIM, in that order, while Islamic North Africa links mostly to EC '92.

The Two-Plus-Ten Military World is an arguable alternative, especially in view of Russian strategic rocket and submarine forces, which exist almost undiminished, while the US giddily devalues its strategic margin.

The "Ten" in this array are the regional powers, selected for regional military impact, not on a descending world military power scale. The "Ten" are, at present: Europe-Germany, France, and the United Kingdom; Asia-China, India, and South Korea; Middle East-Israel and Iran; Latin America-Brazil; Africa-Republic of South Africa.

Obviously, Ukraine, Cuba, Nigeria, Egypt, North Korea, Japan, Pakistan, Iraq and others would find advocates for inclusion, making the paradigm less clean but more durable.

The central idea is that there still are two military superpowers with global projection (the US and Russia), and an array of regional military powers with varied inter-regional projection.

Although the former East-West Power World died politically in 1989, its old paradigmatic rival, the North-South Economic World, is pragmatically alive. It is a by-product of Alfred Sauvey's 1952 First World, Second World, Third World triad, a scheme that still appears in much international relations literature.

Little more than an intellectual parlor game at its inception, Sauvey's paradigm was wildly outdated by the late 1960s and should now be allowed to expire quietly, and not to be confused with an arguably valid North-South Economic World array.

The Northern Constellation is a longitudinal arc stretching from Tokyo across the southern US to London, thence eastward to Warsaw. The Southern Constellation is the Group of 77, abandoned now by a few neo-giants from its original ranks and no longer able to spout with impunity the heady doctrines of neo-Marxist exploitation with supporting cheers from Moscow and Havana.

The central notion in this array, however, remains the Southern Constellation's complaint that their lesser economic development is the fruit of unjust Northern Constellation policy.

Crossing political, economic, and military parameters with abandon is the Theologically Determinist World. Major components are: Protestant Christendom; Roman Catholic Christendom; Sunnite Islam; Shiite Islam; Pacific Islam; Marxist-Leninist Communism; Eastern Orthodox Christendom; Maoist-Leninist Communism; and loose constellations amid the global imprints of Africa's Animism, South Asia's Hinduism, mainland Asia's Buddhism/Confucianism, Southeast Asia's lesser Buddhism, and the Pacific Rim's Shintoism.

Obviously, this paradigm is difficult to conceptualize, and yet threads of political, economic, and military power do, to some degree, track religious alignment. Also, Communism, viewed as a state religion, rates a sector in the calculus and competes for influence against older deistic faith systems.

The Mixed Paradigm World merits consideration. A single issue, say, access to minerals or regional pan-ethnic tension, can define itself within the political, economic, and military triad, and cross-paradigmatic alignments then arise. Thus, there could be, in a period, unification of economic interests with a religious interest, resulting in an altered military calculus. The 1990-1991 Persian Gulf War showed these tendencies.

The largest challenge to world peace, 1989-2025, is Regional Ethnic Conflict, the 200 vs. 4,000 Scenario. Since the 1648 Treaty of Westphalia, nation-states, a Western invention, have directed the world.

They are historically defined as global units of land and people having sovereignty, identified borders and population, acknowledged government, accepted themes of national unity, and functional economy.

While there are about 180 such nation-states in 1993, arguably 200 by the early 2000s, there already existed by 1989 some 4,000 ethnic minorities who do not accept their present nation-state affiliation. Rabid pan-Serbianism, in 1993, covets land in Bosnia and Croatia; comparable pan-Kurdish militancy envisions a kingdom composed of land in five existing nation-states; and French separatists in Canada's Quebec crave autonomy. Non-acceptance of the nation-state fuels perhaps 20 armed conflicts in 1993 and is the greatest threat to world peace until 2025.

The second most likely challenge to world peace is Arms and Engineers for Hire. This syndrome arises from the confluence of three chilling trends: a flood of arms and weapons experts now available from the former USSR, contract-hungry Western arms producers, and the crescendo of regional conflict.

The Tri-Polar Economic World lacks the political and military control mechanisms to restrain this syndrome; indeed, both the Tri-Polar Economic World paradigms, if anything, fuel the arms-cum-engineers-for-cash traffic.

The third most likely cause of world conflict is Regional Pariah Regimes. Prototypical are Panama's Manuel Noriega, Iraq's Saddam Hussein, North Korea's Kim Il Sung, and Serbia's Slobodan Milosevic.

Their support rests upon a mixture of perceived economic deprivation, national political ineptitude, and fantasy material. The ability of these regimes to initiate and sustain armed conflict is heavily dependent upon, and intertwined with, Regional Economic Conflict, and Arms and Engineers for Hire. Mass ideological movements are a factor but lack the determinative force seen in the Cold War, 1947-1989.

The fourth major cause of world conflict is the Focused Economic Grievance Syndrome. Generalized economic conflict, long predicted and advocated by Marxists, is not sustainable. But a single, focused economic issue can be both catalyst and sustaining force behind substantive conflict.

Among these focused economic grievances are famine; control of a valuable natural resource; tariffs and government subsidies; environmental destruction or depletion; contraband marketing; and exploitation of a public fiscal issue, e.g., taxation, corruption, or budget allocation. This syndrome is easily tied to the previous three, and greatly exacerbated by any achievable intermix. The post-Cold War world probably has the same prevalence of flash points as the pre-World War I world, and 1914 was the starting point of generalized or linked multi regional conflict.

Further, the post-Cold War world has nearly five times the population competing for depleting resources, plus mass communication via which to transmit calls to arms and global transport via which to project military power. Yet, on balance the world is probably less conflict prone in 1993 than in 1914.

Mechanisms for arms control, collective security alliances, and the spread of political democracy with privatized economies all militate toward less probable conflict. So does the rise in technically competent, constitutionally obedient armed forces in many regions.

Yet, the ability of a submerged ethnic group to take advantage of the arms flood under the leadership of a rabid power figure suggests a very tough armed challenge to a world oriented on economic polarities.

A permanent World Peacekeeping Force under the United Nations Security Council just might by 2025, become the workable antidote. Such a force would have to be linked to a Security Council and a world of nations more functionally educated about the trade-offs between absolute national sovereignty and early U.N. intervention to avert the start and spread of armed conflict.

Russell W. Ramsey, Ph.D., D.Min.

"LATIN AMERICA: The European Canon and the Black Legend," Lecture at Key Auditorium, St. Johns College, October 29, 1999.

Introduction

Nineteen republics of the Hispano-Luso-Indo-Afro heritage share the Western Hemisphere with the United States and Canada. Collectively, they form the world's most culturally homogenous block, and they possess some rather remarkable characteristics not often heard, especially in academic circles. As a region, they possess the world's longest history of stable borders, have historically devoted the lowest percentage of their treasure to military uses, and are the world's only block that is treaty free of nuclear-toxic-biological weapons. They were the biggest early block of countries to support the United Nations, formed the Organization of American States before the United Nations was born, opposed both Fascism and Communism consistently, and provided, since 1989, the largest per stripes share of United Nations peacekeepers. They are generally the world's model for rapid democratization and privatization in the post-Cold War era. Like the United States and Canada, the Iberian Americas share the western canon with a powerful indigenous heritage, and with an African heritage as well. Yet upon this region, which has no active wars and accounts for ten percent of the U.S. dollar's value, we, their powerful northern neighbor and often their political and economic role model, heap a systematic and almost transcendental scorn.

The Task at Hand

It shall be my task here to outline that portion of Latin American civilization which stems from the Western canon and suggest something of its blending with indigenous and other immigrant cultures. I shall then briefly examine some differences in the United States' own hybrid version of the Western canon. Third, I shall review a particularly lamentable component of North American culture which may be called the "Black Legend," la leyenda negra. (in Spanish) regarding Latin America, and last I shall suggest some future trajectories for our fast evolving Hemisphere. It shall be my admittedly controversial proposition here that many of the U.S. scholars who claim to have devoted their working lives to the moral vindication of Latin American civilization have actually manifested the worst of the "Black Legend" attitude, namely that the region is innately violent, undemocratic, and in need of rescuing by external forces.

Latin America has passed through four periods of historiographical interpretation by scholars in the United States and Western Europe, and arguably, since 1989, has entered a revisionist wind tunnel.

Washington Irving and William H. Prescott, minions of Early National U.S. history writing, created the heroic conqueror image and, incidentally, the first window into the great historical documents by which North American scholars could study their southern neighbors meaningfully. Irving's sabbatical in Spain in the late 1820s resulted in biographies of Christopher Columbus, Ferdinand and Isabella, and several hero figures of the conquest. Prescott's *Conquest of Mexico* (1843) and the *Conquest of Peru* (1847) set the tone literarily for the heroics of the conquest.

A Euro-centric interpretation prevailed until the early twentieth century, when Herbert Eugene Bolton authored the "one hybrid Americas" interpretation. Influenced by Frederick Jackson Turner's 1907 publication, *The Influence of the Frontier in American History*, which ended forever the notion of the United States as a transplanted England with more land, Bolton visualized the borderlands of the southwestern United States as an amalgam of Iberian and Native American culture, known then as the Indian heritage. Latin America, he hypothesized, answered to similar historical determinants. This paradigm made it possible to analyze Latin America's huge racial amalgam, non-existent in North American history: the recognition of a legitimate *mestizo* Latin America was the product. This hybrid *mestizo* Latin America was referred to as being racially Indo-Ibero and became the basis for studies on the contributions of the Incas of Peru, the Aztecs of Mexico, the Mayas of Central America, and the Chibchas of Colombia to the modern countries bearing those names.

The advent of President Franklin D. Roosevelt's "Good Neighbor Policy" in 1933 accompanied a third wave of historiographical perspective, the concept of the "Americas as a Common Heritage" articulated so well by giant historians like the late Professor Lewis Hanke. This view gave rise to optimistic projections of democracy blooming as a universally shared value throughout the Western Hemisphere, a perspective we now believe to have held the roots of validity but which was somewhat exaggerated by its proponents in terms of actualization. It was this rose-tinted view of Latin America that was to come crashing down in the second half of the Cold War.

The 1960s saw the bitterest and most sweeping historiographical revision ever accorded by U.S. scholars to a developing world region, the angry rejection of the "Americas en route to democracy and prosperity" myth and the adoption of the neo-Marxist view. Princeton University's Professor Stanley Stein, at his Presidential Inaugural Lecture to the Conference of Latin American History in 1960, announced that constitutional democracy and free market economics were dead in the Latin American region, and that revolutionary processes were inevitable if democracy and economic justice were ever to be created. This, of course, was precisely what Fidel Castro was proclaiming before the world with telling effectiveness via the newly discovered mass medium of television. Never in my view did so many scholars leap so foolishly, nor so embark upon a bandwagon so faddishly precarious in nature and so manifestly incorrect. The concept held that Latin America was a hopelessly backward region, controlled totally by its own armed forces and police, exploited mercilessly by its own greedy entrepreneurs working in cahoots with vicious U.S. commercial giants, and governed irresponsibly by a class of demagogues who were selected, approved, and sustained in office by the U.S. Department of State and the

Pentagon. I shall devote more attention to this massive collapse in rational academic judgment, which I believe to have been both intellectually dominant and intellectually ridiculous from 1960 until 1989.

The collapse of the Soviet Union in 1989 and 1990 was accompanied by a collapse of both Marxist proxy forces in Latin America and of brutal anti-communist regimes created to prevent or limit the predatory conduct of those Marxist elements within Latin America. The locus of intellectual research, influence, and paradigmatic creativity shifted from the traditional disciplines like history, political science, anthropology, and sociology to a different locus on many college campuses, this being the colleges of business administration and commerce. Bluntly put, the specialists from the traditional theoretical academic fields who study Latin America had kicked the football so far out of the stadium that the analytical work of business administration professors, once scorned as Wall Street baggage and proof of academic complicity with economically predatory evil, has risen to pre-eminence in the study of Latin America. Thus, we find Paul C. Roberts' and Karen LaFollette Araujo's 1997 book *The Capitalist Revolution in Latin America*, and John Williamson's 1990 book *Latin American Adjustment: How Much Has Really Happened?* competing well in the college bookstore with James D. Cockcroft's Marxist introduction to the region, a 1997 update called *Latin America: History, Politics, and U.S. Policy*. Ten years ago, the neo-Marxist interpretive canon would have gone largely unchallenged at the bookstall and elsewhere.

The Western Canon in Latin America

What things, then, comprise the central core of the Western canon in Latin America? The impetus to conquer and convert or banish infidels in God's name is a by-product of the Reconquest of Spain in the 14th and 15th centuries by the Catholic kings. Yet it has a solid Biblical foundation, even if it became distorted into an ultra-nationalistic vehicle for Spanish conquest.

Transmitted through an omni-present church came the doctrines beyond the purely military conquest, namely the catechizing of non-Christians by missionary efforts, this from Genesis 12, John 21, and Acts 2. Spain's machinery for missionary projection was arguably the greatest institutionalized ecclesiastical force in history, spearheaded by the regular orders such as the Augustinians, the Benedictines, the Dominicans, and the Franciscans. Some of this heroic projection may be seen with historical honesty in the Academy Award and Cannes Film Festival Award winning 1986 film "Mission," with Jeremy Irons portraying the committed Jesuit missionary.

Having established the evangelical zeal with which both religious doctrine and Spanish civil authority were disseminated in the Western Hemisphere, it would be well to name exactly what theodicy underlay the effort. Central to all of it is an unyielding belief in the Trinity, the amalgam of God the Father, the Son, and the Holy Spirit, articulated and defended successfully by Athanasius before the Councils of Nicea and Alexandria against the Arian Heresy in the 4th century.

Directly supporting this Credal concept is the notion of the Monarch as God's earthly steward of the Kingdom, seen in the Old Testament as the Royal lineage of David and continued by Roman Emperors starting with Constantine in the early 4th century. A stern doctrinal orthodoxy and a huge institutional hierarchy protected this theodicy from external intrusions and internal heresies.

After theological certainty, mandate for military conquest, and evangelical intensity, in order of importance, came the Spanish commitment to re-create Peninsular civilization and institutions of government, church, and commerce. The layout of towns, the administration of districts and municipalities, and the role of armies and police, all came from the second half of the Roman Empire as it was institutionally configured in the colonies that became the nation-state known as Imperial Spain.

The literary trail for this mix of institutions and ideas about governance is summed up best in Justininian's Code of 534 AD, with much of its fabric interwoven between church and state. The outcome of these values was to transform what was initially a dual culture – Ibero-Americans with Indo-Americans – into a linguistically homogenous, Catholicized society. An example of how Spanish monarchs applied the western canon to their American Empire is seen in the great influence of Julius Caesar's *Gallic Wars*, and the heroic monarch biographies in *Plutarch's Lives*, on Philip II. At the formative stage, in the late 1500s, Philip explicitly forced into existence such Roman civic ideas as the lingua franca – one standard unifying language – a legitimate tool of governance by God's earthly prince, and the universal Catholicizing of the non-believers as the justification for the Empire.

A transcendental concept making all this to work out was the relationship between Church and State established by Ambrose of Milan in 390, when he succeeded in forcing the Emperor Theodosius I to kneel in public and seek penance from the Church, penance for having ordered the massacre of 7,000 citizens at Thessalonica in reprisal for the killing of seven policemen. Bear in mind that this concept meant the moral transcendency of the Roman Catholic Church over the Catholic Monarchs of Spain and was often disputed in application, as may again be seen in that excellent 1986 film "Mission." Ambrose baptized a young African convert from Manicheanism in 386, and this man became known as Augustine, Bishop of Hippo, author of *De Civitata Dei*, completed in 426 in Latin. Known to history as *The Heavenly City*, this work enumerates in some detail the five conditions under which the Christian nation-state may conduct war, a subject we will visit again. But two of the conditions – the existence of the just and Christian monarch, and the principle of proportionality between moral responsibility and levels of civil authority – were extremely influential in founding Latin America. One reads much of inhumane attitudes and acts on the part of the viceroys appointed for Peru; for New Spain, which became Mexico; for New Granada, which became four Andean republics; and for La Plata, which became Argentina. The historical picture needs to be placed in balance with studies, say, on viceroys such as Antonio de Mendoza and Francisco de Toledo, who founded educational institutions and orphanages, ordered reviews of public authority figures, limited the depredations of the Inquisition, and generally applied these lofty Augustinian principles with power and grace. The depredations and cruelty of the early *conquistadores* such as Hernan de Cortez in Mexico and Franscisco Pizarro in Peru reflect more the fact that the early conquerors were not professional soldiers, but rather adventurers and temporary anti-Islamic crusaders from the Reconquest of Spain against the Moors.

With a theological base in the canon somewhat established, we can examine the enduring spiritual climate that was stamped on this region, first by military force and then by one of the world's largest missionary conversion programs ever carried out. The name Ariel is a good symbol to work with, for it touches several cultures and historical periods. Ariel was the lion-like man in 2 Samuel 23:20 and I Chronicles 11:22. In the Book of Ezra 8:16, Ariel is a priestly intercessor for Israel, and in Isaiah, the name identifies a city punished for the great sin which David, the King, once committed there. Around 1607, William Shakespeare borrowed him as a sprite delivered by Prospero for "The Tempest," and John Milton made him a fallen angel in "Paradise Lost," (1665), all this at a time when Miguel de Cervantes was creating visions who tempted the would-be knight errant Don Quixote in Golden Age Spain.

Quixotic sprites, in fact, helped Cervantes get away with satirizing the heroic behavior myths among the Spanish nobility at the same time that these myths were taking root among the colonial administrators and the entrepreneurial class within the American colonies. In 1900, the Uruguayan poet and novelist Jose Emilio Rodo pilloried the United States in his novel *Ariel*, in which the grossly materialistic character Caliban represented the greedy Colossus of the North, and Ariel was the sprite who represented the essential spirituality of Latin America. This symbolism would roar onto the Hemispheric political scene again in 1960, in ways never anticipated.

Spirituality was definitely the central issue in colonial Latin America when Bartolome de las Casas gave up an entrepreneurial role in the early Spanish colonies to take priestly orders, confront the mighty Hapsburg monarchy over the mistreatment of the indigenous natives, and secure better treatment for countless thousands of helpless wretches confined to an early death via servitude in the silver mines.

Dubbed the "Apostle of the Indies," las Casas' record as a humanitarian is brave but checkered, yet he established for Latin America a legitimate, authentic, and significant human rights tradition long before any European emigrants occupied the United States. Las Casas' courageous attack on the machinery of empire included the doctrines of the Christly commandant of brotherly love, the admonitions on this and other doctrines by the Apostle Paul (Titus 1:7-12 is a good example), and the writings of Augustine and Ambrose on kingship.

The Aristotelian worldview, passed through multiple lenses of the Roman Catholic Church, is the place to look for an understanding of the Latin American mind, once the Iberian culture was dominant. One recalls that early Christian harmonization of the eschatological Jesus of Nazareth with Greek philosophy was launched by the Apostle Paul and carried forward by Origin, Justin Martyr, and other Platonists and neo-Platonists. When the armies of militant Islam over-ran

Christian cities with document collections, these documents passed into the hands of such Islamic theologians as Averroes of Cordoba in the 12th century, thence to influence such Christian theologians as Peter Abelard and, most importantly, Thomas Aquinas at Paris. Thonust philosophy and syllogistic methodology became the dominant intellectual mode for Latin America and co-exist today with 20th century intellectual main currents.

Strong elements of the Mediterranean version of the Enlightenment also came across to Latin America. One sees it in the humanistic writings of the 17th century Mexican poet, a nun called Sor Juana Inez de la Cruz. She was heralded as the "Tenth Poet of the World" by the monarch at Vienna during the high age of Baroque. Latin American Enlightenment influence, however, is more artistic than political; it is seen in several churches with glorious golden altars, in paintings, and in a literature that resides now mostly in college courses.

Because we have the benefit of historical hindsight, it is pertinent now to become eclectic and choose two applied values that have affected Latin American politics and economics from earliest colonial times.

The first one is the concept of the *fuero militar*. Meaning literally "the military institution as a law unto itself," the concept is really the medieval European guild concept in the context of the army and the police, the word "guild" being *gremio* in Spanish. In medieval Europe, wherever the hand of the Roman Empire had laid down its imprint, workers banded together by vocational identification to form powerful societal units. They blocked outside competition, guaranteed monopolistic control of sales for their members, and cared for the members literally as a state within the state. Was the daughter of a shoemaker violated by another shoemaker? The Shoemakers' Guild would conduct the trial and punish the guilty member. Was this daughter orphaned at an early age? The Guild would see her raised in a shoemaker family, and, were she a boy instead, apprenticed to a shoemaker at an early age. The external institutions of statehood scarcely penetrated this social system, and within the Hispanic world, both soldiers (*militares*) and police (*serenos* or *vigilantes*) followed the guild model. But given that soldiers and police are accorded monopolistic control over the legitimate means of force within the realm of the just Christian monarch, how big a jump is there between the internal policing of these groups to regulate the behavior of their members, and violations of the rights of citizens and the sovereignty within the body politic? Of this material, given the weak civilian institutions of government that existed following the final defeat of the Spanish Imperial forces in 1830, was born the Latin American tradition of deliberative armies, that is to say armies whose generals have a voice and a legitimate role in deciding who may govern and how.

Strengthening this tradition was the heritage of three orders of soldier-priests who spearheaded the defeat of the Moors in Spain during the Reconquest, these orders being Alcantara, Calatrava, and Santiago. Even though nationalized by Ferdinand and Isabella to help create one central army and church for the newly unified nation-state called Spain, the *conquistadores* of Latin America were steeped in the traditions of the soldier-priest, with a mixed holy and military mission. Hernan Cortes, the conqueror of Mexico, was a Knight Commander in the honorific

Order of Santiago, and his soldiers sometimes spotted St. James the Lesser (James is *Jaime,* in Spanish, the name of the Order) mounted on his white horse amidst the battles against the Aztec hordes. To put the matter in balance, the three orders of soldier-priests began institutional life as social guardians and colonizers within Spain. The Latin American military forces would continue this tradition in modern times through the mechanism of military intervention in times of political crisis, humanitarian assistance during natural disasters, and useful civic action such as construction in the rural areas, sometimes controversial because elected civilians were not necessarily making the decisions for resource allocation. Never far from the surface, in any analysis of this applied institutional value, was the Romano-Hispanic view of the chief executive as God's Prince, divinely appointed to rule the earthly city.

The other applied concept of note here is the Romano-Hispanic view on the stewardship of earthly resources. Gold returned to the Crown had spiritual value because it enriched the Crown to do God's work on earth. Nobles and entrepreneurs chartered to capture, exploit, or create resources were doing this work in God's name. Never far below the surface were Jesus' own personal admonitions in the synoptic Gospels about the good steward, about Joseph's role as Pharaoh's honest and faithful steward. The emphasis lies upon the amassing and accounting for the resources. The Board of Trade (*Casa de Contratacion*) at Cadiz after 1503 often had more to say about daily colonial life in Latin America than the Royal Council at Madrid, the capital. The monarch, who was God's Prince, was the steward of all riches: all wealth redounded to the glory of God. Entrepreneurship by individuals, such as that seen in ancient Phoenecia and Athens, carried little weight in this system. God would provide those resources as needed for the taking by Christians and to His greater glory. The borrowing of money, that necessary act for the expansion of the economy through the vehicle of the corporation, was a venal sin; did not the Jews, in fact, loan money for profit? And had not these same Jews of the Old Dispensation executed Jesus of Nazareth? So this second concept, the institutionalization of the monarch as God's economic agent in the name of the people, was deeply seated and powerful.

Finally, one shines a light upon the other cultures, internal and external, which formed in sum the canon that became Latin American life and culture. The indigenous nations were in fact late Bronze Age civilizations, pagan empires steeped in animistic religions and, to some degree, polytheism. Scholars have done little analytical work on how so small a force of Spaniards, enjoying a technological margin of advantage so narrow, could defeat these empires with their huge military forces. In some ways, one might find an analogy with the occasional stinging defeats which the Israelites inflicted on their Babylonian, Egyptian, and Assyrian neighbors, who had much larger forces. After the conquest, those pockets of indigenous people who remained were strongly controlled by Spanish civil and ecclesiastical administrators, one may again visit the 1986 film "Mission" to see Mozart's music produced on woodwind instruments crafted in the upper Amazonian rain forest by the Guarani nation.

Another way to examine the canonic presence of native Americans and imported Africans upon Latin America is the default system; what things did these people yearn to do that they could not demand to do when they occasionally succeeded in rebelling? And this question has an answer in Spanish, the word being *indinenismo*, loosely translated as "indigenism," "nativism," or the celebration of those cultural manifestations which the indigenous people might want to do. One sees traces of these values in today's struggle in southern Mexico, the Chiapas rebellion; in northern Guatemala, the *indio* movement; and in Peru, in parts of the *Sendero luminoso* (Shining Path) movement. The summation of it is a partially irrational yearning for old customs and values to coexist successfully with the technologically modernist and post-modernist societies that have surrounded them and passed them by. And African culture in Latin America, heavily focused in the Caribbean area, never passed through the cruel racial experience in which the African was property and not human. Latin American slavery was more like indentured servant-hood and passed from the scene in a manner more benign and more civil by a wide margin than the North American experience.

The Latin American colonial canon, then, was complicated and truncated by the later arrivals of Adam Smith's *laissez faire* economics, John Locke's views on constitutional government, Jean Jacques Rousseau's romantic view of natural rights, Jeremy Bentham's "pain and pleasure" paradigm, August Comte's positivism, Karl Marx's dialectical materialism, and the neo-Marxist re-makes of this canon as dependency theory and armed liberation theology. *Laissez faire* economics entered the world scene at the time of the North American rebellion against Britain, when Latin America was still undergoing the effects of the Bourbon dynasty's reforms. These, coupled with traditional Catholic theology on stewardship and money-lending, translated into minimal penetration of entrepreneurship as a philosophy. Similarly, Lockean views on the contract between citizen and government had to compete against Hispanic/Catholic ideas on the Monarch as God's Prince. Locke's three-branch government with executive, legislative, and judicial functions gave way to the Spanish heritage, which included these three plus the fiscal steward and the designated administrator for the executive. Rousseau's views on natural rights were influential but lacking in defined structure, and always at odds with the Thomist worldview.

Benthamist utilitarianism had its Latin American adherents but lost out badly to the inherent spirituality that underlay all regional thinking. Comte's positivism had its adherents in Poffirio Diaz' Mexico and in Brazil during the 1870s, where the somewhat gentler force of Portuguese Catholicism stamped upon that Latin American giant gave in somewhat to positivism's claim to be a scientific order of universality.

Marxism arrived in Latin America in the late 1920s and was weak because the sweaty, blue collar labor force to whom it appealed was relatively small. Neo-Marxism, while blending the spirituality of Ariel with the under-dog militancy propounded by the Argentine revolutionary Ernest "Che" Guevara, was always a recent European import fashionable among the radical intelligentsia sector with little grass roots membership. The super-imposition of neo-Marxism upon older processes such as statist economics and praetorian militarism during the Cold War proxy struggles in Latin America brought back many themes from the Black Legend. These themes acted out in North America and Western Europe, to which we next turn our attention. Even as Fidel Castro struggles to keep his hybrid Marxist experiment afloat, the post-constructionists are trying to put their whimsical spins on Latin America. To do this, they employ floods of wordy ideological speculation and not much quantifiable evidence, nor any syllogistically verifiable paradigm. Against the recent challenges of both neo-Marxism and post-constructionism, I purport here that the ideas of Adam Smith and John Locke, thoroughly inter-mixed with long and honorably executed elements of Latin America's own authentic canon, are going to guide the region rather successfully in the coming century.

Some North American Differences

It is not my task here to evaluate the North American canon, but rather to lay out eclectically those things which are different from the Latin American canon, and then to connect those differences to perceptions of Latin America in the United States. I shall be arbitrary and very specific.

British-American colonials challenged the concept of the King as God's designated Prince, in 1776, at a fairly high minority level, and by the Revolutionary War's end, at a strong majority level. British colonial Americans enjoyed a higher degree of freedom in political and economic life, sometimes called a salutary neglect, than did Latin Americans. British regular army troops in colonial North America were not very numerous, and, when employed, were often disliked and even hated. Local militia units, by contrast, were popular and socially important. In Latin America, Crown troops were not numerous but were seen as legitimate, while local militias were weak. In North America, there existed a well-honed British custom and doctrine by which military and naval commanders both sought and obeyed the orders of the chief civilian executive. In colonial Latin America this was the case, but during the Latin American Wars for Independence, which lasted for twenty years and were much more bloody than in North America, vested civilian authority crumbled and only the military structure survived as a viable public institution. In British North America, the notion of *posse comitatus* was understood to mean that army troops defend the borders, while police guarantee internal order. Literally, the expression means "power of the county" and evolved in long struggles between the nobles and the office of King's High Sheriff in medieval England. In post-independence Latin America there remained the old tradition of the soldier-priests from the Orders of Alcantara, Calatrava, and Santiago, which merged army and police roles. Newly empowered rural politicians in early national Latin America learned to employ military factions for short term power struggles, giving rise to the concept of *caudillismo*, or civilian power figures in Napoleonic garb enjoying some kind of military backing. Would-be *caudillos* in the United States, by contrast, often had names like Andrew Jackson, and they followed the model of George Washington, who chose to delineate a northern European Enlightenment concept of strict separation between the armed forces and the civilian executive with his strong personal example.

In North America, the three branches of government delineated in the Constitution worked out well, whereas in Latin America the hurly-burly politics of the caudillos and the Romano-Spanish notion of the fiscal auditor and the local administrator continued to muddy the waters of democratic governance. The inviolability of the electoral process took root in North America and was codified in North American life.

The African-American, in North American democratic life, would go three centuries and finally have to resort to special legislation to secure this right. The ballot box did not take root as a necessity for free government in Latin America until recent times, but Latin America never has had a systematic denial of full personhood inflicted on one certain racial group. While church and state were never totally separated in North American life, the Latin American church-state relationship came much closer to the theocratic-state model until recently. This is a direct result of the fact that Latin America is nearly two centuries older than North America, and that its Enlightenment canon is the Mediterranean Enlightenment, not the northern European Enlightenment with its powerful strand of Rene Descartes' influence. The Church's influence in the United States became, by historical practice, the imparting of civic morality rather than the wielding of specified authority, another manifestation of our different canon drawn from the north European Enlightenment. 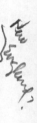 While the greater separation between church and state in the United States left room for many to enjoy a spiritually intensive life, it would be accurate to say that spirituality in Latin America has carried historically a higher order of personal importance. While economic success brought many advantages and many morally admirable dimensions to the United States, it also produced a materialistic outlook which caused Jose Emilio Rodo to characterize the Colossus of the North as Caliban always winning out in power struggles with Ariel who symbolized Latin America.

The United States became the world's most visible crucible for the validity of Adam Smith's *laissez faire* economics and John Locke's system of government by constitutional accord between citizen and state. As Latin America entered the 20th century, the countries there increasingly turned away from the Iberian Peninsula and toward their North American neighbor for a mentor and role model, even though that mentor took military action on their sovereign soil thirty-seven times under the imprimatur of regional order or national security issues. And it is in this context of maturation under the extra-Hemispheric threat, called collectively the Cold War, that the old Black Legend, with new manifestations. The Black Legend was created in Elizabethan England as a way to whip up nationalistic sentiment against the Spanish Armada. Oliver Cromwell fortified it with vicious racial and religious attacks against the Spanish character. Early U.S. figures like George Washington's half-brother Lawrence, President John Quincy Adams, and the statesman Henry Clay all showed respect for Latin America, but the Black Legend strand was always there for opportunistic politicians to use. Thus, recruits were gotten for the War with Mexico, 1846-1848, by appealing in New England to the need for disempowering the dirty Spanish heritage there. Karl Marx opined in an editorial that progressive American workmen should march right on down to Panama and then keep control of the region. Men who volunteered with enthusiasm for the Cuban War of 1898 saw no hypocrisy in volunteering to free Cuba from Spanish cruelty, and later viewing Cuba as a political cesspool in need of extended occupation and total management from without.

The era of the Good Neighbor, 1933 through the end of World War II, saw efforts made by scholars to temper the Black Legend with the notion that Latin America was moving slowly and inexorably but differently towards full constitutional democracy. In their enthusiasm, they overdid it a little. During the early Cold War period, fear of "another Red China in the back yard" propelled men like Secretary of State John Foster Dulles and his brother, CIA Director Allen Dulles, to carry out clumsy interventions in several Latin American social conflicts. The worst case was Guatemala in 1954, totally unjustified by any real threat of Soviet intervention there. Here, we saw conservatives using the Black Legend; they thought they could prop up the militaries, under the praetorian concept already discussed, and block out communist activity. In 1961, came the Kennedy doctrine of counter-insurgency, humane and totally compatible with Augustine's Just War theory as a system of internal defense. The doctrines were effective in Colombia, Bolivia, and Peru, to name a few examples. But in the 1970s, ugly civil wars on the South American continent pitted communist terrorists against state-sponsored terrorism in the name of anti-communist, counter-insurgency doctrine, in reality a French Algerian concept that freely advocated the preemptive killing of citizens identified with the radical left. In the 1980s, Fidel Castro assisted the Sandinista revolutionary socialist regime in Nicaragua in their program to destabilize neighboring El Salvador, Honduras, and Guatemala. In El Salvador, the Army conducted bloody campaigns of reprisal against suspected sympathizers with Marxist insurgents. Fidel Castro mounted a highly effective campaign that identified the Latin American military forces as the true enemy of democracy, and which posited his own social revolutionary doctrines as vehicles to genuine liberation. Ernesto "Che" Guevara is the chief apostle of this movement, the perfect Ariel figure wrapped in the liberationist camouflage fatigue uniform. All of this was accompanied by an economic theory of dependency and a politicized religious theory of liberation theology. Economic dependency, expounded in 1974 by Fernando Cardozo, has now been abandoned by its own original apostle, as he is currently the democratically elected President of Brazil and a strong supporter of free trade reforms. Dependency economics assumes that the Latin Americans are too economically inept to be the masters of their own destiny in the creation and distribution of wealth. Liberation theology, a highly respected doctrine based upon Jesus' compassion for the poor expressed in Luke 4:18-23, preached by giants like Bishop Gustavo Gutierrez of Peru, is distorted by secular Marxist intellectuals into a justification for armed guerrilla warfare. This idea re-opens the old Donatist heresy condemned by the Council of Nicea in 325 AD and by Pope John Paul II in 1991 and 1993. Theologically, this doctrine assumes that Jesus of Nazareth can be separated from the Trinity and made into a guerrilla warfare hero figure, the 4th

century Greek concept here being homo-ousous, or Jesus apart from the Trinity in place of homo-iousous, or Jesus subsumed into the Trinity.

To carry off their intellectualized sleight-of-hand, the neo-Marxists, who are predominantly Caucasian North Americans and Europeans, have resurrected the worst of the old Black Legend. Latin Americans, in their view, are too weak, too lazy, and too incompetent to function in the modern world; so the neo-Marxists have set about liberating the region from oppression. These Latin Americans, they believe, need to have their armed forces and police destroyed, then their governments and economic sectors, all to be replaced by some unidentified amorphous group known to them as "the people." It is a tired, oft repeated doctrine that has failed where tried again and again. No analyst thinks that North Korea, China, or Cuba, the world's most prominent holdouts for Marxist doctrines, are really functioning on Marxist principles. Hundred of analysts, academic and otherwise, have concluded that Latin America is moving on its own set of authentic trajectories towards some kind of position within the new world economy, the neo-liberal economic posture, and that democratization is occurring at a blinding pace. And when all is said and done, the region since 1830 has had the lowest proportion of its resources and manpower devoted to military use, two percent (2%) in both cases, of any world region.

Some Future Trajectories

Predicting the future of a major world region based upon its cultural canon is a whimsical and highly unscientific effort. Nevertheless, we have examined some powerful and enduring main currents here, and it would be worth the game to look for patterns.

The first pattern is that no major cultural trajectory within Latin America was very predictable at the time it began. Who, watching the Incas or the Aztecs the year 1500, would have predicted the relative ease with which a few thousand Spaniards would overcome their huge military formations? And who would have predicted the relative docility with which they underwent Hispanicization and Catholicization?

Nevertheless, once those hybrid cultures were in place, and the African minorities added to the mix, one might have seen the powerful blend of stability and flexibility in their make-up. That fact that they were not industrialized states was seen as weakness when their linguistic and religious homogeneity should have been seen as stability factors. The fact of military interference in government should have been seen in terms of a historical context granting considerable legitimacy to the armed forces as deliberative institutions with an accepted role in social stability. The fact that the Latin American region has by far the fewest wars between its nation-states, and by far the least financial and human resources devoted to warfare and military affairs, should have been seen as an indicator that the region is not and never has been hopelessly mired in militarism. The fact of Spain's once great stature in European affairs, and of the Incas' and the Aztecs' once great prominence in the Western Hemisphere, should have been read as a signal of great and capable populations going through a process of merger and re-orientation, not as a signal of endemic regional weakness.

There are two enormous errors of perception and interpretation regarding Latin America within North America that I consider to be both damaging and inexcusable. The first is the continuation of the Black Legend regarding the people of Latin America by patronizing North Americans. The second is an error which connects to the first one, namely the invalid notion that Latin Americans answer to Marxist and neo-Marxist dynamics. Given the extensive moral foundations that underlie Latin American culture, the idea that the region would need to be rescued from its own military, political, and economic leaders ranges somewhere between the intellectually ridiculous and the arrogantly preposterous.

What factors will tend to debilitate Latin America's otherwise promising adaptation to post Cold War main currents in neo-liberal economics and democratization? One is the drug war, which corrupts and destabilizes with cruel effectiveness. U.S. drug users sent $1.2 billion to Colombia alone in 1990 to purchase illegal hallucinogenic narcotics, mainly cocaine and its derivatives. By 1998, that annual sum of mayhem-producing dollars had reached $6.2 billion, claiming the lives of one Colombian soldier or police officer each day, and seven to ten Colombian civilians per day. The U.S. Senate is still mumbling darkly about different escape formulas by which to blame Colombians for the drug plague that did not exist in their country twenty years ago, and which is an explicit assault on Colombian sovereignty and their national existence. Colombia is the region's longest continuously functioning two party democracy and supported the United Nations efforts in Korea and in the Sinai, thereby earning universal world respect.

A second potential show stopper for Latin America's otherwise bright future would be that their North American neighbors choose to continue the past tendency to make east-west alliances, and to ignore the north-south axis of common interests. The simple fact is that east-west strategic fascination in the United States has produced two bloody wars in Europe and three wars in Asia. Simple analysis of cultures would show that the Latin Americans share most of the early European canon with North America, and enough of the Enlightenment canon by which to pursue a common pair of trajectories oriented on regulated private enterprise and strengthened democratic institutions leading to a highly articulated family of civil societies. Simple economics alone show that Latin America produces ten cents worth of value behind every U.S. dollar, and by the year 2020 will account for about thirty cents worth of world market value behind each dollar. Simple political arithmetic will show that the Latin American region has the least wars, the most stable borders, and the greatest commitment to democratic governance of any world region outside of North America, itself and the western rim of small European nation-states.

We have devoted significant resources in the United States to terminating our ugly prejudice towards the African-American. Most U.S. citizens have learned to give up their negative stereotypes about African-Americans. But the Black Legend, teaching that Latin Americans are innately cruel, dishonest, cowardly, and violent is deeply inculcated into our culture. It is reinforced by things so innocent as the contemptible Sergeant Garcia character in the relatively benign Walt Disney television series "Zorro." It surfaces every time someone initiates a preposterous rumor about Latin American life and the rumor becomes a sensational and largely fictional event in the U.S. news media, another of their infamous "non-event" events. There are twenty-two million Spanish speaking U.S. citizens, more Spanish speakers than live in all the Spanish-speaking countries save Mexico, Spain, Colombia, and Argentina. Yet rumors of misbehavior among these, our own people, are easily blown up and circulated as huge social and moral disorders simply because the Caucasian mainstream culture we have formulated retains its Black Legend lens through which to view Latin America. Bluntly put, I have spoken with journalists for years who tell me, off the record, "Look, the only time our audience gives a damn about Latin America is when we can report that the military are zapping somebody, or that some guerrillas are in the jungle making the Pentagon mad."

I particularly salute this college for its commitment to find and understand the canon that, in sum, forms our country and our lives. I challenge you to apply the same rigorous standards of evidence and logic to the Latin American culture which shares our Hemisphere and discover it for what it really is, a strong, beautiful, and noble bastion of the human spirit.

BIBLIOGRAPHY

Bainton, Roland. *Christendom: A Short History of Christianity and Its Impact on Western Civilization* 2 vols. New York: 1966.

Cavarozzi, Marcelo. "The Left in Latin America: The Decline of Socialism and the Rise of Political Democracy," in *The United States and Latin America in the 1990s: Beyond the Cold War*, Jonathan Hartlyn, et. al., eds. Chapel Hill: University of North Carolina Press, 1992, pp. 101-127.

Cockcroft, James D. *Latin America: History. Politics, and U.S. Policy.* 2d ed. Chicago: Nelson-Hall Publishers, 1997.

Gibson. Charles, ed. *The Black Legend: Anti-Spanish Attitudes in the Old World and the New.* Borzoi Books New York: Alfred A. Knopf, 1971.

Hanke, Lewis, ed. *History of Latin American Civilization: Sources and Interpretations.* 2 vols., 2d ed. Boston: Little, Brown & Co., 1973.

Haring, Clarence H. *The Spanish Empire in America.* New York: Harcourt, Brace, & World, 1947.

Keen, Benjamin. *Latin American Civilization: History and Society, 1492 to the Present.* 6th ed. Boulder, CO: Westview Press, 1996.

Lewis. Paul H. "Review Essay: Political Scholarship," *Journal of Interamerican Studies & World Affairs 38.* Winter 1996, 193-200.

Ramsey, Russell W. 'Addenda to *Guardians of the Other Americas: Essays on the Military Forces of Latin America.* 2d printing, Ft. Benning. GA: Troy State University, 1999.

Guardians of the Other Americas: Essays on the Military Forces of Latin America 2d printing Lanham, MD: University Press of America. 1997.

Russell W. Ramsey, Ph.D., D.Min.

The Strategic Literature on Latin America in the Post-Cold War Era 2d ed. Carlisle Barracks, PA: U.S. Army War College, 1999.

Radu. Michale and Vladimir Tismaneanu. *Latin American Revolutionaries: Groups, Goals, Methods, Foreign Policy Institute Book* Washington D.C.: Pergamon Brassey, 1990.

Rodriguez, Linda Alexander. ed. *Rank and Privilege: The Military and Society in Latin America* The Jaguar Series. Wilmington. DE: Scholarly Resources, Inc., 1994.

Smith, William C., Carlos Acuna and Eduardo Gamarra, eds. *Latin American Political Economy in the Age of Neoliberal Reform:Theoretical and Comparative Perspectives for the 1990s.* University of Miami North-South Center Series New Brunswick. N.J.: Transaction Publishers, 1994.

Wiarda. Howard J. *Democracy and Its Discontents: Development, Interdependence, and U. S. Policy in Latin America.* Lanham, Md.: Rowman &Littlefield, 1995.

Wickham-Crowley. Timothy P. *Guerrillas and Revolutions in Latin America.* Princeton, N.J.: Princeton University Press, 1992.

Reviews of: *The Wealth of The World and the Poverty of Nations,* by Daniel Cohen, Cambridge: M.I.T. Press, 1998; and *The Wealth and Poverty of Nations,* by David Landes, New York: Norton Publisher, 1998. Reviewed in: *Journal of Comparative Strategy,* 1999.

In August of 1993, I organized and directed a conference at the U.S. Army School of the Americas called Privatization and Democratization: The Role of the Military Forces. For the conference logo, two trains were shown on parallel tracks, with a question mark in the center. Eleven professors offered their thoughts on what things the armed forces and police of Latin America could do to enhance the convergence, or reduce the divergence, between the two symbolic trains representing privatization and democratization.

Five years later, conflicts and disorder are occurring in several countries within each of the world's regions, and these disorders appear related to the fact that privatization and democratization occur in disarticulated ways. Some analysts argue that the two things are not even related, that a country can have economic development under autocratic conditions of governance, the Chilean "Chicago Boys" paradigm, or that a political democracy can develop in a chronically impoverished society, the post-Cedras Haitian paradigm.

But there is just enough evidence by which to show that privatization and democratization are somehow connected, if not synergistic, to invite a strategic analysis of the flash points. If privatization translates into neo-liberal economics, and democratization translates into the creation of a civil society with ample empowerment of the individual, what is the relationship between these two processes? Where and how does the mix go wrong? Indeed, Robert W. Hefner argues that civil society is only possible within a modern state, negating the possibility of democratization without economic development. And what, if anything, can public and private decision makers do to keep the twins in harness?

Two new books offer critical analyses of the context in which the privatization and democratization dyad occurs. Daniel Cohen, professor of economics at the University of Paris, has written *The Wealth of the World and the Poverty of Nations*, and Harvard economic historian David Landes has written *The Wealth and Poverty of Nations*. Both borrow in title and content from Adam Smith's 1776 classic *The Wealth of Nations*. Both are interdisciplinary, mixing history with economics and the behavioral sciences, and both are cross-cultural. Both are also a quantum leap forward in understanding the world.

Biblical historians and theologians ponder the mix of governance and economics circa 1900 B.C.E. that allowed an impoverished shepherd named Jacob to leave Haran (northern Iraq), dwell 20 years in a foreign culture called Canaan (modern Israel), and return home as a wealthy tribal prince (Genesis 28:15). Cohen and Landes dare to answer this type of question 39 centuries later.

Russell W. Ramsey, Ph.D., D.Min.

Two great questions endure: What is the relationship between democratization and privatization, and where are the strategic flash points? Cohen offers three coherent and specific conclusions that speak to these questions. First, "Fordism" is over, and the post-industrial revolution economies emerging around the world will not follow the classic neo-liberal development stages that were presumed when the encouragement of economic growth was a major component of U.S. foreign policy towards developing nations. Walt Whitman Rostow's five stages of economic growth, written as the Kennedy administrations answer to Karl Marx and, perhaps, to Ernesto "Che" Guevara, are made almost as obsolete by events as Marxism. Second, although there is a huge gap between the rich and the poor in most countries, this gap is highly fluid, elusive, of definition, and relative rather than absolute. Cohen bids farewell to British economist Barbara Ward's 1962 classic analysis on both the necessity and the techniques for narrowing this gap. Third, a small technologically literate minority actually creates the new wealth in most nations, risk takers who are frequently outside the limelight and the ideological marketplace. Cohen visualizes this process taking place in a way that bears some resemblance to Alfred T. Mahan's theory to justify the expansion of commerce and democracy in the 1980s.

Landes, by contrast, requires the reader to extrapolate conclusions from what are best described as an eclectic collection of historical portraits. Stylistically elegant, they draw upon the best known sources and paint a unique trace of how wealth actually was created, expanded, diminished, or even destroyed. Because Landes' case studies vary widely across time and locale, the probability of idiosyncratic linkage between events and processes is reduced.

Although Landes professes no formula for his vivid portraits in economic modernization, one can discern a pattern. First, he examines the moral system extant in a given culture, and then its values within that system that relate to technology, education, and commerce. Next, he links these values to the thinking and actions of those who made the actual decisions affecting the creation and distribution of wealth. In the process, he effectively wrecks the ideologically driven economic theories of our time.

Landes has little patience with collectivism, whether imposed by governing elites or mass ideology. This view is consistent with the writing of Marx-bashers like Paul B. Johnson and Robert A. Packenham. But before the neo-liberals can raise their flags, he shows the massive human displacement and suffering that have occurred in several cultures wherein great wealth was discovered, amassed, and then squandered for the lack of an efficient distributional and wage-labor system. Like Cohen, he shows how a small number of economic elites have, upon occasion, made risky but successful decisions. Unlike Cohen, he relates these decisions by private economic actors to policies promulgated by public actors; Cohen criticizes wrongful policies, such as taxing farmers to support the burgeoning metropolitan slums, but implies rather than shows how this error occurs.

Landes dismisses geographic determinism outright and thus would have little faith in the statist policies of Raul Prebisch, nor in the dependency theory of Fernando Cardoso. He calibrates the horror and human cost of war but declines to identify armed conflict as the automatic cause of poverty and national decline, thus opposing the conclusions of Paul M. Kennedy in his 1988 study, *The Rise and Fall of the Great Powers* (New York, NY: Random House).

Pragmatically, Landes agrees with Nancy Birdsali that some inequitable gaps in income are a by-product of modernization and the creation of wealth in previously poor countries. Cohen argues that the creation of a strong, equitable wage-labor system is necessary to guarantee both stability and continued economic growth, but that current economic thinking does not understand the origin of declining wages either in developed or in developing nations. Neither author seems to agree with William Greider that government must bridge the gap to equitable income and benefits distribution in a hands-on way that resembles New Deal economics in the *maquiladora*-driven societies. Landes shows historically, as Sonia E. Alvarez' *Cultures of Politics; Politics of Cultures: Revisioning Latin American Social Movements* (Boulder, CD; Westview Press, 1998), shows in the present, that ethnic minorities often do not share in the newfound flood of riches in developing societies, but Landes and Cohen would disagree with Alvarez that the solution is government-mandated proportionate sharing of expanding wealth along ethnic lines.

Over a century ago, Mahan posited the notion that the strong-pointing of maritime centers in underdeveloped regions, most of which were then colonies, was justified because a local merchant class would be created and would, in turn, create a democratic government. "Strong-pointing" often meant naval ports operated by the colonial powers acting in concert with corrupt local officials, so it was later condemned as an imperialistic tool. Cohen would validate Mahanist economic thinking by substituting the globally positioned multinational corporation for the maritime fleets and big navies of the colonial powers. Mahan's philosophical foundation appears well justified in the analyses of both Cohen and Landes, and no more can the world dismiss developmental-economics fiascos as Barbara Ward once did on a television interview in 1963, in which she explained failed economic development as "a jolly bad contractor at work somewhere."

For Landes, the Calvinist work ethic, or some cultural package resembling it, is very likely to produce economic success. For Cohen, understanding the new relationships of capital, labor, and technology is the sine qua non U.S. foreign policy holds that some combination of privatization and democratization must go forward in underdeveloped areas, and thinking is limited to the articulated philosophies of liberals, who favor government interventionism, and conservatives, who favor laissez faire economics. With the arrival of the Cohen and Landes books, U.S. political leaders now have some models, structures, choices, and vocabulary with which to present foreign-policy choices that have a higher probability of producing a politically democratic and economically developed world family of nations.

Russell W. Ramsey, Ph.D., D.Min.

Review of: *Made by the USA: The International System,* by Alex Roberto Hybel, New York: Palgrave-St. Martin's Press, 2001. Reviewed in: *Parameters, Journal of the US Army War College,* Summer, 2002.

Professor Alex Hybel subscribes to the proposition that open and democratic systems have a marked advantage in the acquisition and retention of global influence. He then vitalizes this theory by describing the rise of the United States to world preeminence, employing a highly original structure and a set of sophisticated, internally consistent paradigms.

For six chapters, Professor Hybel describes the political actors and forces, the economic actors and forces, and their relationship. These chapters are chronological, starting with the early 19th century, and the author manages, in amazingly short space, to show cognizance of other known explanations for the outcomes of world power struggles. Without consciously delineating military power as a separate entity, he weaves a succinct and accurate portrait of relative military power in each period. He emphasizes forces over actors, and economics over ideology, without ignoring either actors or ideology.

The seventh chapter describes the United States as the world's fully developed hegemon, and Professor Hybel makes no assertion that is not adequately sustained by the groundwork laid in previous chapters. The scope of Hybel's sources is simply staggering; his massive use of references sustains his far-flung entry into differing economic, political, and military realms. Sometimes excessive footnoting can be tedious to the reader, yet Hybel's prose moves along at a snappy pace and invites the reader to continue.

The book is perhaps the most inclusive short description yet written of how the United States became the world's primary hegemon at Cold War's end. It is also totally convincing, leaving in intellectual tatters the work of those who consider correct ideology to be determinative. The reader will respect Hybel's conclusions even when not in agreement, for the documentation is so powerful and the syllogistic logic so deceptively simple yet airtight.

This reviewer would have liked to see a page on the Spanish Civil War as it illustrates the failed policy of US neutrality during the 20th century's divisively ideological civil wars. Also, a few examples of naval and maritime power application by the United States would strengthen Hybel's thesis, when couched in Mahanist philosophy. But these additions could only make small improvement on what is likely to be the best book of its kind in print.

Professor Hybel's book is strongly recommended for courses at all levels in international relations and world politics or economics. Read in conjunction with Professor David Landes' 1998 blockbuster *The Wealth and Poverty of Nations*, the book would be excellent for a general course on the world in the 21st century. While the general reader would benefit from this book, it is tightly packed with inter-disciplinary facts and analysis, and with answers to intellectual battles about international relations en route to the finish line, all adding up to some heavy lifting.

Other books by Alex Hybel are *The Logic of Surprise in International Conflict* (1986); *How Leaders Reason* (1990); and *Power Over Rationality* (1993). Dr. Hybel is currently a Susan Eckert Lynch Professor of Government at Connecticut College and a well-known lecturer on both world and Western Hemisphere politics.

Russell W. Ramsey, Ph.D., D.Min.

"Strategic Reading on Latin America," Review Essay, *Parameters, Journal of the US Army War College*, Summer, 1994.

Latin America emerges in the 1990s as the post-Cold War world's humane region, exciting in the present and headed for a promising future. While some observers remain pessimistic, a parcel of well-written recent books brings the reader into the geo-strategic vitality of Latin America on a positive note.

Pierre Etienne Dostert's *Latin America 1993* is the 27th edition of the Stryker-Post series on the world's regions. Dostert has unusual credentials. Judge, economist, Africa analyst, and master of four languages, he offers credible descriptions of the conflict zones, country by country, between economic privatization and booming democratization. Complementing this book topically and philosophically are the February and March 1993 issues of *Current History*, edited by William W. Finan, Jr. The February issue highlights Mexico and NAFTA from many viewpoints, and the March number has balanced contents on national security issues such as the Andean narcotics war, Panama's continuing instability, and Brazil's battle to privatize the economy. In 1994, only the March issue is dedicated to Latin America, and the analysis is more pessimistic.

Some analysts consider Latin America's present wave of privatization and democratization to be skin deep. There is historical precedent for this skepticism. Generals Simón Bolívar and José Francisco San Martín, principal military architects of the long independence campaigns against Spain in the 1820s, spoke ardently of a region searching for a constitutional order and free-market economies. San Martín said that his mission as soldier-liberator was "to protect the innocent oppressed, to help the unfortunate, to restore their rights to the inhabitants of this region, and to promote their happiness" (1820, quoted by Henry Brackenridge). In their later years, both San Martín and Bolívar lamented their betrayed dreams when caudillos – a genre of quasi-military, semi-feudal chieftains – emerged instead of democratically elected presidents.

At the dawn of the 20th century, positivist economic and social policies led by strongmen figures again seemed to derail the democratic impulse. US influence during the high age of maritime imperialism, 1898-1932, imparted both modernization and reinforcement for opportunistic strongmen in Central America and the Caribbean. Cold War era democratic impulses were sometimes artificially focused in Latin America into choices between leftist or anti-communist administrations as the USSR and Cuba challenged the West and threatened to install totalitarian systems. Economic policy in the era took its cues form Raúl Prebisch's structuralism, a form of an inefficient economic nationalism that many US analysts wrongly thought to be a preference for socialism.

So it comes as no surprise that academic analysts are hesitant to proclaim deeply institutionalized democracy and effective free enterprise systems in Latin America at Cold War's end. Two books sum up well the entire pattern of revolutionary challenges which occurred during the years of East-West conflict.

Professors Michale Radu and Vladimir Tismaneanu, both Romanian exiles to the United States, produced *Latin American Revolutionaries: Groups, Goals, Methods* in 1990, showing that much of Latin America's highly publicized romance with armed revolutionists during the Cold War was often an inauthentic carbon copy of European radicalism. Professor Timothy P. Wickham-Crowley, in his 1992 *Guerrillas and Revolution in Latin America: A Comparative Study of Insurgents and Regimes Since 1956*, explains with convincing methodology why it is that revolutionary movements succeeded only in Cuba and Nicaragua. Given that Latin America is the world's least militarized region since 1830, measured as percent of gross national product expended on arms, soldiers per thousand citizens, and percentage of deaths in armed conflict, Professor Wickham-Crowley's thesis that Latin America's other guerrilla forces never really had serious legitimacy is consistent and credible.

Professor Abraham Lowenthal's *Partners in Conflict*, written at the height of the Contra-Sandinista war in Nicaragua and the government-FMLN war in El Salvador, was the first major political analysis on the region to identify the positive trends seen in the 1990s. One can see US policy initiatives that follow Lowenthal's blueprint to encourage political and economic integration and discourage externally imposed conflict. Excellent description of democratization in progress is found in Robert A. Pastor's *Whirlpool: U.S. Foreign Policy toward Latin America and the Caribbean*, 1992. Professor Pastor was a policy adviser to President Jimmy Carter and has remained at the Carter Center of Emory University in Atlanta, working with the peripatetic former President in the supervision of controversial elections in Latin America. Panamá, Mexico, Puerto Rico, and the Organization of American States receive strong and unique treatment in this book which is both an analysis and a testimony.

While there is a spate of journal articles on specific economic issues within Latin America, there is not a single book which fully describes the complete economic process, the dimension which most analysts hold central to the survival of democratization. Professor John Williamson edited a collection of essays in 1990 published as *Latin American Adjustment: How Much Has Really Happened?* a cautionary note to the fact that much privatization moves at snail's pace. More optimistic is Michael Novak's *This Hemisphere of Liberty*, also published in 1990. Novak is a Catholic theologian and economist who has found liberation theology to be of exaggerated importance. He shows the cultural shock of converting Indo-Hispanic Latin America to modern neo-liberal economics. Robert Devlin in his 1992 *Debt and Crisis in Latin America: The Supply Side of the Story*, was responding to demands for an explanation of runaway public indebtedness in the region during the 1980s. His study calls into question the assumption that private banking policy helps the privatization process. There is a great need for a book on the family of regional treaties carried out under the principles of the General Agreement on Tariff and Trade (GATT), NAFTA, MERCOSUR (the South American cone), Andean Common Market, Central American Common Market, and CARICOM (the Caribbean). Many national security issues arise from these accords.

Russell W. Ramsey, Ph.D., D.Min.

US scholars often have not discerned that the age of gunboat diplomacy, say from 1898 to 1932, and the Cold War, 1947 to 1989, were two different phenomena. A paradigm of convenience and doubtful intellectual merit was created according to which US Cold War policy in Latin America was a pretense for continuing the old policies of gunboat diplomacy among conveniently authoritarian governments. Latin America was presented as a heavily militarized region that would overthrow most of its own governments if the United States had not strengthened indigenous militarism. The new crop of books on national security topics is more eclectic and covers more topics.

Professor G. Pope Atkins has edited *South America into the 1990s: Evolving International Relationships in a New Era*. This set of essays appeared in 1990 as General Augusto Pinochet was turning over authority to legally elected civilians in Chile, as Paraguay was moving toward its first democratic administration in decades, and as Argentina was modifying its constitution to limit the use of the army to defense against foreign invasion. It shows internal South American security dimensions previously not understood by the national security community. Professor Jonathan Hartlyn edited *The United States and Latin American Relations in the 1990s: Beyond the Inter-American System*, a 1993 volume available in both hard cover and paperback. Two essays on the economic systems rapidly evolving in the region are among the best available. The political essays focus on the outer ends of the political spectrum and neglect the emerging consensus majority in several countries. The essays on the role of the Latin American military forces reflect a change in regional events as well as in author viewpoints. These analysts in the 1980s saw Latin America's own armed forces as a greater threat to democracy than the Soviet-Cuban subversion machine. Today, they visualize limited roles for the air and naval forces but find little use for armies in the region. A shorter, more balanced book on national security issues in the region is *Evolving U.S. Strategy for Latin America and the Caribbean*, essays edited by Professor L. Erik Kjonnerod. Delicate questions about relative US and Latin American military responsibilities for the drug war are carefully stated. Sub-regional assessments address the visible security threats.

During the peak years of the Cold War, the United States dedicated about two percent of its security assistance money and four percent of its official arms sales and transfers to the entire Latin American region. Despite the ugly misbehavior of several uniformed regimes, military professionalism flourished in Latin America during the era, and a cordial network of useful relationships was forged between US and Latin American officers. Today, such questions as the future of US-Latin American military relations and roles revolve around the continuance of the round table, and the maintenance of a seat at the table for all the knights. This concept is institutionally expressed in the Inter-American Defense Board, the military advisory arm of the Organization of American States, and was explained well by Anthony Harrigan in his article "Inter-American Defense in the Seventies" (*Military Review*, April, 1970). The Kjonnerod volume is singular among the recent wave of books on Latin American security topics by making anew the case for the round table. Some of it was visible in August 1993, when the US Army School of the Americas assembled academics, diplomats, and military officials at the 5th Latin American Conference to discuss the military role in the privatization and democratization process.

In the November 1993, issue of the *Hispanic American Historical Review* there appears an essay by Professor Benjamin Keen on the huge contribution made to the study of Latin America by the late Professor Lewis Hanke. The acknowledged dean of Latin American history in the United States, Hanke discovered the humane origins of Latin American society, presenting the struggle waged by the priest Bartolomeo de las Casas to obtain justice for the Indians under the Spanish Empire. In the wake of las Casas' writings came the Black Legend, convenient to British Protestants who wanted a moral basis to wage mayhem against Spain's gold and silver fleets on the high seas. Black Legend proponents like Oliver Cromwell painted all Hispanic men-at-arms as savage cowards, morally incapable of soldierly behavior; neo-liberals and leftists in the US academic community reinvented this convenient paradigm during the Cold War, which is now over. One suspects that Professor Hanke would counsel an end to the vendetta.

The Western Hemisphere has the world's most cordial military-to-military relationships and the fewest wars. Nuclear arms are rejected in Latin America, as are chemical and biological weapons, the irresponsible use of mines, and the practice of *coup d'etat*. Latin American men-at-arms wear blue helmets for the United Nations in worldwide hot spots and uphold human rights at home and abroad. Yet the drug war, several Indian uprisings, Fidel Castro's eventual demise, the complete demilitarization of the Sandinistas and the Contras in Nicaragua, and the future of the Panamá Canal all present national security questions. The books mentioned herein provide interesting and professionally solid reading.

BIBLIOGRAPHY

Atkins, G. Pope, ed. *South America into the 1990s: Evolving International Relationships in a New Era.* Boulder, Colo: Westview Press, 1990.

Devlin, Robert. *Debt and Crisis in Latin America: The Supply Side of the Story.* Princeton, N.J.: Princeton Univ. Press, 1992.

Dostert, Pierre Etienne. *Latin America, 1993.* 27th ed.: Washington: Stryker-Post Publications, 1993.

Fauriol, Georges, ed. *Security in the Americas.* Washington: National Defense Univ. Press, 1989.

Finan, William W., Jr., ed. "Mexico," *Current History*, February 1993; "Latin America," *Current History,* March 1993; and "Latin America," *Current History,* March 1994.

Hartlyn, Jonathan, *et al.*, ed., *The United States and Latin American Relations in the 1990s: Beyond the Inter-American System.* Chapel Hill: Univ. of North Carolina Press, 1993.

Harrigan, Anthony. "Inter-American Defense in the Seventies," *Military Review*, 5. April 1970, 3-9.

Kjonnerod, L. Erik. *Evolving U.S. Strategy for Latin America and the Caribbean.* Washington: National Defense Univ. Press, 1992.

Lowenthal, Abraham. *Partners in Conflict.* Baltimore: Johns Hopkins Univ. Press, 1987.

Novak, Michael. *This Hemisphere of Liberty.* New York: Paulist Press, 1990.

Pastor, Robert A. *Whirlpool: U.S. Foreign Policy Toward Latin_American and the Caribbean.* Princeton, N.J.: Princeton Univ. Press, 1992.

Radu, Michale, and Vladimir Tismaneanu. *Latin American Revolutionaries: Groups, Goals, Methods, Foreign Policy Institute Book.* Washington: Pergamon Brassey, 1990.

Ramsey, Russell W. "The Role of Latin American Armed Forces in the 1990s," *Strategic Review* (Fall 1992). Reprinted in *Proceedings, 5th Latin American Conference.* Ft. Benning, GA.: US Army School of the Americas, 1993.

Schoultz, Lars. *National Security and United States Policy Towards Latin America.* Princeton, N.J.: Princeton Univ. Press, 1987.

Wickham-Crowley, Timothy P. *Guerrillas and Revolution in Latin America: A Comparative Study of Insurgents and Regimes Since 1956.* Princeton, N.J.: Princeton Univ. Press, 1992.

Williamson, John, ed. *Latin American Adjustment: How Much Has Really Happened?* Washington: Washington Inst. for International Economics, 1990.

"Strategic Reading on Latin America: 1995 Update," *Parameters, Journal of the US Army War College*, Winter, 1995-1996.

Appraising comparatively the post-Cold War national security literature on Latin America in my essay "Strategic Reading on Latin America" (*Parameters*, Summer, 1994), made sense intellectually in view of the quest for a new paradigm. One year later, two clearly opposed viewpoints are established: the neo-liberal optimists and the neo-collectivist pessimists. Both voices merit the careful attention of strategists and national security architects.

Setting the Sails

Pierre Etienne Dostert's *Latin America 1994* is the best one-volume regional description in the English language. The earlier annual issues still read with authenticity since their origin in 1967. Part of the unique Stryker-Post "World Today" series on the world's regions, the Latin America volume integrates economic, political, and military trends and gives a menu for deeper reading. Longer and more topically oriented is *Security, Democracy, and Development in U.S.-Latin American Relations* (1994, edited by Lars Schoultz et al). Where Dostert shows the restrained case for the neo-liberal optimist view, Schoultz and his author team are guarded pessimists, with an occasional glimpse of the neo-Marxist themes oft trumpeted by US Latin Americanists in the 1980s. William W. Finan, Jr., displays an intellectual reversal and a structural peregrination of importance to regional security issues. His February 1995, *Current History* issue on Latin America is a gloomy appraisal indeed, in contrast with his hopeful March 1993, *Latin America* issue. And he has thrown his hat into the ring on the contentious old debate over what defines Latin America; since the early 1500s scholars have disputed the geographic, political, ethnic, linguistic, economic, religious, and cultural determinants of the region. Editor Finan has dedicated his March 1995, issue of *Current History* to an assessment of *North America including Mexico*, a paradigm guaranteed to sting both Ross Perot and the enthusiasts of regional *indigenismo* (translate as "native Americanism") and *Hispanidad* (translate as "Hispanic pride").

National security specialists were long hampered by the relatively fuzzy strategic literature on Latin America. Ironically, in the post-Cold War era there are now three research tools available to those who would calculate power questions about arms, soldiers, money, and resources. The volume *South America, Central America, and the Caribbean: 1995*, from the 5th edition (1994) of Europa Publications' Regional Surveys of the World, is simply the most comprehensive thing of its kind ever done. Another British series, known colloquially as "Brassey's Annuals," offers *The Military Balance* from the International Institute of Strategic Studies, and the "Caribbean and Latin America" section in the 1994-1995 volume is the strongest current analysis on Latin America's greatly reduced and rapidly changing military institutions. Professor Claude C. Sturgill's three Latin America chapters in *The Military History of the Third World Since 1945* (1994) is the best work yet done on US security assistance linkage with the military institutions of all the world's developing regions.

Economics: The Science No Longer Dismal

A big movement in Latin American studies not applauded by many academics is the arrival of business administration experts and applied economists. Your reviewer, a historian, welcomes this development, having watched his history colleagues, the social scientists, and the humanists miss the interpretive boat on Latin America for four decades by stressing politics and ideology at the expense of economics. A lively economic literature now emerges, one that is definitely not a dismal science.

Paul W. Drake has edited *Money Doctors, Foreign Debts, and Economic Reforms in Latin America from the 1890s to the Present* (1994). Part of the impressive new Jaguar series from Scholarly Resources, Inc., the essays show how Latin America has been affected by classical laissez-faire commerce, positivism, Keynesian ideas, wartime commodity price guarantees, structuralism and statist economics, neo-Marxism and dependency theory, foreign investment and multinational corporations, raging inflation and indebtedness, mass unemployment, and now the neo-liberal philosophy of privatization and tariff minimization. If Drake's readings tip slightly toward the historical side, readers may spot a more purely economic viewpoint in William C. Smith et al., *Latin American Political Economy in the Age of Neo-liberal Reform: Theoretical and Comparative Perspectives for the 1990s* (1994), again part of an excellent series, this one from the University of Miami North-South Center.

Jaime Suchlicki, editor of *North-South: The Magazine of the Americas*, devoted the entire November-December 1994, issue to the December 1994, Economic Summit of the Americas in Miami. Several of the articles relate trade and privatization to national security issues. Sadly, *North-South Magazine* ceases to exist with that issue, which will stand for years as a period statement on Latin American policy questions.

Soldiers & Cops in New Roles

Linda Alexander Rodríguez has edited *Rank and Privilege: The Military and Society in Latin America* (1994), another gem from the Jaguar series. These essays fill the vacuum on such questions as how the great *caudillos* (strongmen) gave way to professional military officers in the 20th century, and whence came the cultural ethos of the Latin American military officer. Professor Rodríguez's introductory essay is definitive and should be incorporated into a general book of readings on the region. The annotated bibliography is the best short piece of its kind in print. G. Pope Atkins, Professor Emeritus at Annapolis, offers a new 1995 update of his

Latin America in the International Political System, still the best regional entry in its field.

Scoffers at the notion that Latin America's men-at-arms have changed fundamentally will support Brian Loveman's "Protected Democracies and Military Guardianship: Political Transitions in Latin America, 1978-1993," in the *Journal of Inter-American Studies and World Affairs* (Summer, 1994). In meticulous detail, he categorizes the countries of the region by the degree to which their armed forces accept civilian control over the military forces in several areas, and he concludes that most of them are still *golpistas* (soldiers who overthrow governments) at heart. Pericles Gasparini Alves examines Latin American regional arms limitation and military role restructuring in his edited volume *Proceedings of the Conference of Latin American and Caribbean Research Institutes, 2-3 December 1991, Sao Paulo* (1993). Discussions relating weapons and defense to economic development are excellent. Carlos Molina Johnson has often defended in modern words the doctrine of Diego Portales, a 19th-century Chilean cabinet minister, who argued that it is correct for the armed forces to guarantee a constitutional form of government by force, if necessary. In Molina's "Iberoamérica 2001," published in the School of the America's Magazine *Adelante* (Summer, 1992), he outlines the several roles for Latin America's armed forces in the next century. A similar taxonomy of future Latin American military roles is offered by Venezuela's Virgilio Rafael Beltrán in "La Seguridad Hemisférica y el Nuevo Orden Internacional," *Military Review* (Hispanic ed., September-October, 1992). The political economist Margaret Daly Hayes reveals some positive and generally unknown trends in South American naval affairs in her 1995 study *By Example: The Impact of Recent Argentine Naval Activities on Southern Cone Naval Strategies*.

For a US academic appraisal of what soldiers and police south of the Río Grande ought to be doing, see Gabriel Marcella's edited volume *Warriors in Peacetime: The Military & Democracy in Latin America* (1994). He is less pessimistic than Loveman, to be sure, but also less rosy than Molina and Beltrán. And he offers a short menu of his ideas on this vital topic in his essay "Forging New Strategic Relationships" which appeared in *Military Review* (October, 1994). William Perry and Max Primorac pull in US regional security policy with their essay "The Inter-American Security Agenda" appearing in the *Journal of Inter-American Studies and World Affairs* (Fall, 1994), as does your present reviewer in his article "US Strategy for Latin America" in *Parameters* (Autumn, 1994).

And Still From the Left...

Scholars looking at leftist influence and security threats within Latin America during the Cold War tend to divide into two groups: those who applaud or bewail the demise of the radical left, and those who find it alive but differently arrayed.

Barry Carr and Steve Ellner edited *The Latin American Left: From the Fall of Allende to Perestroika* (1993), one of many titles from Westview Press on the interplay of leftist revolution and national security policy in Latin America. While they are not ready to abandon some of the heady romanticism which gave US academics an exaggerated view of Karl Marx's influence in Latin America during the Cold War, they nonetheless make a solid case for the part played by the political left in bringing about the era of political pluralization and economic privatization. For a more purely descriptive view, see Marcelo Cavarozzi, "The Left in Latin America: The Decline of Socialism and the Rise of Political Democracy," in Jonathan Hartlyn et al., *The United States and Latin America in the 1990s: Beyond the Cold War* (1992). Finally, for an unrepentant view that the far left has done mighty things with more still to come, read Eric Selbin's *Modern Latin American Revolutions* (1993), another Westview title.

Individual Security Topics

Donald E. Schulz and Deborah Sundloff Schulz coauthored in 1994, *The United States, Honduras, and the Crisis in Central America*, still another Westview volume. While focused upon war's havoc in Honduras during the 1980s, the authors achieve a coherent portrayal of the Central American region. It is meticulously supported and forms a caveat to future US Presidents who might decide to go a-filibustering once more. Louis W. Goodman and Gabriel Marcella have edited a short summary of their *Conference on Peace and Reconciliation in El Salvador, Sept. 8-9, 1994*, a joint product of the American University School of International Service Democracy Project and the US Army War College. A full-length volume containing the speeches is projected and would be a great contribution to scholarship.

Anthony P. Maingot shows why he is the emerging dean of Caribbean scholarship in the United States with his 1994 title *The United States and the Caribbean*, one of Westview's best ever. Maingot's article on Haití in the February 1995 issue of *Current History* (previously mentioned herein) is a classic. Two other pieces on the recent US/UN operation in Haití accompany the Maingot article. An excellent set of essays on Haití by a mix of diplomats and scholars is found in Georges A. Fauriol, ed., *Haitian Frustrations: Dilemmas for U.S. Policy* (1995). This reviewer's "On Castro and Cuba: Rethinking the 'Three Gs,'" appeared in *Parameters* (Winter, 1994-1995). Ten blue-chip national security pieces on the future of Fidel Castro and his role in the Cold War are reviewed there in detail. The October-November 1993, issue of *North-South: The Magazine of the Americas* was devoted to trends in the southern cone: Argentina, Brazil, and Chile. Subsequent events have shown those articles to have been prescient indeed. Your present reviewer's "Reading Up On the Drug War" in *Parameters* (Autumn, 1995), puts that melancholy literature into three categories: participant accounts, policy analysis, and political soapbox oratory.

Barry L. Brewer finds positive linkage between US military training conducted in Spanish for Latin American armed forces, and the long-range growth of professionalism. His study is called *U.S. Security Assistance Training of Latin American Militaries: Intentions and Results* (1995). Your reviewer's article "Forty Years of Human Rights Training" (*Journal of Low Intensity Conflict*, Autumn,

1995) examines this sensitive topic in the context of Hemispheric involvement in the Cold War.

Books in Series

In the 1950s Columbia University's Professor Lewis Hanke edited a series of topical books in English on Latin America, known as the Borzoi series (Alfred A. Knopf Publisher). They were the first affordable paperbacks on the region, and the scholarship was superb. For military and national security professionals, several of the Borzoi classics are still germane. Hugh M. Hamill, Jr., edited *Dictatorship in Latin America;* Luis E. Aguilar edited *Marxism in Latin America*; and British historians R. A. Humphreys and John Lynch edited *The Origins of the Latin American Revolutions, 1808-1826.* Donald M. Dozer edited *The Monroe Doctrine: Its Modern Significance*, and Marvin Bernstein assembled *Foreign Investment in Latin America.* The series collected essays on key countries such as Cuba, Mexico, and Brazil. Now, in the post-Cold War environment, come three excellent series of books on Latin America.

The Scholarly Resources Press of Wilmington, Delaware, offers its Jaguar Series under the editorship of William H. Beezley and Colin M. MacLachlan. Richard Hopper, Editorial Director at Scholarly Resources, is the architect of the series. The North-South Center at the University of Miami, under the leadership of Ambler H. Moss, Jr., has no single name for its recent books on security and economic issues in Latin America. But the titles recently edited by William C. Smith and reviewed herein constitute a topical series of great merit. The North-South Center's *Journal of Inter-American Studies and World Affairs* remains the best thing of its kind. Finally, the Westview titles continue to appear with regularity, and they seem to veer from their previous ideological trendiness into ramparts more enduring.

The Stryker-Post World Today series provides dependable and affordable country-by-country introductions, regionally organized. While the Latin America volume has been excellent since 1966, one gets a better perspective of Latin America by reading the other Stryker-Post works on Asia, Africa, the Middle East, and Europe. *Military Review*, of the US Army Command and General Staff College, continues to feature regular and excellent pieces on Latin America; its Spanish and Portuguese language editions carry different articles and play a vital hemispheric role in education and outreach.

Perhaps the most optimistic news is that the demise of the Cold War seems to have fostered a better quality of military and national security issues literature on Latin America than existed from 1947 to 1989. Since failure to understand those issues led to policy blunders by the United States during the Cold War, the trend bodes well for those who love peace, democracy, and economic plenty.

BIBLIOGRAPHY

Atkins, G. Pope. *Latin America in the International Political System.* 3d ed. Boulder, Colo.: Westview Press, 1995.

Alves, Pericles Gasparini, ed. *Proceedings of the Conference of Latin American and Caribbean Research Institutes, 2-3 December 1991,* Sao Paulo. Geneva: United Nations Institute for Disarmament Research, 1993.

Beltran, Virgilio Rafael. "La Seguridad Hemisferica y el Nuevo Orden Internacional." *Military Review,* Hispanic ed. September-October 1992, 2-17.

Brewer, Barry L. *U.S. Security Assistance Training of Latin American Militaries: Intentions and Results.* Wright-Patterson Air Force Base: US Air Force Institute of Technology, 1995.

Carr, Barry, and Steve Ellner, eds. *The Latin American Left: From the Fall of Allende to Perestroika.* Boulder, Colo.: Westview Press, 1993.

Cavarozzi, Marcelo. "The Left in Latin America: The Decline of Socialism and the Rise of Political Democracy." In *The United States and Latin America in the 1990s: Beyond the Cold War,* ed. Jonathan Hartlyn et al. Chapel Hill: Univ. of North Carolina Press, 1992. 101-127.

Chipman, John, ed. "The Caribbean and Latin America." *The Military Balance, 1994-1995.* London: International Institute of International Studies, 1994. 194-222.

Dostert, Pierre Etienne. *Latin America, 1994.* The World Today Series. Harper's Ferry, W.Va.: Stryker-Post Publications, 1994.

Drake, Paul W., ed. *Money Doctors, Foreign Debts, and Economic Reforms in Latin America from the 1890s to the Present.* The Jaguar Series. Wilmington, Del.: Scholarly Resources, 1994.

Fauriol, Georges A., ed. *Haitian Frustrations: Dilemmas for U.S. Policy.* Washington: Center for Strategic and International Studies, 1995.

Finan, William W., Jr., ed. "Latin America," *Current History,* February 1995 and "North America," *Current History,* March 1995.

Goodman, Louis W., and Gabriel Marcella, eds. *Proceedings of the Conference on Peace and Reconciliation in El Salvador, Sep. 8-9, 1994.* Washington: American Univ. School of International Service Democracy Project, 1995.

Hayes, Margaret Daly. *By Example: The Impact of Recent Argentine Naval Activities on Southern Cone Naval Strategies.* Alexandria, Va.: Center for Naval Analyses, 1995.

Loveman, Brian. "'Protected Democracies' and Military Guardianship: Political Transitions in Latin America, 1978-1993." *Journal of Inter-American Studies and World Affairs* (Summer 1994), 105-89.

Maingot, Anthony P. *The United States and the Caribbean.* Boulder, Colo.: Westview Press, 1994.

Marcella, Gabriel. "Forging New Strategic Relationships." *Military Review,* October 1994, 31-42.

Marcella, Gabriel, ed. *Warriors in Peacetime: The Military & Democracy in Latin America.* Portland, Ore.: Frank Cass, 1994.

Molina Johnson, Carlos. "Iberoamerica 2001." *Adelante,* Summer 1992, 17-24.

Perry, William, and Max Primorac. "The Inter-American Security Agenda" *Journal of Interamerican Studies and World Affairs,* Fall 1994, 111-27.

Ramsey, Russell W. "Forty Years of Human Rights Training." *Journal of Low Intensity Conflict,* Autumn 1995.

Ramsey, Russell W. "On Castro and Cuba: Rethinking the 'Three Gs.'" *Parameters,* 24, Winter 1994-1995, 138-41.

Ramsey, Russell W. "Reading Up On the Drug War." *Parameters,* 25, Summer 1995, 104-07.

Ramsey, Russell W. "Strategic Reading on Latin America." *Parameters,* 24, Summer 1994, 133-36.

Ramsey, Russell W. "US Strategy for Latin America." *Parameters,* 24, Autumn 1994, 70-83.

Rodríguez, Linda Alexander, ed. *Rank and Privilege: The Military and Society in Latin America.* The Jaguar Series. Wilmington, Del.: Scholarly Resources, 1994.

Schoultz, Lars, William C. Smith, and Augusto Varas, eds. *Security, Democracy, and Development in U.S.-Latin American Relations.* North-South Center Series. University of Miami, New Brunswick, N.J.: Transaction Publishers, 1994.

Schulz, Donald E., and Deborah Sundloff Schulz. *The United States, Honduras, and the Crisis in Central America.* Boulder, Colo.: Westview Press, 1994.

Selbin, Eric. *Modern Latin American Revolutions.* Boulder, Colo.: Westview Press, 1993.

Smith, William C., Carlos Acuna, and Eduardo Gamarra, eds. *Latin American Political Economy in the Age of Neoliberal Reform: Theoretical and Comparative Perspectives for the 1990s.* University of Miami North-South Center Series. New Brunswick, N.J.: Transaction Publishers, 1994.

South America, Central America, and the Caribbean: 1995. Europa Publications' Regional Surveys of the World. 5th ed.; London: Europa Publications, 1994.

Sturgill, Claude C. "The Caribbean" 131-142, "Central America" 143-170, and "South America" 171-194. *The Military History of the Third World Since 1945: A Reference Guide.* Westport, Conn.: Greenwood Press, 1994.

Suchlicki, Jaime, ed. *North-South: The Magazine of the Americas* (October-November 1993, "The ABCs;" and November-December 1994, "Summit of the Americas 1994 Miami," publication of the North-South Center, University of Miami.

Russell W. Ramsey, Ph.D., D.Min.

"Strategic Reading on Latin America: Long on Quality, New Rumbles from the Left," *Parameters, Journal of the US Army War College*, Winter, 1996-1997.

In the post-Cold War era, the need for rational consideration of ends-means linkage and the possible use of military force in the Latin American region is unclear. Ironically, the strategic literature on Latin America in 1996, is much better in quality than at any time during the Cold War, even though the Cold War produced a menu of issues that most national security analysts considered to be more truly "strategic."

An admittedly arbitrary menu of books and articles for 1996 can be organized into four categories: interpretive, US policy, anti-drug war, and Cuba and the radical left. This article is an update on previous offerings by your reviewer in *Parameters*: "Strategic Reading on Latin America" (Summer, 1994), and "Strategic Reading on Latin America: 1995 Update" (Winter, 1995-96).

Interpretive Works

The best starting point for analyzing Latin America's post-Cold War boom in privatization and democratic pluralization is the unheralded 1974 volume *Beyond Cuba: Latin America Takes Charge of Its Future,* edited and largely authored by Luigi Einaudi. Professor Einaudi et al opined, under sponsorship of the RAND Corporation during a low point in US foreign relations, that Latin America would opt for constitutional democracy and a mixture of regulated free economies. They also held that the flamboyant militarism of the day was an evolving institution, its blatant interventionism caused by Latin America's entrapment in the Cold War, coupled with too-rapid urbanization amid weak civilian bureaucratic structures. Einaudi subsequently became US Ambassador to the Organization of American States (1989-1993) and is now a senior Latin America policy adviser. His 1974 book is to the post-Cold War interpretation of Latin America what Ambassador George Kennan's "Mr. *'X'*" article in *Foreign Affairs* was to the Cold War: seminal, prophetic, and unique.

The best one-volume summary of the Latin American region is Pierre Etienne Dostert's *Latin America 1996,* the 30th edition in Stryker-Post's excellent World Today Series. Maps, bibliography, intellectual balance, photographs, good writing, and low price all combine to make this the textbook of choice for regional introductory courses. Abraham F. Lowenthal and Gregory F. Treverton are author-editors of *Latin America in a New World* (1994). These essays do the best job of relating politics, economics, and national security issues. Scott B. MacDonald et al are the authors and editors of *Fast Forward: Latin America on the Edge of the Twenty-First Century.* Produced in 1996 at the Washington D.C. Center for Strategic and International Studies, these essays mix sound regional analysis with the Heidi and Alvin Toffler futuristic scenario; this volume and the Lowenthal work are good candidates for seminar textbooks at the war college and staff college levels and for graduate programs in regional area studies. Your reviewer's piece "Latin American Military Affairs" in the March-April 1996 issue of *Military Review* evaluates several new strategic reference volumes of interest to the national security affairs student.

David Sheinin has written a 1995 work called *The Organization of American States,* a welcome addition that shows the regional organization's efforts in democracy-building, peace-making, and treaty negotiations. Another welcome and long overdue book is a 1995 collection of essays authored or edited by William H. Swatos entitled *Religion and Democracy in Latin America.* The role of evangelical Protestantism is fully evaluated, the changing nature of Roman Catholicism is examined, and liberation theology is put into a balanced context. The relationship between economic motivations and political behavior is analyzed closely in a 1992 study called *The Economics of Violence in Latin America: A Theory of Political Competition,* by Wilber A. Chaffee, Jr.

Howard J. Wiarda gives his customary balanced judgment to the politico-economic relationship in "After Miami: The Summit Crisis, the Peso Crisis, and the Future of U.S.-Latin American Relations," in the Spring 1995 issue of the *Journal of Inter-American Studies and World Affairs.* Benjamin Keen presents, in 1996, the sixth edition of his distinguished textbook, *Latin American Civilization: History and Society, 1492 to the Present.* It contains beautifully edited translations of the writings of key figures throughout Latin American history. Beginning Latin American history students in the United States, however, are going to get a highly unbalanced treatment if this becomes their only textbook, for Professor Keen has chosen to include only the writings of the democratic and revolutionary political left in his section on recent decades. Finally, your reviewer sorted out recent books on Latin America into two schools of thought in an essay called "Hopeful Neoliberals, Derailed Collectivists—Emerging Paradigms on Latin America," in the January-March 1996 issue of *Comparative Strategy.*

On US Policy

David W. Dent made a huge contribution to Western Hemispheric scholarship in 1995 by editing *US-Latin American Policymaking: A Reference Handbook.* It is the first objective, systematic treatment of the US national security process as it affects Latin America, and it becomes the reference tool of choice for scholars in this field. A companion volume for the library of all institutions teaching US-Latin American relations is another 1995 offering, a collection of essays edited by John D. Martz under the title *United States Policy in Latin America.* Finally, Howard J. Wiarda's *Democracy and Its Discontents: Development, Interdependence, and US Policy in Latin America* (1995) is arguably the best volume by a single author ever done on contemporary US policy in Latin America.

Four journal articles highlight strategic application of these three excellent books. Raymond M. O'Brien's "Regional Security in Latin America: U.S. Economic and Military Options," in the Fall, 1992 issue of *Strategic Review,* is a

Mahanist analysis. Paul G. Buchanan wrote "U.S. Defense Policy for the Western Hemisphere: New Wine in Old Bottles, Old Wine in New Bottles, or Something Completely Different?" in the *Journal of Inter-American Studies & World Affairs* (Spring, 1996), and your reviewer offered "US Strategy for Latin America" in the Autumn 1994 issue of *Parameters*. These articles present US regional strategy essentially as applied military policy. Walter S. Clarke and Arthur E. Dewey crafted "Peace/Humanitarian Operations: Introducing the 'Comprehensive Campaign Plan," a 1996 paper based on their work in Latin America that is well worth reading.

Since the US Army took on a tutorial role with the Latin American armies during World War II, and gradually included the region's internal security forces in its doctrinal training umbrella, US policy toward the Latin American armed forces has been a critical issue for national security students. Geoffrey B. Demarest discusses the *posse comitatus* principle, under which armed forces defend the national sovereignty and police defend society, in his article "The Overlap of Military and Police Responsibilities in Latin America," in the *Journal of Low Intensity Conflict & Law Enforcement* (Autumn, 1995). J. Patrice McSherry's "Military Political Power and Guardian Structures in Latin America," in the *Journal of Third World Studies* (Spring, 1995), makes the case for enduring and hopelessly predatory militarism in contemporary South America. Despite five pages of footnotes, McSherry's force ratios and structural portrayals are wildly inaccurate.

Your reviewer examined the economic role of those same armed forces in the Fall 1992 issue of *Strategic Review* in an article entitled "The Role of Latin American Armed Forces in the 1990s." Three other pieces by your reviewer examined the delicate issue of transmitting professional values from US to Latin American military personnel via training programs offered in the Spanish language. These are "Forty Years of Human Rights Training" in the Autumn 1995 issue of the *Journal of Low Intensity Conflict & Law Enforcement*; "U.S. Military Courses for Latin Americans Are a Low-Budget Strategic Success," in *North-South: The Magazine of the Americas* (February-March, 1993); and "A Military Turn of Mind: Educating Latin American Officers," in the August 1993 *Military Review*.

Several new books critique US policy on specific thorn-in-the-side countries. Former Ambassador (to Haiti) Ernest H. Preeg posits a fascinating theory about the relationship of arable land, land tenure, population, and US Haitian policy. His 1996 volume *The Haitian Dilemma* was sponsored by the Center for International and Strategic Studies. Joseph S. Tulchin authored and edited with Gary Bland in 1992 the excellent study *Is There a Transition to Democracy in El Salvador?* Tentative optimism at that time required courage, and subsequent events seem to bear out the author-editors' conclusion that a genuine political democracy is slowly emerging in that once war-torn land. Saul Landau gives Uncle Sam a mighty buffet in his 1993 polemic *The Guerrilla Wars of Central America: Nicaragua, El Salvador, and Guatemala*. This book could have been written from the New York Public Library, employing the articles in *Nation* and *The Progressive* as sources; there is hardly any material on guerrilla warfare in it. Stephen C. Benz's *Guatemalan Journey* (1996) displays critical scholarly objectivity, while Victor Perera's *Unfinished Conquest: The Guatemalan Tragedy* (1995) offers a native leftist's views. While indicting the

Guatemalan army for human rights abuses, Perera also blames the leftist guerrillas for dragging the indigenous Guatemalans into their bloody and unwinnable struggle.

The Anti-Drug War

Your reviewer examined this melancholy literature in an essay called "Reading Up on the Drug War," in *Parameters* (Autumn 1995). Some important new writing has appeared.

Starting close to home, Timothy J. Dunn has produced a 1996 book called *The Militarization of the US-Mexico Border, 1978-1992: Low Intensity Conflict Comes Home*. His work is part of the Border and Migration Studies Series, sponsored by the University of Texas' Center for Mexican-American Studies. Since a heightened US military role in the US-Mexican border scenario is an issue for the November 1996 US presidential election, the importance of this study can hardly be exaggerated. Historian William O. Walker, III has written several prominent studies on US drug war policy. Now comes his 1996 *Drugs in the Western Hemisphere*, part of the distinguished Jaguar Series from Scholarly Resources, Inc. This book is simply the best in its field.

A strategy of the drug lords in Colombia for years has been to forge an unholy alliance with the leftist guerrillas; the narco-thugs have the cash, while the guerrillas have manpower, an elegant propaganda machine, and quasi-respectability. Such distinguished entities as Amnesty International and *The New York Times* have been regularly deceived into believing that the Colombian Army and National Police, plus a fictitious "right-wing militia" are the perpetrators of human rights violations. Retired Major General Miguel Sanmiguel, a highly decorated human rights hero and military historian, lays bare the defamatory plot in his article "Human Rights Violations in Colombia: "Colombian Government and Military Perspectives," in the *Journal of Low Intensity Conflict & Law Enforcement* (Autumn, 1995). Sanmiguel's article can be read in its original Spanish in the March-April 1995, "50th Anniversary" issue of *Military Review (Hispanic Edition).* Easily located opinion surveys in Colombia reveal that public confidence in the Army has never wavered, but great damage has been done internationally when major US news chains allude to the "killings by the Colombian military" as if they were discussing the Salvadoran Army or National Guard of 1981.

Cuba and the Far Left

Your reviewer has been making the point for several years that Fidel Castro considers himself to be neither historically idiosyncratic nor erroneous. The 1962 film *El Cid* ended with the hero's cadaver strapped upon his horse in full armor, leading the troops to victory and then being cantered off down the Mediterranean beach into immortality. Charlton Heston played the role of this medieval Spaniard grandly. Fidel Castro, son of a Spanish multimillionaire, is no slouch of an actor, but neither has he any intention of being trotted down the beach into the Caribbean.

Russell W. Ramsey, Ph.D., D.Min.

US Latin American specialists have extolled and fawned over the Castro revolution since late 1960, when Professor Stanley Stein pronounced the death of constitutional democracy in Latin America before the Conference on Latin American History *(Hispanic American Historical Review,* August, 1961), yet since the Cold War's end, they've lined up to predict his imminent downfall. The big question is how to explain his apparent staying power, and several scholars are doing it well.

Enrique A. Baloyra and James A. Morris are author-editors of the 1993 work *Conflict and Change in Cuba,* a multidisciplinary collection of essays which reveal adaptability and toughness within the beleaguered Cuban revolution. Carolee Bengelsdorf shows in her 1994 book, *The Problem of Democracy in Cuba: Vision and Reality,* that Castro has often balanced pragmatism with idealism in order to survive. Frank T. Fitzgerald's 1994 study, *The Cuban Revolution in Crisis: From Managing Socialism to Managing Survival,* makes a similar case from a different perspective. Jorge F. Perez-Lopez offers previously unknown material about recent policy shifts in Havana in his 1994 volume, *Cuba at a Crossroads: Politics and Economics After the Fourth Party Congress.*

The best literary action pertaining to Cuba is easily Mary-Alice Waters' pair of edited volumes containing Ernesto "Che" Guevara's essays and field notes from the Cuban (1957-1959) and Bolivian (1967) campaigns. Guevara belongs to the select company of revolutionary architects who also commanded in the field, died for the cause, and polarized the forces of history for a generation or more. Waters' books – *The Bolivian Diary of Ernesto Che Guevara* (1994) and *Episodes of the Cuban Revolutionary War, 1956-58* (1996) – create the same level of literary immortality for the Argentine apostle of neo-Marxism that US Marine Corps General Samuel B. Griffith did for the works of Mao Tse-tung, and the Roman General Flavius Arrianus did for Alexander the Great. Her two cross-referenced and beautifully annotated volumes belong in all library collections pertaining to Latin America. Your reviewer's "On Castro and Cuba: Rethinking the 'Three Gs,'" in the Autumn 1995 issue of *Parameters* evaluates several more studies and memoirs of importance on the Cuban revolution.

BIBLIOGRAPHY

Baloyra, Enrique A., and James A. Morris, eds. *Conflict and Change in Cuba.* Albuquerque: Univ. of New Mexico Press, 1993.

Bengelsdorf, Carolee. *The Problem of Democracy in Cuba: Vision and Reality.* New York: Oxford Univ. Press, 1994.

Benz, Stephen Connely. *Guatemalan Journey.* Austin: Univ. of Texas Press, 1996.

Buchanan, Paul G. "U.S. Defense Policy for the Western Hemisphere: New Wine in Old Bottles, Old Wine in New Bottles, or Something Completely Different?" *Journal of Inter-American Studies & World Affairs,* 38 (Spring 1996).

Chaffee, Wilber A., Jr. *The Economics of Violence in Latin America: A Theory of Political Competition.* Westport, Conn.: Greenwood Publishing Group, 1992.

Clarke, Walter S., and Arthur E. Dewey. "Peace/Humanitarian Operations: Introducing the 'Comprehensive Campaign Plan.'" Occasional Paper, US Southern Command & Congressional Hunger Center, 1996.

Demarest, Geoffrey B. "The Overlap of Military and Police Responsibilities in Latin America," *Journal of Low Intensity Conflict & Law Enforcement,* 4 (Autumn 1995).

Dent, David W., ed. U.S-Latin American Policymaking: A Reference Handbook. Westport, Conn.: Greenwood, 1995.

Dostert, Pierre Etienne. *Latin America 1996.* The World Today Series. Rpt.; Harpers Ferry, W.Va.:Stryker-Post Publications, 1996.

Dunn, Timothy J. *The Militarization of the U.S-Mexico Border, 1978-1992: Low Intensity Conflict Comes Home.* Center for Mexican-American Studies, "Border & Migration Studies" Series. Austin: Univ. of Texas Press, 1996.

Einaudi, Luigi, ed. *Beyond Cuba: Latin America Takes Charge of Its Future.* The RAND Corporation. New York: Crane Russak, 1974. Out of print.

Fitzgerald, Frank I. *The Cuban Revolution in Crisis: From Managing Socialism to Managing Survival.* New York: Monthly Review Press, 1994.

Gross, Lisa. *Handbook of Leftist Guerrilla Groups in Latin America and the Caribbean.* Boulder, Colo.: Westview Press, 1995.

Keen, Benjamin, ed. *Latin American Civilization: History and Society, 1492 to the Present.* Rpt.; Boulder, Colo.: Westview Press, 1996.

Landau, Saul. *The Guerrilla Wars of Central America: Nicaragua, El Salvador, and Guatemala.* New York: St. Martin's Press, 1993.

Lowenthal, Abraham F., and Gregory F. Treverton, eds. *Latin America in a New World.* Inter-American Dialogue Series. Boulder, Colo.: Westview Press, 1994.

MacDonald, Scott B., et al. *Fast Forward: Latin America on the Edge of the Twenty-First Century.* Center for Strategic and International Studies. New Brunswick, N.J.: Transaction, 1996.

Martz, John D., ed. *United States Policy in Latin America.* Lincoln: Univ. of Nebraska Press, 1995. McSherry, J. Patrice. "Military Political Power and Guardian Structures in Latin America," *Journal of Third World Studies,* 12 (Spring 1995).

Miranda, Roger, and William Ratliff. *The Civil War in Nicaragua: Inside the Sandinistas.* Rpt.; New Brunswick, N.J.: Rutgers Univ. Press, 1993.

O'Brien, Raymond M. "Regional Security in Latin America: U.S. Economic and Military Options," *Strategic Review,* 20 (Fall 1992).

Perera, Victor. *Unfinished Conquest: The Guatemalan Tragedy.* Berkeley: Univ. of California Press, 1995.

Perez-Lopez, Jorge F. *Cuba at a Crossroads: Politics and Economics After the Fourth Party Congress.* Gainesville: Univ. of Florida Press, 1994.

Preeg, Ernest H. *The Haitian Dilemma: A Case Study in Demographics, Development, and U.S. Foreign Policy.* Center for Strategic and International Studies, "Significant Issues" Series. Washington: CSIS Press, 1996.

Ramsey, Russell W. "Forty Years of Human Rights Training." *Journal of Low Intensity Conflict & Law Enforcement,* 4 (Autumn 1995).

— "Hopeful Neoliberals, Derailed Collectivists-Emerging Paradigms on Latin America." *Journal of Comparative Strategy,* 14 (Winter 1996).

— "Latin American Military Affairs." *Military Review,* 76 (March-April 1996).

— "A Military Turn of Mind: Educating Latin American Officers." *Military Review.* 73 (Aug. 1993).

— "On Castro and Cuba: Rethinking the 'Three *Gs.*'" *Parameters,* 24 (Winter 1994-95).

— "Reading Up on the Drug War." *Parameters,* 25 (Autumn 1995).

— "The Role of Latin American Armed Forces in the 1990s." *Strategic Review,* 20 (Fall 1992).

— "Strategic Reading on Latin America." *Parameters,* 24 (Summer 1994).

— "Strategic Reading on Latin America: 1995 Update." *Parameters,* 25 (Winter 1995-96).

— "U.S. Military Courses for Latin Americans Are a Low-Budget Strategic Success." *North-South: The Magazine of the Americas,* 2 (February-March 1993).

— "US Strategy for Latin America." *Parameters,* 24 (Autumn 1994)

Sanmiguel Buenaventura, Manuel. "Human Rights Violations in Colombia: Colombian Government and Military Perspectives." *Journal of Low Intensity Conflict & Law Enforcement,* 4 (Autumn 1995).

Sheinin, David. *The Organization of American States.* International Organizations Series, Vol. II. New Brunswick, N.J.: Transaction, 1995.

Swatos, William H., ed. *Religion and Democracy in Latin America.* New Brunswick, N.J.: Transaction, 1995.

Tulchin, Joseph S., ed., with Gary Bland. *Is There a Transition to Democracy in El Salvador?* Boulder, Cob.: Lynne Rienner, 1992.

Walker, William O., III. *Drugs in the Western Hemisphere.* The Jaguar Series. Wilmington: Scholarly Resources, 1996.

Waters, Mary-Alice, ed. *The Bolivian Diary of Ernesto Che Guevara.* New York: Pathfinder Press, 1994.

— ed. *Episodes of the Cuban Revolutionary War, 1 956-58.* New York: Pathfinder Press, 1996.

Wiarda, Howard J. "After Miami: The Summit Crisis, the Peso Crisis, and the Future of U.S-Latin American Relations." *Journal of Interamerican Studies and World Affairs,* 37 (Spring 1995).

Wiarda, Howard J. *Democracy and Its Discontents: Development, Interdependence, and U.S. Policy in Latin America.* Lanham, Md.: Rowman & Littlefield, *1995.*

"Strategic Reading on Latin America, 1998 Update," *Parameters, Journal of the US Army War College*, Spring, 1998.

The entries in this fourth annual appraisal of the strategic literature pertaining to Latin America are presented in six categories, all of which have some degree of overlap. Three themes previously established in this review essay series continue here. The first is that the post-Cold War era offers a disparate set of regional strategic challenges. The second is that Latin America is moving solidly along the twin trajectories of democratic pluralization and neo-liberal economic development, despite a lingering neo-Marxist and frequently pessimistic mind-set among US academic specialists on Latin America. The third is the ironic fact that despite the first two trends, strategic assessments of Latin America are of decisively better quality than comparable studies written during the Cold War.

Political and Philosophical Issues

Charles D. Brockett and a team of southeastern US Latin Americanists produced a Reserve Officers Association National Security Report called "Latin America in Transition: Politics and Democracy." Excerpted from a longer study, the piece is a superb strategic introduction to the region for professional and academic readership alike. Latin America specialists in the Atlanta region have cooperated with business leaders to create the Southern Center for International Studies, and the paper by Brockett et al is the introduction from a textbook bearing the same title. A full agenda of regional challenges prevents rose-tinted optimism from dominating the text. Jorge I. Dominguez invokes the Latin American political buzzword fracasomania (translates loosely as "obsession with the idea that things are politically chaotic") as the theme for his essay "Latin America's Crisis of Representation," which cautions against excessive political optimism. Lawrence B. Harrison relies on the old "Pan-American dream" for a book title; he examines a 125-year-old regional paradigm for economic cooperation in the post-Cold War context. Since President Benjamin Harrison's support for the conference series that became the Pan-American Union in 1889, the United States has periodically spearheaded campaigns to nurture a neo-liberal economic system in the Western Hemisphere. Lawrence Harrison gives the post-Cold War regional privatization and tariff reduction movement an important historical rung on this ladder.

Elizabeth Jelin and Eric Hershberg offer a set of essays that examine the key aspects of regional democratization in their book *Constructing Democracy: Human Rights, Citizenship, and Society in Latin America*. They represent a viewpoint often expressed by nongovernmental actors on a reformist mission. Eldon Kenworthy identifies excessive focus upon sovereignty as a limiting force in *America/Americas: Myth in the Making of U.S. Policy Toward Latin America*. Paul H. Lewis flies a powerful salvo against neo-Marxist bias among US Latin American political science specialists in his "Review Essay: Political Scholarship." Professor

Russell W. Ramsey, Ph.D., D.Min.

Lewis believes that Latin Americanists in the United States rejected the optimistic worldview prevalent in the early 1960s as pseudo-scientific. They dumped this neo-positivistic outlook for an even more distorted outlook, Ernesto "Che" Guevara's neo-Marxism, which prescribes armed revolution and one-party dictatorship for all of Latin America. Scott B. MacDonald and Georges A. Fauriol offer detailed analyses of seven important Latin American countries in *Fast Forward: Latin America on the Edge of the 21st Century*.

Military Activities

A literature generally less emotional and less politically biased has emerged on this topic. Tom Farer provides an excellent set of essays in his book *Beyond Sovereignty Collectively Defending Democracy in the Americas*. Professor Farer correctly identifies sovereignty as the value that defines the approach that Latin American nations have taken to the inter-American system. Since the Cold War's end, he opines, the United States must grant a larger, more sovereign role to the "other Americas" if there is to be an effective system of regional security. John T. Fishel's *Civil Military Operations in the New World* analyzes hemispheric use of military forces for operations other than war. Examples drawn from both north and south allow a comparison of Latin America with other, more turbulent world regions. Fishel has also coauthored with Kimbra L. Fishel the monograph "The Impact of an Educational Institution on Host Nation Militaries," a sophisticated rationale for sustaining the US Army School of the Americas as an instrument of US military policy, and revealing the human rights protest to be a disguise for deeper political agendas. Joseph C. Leuer's "School of the Americas and U.S. Foreign Policy Attainment in Latin America" covers much of the same ground by matching the school's curriculum against foreign policy goals of the Clinton Administration.

Michael Klare and David Anderson suggest in *A Scourge of Guns: The Diffusion of Small Arms and Light Weapons in Latin America* that all social sectors within the region are inundated by easily accessible small arms. Their solutions are the statutory limitation of arms importation and a vast reduction in military forces, which are already the smallest per capita (save in Cuba) among the world's regions.

Brian Loveman and Thomas M. Davies, Jr., have updated their collection of essays called *The Politics of Anti-Politics: The Military in Latin America*. The central thesis remains: Latin American military leaders claim their governmental takeovers to be politically neutral stewardship regimes, while in fact these regimes generate their own negative politics. The essays are outdated, even if updated. Richard L. Millett and Michael Gold-Bliss, by contrast, have edited what promises to be the most significant book on Latin American military forces in three decades. Called *Beyond Praetorianism: The Latin American Military in Transition*, the title is self-explanatory, and the tone is guardedly optimistic. The volume includes essays by a balanced group of analysts skilled and experienced in civil-military relationships in Latin America. Emerging roles, force structures, and police-military relationships are analyzed, as is the ever-emotional topic of US security assistance and its linkage to human rights issues.

Your reviewer recently published *Guardians of the Other Americas: Essays on the Military Forces of Latin America*; the real value of the essays lies in noting the date of original publication and the context. Glenn R. Weidner and a group of writers offer "United States Military Group—Honduras: Supporting Democracy in Central America" in *The DISAM Journal of International Security Assistance Management*. Weidner played an important role in negotiating a truce during the recent Ecuador-Peru border flare-up. The *DISAM Journal*, in which Weidner's article appears, represents the only effort by a country operating an international security assistance program to make that program fully known in costs, staffing, weapons and equipment, training, and rationale, thus negating the oft-expressed neo-Marxist claim that US security assistance is a secret and sinister affair.

Drug War

Sewall H. Menzel's *Fire in the Andes: U.S. Foreign Policy and Cocaine Politics in Bolivia and Peru*, is an insider's powerful argument that only by significantly reducing demand for narcotics in the United States can the drug war be won in the Andean region. Menzel's companion volume *Cocaine Quagmire: Implementing the U.S. Anti-Drug Policy in the North Andes-Colombia*, is the best work to date on this topic. The final chapter should be mandatory reading for all US national security community personnel who work on or want to understand the Andean drug-war scene. Menzel examines supply-side and demand-side arguments and shows how the shower of drug money arriving in Colombia from the United States has corrupted a previously model political system, leaving the army and national police to fight on alone at the cost of over 300 combat casualties per year. Luis Alberto Villamarin Pulido's translated revelation *The FARC Cartel* lays bare the marriage of two evil empires, the leftist "FARC" guerrillas of Colombia and the former drug cartels. North Americans who read this honest account may feel remorse over the distortions about the Colombian drug war regularly produced by such distinguished sources as *The New York Times, The Washington Post*, and *National Public Radio*. Your reviewer's bibliographic essay on this melancholy topic appeared in *Parameters* (Autumn, 1995).

Indigenous Peoples

Hector Diaz Polanco has authored the excellent book, *Indigenous Peoples in Latin America: The Quest for Self-Determination*. While several trapped minority populations have a potential for national security concerns, the Latin American region is vastly better off than, say, the Balkans, Cyprus, Rwanda and Burundi, or Northern Ireland. Donna Lee Van Cott's *Defiant Again: Indigenous Peoples and Latin American Security* is an excellent and trenchantly worded analysis of this topic. Von Cott's work shows how Latin America's long history of tolerance for its ethnic minorities has nevertheless left the minorities largely outside the economic growth of past decades. Druglords and Marxist guerrillas will continue to arm the unlanded minorities against their governments, she concludes, until an equitable land tenure and market participation formula is found for each ethnic group.

Economics

Thomas I. Desrosier's monograph "Neo-Liberal Economics and the Latin American Military," which relates military roles to economic development, is based upon a survey of mid-career Latin American officers. The 5th LATAM Conference at the US Army School of the Americas in 1995 offered a dozen guest lectures by experts on this topic, and a summarized "Conference Proceedings" was published.

Sandor Halebsky and Richard L. Harris have edited *Capital, Power, and Inequality in Latin America*. The authors included are generally skeptical that neo-liberal economics are anything but one more scheme by which the rich despoil the poor in Latin America. Ricardo Hausmann and Liliana Rojas-Suarez have written a short and somewhat technical book, *Banking Crisis in Latin America*, which should be read alongside recent articles in *The London Economist* on the same topic for a fuller and more balanced view of events.

Paul Craig Roberts and Karen LaFollette Araujo offer a technically impressive, if somewhat dubious, critique in *The Capitalist Revolution in Latin America*. Their data allow the reader to make a full evaluation of Latin America's current privatization movement. While the authors do not seem to advocate a return to state-owned enterprises, or to a neo-Marxist system, they show clearly that capitalism in Latin American societies has always exacted a price in human suffering. Thomas E. Skidmore and Peter H. Smith offer the third edition of their introductory textbook *Modern Latin America*, with a heavily negative economic view of the post-Cold War era. Jeffrey Stark's monograph entitled "Health" in the University of Miami's *North-South Issues* series is a good survey of a critical issue, as is his "Sustainable Development," in the same series.

Specific Countries and Sub-Regions

Roderic Ai Camp is a highly regarded specialist on the Mexican military institution. His *Politics in Mexico* is fundamental reading on that rapidly changing milieu. Professor Camp is also the author of important studies on Mexican military officer behavior and values. As the Partido Revolucionario Institucionalizado (PRI) loses its one-party power grip, its 75-year span of control over the officer corps is a collateral casualty. A new civil-military paradigm emerges, just as the drug war projects the Mexican Army into new internal roles. T. R. Ferenbach's *Fire and Blood: A History of Mexico* presents the country as a historical cauldron of unresolved social conflicts. Gerardo Otero's collection of essays entitled *Neoliberalism Revisited: Economic Restructuring and Mexico's Political Future* is fundamental strategic reading.

Alex Dupuy's *Haiti in the New World Order* rests on the highly debatable viewpoint that US imperialism created Haiti's endemic problem with repressive military and police institutions. Ivelaw L. Griffith offers an excellent strategic analysis in the monograph "Caribbean Security on the Eve of the 21st Century." Griffith teamed up with Betty N. Sedoc-Dahlberg to edit *Democracy and Human Rights in the Caribbean*, a reasonably balanced treatment of the subject. Lester D. Langley and Thomas Schoonover offer *The Banana Men: American Mercenaries & Entrepreneurism in Central America, 1880-1930*, which explores the political and commercial side of the banana diplomacy era in that region. Their work seems intended to complement Ivan Musicant's *The Banana Wars: A History of United States Military Intervention in Latin America from the Spanish-American War to the Invasion of Panama*. J. Patrice McSherry's *Incomplete Transition: Military Power and Democracy in Argentina* reveals a fundamental dislike of Argentina's military institutions, so strong that no amount of reform will satisfy the author. The evidence offered in support of her dismal conclusions is thin, negatively selective, and outdated. Tommie Sue Montgomery's article "Constructing Democracy in El Salvador" is the best analysis yet on this emotion-laden topic.

Louis A. Perez, Jr., authored *Cuba: Between Reform and Revolution*. The title is self-explanatory, and the book helps explain Fidel Castro's remarkable capacity to remain in power. Marifeli Perez-Stable's *The Cuban Revolution: Origins, Course, and Legacy* is but one of many interpretive works on a topic that seems to fascinate authors.

Nazih Richani's "The Political Economy of Violence: The War System in Colombia," is based on limited evidence. The article reaches the remarkable conclusion that the Colombian armed forces, presently losing about 300 soldiers annually in combat with narco-terrorists, are part of a giant interest-group conspiracy to keep the drug war afloat because it provides good salaries.

BIBLIOGRAPHY

Brockett, Charles D., et al. "Latin America in Transition: Politics and Democracy." Excerpt from text by Southern Center for International Studies/ROA National Security Report, *The Officer*. November 1996, pp. 31-34, 38.

Camp, Roderic Ai. *Politics in Mexico*. New York: Oxford Univ. Press, 1993.

Desrosier, Thomas J. "Neo-Liberal Economics and the Latin American Military." Occasional paper, Troy State University. June 1997.

Diaz Polanco, Hector. *Indigenous Peoples in Latin America. The Quest for Self-Determination*. Latin American Perspective Series, No. 18. Trans. Lucia Rayas. Boulder, Cob.: Westview Press, 1997.

Dominguez, Jorge I. "Latin America's Crisis of Representation." *Foreign Affairs*, 76, January-February 1997, 100-13.

Dupuy, Alex. *Haiti in the New World Order*. Boulder, Colo.: Westview Press, 1997.

Farer, Tom, ed. *Beyond Sovereignty: Collectively Defending Democracy in the Americas.* Baltimore: Johns Hopkins Univ. Press, 1996.

Ferenbach, T. R. *Fire and Blood: A History of Mexico.* New York: Da Capo Press, 1995.

Fishel, John T. *Civil Military Operations in the New World.* Westport, Conn.: Greenwood, 1997.

Fishel, John T., and Kimbra L. Fishel. "The Impact of an Educational Institution on Host Nation Militaries." Monograph, Ft. Leavenworth, Kans., 1996.

Griffith, Ivelaw L. *Caribbean Security on the Eve of the 21st Century.* Institute for National Strategic Studies, McNair Paper, 54. Washington: National Defense Univ., 1996.

Griffith, Ivelaw L., and Betty N. Sedoc-Dahlberg, eds. *Democracy and Human Rights in the Caribbean.* Boulder, Colo.: Westview Press, 1997.

Halebsky, Sandor, and Richard L. Harris, eds. *Capital, Power, and Inequality in Latin America.* Boulder, Colo.: Westview Press, 1995.

Harrison, Lawrence E. *The Inter-American Dream.* New York: Basic Books, 1997.

Hausmann, Ricardo, and Liliana Rojas-Suarez. *Banking Crisis in Latin America.* Washington: Inter-American Development Bank, 1996.

Jelin, Elizabeth, and Eric Hersliberg, eds. *Constructing Democracy: Human Rights, Citizenship, and Society in Latin America.* Boulder, Colo.: Westview Press, 1996.

Kenworthy, Eldon. *America/Americas. Myth in the Making of U.S. Policy Toward Latin America.* University Park: Pennsylvania State Univ. Press, 1995.

Klare, Michael, and David Anderson. *A Scourge of Guns: The Diffusion of Small Arms and Light Weapons in Latin America.* Washington: Federation of American Scientists/Arms Sales Monitoring Project. 1996.

Langley, Lester D., and Thomas Schoonover. *The Banana Men: American Mercenaries & Entrepreneurism in Central America, 1880-1930.* Lexington: Univ. of Kentucky Press, 1995.

Leuer. Joseph C. "School of the Americas and U.S. Foreign Policy Attainment in Latin America." Monograph, Ft. Benning, Ga., 1996.

Lewis, Paul H. "Review Essay: Political Scholarship." *Journal of Interamerican Studies & World Affairs.* 38 (Winter 1996), 193-200.

Loveman. Brian. and Thomas M. Davies, Jr., eds. *The Politics of Anti-politics: The Military in Latin America.* Wilmington, Del.: Scholarly Resources, 1997.

MacDonald, Scott B., and Georges A. Fauriol. *Fast Forward: Latin America on the Edge of the 21st Century.* New Brunswick. N.J.. Transaction Publishers, 1997.

McSherry, J. Patrice. *Incomplete Transition: Military Power and Democracy in Argentina.* New York: St. Martin's Press, 1997.

Menzel, Sewall H. *Cocaine Quagmire: Implementing the U.S. Anti-Drug Policy in the North Andes-Colombia.* Lanham, Md.: Univ. Press of America, 1997.

Menzel, Sewall H. *Fire in the Andes: U.S. Foreign Policy and Cocaine Politics in Bolivia and Peru.* Lanham, Md.: Univ. Press of America, 1996.

Millett, Richard L., and Michael Gold-Biss, eds. *Beyond Praetorianism: The Latin American Military in Transition.* Coral Gables, FL.: North-South Center, Univ. of Miami Press, 1996.

Montgomery, Tommie Sue. "Constructing Democracy in El Salvador," *Current History,* 96, February 1997, 61-68.

Musicant, Ivan. *The Banana Wars: A History of United States Military Intervention in Latin America from the Spanish-American War to the Invasion of Panama.* New York: Macmillan, 1990.

Otero, Gerardo, ed. *Neoliberalism Revisited: Economic Restructuring and Mexico's Political Future.* Boulder, Colo.: Westview Press, 1996.

Perez, Louis A., Jr. *Cuba: Between Reform and Revolution.* 2d ed. New York: Oxford Univ. Press, 1995.

Perez-Stable, Marifeli. *The Cuban Revolution: Origins, Course, and Legacy.* New York: Oxford Univ. Press, 1993.

Ramsey, Russell W. *Guardians of the Other Americas: Essays on the Military Forces of Latin America.* Lanham. Md.: Univ. Press of America, 1997.

Richani Nazih. "The Political Economy of Violence: The War System in Colombia," *Journal of Jnteramerican Studies & World Affairs,* 39, Summer 1997, 37-82.

Roberts, Paul Craig, and Karen LaFollette Araujo. *The Capitalist Revolution in Latin America.* New York: Oxford Univ. Press, 1997.

Skidmore, Thomas E., and Peter H. Smith. *Modern Latin America.* 3d ed. New York, Oxford Univ. Press, 1992.

Stark. Jeffrey. *North-South Issues: Health.* 6 (No. I, 1997).

__*North-South Issues: Sustainable Development,* 6 (No. 2. 1997).

Van Cott, Donna Lee. *Defiant Again: Indigenous Peoples and Latin American Security.* Institute for National Strategic Studies. McNair Paper p53. Washington: National Defense Univ. 1996.

Villamarin Pulido. Lois Alberto. *The FARC Cartel.* Trans. Alfredo de Zubiria Merlano. Bogota: Ediciones "El Faraon," 1996.

Weidner. Glenn R., et al., "United States Military Group – Honduras; Supporting Democracy in Central America." *The DISAM Journal of International Security Assistance Management,* 18, Summer 1996, 1-34.

Russell W. Ramsey, Ph.D., D.Min.

"Latin America: A Booming Strategic Region in Need of an Honest Introductory Textbook," *Parameters, Journal of the US Army War College*, Spring, 1999.

According to the Administration's *A National Security Strategy for a New Century* (May, 1997), "Our hemisphere enters the twenty-first century with an unprecedented opportunity to build a future of stability and prosperity – building on the fact that every nation in the hemisphere except Cuba is democratic and committed to free market economies." Yet two textbooks commonly used for introductory college courses on Latin America present the region in 1998 as a revolutionary cauldron where democracy is a sham, and where the people are pauperized by greedy US corporations and often murdered by huge US-trained armies. This fifth annual *Parameters* essay on the strategic literature on Latin America will examine the question of ideological interpretation.

Regional Surveys and References

Robert T. Buckman's *Latin America, 1998* is the 32d annual entry into the Latin American field by the distinguished Stryker-Post series on world regions. It is packed with detail, yet readable; philosophically ample, yet focused; historically rooted, yet very contemporary. These factors, plus its inexpensive paperback format, make Buckman's volume the regional survey of choice. Simon Collier, Thomas E. Skidmore, and the late Harold Blakemore edited the 2nd edition of *The Cambridge Encyclopedia of Latin America and the Caribbean* in 1992. Neither a text nor a reference encyclopedia, this costly hardback follows the topical commentary format pioneered by the French encyclopedist Denis Diderot in the 1750s. It is, therefore, neither a complete reference tool nor a purely factual commentary, innocent of ideological slant. The Europa Publisher, Brassey's Ltd., and the International Institute for Strategic Studies, all of London, publish annually updated reference volumes that better accomplish the regional strategic reference task.

Regional Histories and Interpretations

Thomas E. Skidmore is a well-established Latin American historian and, coincidentally, a coeditor of the Cambridge Encyclopedia just mentioned. His article "Studying the History of Latin America: A Case of Hemispheric Convergence," in the Winter 1998 issue of *Latin American Research Review*, is a long-needed contribution. Skidmore's title reflects his conclusion that the bitterly divisive historiographical wars of the 1960s have faded, and so they have. Yet Skidmore makes a fascinating case for a newer and richer fabric in the post-Cold War era. Benjamin Keen is one of the grand old men of Latin American history.

The 6th edition of his edited *Latin American Civilization: History & Society, 1492 to the Present* (1996) has long since replaced *A History of Latin America from the Beginnings to the Present* (3d edition, 1968), by the late Hubert Herring, as the North American college student's standard introductory textbook. Contents up to 1947 emphasize social history and conflict issues, with reason and balance. Thereafter, Keen abandons his scholarly stance and includes nothing but paeans to socialism, a political and economic option which clearly was rejected within Latin America by 1996. The reader not only gets an artificially-inflated view of socialism's legitimacy in the region, but also is left with a void about what everyone else was thinking and doing during the Cold War.

James D. Cockcroft's 1997 volume, *Latin America: History, Politics, and U.S. Policy* (2d edition), is a costly paperback that will pass as an academic textbook for many in an era when the lines between adversarial journalism and scholarly appraisal have been blurred. However, should this be the only text used by college students in an introductory course on Latin America, those students will be taught, under the guise of academic legitimacy, a large number of explicit falsehoods about Latin America, the United States, and the relationships between the two bodies. Cockcroft uses a standard format by which to pass off his spin-doctored commentary. Each topical portion uses selected historical strands to show the need for bloody socioeconomic revolutions to remedy centuries of injustice. Then comes a descriptive portion showing the local Marxists as the only people who understand the public and have any support. Finally, there is a de rigueur passage which villainizes US regional policy in regard to each topic, showing how Wall Street, the Pentagon, and the oligarchs who govern the United States conspire with evil Latino power figures to abuse nearly everyone.

Splendid fiction, this material: authors who blame all troubles in Latin America on US Cold Warriors leap quickly from the cognitive to the affective, thence to the realm of entertainment. Some of the sophomores may actually read it. An intellectual explanation for the apparent popularity of this neo-Marxist fantasy, ten years after its universal rejection at the grass roots throughout Latin America, is the object of your reviewer's 1997 article "Neo-Marxism Rides the Black Legend." Only by accepting that the people of Latin America are so functionally inept as to be historically dominated by their own entrepreneurs, generals, and politicians could anyone conclude that the region needs US Marxists to ride to its rescue with revolutionary cadres and a Utopian formula.

Political and Economic Studies

How is democratization faring in the wake of global neo-liberal economics within Latin America? Howard J. Wiarda and Harvey F. Kline have edited the 4th edition (1996) of their volume *Latin American Politics and Development* to reflect the massive post-Cold War changes. For the national security analyst, strategist, or graduate student, this is the volume of choice. Wiarda and Kline are political scientists, but they amply build in the sweeping effects of the global neo-Liberal economic movement and its political influence on Latin America. A splendid complement is the 1995 volume by Scott Mainwaring and Timothy R. Scully, *Building Democratic Institutions: Party Systems in Latin America*. These authors show how emerging Latin American political parties are moving from a single-issue orientation (borrowed from French models) to the inclusive "party as a tent" model seen in the United States. Finally, Ernest Bartell and Leigh A. Payne edited *Business and Democracy in Latin America* in 1995, showing how the giddily optimistic "trickle-down" prescriptions and predictions failed partially in the 1980s, but also how the enhanced base of entrepreneurship has indeed produced a broader set of political constituencies.

Civil-Military issues

Brian Loveman wrote *The Constitution of Tyranny: Regimes of Exception in Spanish America* in 1993, an important reinterpretation of early national Latin America. He shows how the 19th-century elected administrations often gave way to "regimes of exception," which were usually dictatorships by military-looking caudillo figures. Accurate history it is, but Loveman's non-recognition of the same slow and irregular departure of authoritarian regimes in Europe, Asia, Africa, and the Middle East once again resurrects the old Black Legend, namely that Latin Americans manifest a unique preference for flag-waving pseudo-generals on horseback as chief executives.

David R. Mares corrects Loveman's otherwise valuable historical analysis with his 1998 edited volume of essays, *Civil-Military Relations: Building Democracy and Regional Security in Latin America, Southern Asia, and Central Europe*. These cross-cultural essays leave little doubt that militarism is not the dominant issue when developing countries with weak democratic traditions occasionally vest political leadership in their armed forces. Further, the Latin American region comes off as problematic but rapidly improving in this regard, not nearly so likely as other world regions to call out for the men-at-arms in times of political turmoil.

Jorge I. Dominguez's edited book of essays, *International Security & Democracy: Latin America and the Caribbean in the Post-Cold War Era*, makes no attempt to set a single paradigm. But the quality of the writers whose essays comprise this book make it a classic: Caesar D. Sereseres on Central America, Carlos Escude and Andres Fontana on Argentina, and Ivelaw L. Griffith on regional security collaboration all provide blue-chip contributions. Dominguez concludes his summary essay with a recommendation that the United States needs to recognize the external missions of the Latin American armed forces and legitimize these roles through professional help, a sermon your reviewer has preached for many years without many amens from the congregation. In this regard, my 1997 book *Guardians of the Other Americas: Essays on the Military Forces of Latin America* details the efforts of the US Army to help the Latin Americans give up their periodic dependency on military strongmen during the worst of all possible times, the defense against Soviet-Cuban subversion directed against their governments.

Donald E. Schulz's 1998 volume *The Role of the Armed Forces in the Americas Civil-Military Relations for the 21st Century* is an update on the search for new missions as the Latin Americans shift toward the *posse comitatus* principle of civil-military relations. Glenn R. Weidner's paper titled "Overcoming the Power Gap: Reorienting the Inter-American System for Hemispheric Security" (1998) traces and analyzes the quest for a functional regional security apparatus. Weidner, who was involved in conflict prevention during the 1994 Peru-Ecuador border dispute, concludes that old scars, internal and external, tend to prevent the political support that could yield a world model for conflict prevention.

Social Movements and Revolution

Sonia E. Alvarez, Evelina Dagnino, and Arturo Escobar examine several of Latin America's indigenous peoples and the effects of globalizing economics upon them. Their *Cultures of Politics, Politics of Cultures: Re-visioning Latin American Social Movements* (1998) is a collection of essays by anthropologists from both Latin America and the United States. During the Cold War, Fidel Castro planted Cuban cadres within several Latin American ethnic minority regions with the mission of fomenting revolutionary conflict. Post-Cold War Latin America has seen the continuation of some of these struggles, featuring both domestic and external leadership and support. The Alvarez et al volume is therefore important strategic reading. Its essays confirm two points. First, the neo-liberal economic movement is not enriching Latin America's ethnically distinct regions very much. Second, there is authentic leadership within the non-assimilated regions that is working to adapt old customs and dreams to economic modernity, while sacrificing neither ethnic honor nor authenticity.

Ofelia Schutte's 1993 study *Cultural Identity and Social Liberation in Latin American Thought* reached similar conclusions. Ways must be found, she concluded, to preserve the ethnic dignity and authenticity of old submerged cultures, even as those same cultures must learn to accept some aspects of modernity in order to enjoy its economic and technological advantages. Finally, Cynthia McClintock's *Revolutionary Movements in Latin America: El Salvador's FMLN and Peru's Shining Path* (1998) achieves two goals. It is the latest and best interpretation of El Salvador's 1980s civil war and of Peru's long struggle to contain the Shining Path movement. Additionally, McClintock sets a new standard of scholarly excellence for this kind of narrative, eschewing emotion yet retaining empathy with the wretched victims of those struggles. Your reviewer found no fact to discount, and few conclusions to dispute.

Summary

Post-Cold War Latin America seems to be following a strong if irregular trajectory to full political and economic modernity. En route, old customs and values from Indo-America, the Iberian Peninsula, and Africa are being modified and sensibly adapted to a careful pursuit of that goal. Latin America may not end up looking like US beltway communities with street signs in Spanish or Portuguese, but it may well do a better job than the Colossus of the North has done in melding the old with the new. The estimate from this corner is that readers of these books, and keen observers of Latin America, will see that neither the Black Legend nor the neo-Marxist world-view ever did have any real connection to this vital region.

BIBLIOGRAPHY

Alvarez, Sonia E., Evelina Dagnino, and Arturo Escobar. *Cultures of Politics, Politics of Cultures: Re-visioning Latin American Social Movements.* Boulder, Colo.: Westview Press, 1998.

Bartell. Ernest, and Leigh A. Payne, eds. *Business and Democracy in Latin America.* Pittsburgh: Univ. of Pittsburgh Press, 1995.

Buckman, Robert T. *Latin America, 1998.* 32d ed.; Harper's Ferry, W.Va.: Stryker-Post, 1998.

Clinton, William J. *A National Security Strategy for a New Century.* Washington: The White House. 1997.

Cockcroft, James D. *Latin America: History, Politics, and U.S. Policy.* 2d ed.; Chicago: Nelson-Hall Publishers, 1997.

Collier, Simon, Thomas E. Skidmore, and Harold Blakemore, eds. *The Cambridge Encyclopedia of Latin America and the Caribbean.* 2d Cd.: New York: Cambridge Univ. Press, 1992.

Dominguez. Jorge I., ed. *International Security & Democracy: Latin America and the Caribbean in the Post-Cold War Era.* Pittsburgh: Univ. of Pittsburgh Press, 1998.

Herring, Hubert. *A History of Latin America from the Beginnings to the Present.* 3d ed.; New York: Knopf, 1968.

Keen, Benjamin, ed. *Latin American Civilization: History & Society, 1492 to the Present.* 6th ed.; Boulder, Colo.: Westview Press, 1996.

Loveman, Brian. *The Constitution of Tyranny: Regimes of Exception in Spanish America.* Pittsburgh: Univ. of Pittsburgh Press, 1993.

Mainwaring, Scott, and Timothy R. Scully. *Building Democratic Institutions: Party Systems in Latin America.* Stanford, Calif.: Stanford Univ. Press, 1995.

Mares, David R.. ed. *Civil-Military Relations: Building Democracy and Regional Security in Latin America, Southern Asia, and Central Europe.* Latin America in Global Perspective Series. Boulder, Colo.: Westview Press, 1998.

McClintcck. Cynthia. *Revolutionary Movements in Latin America: El Salvador's FMLN and Peru's Shining Path.* Washington: US Institute of Peace Press, 1998.

Ramsey, Russell W. *Guardians of the Other Americas: Essays on the Military Forces of Latin America.* Lanham, Md.: Univ. Press of America, 1997.

— "Neo-Marxism Rides the Black Legend," *Journal of Low Intensity Conflict & Law Enforcement,* 6, Winter 1997, 41-47.

Schulz, Donald E. *The Role of the Armed Forces in the Americas: Civil-Military Relations for the 21st Century.* Carlisle Barracks, Pa.: US Army War College, Strategic Studies Institute, 1998.

Schutte, Ofelia. Cultural Identity and Social Liberation in Latin American Thought. Albany, N.Y.: SUNY-Albany, 1993.

Skidmore, Thomas E. "Studying the History of Latin America: A Case of Hemispheric Convergence," *Latin American Research Review.* 33 (Winter 1998).

Weidner, Glenn R. "Overcoming the Power Gap: Reorienting the Inter-American System for Hemispheric Security." Occasional paper, Wetherhead Center for International Affairs. Boston: Harvard Univ., 1998.

Wiarda, Howard J. and Harvey F. Kline, eds. *Latin American Politics and Development.* 4th ed.; Boulder, Colo.: Westview Press, 1996.

Russell W. Ramsey, Ph.D., D.Min.

"Strategic Reading on Latin America," Review Essay, *Parameters, Journal of the US Army War College*, Spring, 2000.

As we begin a new century, a bright shining star in Latin American history is an edited work from professors Lewis Hanke and Jane M. Rausch entitled *People and Issues in Latin American History: From Independence to the Present* (2d ed., 1998). All the great names and issues both salutary and troubling in the region's history since the early 1800s are here in short, pithy readings, edited with honesty and elegance. Sadly, Professor Hanke, one of Latin American history's grand old men and certainly the premier scholar of the Western Hemisphere's human rights tradition, passed away before this superb volume was published. Here we can read Simon Bolivar's appeal to Bolivians to proclaim a constitution based on principles traced from ancient Greece, and we can find three different appraisals of Fidel Castro's Cuban revolution. Also in the mix are short, pertinent readings on land tenure, caudillismo, urban society, industrialization, Latin American views of the North America giant, and much more. For any introductory course on Latin America, this is the perfect book to be read in conjunction with Robert T. Buckman's regional introduction, *Latin America 1999*, from the excellent Stryker-Post Series.

Thomas O'Brien's 1998 work *The Century of U.S. Capitalism in Latin America* and Terry L. McCoy's *The 1999 Latin American Business Environment: An Assessment* offer the reader a nicely opposed pair of views on the region's current economic situation. For Professor O'Brien, all US investment in Latin America has been a manipulative, profit-seeking venture that has contributed to undemocratic governments and societies. His factual descriptions of US investment and its political consequences are quite good. For Professor McCoy, the regional economic climate is guardedly optimistic, and neo-liberalism is an authentic world trend with overall positive trajectories for Latin America.

Daniel Castro's edited volume *Revolutions and Revolutionaries* (1999) and Kevin J. Middlebrook's edited collection *Electoral Observation and Democratic Transitions* in Latin America (1998) offer comparative strategic insights on the political condition of the region. Castro's revolutionary potpourri shows how the indigenous social and economic injustice issues within Latin America were manipulated by both giants during the Cold War, and have now died back into specific armed challenges heavily connected to the drug war in Colombia and Peru. Middlebrook's work is a good portrait of what election supervision efforts can do with their often limited resources; one is struck by how much more successful these efforts have been in the Western Hemisphere than in the Eastern Hemisphere.

Brian Loveman's 1999 volume *For la Patria: Politics and the Armed Forces in Latin America* revisits the tempestuous field of the Latin American military forces and their role in modern politics. He examines their historical status as independent actors functioning in politically and economically nonintegrated societies, concluding that military attitudes now tend to accept democracy but that military *coups d'etat* could reoccur if economic development fails in the region. Your reviewer examines the history of Latin American military behavior and the US mentorship role in the second printing of the 1997 volume *Guardians of the Other Americas: Essays on the Military Forces of Latin America.* A 1999 follow-up volume, *Addenda to Guardians of the Other Americas* offers several recently published essays examining policy and behavioral aspects of the Latin American armed forces. These essays will be incorporated into the next edition of the original work, which is currently under publication in Spanish in Quito, Ecuador, by the Defense Ministry.

Stephen C. Rabe's 1999 work *The Most Dangerous Area in the World: John F Kennedy Confronts Communist Revolution in Latin America,* continues his 1988 critique of the Eisenhower-era anti-communism policy in Latin America. In the present work, he pounds on the Kennedy counterinsurgency doctrine as basically unnecessary and productive of abusive, retrograde regimes, in total contravention of the noble ideals presented in the Alliance for Progress. Professor Rabe's historical trace of the Kennedy-era counterinsurgency doctrine is excellent; your reviewer can attest to this as a first-person participant as well as a historian of the issue. The harsh historical judgment seems unwarranted, however, given the fact that the end product of the counterinsurgency policy in 1990 was a region ready for and generally accepting of democratization and economic liberalization, and given that the internal defense of small societies during great-power struggles is never pretty to watch. One can conclude that without the counterinsurgency policy started by President Kennedy and continued by every President thereafter, Latin America would have suffered a half dozen communist regimes, and the "basket-case country in the backyard" population would be much larger than merely Cuba and Haiti. Richard D. Downie's 1998 *Learning from Conflict: The U.S. Military in Vietnam, El Salvador, and the Drug War* is the best operational description yet written on the US counterinsurgency policy. However, his quest for the correct universal application that would have worked well in El Salvador and in the Colombian drug war is perhaps quixotic.

We shift now to individual country situations. Richard C. Thornton's 1998 book *The Falklands Sting: Reagan, Thatcher, and Argentina's Bomb* is a real James Bond story at the national security policy level. He examines the idea that not only did Prime Minister Margaret Thatcher invent her "splendid little war" in 1981 to shore up sagging Conservative policies, but also that President Ronald Reagan's national security team actually supported Dame Margaret's war as a way of defusing the production of nuclear weapons in the Southern Cone of South America. The review of diplomatic events is solid history; one can accept or reject Thornton's Byzantine explorations.

Lee K. Durham's occasional paper "Reality v. Perception: Democracy Under President Fujimori" (1999) is one of the few pieces extant that examines what Latin American military professionals and their families actually think about incomplete democracies such as Peru under President Aiberto Fujimori. Professors Gabriel Marcella and Richard Downes edited *Security Cooperation in the Western Hemisphere: Resolving the Ecuador-Peru Conflict* (1999). It shows how US

Ambassador Luigi Einaudi and US Army Colonel Glenn R. Weidner led peacemaking efforts that resolved the 1995 border conflict between Ecuador and Peru in a manner that should become a world model for conflict resolution (for a full review, see the Winter 1999-2000 issue of *Parameters*, pp. 137-39).

Professor Harvey F. Kline's 1999 study *State Building and Conflict Resolution in Colombia, 1986-1994*, deals with the troubling question of why a country so excellent in rural peacemaking in the 1960s could have fallen victim to the FARC narco-guerrillas in the 1990s. He traces the ways in which Presidents Virgilio Barco (1986-1990) and Cesar Gaviria (1990-1994) failed to build a unified civil-military peacemaking system in the rural zones long flagellated by the earlier banditry and guerrilla violence. Canadian Professor Dennis Rempe has recently produced two important articles on Colombia, en route to a full-length treatment on rural violence in Colombia since the 1970s. "The Origin of Internal Security in Colombia" will appear in the Winter 1999 issue of *Small Wars & Insurgencies*, and "An American Trojan Horse? Eisenhower, Latin America, and the Development of U.S. Internal Security Policy, 1954-60" appeared in the Spring 1999 issue. Rempe's work will ultimately be phase two of your reviewer's forthcoming *Soldados y Guerrilleros, the History of the Colombian Violence from 1946 to 1965*.

Thomas L. Percy's 1999 work *We Answer Only to God: Politics and the Military in Panama, 1903-1947* provides a vital and completely original theory of civil-military relations in Latin America. Percy opines that the US policy of demilitarizing Panama by means of institutionalizing a national police resulted in a highly politicized police institution which, in fact, made and broke governments in Panama during the years when textbooks tended to label Panama a democracy.

The quality of scholarly books about Latin America which examine national security issues is much higher than it was during the Cold War. Little by little, the scholarly world is abandoning the lamentable predisposition to see the region through the eyes of neo-Marxism and dwell more on the actual political and economic settings, with sincere analysis of US regional policy. All of this bodes well for the US policy of military-to-military engagement. Despite vicious accusations from bitter neo-Marxists who cannot admit that Latin America rejected their millenarian dream, the US Army's tutorial role in Latin America since 1940, when it took on that role, is an achievement that redounds heavily to the institution's credit.

BIBLIOGRAPHY

Buckman, Robert T. *Latin America 1999*. 33d ed. Harpers Ferry, W.Va.: Stryker-Post Publications, 1999.

Castro, Daniel, ed. *Revolution and Revolutionaries*. Jaguar Books Series. Wilmington, Del.: Scholarly Resources, 1999.

Downie. Richard D. *Learning from Conflict: The U.S. Military in Vietnam, El Salvador, and the Drug War*. Westport, Conn.: Praeger, 1998.

Durham., Lee K. "Reality v. Perception: Democracy Under President Fujimori." Occasional paper, Troy State University, Ft. Benning, Ga., 1999.

Hanke, Lewis, and Jane M. Rausch, eds. *People and Issues in Latin American History from Independence to the Present.* 2d ed. Princeton, N.J.: Marcus Wiener Publishers, 1998.

Kline, Harvey F. *State Building and Conflict Resolution in Colombia, 1986-1994.* Tuscaloosa: Univ. of Alabama Press, 1999.

Loveman, Brian. *For la Patria: Politics and the Armed Forces in Latin America.* Jaguar Books Series. Wilmington, Del.: Scholarly Resources, 1999.

Marcella, Gabriel, and Richard Downes, eds. *Security Cooperation in the Western Hemisphere: Resolving the Ecuador-Peru Conflict.* Coral Gables, Fla.: North-South Center Press, Univ. of Miami, 1999. McCoy, Terry L. *The 1999 Latin American Business Environment: An Assessment.* Center for International Business Education and Research. Gainesville: Univ. of Florida Press, 1999.

Middlebrook, Kevin J., ed. *Electoral Observation and Democratic Transitions in Latin America.* San Diego: Univ. of California, San Diego, 1998.

O'Brien, Thomas. *The Century of U.S. Capitalism in Latin America.* Albuquerque: Univ. of New Mexico Press, 1998.

Pearcy, Thomas L. *We Answer Only to God: Politics and tire Military in Panama, 1903-1947.* Albuquerque: Univ. of New Mexico Press, 1999.

Rabe, Stephen C. *The Most Dangerous Area in the World: John F Kennedy Confronting Communist Revolution in Latin America.* Chapel Hill: Univ. of North Carolina Press, 1999.

Ramsey, Russell W., ed. *Addenda to Guardians of the Other Americas: Essays on the Military Forces of Latin America.* Columbus, Ga.: VIP Publishing, 1999.

— ed. *Guardians of the Other Americas: Essays on the Military Forces of Latin America.* Lanham, Md.: Univ. Press of America, 1997.

— ed. *Soldados y Guerrilleros.* 2d ed. Bogota, Colombia: Presna Tercer Mundo, 2000.

Rempe, Dennis. "The Origin of Internal Security in Colombia." *Small Wars & Insurgencies,* 10 (Winter 1999).

— "An American Trojan Horse? Eisenhower, Latin America, and the Development of U.S. Internal Security Policy, 1954-60." *Small Wars & Insurgencies,* 10 (Spring 1999). 34-64.

Thornton, Richard C. *The Falklands Sting: Reagan, Thatcher, and Argentina's Bomb.* Washington: Brassey's, 1998.

Russell W. Ramsey, Ph.D., D.Min.

"Strategic Reading on Latin America," Review Essay, *Parameters, Journal of the US Army War College*, Winter, 2000-2001.

The quality of strategic literature in the English language on Latin American security issues continues to improve. While the success of democratization and privatization in Latin America is the subject of wholesome debate, there can be little doubt that better books on regional security issues now exist for productive use by the military analyst, policymaker, professor, or entrepreneur than could be found during the Cold War.

Once again, Robert Buckman's annual entry from the Stryker-Post Series, *Latin America, 2000*, wins the prize as the one-volume book of choice for the strategic analyst. This is the 35th edition on the Latin American region, updated annually by the professor of journalism from the University of Louisiana at Lafayette. Buckman is also an Army Reservist with a Joint Chiefs of Staff billet. His thumbnail regional introduction is guardedly optimistic; his country-by-country presentations give historical sketches followed by recent economic, political, and national security trends. Editor Phil Stryker has made this series remarkable for ideological neutrality, factual integrity, and low cost; Buckman's summary on the Colombian drug war is excellent.

The next book in order of value is Patrice Franko's unique volume, *The Puzzle of Latin American Economic Development*. Franko has translated the jungle of economic terminology about Latin America, often distorted by the writer's own ideological slant, into clear, objective words, showing the humanistic dimension of the various policies. Thus, Raul Prebisch's import substitution and ultra-nationalistic economic policies are explained as an unsuccessful alternative to economic liberalism in the late 1950s. Professor Franko connects these policies to the dependency theory of Fernando Henrique Cardoso and others, showing how this interpretation led to unsuccessful experiments with Marxist economics in the Western Hemisphere. After detailing the paradigm shift to the neo-liberalism of the 1980s, she revisits her five-point agenda for modernization stated at the outset of the book. These issues are: balance between internal and external economic activity, promoting stability alongside change in economic policy, balancing the needs of the poor with those of the entrepreneurial sector, the role of the state in development, and the conflict between contemporary economic success and future strength. For any course or seminar on the economics of regional security in the Western Hemisphere, this is the book of choice.

Professors Michael LaRosa and Frank O. Mora have jointly written and edited *Neighborly Adversaries: Readings in U.S.-Latin American Relations*. It includes a survey essay by LaRosa and Mora, followed by six sections of readings on US-Latin American relations, each with a summary essay by the editors. The six sections include a philosophical overview, the 19th century, the 20th century to World War II, the early revolutions following World War II, the regional conflict era when the Cold War spilled over into Latin America, and the post-Cold War period. By carefully culling the best and most typical portrayals of US-Latin American relations in each of these eras, the authors bring sunlight and logic to much that has been dark and polemical within the scholarly community. They quote Ambassador George Kennan's 1950 analysis of communism in *Latin America*, attempting to tie the region to his earlier Cold War paradigm known as the "Mr. X" article, that great 1947 policy watershed which initiated the era of deterrence and containment. They extract the core of President John F. Kennedy's rationale for the Alliance for Progress, and also a salient critique on why the alliance did not create political democracies capable of withstanding the impetus to military dictatorship during the Cold War assault on several governments by Soviet-sponsored Cuban subversion. This excellent book gives the reader a way to view US relations with Latin America without diving into the murky waters of ideology; Professors LaRosa and Mora show the strengths and the weaknesses of the US national security policies, the region's governments, and the several kinds of revolutionaries who challenged the existence of some governments. Again, this is the clear choice for a single-volume reader on US-Latin American relations.

John Peeler's 1998 volume *Building Democracy in Latin America* examines the elusive question that scholars and policymakers alike have examined so often, namely, the fact that Latin America has historically tried to portray itself as a region of peace-loving democratic republics but has produced several brutal dictatorships and a larger number of partial democracies. He establishes his position early that democracy in Latin America is possible but not inevitable. In the introductory chapter he examines the political theory extant in the establishing of Latin America's nation-states, concluding that shortcomings of implementation are the cause of Latin America's departure from the theoretical models of democracy. Professor Peeler's subsequent chapter on early Latin American democracies concludes that variegated evolution from a "civil oligarchy" into a full democracy occurred in Costa Rica, Colombia, Chile, and Venezuela. Choosing Paraguay, Mexico, and Cuba for his chapter on authoritarian regimes, the author suggests that none of these three countries rests upon an inevitable trajectory toward full democracy, yet that each has provided some important democratic features. In his overall evaluation, he equates democratic success with strong linkage between electoral choice and public policy, concluding that Latin America's history of balancing radical reform with governmental stability under a constitution will provide some successful governing systems. But Peeler finds neither populism nor neo-liberalism to be acceptable panaceas, returning again to the paradigm of a successful linkage between voter will and public policy. This book is not comprehensive, save for its superb bibliography, but it does offer vital new ways to evaluate emerging democracy in post-Cold War Latin America.

A longer book of edited readings with commentary is Larry Diamond, et al, *Democracy in Developing Countries: Latin America*. For Central America, the authors address Mexico and Costa Rica; the Dominican Republic is the Caribbean entry; and the South American continent is represented by essays on Argentina, Brazil, Chile, Colombia, Peru, and Venezuela. Although not written to a precise format, each essay includes historical trends, recent economic development, recent political evolution, and evaluation of overall political-economic integration. Some include a discrete section on US policy toward the subject country, and some include a prognosis for future democratic performance. The introduction is, in essence, an essay on what constitutes a democracy in Latin America. It follows the methodology and contents seen in Professor Seymour Martin Lipset's 1981 classic *Political Man: The Social Bases of Politics*. (While Lipset, the nation's professor emeritus of socio-political integration is one of the editors of this collection, none of the essays appears under his by-line.) The introduction and nine-country analyses are strong, but the book fails in lacking a final essay that synthesizes the trends. Each essay, nevertheless, is a stand-alone gem, written by an acknowledged national expert. The book would serve well for a course on comparative politics in Latin America, and as background reading for national security professionals who will work in the countries analyzed.

Joseph S. Tulchin and Ralph H. Espach are coauthors and coeditors of *Security Cooperation in the Caribbean Basin*. This region is the maritime front door of the United States, over whose stability and control a century ago the United States became a world-ranked naval power. Following the authors' joint introductory essay about the region's strategic importance, there are three topical sections: the post-Cold War Caribbean security agenda, nontraditional threats to that region, and cooperative security measures extant or planned. "Drugs and the Emerging Security Agenda in the Caribbean," by Professor Ivelaw L. Griffith, is one of the finest essays available on the topic. Item by item, Professor Griffith names a condition pertaining to the illicit drug problem, derives the security threat it imposes, and then connects it to Caribbean and US societies. At the essay's end, the reader can see how comprehensive and overwhelming the illegal narcotics plague really is, yet can also see the sectoral linkage behind both the threat and the possible solutions. "A Call for the Redefinition of Regional and National Interests," is a short essay by Dominican Republic General Jose E. Noble Espejo. He points out that most security measures in the Caribbean have traditionally been taken bilaterally between the United States and each of the small countries, and calls for the adoption of a truly regional anti-narcotics strategy. The summary essay by Tulchin and Espach posits that the Caribbean Economic Community (CARICOM) and a Caribbean anti-narcotics strategy cannot succeed independently, and that each must be coordinated politically with the other. They also opine that the United States' "anachronistic stalemate with Cuba" is counterproductive to overall regional security. This book should be mandatory reading for any college course on the Caribbean region and is a model for short, excellent texts in regional security studies.

MERCOSUR: Regional Integration, World Markets is a 1999 study authored and edited by Professor Riordan Roett. MERCOSUR is the world's only regional trade agreement under the World Trade Organization concept which uses a Spanish acronym – for Mercado Comun Sureño (in English, "Southern Common Market") based on its primary members Argentina, Brazil, and Chile, with Paraguay and Uruguay in an affiliated status. The issue is vital to Western Hemisphere security, for the so-called "ABC" countries (Argentina, Brazil, and Chile) anchor the South

American continent, and upon them depends the region's stability and future growth. Following an introduction by Roett, there are essays by experts on trade, Brazil, industrialization, membership, and relationships with the European Economic Union. The chapter on Brazil is critical to any study of regional security, for the South American giant conducts 70 percent of all MERCOSUR's trade and is the world's 9th-ranked economic power. In his summary essay, Roett shows how partisan squabbling and petty nationalistic posturing in the United States damages MERCOSUR as well as US interests in that potentially powerful region. This book provides invaluable readings for a course on Latin American economics, as well as for studying regional security.

While other excellent English-language books exist, this collection will take the serious student of Latin American security issues deeply enough into the milieu to formulate solid policy ideas.

BIBLIOGRAPHY

Buckman, Robert T. *Latin America, 2000*. 35th ed. Harpers Ferry, W.Va.: Stryker-Post, 2000.

Diamond, Larry, Jonathan Hartlyn, Juan J. Linz, and Seymour Martin Lipset, eds. *Democracy in Developing Countries: Latin America*. 2d ed. Boulder, Colo.: Lynne Rienner, 1999.

Franko, Patrice. *The Puzzle of Latin American Economic Development*. Lanham, Md.: Rowman & Littlefield, 1999.

Henderson, James D., Helen Delpar, and Maurice P. Brungardt. *A Reference Guide to Latin American History*. Armonk, NY: M.E. Sharpe, 2000.

LaRosa, Michael, and Frank O. Mora, eds. *Neighborly Adversaries: Readings in US-Latin American Relations*. Lanham, Md: Rowman & Littlefield, 1999.

Peeler, John. *Building Democracy in Latin America*. Boulder, Colo.: Lynne Rienner, 1998.

Roett, Riordan, ed. *MERCOSUR: Regional Integration, World Markets*. Boulder, Colo: Lynne Rienner, 1999.

Tulchin, Joseph S., and Ralph H. Espach. *Security Cooperation in the Caribbean Basin*. Boulder, Colo: Lynne Rienner, 2000.

Russell W. Ramsey, Ph.D., D.Min.

"War and Its Aftermath: New Writing on Latin America," *Parameters, Journal of the US Army War College*, Spring, 2002.

This cluster of books on Latin America deal with war, civil-military relations, and the social aftermath of conflict. The works are literarily important, strategically significant, uneven in scope, and likely to enjoy an enduring place in library collections. My new volume *Strategic Reading on Latin America* (2001) is offered as a compilation of my previous essays on this topic in *Parameters*, plus several more from the *Hispanic American Historical Review, Military Review, Strategic Review*, and *Journal of Comparative Strategy.*

We jump quickly into the ideological frying pan with John Charles Chasteen's new work called *Born in Blood and Fire: A History of Latin America* (2001). In short and literarily superb chapters, Professor Chasteen profiles a survey sketch of Latin American history which emphasizes both military and social conflicts in each major period. The ensuing view which the reader obtains is thereby unbalanced, since cultural history and civil society get little space. Author Chasteen's outlook is distinctly at odds with well documented facts (e.g., Ruth L. Sivard's *World Military and Social Expenditures*, 1991, pp. 22-23; 50-51) revealing Latin America to be the world region historically possessing the fewest casualties due to war, the fewest soldiers as a percent of the population, and the smallest percent of the gross domestic product devoted to military spending.

Professor Patricio Silva has edited *The Soldier and the State in South America: Essays in Civil-Military Relations* (2001), the title deriving from Professor Samuel P. Huntington's 1957 classic on civil-military relations. Professor Silva's book fills the gap between the definitive writing on this topic by Professor Lyle N. McAlister in the 1960s and the present day. The essays deal with Argentina, Brazil, Chile, and Peru and are descriptively valuable, but not structurally definitive. Professor Paul Cammack's contribution characterizes these Latin American countries as "state-managed democracies" with the armed forces being increasingly less praetorian, yet retaining social roles not fully consistent with the *posse comitatus* model. Complementing this book is the Fall 2000 edition of the *Journal of Inter-American Studies and World Affairs* (Volume 42, Number 3). These essays cover civil-military relations in Argentina, Brazil, Chile, and Venezuela. They show an expansion of civil society, a growth in constitutionalism, and occasional forays into military populism.

Manual G. and Cynthia M. Gonzales have written *En Aquel Entonces* (2000) which translates loosely as *Way Back Then*. They depict the post conflict conditions under which Mexican citizens lived during the transition into immigration to the United States, or to living in proximity to the United States. They capture unforgettably the racially negative stereotypes which North Americans have usually held about Mexicans, a racism best understood as the "Black Legend" (see my article "Neo-Marxism Rides the Black Legend," *Journal of Low Intensity Conflict & Law Enforcement*, Winter, 1997). Shifting from the world's most populous

Spanish speaking country to the overwhelmingly dominant Portuguese speaking nation, we examine Professor R. S. Rose's *One of the Forgotten Things: Getulio Vargas and Brazilian Social Control, 1930-1954*. For a period of time in the late 1930s, Vargas was evidently more akin to Adolph Hitler than to the benign autocrat the distinguished liberal Brazilian historian Gilberto Freyre has portrayed him to be. This book offers intimate detail on the centralization of power from the state capitals to the national capital then located in Rio de Janeiro, supported with sickening accounts of torture administered to alleged communists in select prisons. The author shows how vicious struggles between the political right and the left of that era somewhat resembled events in the streets of Rome and Berlin a decade earlier. The author does not implicate the Brazilian armed forces but rather identifies terroristic police entities resembling the German Gestapo.

In 1970 my *History of the Rural Violence in Colombia, 1946 – 1965* (Gainesville, Florida: University of Florida Center for Latin American Studies, 1970) invited future scholars to extend the analysis. The 2d edition of this book, in Spanish, *Guerrilleros y Soldados*, (Bogota: 3d World Press, 2000) sold out within six weeks in Colombia; and vital, excellent new research is taking place. Bradley L. Coleman has written *The Colombian-American Alliance: Colombia's Contribution to U.S.-Led Multilateral Military Efforts, 1938-1953* (2001) in which he portrays the United States and Colombian armed forces as senior and junior partners in a cooperative military partnership which effectively boosts the national security goals of both countries, to include the strengthening of democracy. Dennis Rempe has authored *Counterinsurgency in Colombia: A U.S. National Security Perspective, 1958-1966* (2001), showing convincingly that the transmission of the oft-controversial U.S. version of counterinsurgency doctrine in the John F. Kennedy era was a humane and effective tool of democracy and stability when applied by the Colombian armed forces. This is critically important in 2001, for the so-called Revolutionary Armed Forces of Colombia (whose Spanish acronym is FARC) have invested in a multi-million dollar program to portray the myth that they are innocent social reformers when their chief products are, in fact, murder, social mayhem, and illegal narcotics (*Columbus Ledger-Enquirer*, p. A-12, October 14, 2001). Professors Gonzalo Sanchez and Donny Meertens have just published *Bandits, Peasants, and Politics: The Case of La Violencia in Colombia* (2001). These authors build upon my earlier work, studies by Professor Eric Hobsbawm, and Colombian Professor German Guzman's field interviews to create a social portrait of Colombia's socially rebellious rural sector. The detail is exacting and valuable, but there is little commentary on the somewhat skewed connections these people have with Colombia's national institutions. Finally, Professor Charles Berquist et al have edited *Violence in Colombia, 1990-2000* (2001). This book, in its original Spanish form, is influential in the current Colombian policy of negotiating with the FARC, although that arrangement may soon end. It covers Colombia's tempestuous rural violence in the most recent decade with great detail and precision; its biggest limitation is the minimal commentary on the armed forces and police, which are obviously vital in any serious discussion of rural violence in Colombia.

Russell W. Ramsey, Ph.D., D.Min.

Emerging civil-military relations in Latin America are a key element in the region's democratization, and in the success of neo-liberal economics in a region that resisted free market economics for many years due to its Hispano-Catholic colonial heritage. No discussion of civil society, as pioneered so vitally by the late Professor Seymour Martin Lipset, is complete without it. These books relating to conflict and the social consequences of its aftermath open important windows into civil-military relations in Latin America. The Western Hemisphere Institute for Security Cooperation offers a college-accredited course called Democratic Sustainment which brings field grade officers, defense ministry civilians, and non-governmental civilians to the United States to study the field. Since the retirement of Professor Lyle McAlister, no one has done systematic, non-polemical original research on this topic at the same level. What is needed, for a fuller understanding of 21st century Latin America, is a Professor Charles Moskos, Northwestern University's luminous star in military sociology, to direct a research assault on the Latin American region. Until that occurs, the books reviewed here are recommended reading on conflict and its civil-military aftermath in Latin America.

BIBLIOGRAPHY

Berquist, Charles et. al. *Violence in Colombia, 1990-2000: Waging War and Negotiating Peace.* Latin American Silhouettes Series. Wilmington, Del.: Scholarly Resources, Inc. 2001.

Chasteen, John Charles. *Born in Blood and Fire: A Concise History of Latin America.* New York: W.W. Norton Co., 2001.

Coleman, Bradley Lynn. "The Colombian-American Alliance: Colombia's Contribution to U.S.-Led Multilateral Military Efforts, 1938-1953," Unpublished Ph.D. dissertation. Athens: University of Georgia, 2001.

Gonzales, Manual G. & Cynthia M. Gonzales. *En Aquel Entones (trans.) Way Back Then.* Bloomington: Indiana University Press, 2000.

Journal of Interamerican Studies & World Affairs, Miami, Florida (Vol 42, No 3) Fall 2000.

Ramsey, Russell W. *Strategic Reading on Latin America*, 3d ed. Bloomington, In.: 1st Books, Inc., 2001.

Rempe, Dennis. "Counterinsurgency in Colombia: A US National Security Perspective, 1958-1966," Unpublished Ph.D. dissertation. Coral Gables, Fl.: University of Miami, 2001.

Rose, R. S. *One of the Forgotten Things: Getulio Vargas and Brazilian Social Control, 1930-1954.* Westport, Con.: Greenwood Press, 2000.

Sanchez, Gonzalo and Donny Meertens. *Bandits, Peasants, and Politics: The Case of La Violencia in Colombia.* Trans. into English by Alan Hynds. Austin: University of Texas Press, 2001.

Silva, Patricio, ed. *The Soldier and the State in South America: Essays in Civil-Military Relations.* New York: St. Martin's Press, 2001.

Strategic Reading on Latin America: Economic, Political, & Military
Russell W. Ramsey, Ph.D., D. Min.
Visiting Professor of Latin American Security Studies
Troy State University to the Western Hemisphere Institute for Security Studies

ECONOMIC:

Tremendously important to strategic planners and international developers is Hernando de Soto's work called The Mystery of Capitalism: Why Capitalism Triumphs in the West and Fails Everywhere Else. Published in 2000 when the first blush of neo-liberal economic success was clearly off the rose in Latin America, Soto's thesis is that most Latin American countries have huge reservoirs of unused investment capital right at home in the form of houses and family properties which cannot be converted into lines of credit. Soto painstakingly traces the process for a Peruvian homeowner who wants to obtain a bank loan with which to invest or to start a business. He depicts mountains of bureaucracy, corruption, inefficient government controls, and other barriers which effectively deny this source of capitalization to the fledgling entrepreneur. The process works well in North America and Western Europe, he shows, and is disastrously non-existent in most of Latin America, Africa, and other developing regions. Clearly the strengthening of property value infrastructure in developing regions would enhance the economics of national development and security.

Michael C. Desch et. al. present in their 1998 collection of essays From Pirates to Drug Lords: The Post-Cold War Caribbean Security Environment an inventory of security challenges that are primarily economic. The combination of money laundering, drug trafficking, corruption, and the completely legitimate but morally questionable practice of off-shore banks drawing huge U.S. cash flow makes the Caribbean a 21st century electronic clone of the 18th century age of piracy. The unwillingness of the U.S. Congress to regulate or prevent money hiding in fairyland Caribbean island "countries" is an ugly tale of moral hypocrisy, since many figures in the U.S. Congress who protect this irresponsible commerce are the loudest champions of enhanced national security. Michael R. Hall's study in 2000 called Sugar and Power in the Dominican Republic: Eisenhower, Kennedy, and the Trujillos shows the 1950s version of this ugly process, wherein Senator Allen J. Ellender (D., Louisiana) and Representative Harold J. Cooley (D. North Carolina) were heavily bribed by the corrupt administration of Rafael Leonidis Trujillo to rig the U.S. sugar importation quota in ways which even the highly respected President Dwight Eisenhower could not overcome, as he belatedly tried to reduce the powers of Caribbean dictators (p. 98, 113). The ability of these dishonest Congress members to damage U.S. national security while posturing to support it was made clear when General Trujillo appointed his son "Ramfis" a phony military officer, sent him to the U.S. Army Command and General Staff College to obtain legitimacy, and was rebuffed when a courageous Commandant there refused young Trujillo his diploma because he seldom bothered to attend class (p. 87). Senator Ellender's threats against the US Army C&GSC Commandant, Major General Lionel C. McGarr, and Deputy Commandant, Brigadier General Frederick R. Zieraph, were resisted by both officers at considerable risk to their careers. These actions form a brave page in the U.S. Army's historical role in civil-military relations. Finally, Donald E. Schulz' article "The Growing Threat to Democracy in Latin America," Parameters (Spring 2001) draws these economic threats together with the wave of ultra-patriotic military populism within Latin America to show how democracy is being short-circuited via the unwholesome admixture of neo-liberal world economics and old domestic power trends in Latin American countries.

POLITICAL:

Legal reform has a major role in political reform and consequently in regional security, according to Christina Blebesheimer et. al. in their 2000 book Justice Beyond Our Borders: Judicial Reforms for Latin America and the Caribbean. Chapter 2, by Robert H. Rhudy, traces legal aid models for Latin America. The rest of the book is devoted to essays on the theory of legal reform, and its application in Spain. William C. Prillaman's study in 2000 called The Judiciary and Democratic Decay in Latin America: Declining Confidence in the Rule of Law contains case studies and commentary on Argentina, Brazil, Chile, and El Salvador. The conclusions are uneven, but the author is pessimistic about democracy's future in the Southern Cone, and in Central America. Paul H. Gelles' 2000 book Water and Power in Highland Peru: The Cultural Politics of Irrigation and Development may be termed the "TVA Story" for Peru. It shows how culturally remote people want the benefits of electric power, but will fight the system when electrification creates physical and political structures that impinge on ancient and local lands, customs, and rights, an obvious potential for armed rebellion. Kevin J. Middlebrook's edited 2000 book Conservative Parties, the Right, and Democracy in Latin America is an edited set of essays on post Cold War conservative parties in Argentina, Brazil, Colombia, El Salvador, Peru, and Venezuela. The writers show variegation and a generally democratic disposition; they define core interests; they reveal some degree of uncertainty; and they herald an end of conservative parties that trumpet rightwing salvationist revolutions.

Continuing with politically oriented works, Merilee S. Grindle asks, in her 2000 study Audacious Reforms: Institutional Invention and Democracy in Latin America, if there is any reason why political leaders in existing roles should agree to cede power to reformers and new structures. This is a refreshing viewpoint, since many U.S. political analysts have naively prescribed reforms for the Latin Americans across the years with no respect for incumbents who operate existing systems. Focusing on Argentina, Bolivia, and Venezuela, she also examines how legitimacy for political reform is to be obtained, and how these reforms would work. Anna L. Peterson offers a theological and social analysis of the Catholic left in El Salvador during the 1980s. Her 1997 volume <u>Martyrdom and the Politics of Religion: Progressive Catholocism in El Salvador's Civil War</u> concludes that supporters of the now defunct Faribundo Marti Liberation Front (FMLN, Spanish acronym) re-discovered a Biblical concept of martyrdom on behalf of the poor and the abused in El Salvador. Finally, Eric Selbin's "Resistance, Rebellion, and Revolution in Latin America at the Millenium," <u>Latin American Research Review</u> (2001) is a detailed analysis of six new books on revolution and protest politics in Latin America since the Cold War. Selbin concludes that social and economic injustice remain the defining political issues of the region and that, even though the Cold War dynamics may be outdated, revolutionary ferment is the dominant political variable.

MILITARY:

Thomas L. Whigham's 2002 work <u>The Paraguayan War: Causes and Early Conduct</u> [Vol. I] is the first of two volumes in what promises to become the standard work on Latin America's largest 19th century war. Often called the War of the Triple Alliance in which Paraguay fought to the death against Argentina, Brazil, and Uruguay from 1866 to 1870, it is reinterpreted here through modern eyes and methods here by an eminent historian. Painstakingly accurate, Whigham's prose reads like the late Bruce Catton's descriptions of battles in the US Civil War; he lays the groundwork for some important revisionist views on national defense institutions and values in the four countries affected. Peter M. Beattie's 2001 study <u>The Tribute of Blood: Army, Honor, Race, and Nation in Brazil, 1864-1945</u> is the type of historical sociology that has long been lacking among the works of Latin American specialists. Beattie re-visits some of the old shibboleths about draconian militarism in the region's largest country and shows a progression of modernization in recruiting, manning, and employment of the Brazilian Army. He starts with the highly determinative impact of the War of the Triple Alliance (see Whigham, above) and ends in 1945, just when U.S. tutelage had maximized its impact through the training provided to the Brazilian Brigade that fought with the Allies in Italy against the Axis forces in World War II. Beattie traces the growth of civil-military institutions appropriate to a large political democracy, with hitches along the way not unlike the rough-and-tumble practices conducted by the U.S. Army during the frontier war era.

Jeffrey F. Addicot and Guy B. Roberts are two highly educated military lawyers who were involved with legal reform in the Latin American military forces in the 1990s. Their 2001 article "Building Democracies with Southern Command's Legal Engagement Strategy" in <u>Parameters</u> is a fascinating description of the work being done, and yet to be done. Obviously, a fully transparent and legally accountable set of armed forces and police are necessary for the continuation of any genuine political democracy; Addicot and Roberts are guardedly optimistic. Ernesto Alayza Mujica, <u>et. al.</u> collected their essays entitled <u>Military Service in Latin America</u> under sponsorship of the CEAPAZ Institute in Lima, and they were translated for English speaking readers in 2001. The essays deal with religious and other legal freedoms allowed to soldiers in Bolivia, Brazil, Chile, Colombia, Ecuador, Paraguay, Peru, and Venezuela, by scholars from these countries. The CEAPAZ Institute is an affiliate of the (Quaker) US Friends Service Committee. Military sociology in Latin America in the style of Morris Janowitz (University of Chicago), Lyle N. McAlister (University of Florida), and John J. Johnston (Stanford University) in the United States has been sorely lacking, and the Alayza Mujica work is a small but welcome contribution from the region.

Goeffrey Demarest at Ft. Leavenworth, Kansas has negotiated with Frank Cass Ltd., a distinguished British publisher of academic journals, to edit a new quarterly journal which will be called Ibero-American Security. This magazine will appear in 2003, will offer articles primarily in English but occasionally in Spanish and Portuguese, and will fill a huge yawning gap in Western Hemisphere scholarship. All submissions will be subjected to the standard academic referee process. Your reviewer here has been honored as an Editor Emeritus. Finally, your reviewer's collected writings on Latin American regional security issues, across four decades of scholarship and military collaboration, will be published in 2003 as Essays on Latin American Security Issues. This work will replace the somewhat outdated book Guardians of the Other Americas: Essays on the Latin America Military Forces (1997).

BIBLIOGRAPHY

Addicot, Jeffrey F. & Guy B. Roberts. "Building Democracies with Southern Command's Legal Engagement Strategy," Parameters XXXI,1 (Spring 2001)

Alayza Mujica, Ernesto, et. al. Military Service in Latin America (Lima: Centro de Estudios y Accion para la Paz CEAPAZ, 2001).

Beattie, Peter M. The Tribute of Blood: Army, Honor, Race, and Nation in Brazil, 1864-1945 (Durham, N.C.: Duke University Press, 2001).

Blebesheimer, Christina, and Francisco Mejia (eds.). Justice Beyond Our Borders: Judicial Reforms for Latin America and the Caribbean (Washington D.C.: Johns Hopkins Press/Inter-American Development Bank, 2000).

Demarest, Goeffrey, Editor. IberoAmerican Security (Frank Cass, Publisher, London).

Desch, Michael C; Jorge I Dominguez; & Andres Serbin (eds.) From Pirates to Drug Lords: The Post-Cold War Caribbean Security Environment (Albany, N.Y.: State University of New York Press, 1998).

Gelles, Paul H. Water and Power in Highland Peru: The Cultural Politics of Irrigation and Development. (New Brusnwick, N.J.: Rutgers University Press, 2000)

Grindle, Merilee S. Audacious Reforms: Institutional Invention and Democracy in Latin America (Baltimore: The Johns Hopkins University Press, 2000).

Hall, Michael R. Sugar and Power in the Dominican Republic: Eisenhower, Kennedy, and the Trujillos. (Westport: Greenwood Press, 2000).

Middlebrook, Kevin J. (ed.). Conservative Parties, the Right, and Democracy in Latin America. (Baltimore: The Johns Hopkins University Press, 2000).

Peterson, Anna L. Martyrdom and the Politics of Religion: Progressive Catholocism in El Salvador's Civil War (Albany: State University of New York Press, 1997.

Prillaman, William C. The Judiciary and Democratic Decay in Latin America: Declining Confidence in the Rule of Law (Westport: Praeger Publisher, 2000).

Ramsey, Russell W. Essays on Latin American Security Issues (Bloomington, Indiana: 1stBooks Library, 2003)

Schulz, Donald E. "The Growing Threat to Democracy in Latin America," Parameters XXXI,1 (Spring 2001)

Selbin, Eric. "Resistance, Rebellion, and Revolution in Latin America at the Millenium," Latin American Research Review (36:1) 2001.

Soto, Hernando de. The Mystery of Capitalism: Why Capitalism Triumphs in theWest and Fails Everywhere Else. (New York: Basic Books, 2000).

Whigham, Thomas L. The Paraguayan War: Causes and Early Conduct [Vol. I] (Lincoln: The University of Nebraska Press, 2002).

Russell W. Ramsey, Ph.D., D.Min.

U.S. POLICY

"United States Security Assistance Influence in Latin America – the Unheralded Treasure," Lecture at the *Civil Society and Security Issues for the 21st Century Conference,* Western Hemisphere Institute for Security Cooperation, Ft. Benning, Georgia, November 28 – 30, 2001.

In early 1940, the U.S. Army posted twenty officers in the Latin American republics in the capacity of Military Attaché or Senior Military Advisor to the host nation's army, and the U.S. Navy and Marine Corps similarly fielded a smaller network. The Army officers so assigned came here to this building at Fort Benning for a conference in November of that year, just sixty-one years ago this week, to give their new Latin American counterparts a tour of the U.S. Army Infantry Center. U.S. Navy officers conducted comparable visits to port facilities in Florida and Virginia.

The impetus to signing the executive agreements resulting in these relationships was the pressure applied by British Prime Minister Winston Churchill to U.S. President Franklin D. Roosevelt about possible German incursions into the Western Hemisphere through previously existing security assistance relationships with German officers. Churchill also exaggerated the probability that Adolph Hitler might order an invasion from Africa across the Atlantic to the hump of Brazil. U.S. Federal Bureau of Investigation Director J. Edgar Hoover pointed out the very real threats of German U-boats gaining intelligence information with which to sink Allied ships in the Atlantic after leaving Latin American ports and inserting clandestine spy operatives in several Latin American countries. Furthermore, Hoover demonstrated, the Colombian SCADTA Airline employed pilots who were German Luftwaffe reservists and might later bomb the Panama Canal.

By 1945, at the successful conclusion of World War II, the U.S.-Latin American military advisory structure set up in 1940 had far exceeded its value in cost, many times over. Brazil sent a huge Expeditionary Force which fought well with the U.S. IXth Army in Italy, Mexico sent an Air Force Squadron to fight with U.S. 20th Air Force against Japan in the Philippines, Ecuador placed troops to guard radar sites on the strategic Galapagos Islands, coastal navies performed efficient anti-U-boat screening, Colombia took control of SCADTA and the German pilots, and several countries worked closely with the U.S. armed forces and the F.B.I to arrest and dismantle the Nazi German spy apparatus in their midst.

From 1946 until 1950, two unfortunate U.S. policies drove the relationship between the Pentagon and its Latin American allies. One was the disappointing decision by the Harry S. Truman administration not to invest heavily in Latin America at the same time that billions of dollars were invested in Europe and Asia. This decision was based on the idea that re-starting damaged industrial economies was possible, while placing investment capital in developing nations that lacked basic industrial infrastructure was a waste of money. The other regrettable policy was the rapid turnover of excess war material to host nations willing to accept it. The policy was moderately useful in countries like Colombia and Mexico, where civilian control of the armed forces was well established, but in countries like Cuba, Nicaragua, and the Dominican Republic, the U.S. surplus war material program tended to strengthen anti-democratic elements and position the U.S. military mission in the anti-democracy camp.

To their great credit, the U.S. Army and Navy, and the newly independent Air Force after 1948, decided on their own to foster excellent military-to-military relationships in the Western Hemisphere, creating a useful, democratically oriented cultural presence, and a constitutionally obedient role model. This fact is an unheralded treasure awaiting discovery by historians, and blurred by Cold War actions that cast shadows on a worthy relationship. Also lost today is the valuable aggregate of lessons the United States was to learn from the sixty-year relationship with their Latin American friends.

The closing of the Berlin Air Corridor in 1948 by the Soviet Union, and the fall of Nationalist China to Mao Tse-tung's communist revolutionary forces, combined to cause a politically retrograde U.S. policy in the Latin American region until 1961. George F. Kennan, the "Mr. 'X'" of the U.S. State Department and author of the anti-communist manifesto article that became the policies of containment and deterrence, wrote a follow-up memorandum equating social disorder in Latin America with communist revolutionary subversion. With high unemployment, high inflation, and depression owing to post-war economic adjustment, several countries were having riots and challenges in favor of a broader and more responsive type of democracy. The U.S. military advisory groups therefore became expressions of a simplistic anti-communist rhetoric which advocated not only the professionalization of the host armed forces – a valid goal in any democracy – but also the use of those armed forces as internal police forces. This second concept was compatible with a medieval governmental philosophy in the Hispanic world called the *fuero militar*, in which the armed forces operate under a separate law external to the Constitution and have a legitimate and determinative policy making role. Anti-communism as a policy goal became understood in the region, then, as U.S. support for military dictatorship and the practice of *coup d'etat* in Latin America.

In 1961, President John F. Kennedy articulated the new U.S. policy of counterinsurgency through the military advisory groups in Latin America. His brother, Attorney General Robert F. Kennedy, headed the national Counterinsurgency Task Force, largely a response to the new threat of Fidel Castro's stated intention to export communist subversion throughout the region and topple Constitutional governments. The 1961 National Security Act also partially unified the U.S. armed forces more strongly than the original 1948 Unification Act had done, and all security assistance was placed under State Department oversight by the Security Assistance Act of 1961. The U.S. military advisory groups were directed to support a counterinsurgency doctrine that respected democracy and human rights, and whose final political goal was stable democracy, not military dictatorship. Yet by 1975, when the U.S. supported non-communist government in South Vietnam had collapsed under North Vietnam's huge and renewed military assault, the U.S. counterinsurgency concept was generally held in disrepute. This misunderstanding is sad, for U.S. military advisors and their State Department colleagues had explained for years that they were not advocating the French Algerian counterinsurgency policy, which advocated killing suspected communists first and creating stable government later. The U.S. military advisory groups played no determinative role whatsoever in the internal South American wars of the 1970s, but worldwide misperception of differing counterinsurgency doctrines has created the opposite impression in much interpretive writing.

By the advent of the 1980s, counterinsurgency plus military professionalism had made the transition to nation building, and the U.S. military advisory groups articulated this policy as part of a multi-agency team. While methodologically cleaner to explain, the nation-building policy became overshadowed in Central America by the civil wars provoked there when Fidel Castro inserted Soviet-trained and Soviet-equipped Cuban military advisors into Nicaragua, and provided guerrilla training for the Salvadoran FMLN. Consequently, once again, the U.S. military advisory structure in Latin America found itself embroiled as an apparent opponent of popular protest, for by the 1980s virtually every Marxist group in the world outside the communist countries had learned the deceptive art of pretending to be fighters for freedom, and denouncing the Pentagon and its agents as right-wing reactionaries. Yet it was, indeed, this same U.S. military advisory structure in Central America which presented the newly elected Bush Administration, in January 1989, with the recommendation that negotiated settlements were the only rational outcomes possible in Central America. There is a great irony here, for radical Marxist elements in the United States continue to trumpet to this very day that the U.S. military advisory structure caused the most violent and brutal aspects of both the South American civil wars in the 1970s, and the Central American civil wars in the 1980s.

The 1990s saw a great change in U.S. policy within Latin America. Anti-communism, as a battle cry, gave way to the furtherance of human rights, democratization, structural adjustment to privatization, and the discovery of new humane roles for the armed forces. With the United States also searching with some doubt for its exact leadership role in the post Cold War world, the U.S. military advisory groups functioning in Latin America were free to do some pragmatic experimentation. Thus, the Latin American armed forces and police found themselves conducting previously unknown discussions about the employment of basic military trainees to plant trees, about the use of security troops to police the troublesome Balkans region, and the reduction in total size of the armed forces concurrent with a modest degree of technological modernization. The military advisory group structure had a vital role in helping Ecuador and Peru resolve the border conflict of 1995, in helping Colombia's neighbors plan for the non-proliferation of the illegal narcotics plague, and in helping several disaster relief efforts in response to hurricanes, fires, and floods.

Today, as we address the 21st century, the U.S. relationship between its military advisory groups in Latin America and the host country armed forces and police is a world model of propitious excellence. These U.S. military advisory groups are small and often have excellent linguistic and cultural credentials; they tend to be trusted friends and advisers of their Latin American counterparts. If Latin America enters the 21st century as the world's least militarized region, measured in percentage of manpower and money devoted to state preparation for conflict, what has the United States gained in exchange for its commitment to maintain this role which has been, admittedly, a source of controversy? First, the United States has gained a region of allies who prohibit the existence of chemical, nuclear, and biological weapons by statute. Second, the United States is flanked by the region which renders the greatest per capita support to United Nations peacekeeping forces. Third, the United States lives in a region where a sane, professional conversation may be conducted on any given day about any sort of regional security issue. Thus, whether the topic is tracking down radical Islamic terrorists, separating out the combatants and the victims in the drug war, or planning a relief campaign for earthquake victims, there is a body of professionally educated people in uniform, backed by informed policy-making civilians, who can implement sane bi-lateral or multi-lateral policy in a democratic manner. This capability is Latin America's unseen gift to the United States. The unheralded gift from the United States to Latin America, perhaps, is the network of U.S. military professionals who have actualized, since 1940, the dreams of George Washington and Simon Bolivar to create a Hemisphere that was both free and stable.

On this 61st Anniversary of the Latin American Military Conference conducted right here in this room, we recognize the good work which has been done by those who dared to dream here when the world looked very different. Today's challenges are greater, but so are the resources at our disposal, and we have 61 years' experience in a climate of professionalism, trust, and mutual confidence upon which to draw.

BIBLIOGRAPHY

Ramsey, Russell W. *Guardians of the Other Americas: Essays on the Military Forces of Latin America.* Lanham, Md.: University Press of America, 1997.

Ramsey, Russell W. *Strategic Reading on Latin America.* 3d Ed. Bloomington, In.: 1st Books Press, 2001.

Russell W. Ramsey, Ph.D., D.Min.

"US Strategy for Latin America," *Parameters, Journal of the US Army War College*, Autumn, 1994.

"My mission is to protect the innocent oppressed, to help the unfortunate, to restore their rights to the inhabitants of this region, and to promote their happiness," wrote General Jose Francisco de San Martín, the military architect of independence for southern South America, on 8 September 1820.1 General Simón Bolívar, the emancipator of northern South America, opined in 1826, "The man of honor has no country save that in which the citizen's rights are protected and the sacred character of humanity is respected."2 Colombia's first President, the lawyer-General Francisco de Paula Santander, stated repeatedly in the 1820s that "arms have given us independence; laws will give us freedom" as he established the principle of civilian control over the armed forces.3

Yet Bolívar himself expressed anguish over the apparent triumph of *caudillismo* – rule by para-military strongmen – that frustrated constitutional democracy in several Latin American countries for a century. The movement to professionalization of Latin America's small armed forces, after 1880, included a tendency during the Cold War years for military leaders in several countries to exert an extra-constitutional praetorian role.4 At various points in the Cold War, military and police forces in a dozen Latin American countries carried out human rights abuses under the guise of national security. Marxist-Leninist regimes in Nicaragua and Cuba engaged in massive increases in troops and armaments, achieving force levels not previously seen in the region.

Redeeming the Dream

Latin America's armed forces now emerge at the end of the Cold War as a positive force amid bold democratization and economic development within the world's oldest and largest homogeneous block of constitutional and independent nation-states. Measured since 1830 by percent of the gross domestic product spent on the armed forces, percent of the national manpower in military uniform, the number of wars, relative levels of armaments, and percent of citizens killed or displaced by war, Latin America is also the world's least bellicose and least militarized region.5

Military praetorianism under all banners is today in disrepute, and the *posse comitatus* principle is now the law throughout Latin America except in Haiti and Cuba.6 There are 12 Latin American military contingents serving in the 26 international peacekeeping forces operational in 1994.7 Shared linguistic, training, and operations experiences between US and Latin American military officers today contribute to democratically obedient armed forces relationships.8 Finally, a case can be made that Latin America's armed forces, since 1961, are among the world's regional leaders in low-cost civic action programs that improve the quality of life for remote populations and help the general public in times of civil disaster.9

The Core of a US Policy

US military policy for Latin America in the 1990s, and into the 21st century, calls for quiet, inexpensive steps through which to institutionalize and strengthen the functional linkage among the Western Hemisphere's military leaders. The strategic applications all flow from that policy, save in the cases of Cuba, Nicaragua, Haití, and Panamá, whose military and public security officers are estranged from their US counterparts for differing historical reasons. A renewal of the once cordial military-to-military relations with these four nations is attainable during the remaining years of the 1990s.

The possible strategies emanating from this *hermandad* (translated as "brotherhood" without gender, the name for a defensive municipal structure in medieval Spain) hold bright hopes for regional peace. With a tiny per capita regional investment of national security funds, this "brotherhood of the Americas" can be an exportable model by which to secure democratic liberties and open-market economic success in a climate free of international wars, unilateral military interventions, class revolutions, ethnic and religious conflict, and organized crime.

Much analytical literature on Latin America stresses the praetorian and abusive nature of its armed forces. US national security programs during the Cold War era often are blamed for having fostered both tendencies. Yet one analyst concluded in a multi-regional analysis that the United States had little leverage through which to force behavioral change. Careful analysis of these US programs in Latin America reveals that they rarely exceeded two percent of all security assistance allocations and four percent of authorized foreign military sales carried out worldwide during the period. The programs had little effect on armed revolutions led by the military.10

Current US security assistance programs in the region barely total one-half billion dollars annually, most of which is concentrated in closing out the Central American conflicts of the 1980s, and in the Andean counter-narcotics campaign, two areas where the United States bears indisputable moral responsibility to assist.11 The total cost of continuing the policy of cordial, constructive US-Latin American military-to-military relations would remain a tiny fraction of the US national defense budget. If this sum could be divided into the total strategic value of the region,12 the ensuing ration would reveal a highly cost-effective defense policy.

A Permanent Military Dialogue

The first item on the strategy agenda is to build an institutionalized future for the continued relationship. The Organization of American States (OAS) is the world's oldest regional assembly. The Inter-American Defense Board (IADB), a military advisory body, has only a consultative relationship with the OAS. There is much preoccupation in Western Hemispheric political circles about militarism within Latin America and about armed interventionism by the United States in Latin America. While a factual case can be made that these concerns are outdated by events, the future of the IADB is under debate. Some see it as a positive vehicle for international peacekeeping operations, while to others it is warmed-over Cold War baggage.13

The United States is only one actor on the state. Clearly, the era of gunboat diplomacy (1870-1933) and the era of Cold War preemptive interventionism (1947-1989) are over; Uncle Sam neither can nor should attempt to force a regional security regime upon nations which reject the structure. But to the extent that quiet diplomacy can prevail, the United States should work actively to preserve and enrich the existing Western Hemispheric security policy and structure.

Under the Carter-Torrijos Treaties ratified in 1979, US Southern Command (SOUTHCOM) in Panamá must depart or have its presence renegotiated prior to the last day of 1999. A useful US policy, therefore, would be to work for the creation of a regional structure that provides focused national security planning for the United States in a cooperative hemispheric security setting. A US-Western Hemisphere Command (WHC) should be created to replace SOUTHCOM, and an OAS Security Commission, an enhanced version of the IADB, should be created by amending the OAS Charter. The WHC would be structurally located within the newly empowered OAS Security Commission, whose geographic headquarters should be in a convenient, neutral, and uncontested location. Five sub-regional planning elements of this proposed OAS Security Commission would structurally parallel the current family of trade pacts organized under the General Agreement on Tariff and Trade (GATT).14

Region	Members	Economic Parallel
North America	Canada, USA, Mexico	NAFTA
Caribbean	Caribbean Ind. Nations	CARICOM/CAFTA
Central America	Guatemala, Honduras, Nicaragua, El Salvador, Costa Rica, Panamá	Central American Common Market
Andean Region	Colombia, Venezuela, Ecuador, Perú, Bolivia	Andean Regional Free Trade Pact
Southern Cone	Brazil, Paraguay, Chile, Uruguay, Argentina	MERCOSUR

Thus, the North American Region would manage security planning for the North American Free Trade Alliance (NAFTA) countries (Canada, the United States, and Mexico); the Caribbean Region would do the same task for the Caribbean Common Market and Caribbean Free Trade Agreement countries (CARICOM/CAFTA); the Central American Region for the Central American Common Market nations; the Andean Region for the Andean Regional Free Trade

Pact countries; and the Southern Cone Region for this sub-region's trade pact members (called MERCOSUR, by the Spanish acronym). The creation of a small, sub-regional headquarters for each of these elements would help to reduce fears of a "military monolith" on Latin American soil.

Any successful national security system depends upon the balanced triad of political, economic, and military objectives and policies. Discussions of future US-Latin American relations call for the fostering of cordial, consultative relationships in the political sphere, a goal quite achievable given the excellent quality of US State Department career service diplomats who worked in Latin America during the last decade of the Cold War. The economic dimension of the triad may be more difficult to achieve. Economic power is clustered in bewildering arrays of multinational corporations, governmental agencies, regional trade treaty boards, national companies with private and public ownership, and, to be sure, powerful extra-hemispheric interests which neither parallel nor owe allegiance to the political structures in the region.15 Nevertheless, the emergence of a subculture of economic superstars in a dozen Latin American countries in the past decade suggests that a consultative hemispheric network in the economic sphere is already taking form and will not lack for competent personnel.16

The Possible Strategy Agenda

With the political, economic, and military spheres of the Western Hemisphere moving toward structural collegiality, the military strategies for maintaining peace and defense at minimum cost are workable. The military and law enforcement strategy agenda for the remaining years of the 20th century and the early 21st century contains ten objectives. These are:

1. Maintain and improve the hemispheric national security framework, with seats at the round table for every country
2. Bolster military professionalism
3. Reduce the power of the region's drug cartels
4. Cope humanely with mass migration
5. Increase Latin American participation in protection of air and sea lanes of communication, with special emphasis on the Panama Canal
6. Foster the blue-helmet and civic action capabilities of Latin America's armed forces
7. Institutionalize the protection of human rights by the armed forces
8. Maintain a regional defense philosophy which opposes the use of nuclear, chemical, biological, and other inhumane weapons
9. Secure peace and democratic stability in Central America and the Caribbean
10. Develop military and police capabilities to protect both the natural environment and the use of financial resources 17

Political and economic policies must be congruent if the military and law enforcement systems of the hemisphere are to meet these objectives.

Hemispheric National Security Framework

Perfecting the hemispheric national security framework, and the US role in it, calls for a mix of political and military diplomacy. This topic is ranked first in priority because, while parts of the other nine agenda items are possible through bilateral and sub-regional accords and programs, the goal of a peaceful, democratic, and prospering Western Hemisphere requires a structure that no major sector of the world has ever had: a multinational security round table without a perceived immediate foreign military threat. Circumstances are right for creating this mechanism.

Foster Military Professionalism

The immediate concomitant to the structural imperative is the strategy of fostering military and law enforcement professionalism. The conceptual dimension is a continuing process of cognitive (dealing with facts) and affective (dealing with values) professional education. The delivery means have existed in part for half a century. These are the US Army School of the Americas at Ft. Benning, Georgia; the Inter-American Air Force Academy at Lackland Air Force Base, Texas; and the Naval Small Craft Instruction and Technical Training School at Rodman Navy Base in Panamá. These three institutions all present, in Spanish, professional courses that use US curriculum models filtered through the platform delivery of a sophisticated inter-American faculty. Since the early 1960s, the Inter-American Defense Board has operated the Inter-American Defense College (IADC) at Ft. McNair in Washington, D.C. While not entirely analogous, the IADC in many ways resembles the NATO Defense College in Rome.18

Cognitive professional education is available to most Latin American military and police personnel through a wide spectrum of schools and foreign advisory mechanisms, both at home and abroad. What makes the IADC and the family of US-operated schools so valuable is the affective dimension of the education they provide. Students study military and police topics in Spanish, as the most universal of the region's native languages, sharing the experience with hemispheric classmates who face differing challenges but who share cultural bonds.19 An officer or a sergeant can memorize a tactical or technical procedure in the cognitive domain, but one converts those procedures into functional morality and professionalism via the affective learning chance.

The existing family of US-operated professional military education schools should be expanded to permit all participating nations, not just the United States, to serve as teachers and role models. The Colombian army, for example, is a world leader in humane peacekeeping operations, both at home and abroad, with a long record of public affirmation to prove it. The Costa Rican civil guard and the

Barbadian defense force are world-reputed models for the national defense institution in a small, democratic country. The Brazilian navy is effective in both fluvial and blue-water regional security operations. Canada and Colombia are world leaders in blue-helmet operations. In an expanded learning environment, these countries would share their areas of military and law enforcement success with officers and noncommissioned officers of the hemisphere.

US strategy should include the expansion and inter-Americanization of the School of the Americas concept to embrace several campuses in a variety of host countries. One campus, with a heavily civilian faculty, should offer a one-year professional foundations course, "Military and Police Professionalism in the Americas," with a strong curriculum in history, law, ethics, human rights, democracy, economics, and the inter-American system. A subculture of civilians from the Latin American defense and law enforcement ministries should attend these schools regularly with their military counterparts, just as US civilian security careerists now attend the Department of Defense family of senior service colleges. The hemispheric nations should be encouraged to provide modest financial support plus administrative machinery to encourage attendance at the courses and career tracking of the graduates.

Marginalize the Narco-traffickers

Reducing the violent and inherently destabilizing effects of the narcotics empires is a task that cuts across political, economic, and military interests. US strategy should acknowledge that much of the problem begins in the United States, among the cocaine users who have the cash to buy the drugs.[20] Any counter narcotics strategy must recognize that Mexico or the Andean Region is just one facet of the worldwide supply and distribution network, and that any solution must attack the challenge at every level from grower to consumer.

The narcotics kingpins operate bogus nation-states, heavily armed and ruthless beyond description. Colombia alone, for example, has lost more troops in fighting the narco-traffickers since 1983 than the United States lost in all foreign conflict during the same period. Each of the three Inter-American networks for dialogue – political, economic, and military – must work for a coordinated solution that matches resources to measured effectiveness. The round table principle means that within Latin America, at least, US views on how to conduct anti-drug operations within sovereign countries would rest upon the wishes of the host nation.[21]

The drug scourge can never be ended; it is a dimension of human vice that can be changed only in degree through applied public policy. But much of the military training and force configuration that has proved useful in fighting the drug war is also appropriate for other military and security scenarios such as border control, disaster relief, anti-terrorism efforts, regional and international peace operations, and small coalition force campaigns.

Russell W. Ramsey, Ph.D., D.Min.

Humane Migration Control

Coping with migration as a national security problem translates into close dialogue between armed forces and police forces. Armed forces participation on this topic may include the occasional dedication of surveillance, communications, and transportation equipment to back up what is clearly a law enforcement challenge. Several Latin American countries have paramilitary forces, such as the Venezuelan National Guard and the Argentine National Gendarmerie, who do these tasks skillfully; the US role in the regional effort would be to serve as supporting logistics provider, not as primary operator. US law enforcement agencies, such as the Customs and Immigration Service, the Drug Enforcement Administration, the Federal Bureau of Investigation, and state and local police organizations across the sunbelt states, should be major participants in this effort. Clearly, long-term victory over this particular challenge would be enhanced by the success of the GATT family of trade accords, especially NAFTA, CARICOM, and the Central American Common Market. History suggests that there will always be problematic countries within a region, and therefore mass migration remains a mixture of humanitarian, legal, and national security challenges. The national security role in mass migration is professionally underdeveloped and should become a curriculum initiative within the hemispheric system of schools for military and police leaders.22

Sea Lanes, Air Lanes

The future strategic task on the seas adjacent to Latin America is to enhance the region's navies as they assume increased roles during an era of economic development and industrialization, without stimulating a costly and disruptive naval arms race. The blue-water navies of Argentina, Brazil, and Chile have been influential in the region since the 1880s. US naval captains have played a quiet role in bilateral and multilateral maritime diplomacy with these three navies ever since that era.23 Just prior to World War II, US Navy policy added the Andean Region navies in coastal and blue-water security missions, and, as Cuba became a mid-range military threat late in the Cold War, the Caribbean navies joined US naval security activities in that sub-region.24

Latin America's air forces find their principal employment, at present, in logistical support of land forces. One of Latin America's most important decisions during the Cold War was not to emulate the air power arms races in progress in the Middle East, much of Asia, parts of Africa, and all of Europe. The Andean Region air forces have roles in the anti-narcotics conflict, although the growth of national police forces in the region has brought about a proliferation of aviation assets among the national security forces, some of it is duplicative and inefficient. While the role of the Latin American armed forces in developing a technical sector within the educational sphere is well known, a less known aspect is the role of the air forces in stimulating a multi-sectoral aviation industry.25

Discussion of future sea power and air power strategies within Latin America during a time of economic growth must address the issue of persuading the region to take on a sense of importance about protecting the neutrality of the Panama Canal always have evoked mixed perceptions in both the United States and in Latin America.26 The Carter-Torrijos Treaties and the Cold War's end now offer the perfect opportunity for Washington to divest itself of this chronic national security dilemma. A future strategy is for US diplomats, in coordination with US air and sea officers, to encourage the region's own air forces and navies to proclaim and maintain the neutrality of the Panama Canal. The locus of Panamanian foreign relations concerns then becomes the OAS.

Military Civic Action and Blue-Helmet Operations

Enhancing Latin America's blue-helmet and civic action roles is a strategy of value to the region and to the world. The effectiveness of Colombian soldiers in Korea (1952-1954, UN) and in the Sinai (1956-1958, UN; 1981-present, Multinational Force and Observers) has caused village mayors in turbulent regions to ask for them by name.27 Several measures would take advantage of the skills and experiences developed in those kinds of operations. First, curriculum units in peacemaking and peacekeeping operations, taught by Colombians and Canadians with actual blue-helmet experience, should be added to the curriculum of the hemispheric professional military schools. Second, as other nations join in the teaching process, a pilot staff for an Inter-American Defense Force (IADF) should be set up within the OAS Security Council. Third, the hemisphere's political and economic structures should be provided with a statement of capabilities and control measures for this IADF in order to defuse concerns about the force becoming a new kind of gunboat diplomacy.28

The civic action role for the Latin American military forces was well established, legally and morally, in the early 1960s.29 Core curriculum programs at the hemisphere's professional military schools can highlight specific abuses that have occasionally tainted an otherwise excellent civic action record. Civic action programs should not compete with civilian economic activity, should only function where civilian government and the private sector cannot operate, and should not be used as a philosophical cover for military-operated arms factories. The maturation of democratic governmental institutions and free enterprise economic systems now alleviates many of these concerns in the region. The Colombian National Civic Action Council, where the Minister of Defense is the only voting military representative among 16 members, is the best functional mode.30 Civic action by military forces, done efficiently under civilian control, can be a vital contributor to Latin American regional economic and political development.

Guaranteeing Human Rights

The securing of human rights by the armed forces of the Americas is a universally attainable goal by the end of the 20th century. Human rights as an academic subject is taught at the School of Americas. It is really a mixture of several international accords (Hague, 1907; Geneva, 1949), military and civil laws of each country, and an expanding body of ideas based upon the United Nations Declaration of Human Rights. Public knowledge about the subject comes from government sources of mixed accuracy, international humanitarian groups such as the Red Cross, nongovernmental organizations (called "NGOs" in the literature) dedicated to human rights advocacy, news media sources of widely varying credibility, political groups often having ideological agendas, and criminal organizations such as the Andean narco-traffickers. While controversy and emotion attend every facet of the process, Latin America has produced legitimate, battle-decorated human rights heroes like General Manuel Sanmiguel Buenaventura of Colombia and police General Antonio Ketin Vidal of Perú; unfortunately, the deeds of these men rarely appear in the news.31

Developing respect for human rights among uniformed personnel lies more in the affective psychological domain than in the cognitive domain. Further, the contextual authority setting, the state of troop training, and the level of the armed threat all play strong roles. It is one thing to posture for the concept of human rights from the safety of the podium and quite another to place one's life at risk among murderous drug cartel gunmen. Each country needs training initiatives such as the 1993 contract between the Ecuadorian armed forces and the Latin American Association for Human Rights.32 The hemisphere's armed forces could then share techniques for training troops in this matter, while their political counterparts ensure parallel commitment to human rights training by law enforcement agencies. The case for terminating US training assistance, currently called Enhanced International Military Education and Training (IMET), to punish Latin American human rights violators in uniform may be viewed as another example of the *a priori* assumption that all US military actions in the region are morally tainted, or are corrupted by exposure to the Latin American military profession.33

Arms Limitations

Latin America is the world's only region having no inventory of nuclear, biological, and chemical weapons. Despite some controversy in the 1980s about nuclear arms and nuclear power development in the Southern Cone, Latin America's governments without exception stand opposed to the existence of weapons of mass destruction in the region. Further, there is a strong initiative under way in Central America to remove the land mines implanted by several antagonists during the 1980s.34 The US Army School of the Americas has trained packets of Latin American military and police to do some of this dangerous work. One of the strongest ways to build confidence in the region's armed forces and police is for all commanders to declare and show opposition to human rights violations and inhumane weapons.

Burying Hatchets

Putting to rest the earlier conflicts and repressions in Central America and the Caribbean is an agenda which cannot be avoided, if the proposed OAS Security Council is to be taken seriously. Burying old hatchets in Central America is not enough; new political and economic thinking, protected by a new breed of military and police personnel, is an urgent necessity. Those who work directly with Central America's younger generation of military officers see hopeful signs: armies are getting smaller, police forces are being created, and the rising junior officers in many forces now concern themselves with professionalism, not ideology. The hemispheric political community must give change a chance to occur. Demilitarization of former combatants in Nicaragua and El Salvador has been helpful and must continue; supervised electoral processes that seem to work must be affirmed by accompanying economic growth.35

Two current problems threaten the impulse to move away from armed interventions – the situation in Haiti and the continuing deterioration of Cuba under Castro. The United States must restrain the understandable urge to employ its own military force unilaterally in Haiti. A combination of coercive diplomacy and negotiation must first restore a constitutional government, and peacekeeping commitments must come from the hemisphere at large.36 Training of a new Haitian police force by the Royal Canadian Mounted Police in 1993 and 1994 is precisely the right kind of foundation step required for ultimate success.

With regard to Cuba, military invasion would be the one certain way to foster Cuban and hemispheric sympathy for Fidel Castro and thereby lengthen his faltering stay in power. Any national security measures attending the ultimate collapse of Castro's regime must be hemispheric.37

In all these cases, the divisive leftist vs. rightist rhetoric pertaining to US policy in Latin America must be put aside if Uncle Sam is to retain post-Cold War leadership among equals in the region. Full but self-restrained participation in the triad of hemispheric political, economic, and military round tables, however constituted, is in the US national interest. US leaders and Latin American interest lobbies within the United States can scarcely expect Latin Americans to end feuds if US policy toward the region is made with moralistic zealotry.38

Environment and Resources

The Western Hemisphere's military leaders must become champions of the natural environment and of scarce economic resources within their countries. The dismal environmental record of the communist armed forces in Eastern Europe and the former Soviet Union has sent the world a shocking message, one which probably helps nail down the coffin of Marxist ideology. Their unexploded shells, unregistered land mines, spilled toxic wastes, rusting junkyards, and crudely managed nuclear programs will cost the world countless casualties and billions of dollars in restoration. Similarly, the Western world's armed forces consume too much fuel, emit excess toxic wastes, and often fail to budget funds for cleaning up discarded military sites. Latin American militaries are not alone in having lessons to learn.

The Latin American armed forces already have done some good work in the environmental area. Brazilian troops have turned up in the frontier zones in recent years to confront environmental abusers who were laying waste the land and killing workers who dared to object. Colombian troops in the field have always been a model case for leaving their area of operations just a bit better than before they arrived.39 Ecuadorian army troops were fighting fires in the Galapagos Islands in April 1994, rescuing one of the earth's most important natural habitats.

Resources management is another topic now taking root among the Western Hemisphere's armed forces and police. It is defined as the distribution of scarce resources among abundant alternatives; scholastically, it embraces microeconomics, decision science, operations research, scientific management theory, and cyclical budgetary processes. Like human rights, resources management must penetrate the affective realm of the learner to have value. The military officer or police commander must learn to do the most with the least, and to do rational cost and benefit analysis as a matter of routine. For Latin America's small armed forces, this could mean comparing five different ways to interdict border-smuggling, combining the measures with illegal immigration control and the anti-narcotics campaign, and then blending the resources of land, sea, air, and police forces in the most effective, and hopefully efficient, mix. By stretching scarce cash during an era of economic privatization, the Latin American militaries can set a good example and help their governments provide desperately needed social services with the money not spent on military things.40

US Influence on the Region's Militaries

US land, sea, and air officers have done excellent work with Latin America. They have been perceived as helpful modernizers more than as invaders. Illustrious officers like Colonel George W. Goethals, General Leonard Wood, and General Matthew B. Ridgway served with distinction in Latin American long before the Cold War. General Ridgway figured prominently in the early days of the Inter-American Defense Board and the transition to Cold War policy era. General Vernon L. Walters was influential in linking Latin America's armed forces to appropriate Cold War roles. General John R. Galvin and General Frederick F. Woerner were senior Latin American experts during the height of the Cold War challenges; both officers served prominently in other theaters. General George A. Joulwan and General Barry R. McCaffrey combined military success in other world theaters with great knowledge of Latin America's changing security challenges at Cold War's end.

The US Navy and the US Marine Corps bore the brunt of US military policy in Latin America during the age of gunboat diplomacy (1870-1933). Both developed a cadre of senior officers who knew Latin America well, and who are remembered positively in the region despite the military interventionist roles they often played. The US Army was the major actor that linked Latin America to the Cold War challenges (1947-1989), mostly through countering armed subversion, and simultaneously served as role model and teacher for professionalization and acceptance of civilian authority. Those two missions were done with devotion and skill, and with limited resources, since neither had high priority for defense expenditures.

In the 1990s, the repository of US Army national security knowledge about Latin America must not be discarded for lack of a strategic initiative, nor lost through attrition of personnel. Working cooperatively with the other armed forces and federal law enforcement agencies, the US Army is the logical senior executive agent to carry out the ten strategic initiatives, to build the military linkage (*hemandad*) that will make the Americas, once and for all, the bastion of freedom and opportunity that George Washington and Simón Bolívar both fought to achieve and labored to build.

NOTES

1. Henry M. Brackenridge, *Voyage to South America* (London: T. and J. Allman, 1820), pp. 212-16.
2. Bernardo Jurado Toro, *Bolívar y la ley* (Caracas: Direccion de Artes Graficas M.D., 1991), pp. 166-69.
3. David Bushnell, *The Making of Modern Colombia* (Berkeley: Univ. Of California Press, 1993), pp. 55-56
4. Russell W. Ramsey, "The Spanish Military Orders: Alcantara, Calatrava, and Santiago," (British) Army *Quarterly & Defence Journal*, 113 (June 1983), 345-46.
5. Russell W. Ramsey, "A Military Turn of Mind: Educating Latin American Officers," *Military Review*, 73 (August 1993), 13.
6. Literally, "power of the county"; contextual praxis connotes that the army may be used only for national defense, and police who answer to judges must be used for domestic law enforcement.
7. John T. Currier, "The Role of Latin American Armed Forces in Peacekeeping Operations," unpublished paper, Troy State Univ. at Ft. Benning, March 1994, p. 3; and International Institute of Strategic Studies, *The Military Balance*, 1993-1994 (London: IISS, 1994),pp. 253-60. Three of these peacekeeping forces are multinational but not under the United Nations.
8. Russell W. Ramsey, "U.S. Military Courses for Latin Americans Are a Low-Budget Strategic Success," *North-South, the Magazine of the Americas*, 2 (February-March 1993), 38-41.
9. Richard L. Sutter, "The Strategic Implication of Military Civic Action," in *Winning the Peace: The Strategic Implications of Military Civic Action*, ed. John W. DePauw and George A. Luz (New York: Praeger, 1992), pp. 185-89; and Russell W. Ramsey, "The Role of Latin American Armed Forces in the 1990s," *Strategic Review*, 20 (Fall 1992), reprinted in *Proceedings,*

5th Latin American Conference (Ft. Benning, Ga.: US Army School of the Americas, 1993).
10. Timothy P. Wickham-Crowley, *Guerrillas & Revolutions in Latin America* (Princeton, N.J.: Princeton Univ. Press, 1992), pp. 68-85; and Jennifer Morrison Taw, "The Effectiveness of Training International Military Students in Internal Defense and Development," National Defense Research Institute (Santa Monica, Calif: RAND, 1993), pp. 15-22.
11. US Congress, *Congressional Record*, Security Assistance Programs, Fiscal Year 1994 (Washington: GPO, 1994), pp. 3-16, 19-21, 27-28, 38, 44-46, 48-60.
12. Abraham F. Lowenthal, "Changing U.S. Interests and Policies in a New World," in *The United States and Latin American Relations in the 1990s: Beyond the Inter-American System*, ed. Jonathan Hartlyn, et al. (Chapel Hill: Univ. of North Carolina Press, 1993), pp. 65-85. This article is easily the best short calculus of US strategic interests in Latin America.
13. James R. Harding, "Security Challenges and Opportunities in the Americas," *North-South, the Magazine of the Americas*, 3 (February-March, 1994), 48-51.
14. Peter Hakim, "NAFTA and After: A New Era for the US and Latin America?" *Current History*, 93 (March 1994), 97-102.
15. Robert Devlin, *Debt and Crisis in Latin America: The Supply Side of the Story* (Princeton, N.J.: Princeton Univ. Press, 1992), 7-8, 253-56; and Sidney Weintraub, "The Economy on the Eve of Free Trade," *Current History*, 92 (February 1993), 72.
16. J. Benjamín Zapata, "The Honduran View," in Russell W. Ramsey, ed., *Proceedings, Eighth Latin America Symposium* (Maxwell AFB, Ala.: Air Command & Staff College, 1991), pp. 19-21. Minister-Counselor Zapata's ability to explain national security in terms of the political economy is but one example of these economic "superstars" in action.
17. Gabriel Marcella and Fred Woerner, "Mutual Imperatives for Change in Hemispheric Strategic Policy: Issues for the 1990s, *Evolving US Strategy for Latin America and the Caribbean,* ed. L. Erik Kjonnerwood (Washington: National Defense Univ. Press, 1992), 56. The inventory of Inter-American strategic agenda items in this article is the most complete and coherent in the literature to date.
18. "The Inter-American Defense College," *Military Review*, 50 (April 1970), 20-27.
19. This explains the "Manuel Noriega Syndrome," namely, that the School of the Americas produced an academically superior graduate whose personal standards were vicious. Noriega avoided the affective education environment, filtering out useful technical information for his own purposes. All schools have conspicuous failures among their alumni.
20. Russell W. Ramsey, "U.S. Narcotics Addiction Wrecks Colombian Democracy," (British) *Army Quarterly & Defence Journal*, 120 (January 1990), 27-34. US cocaine cash intercepted in Colombia during 1990 was

$1.2 billion dollars, the annual worldwide profit of Coca-Cola International that year.

21. Kate Doyle, "The Militarization of the Drug War in Mexico," *Current History*, 92 (February 1993), 36-88; James van Wert, "Bush's Other War," in *War on Drugs: Studies in the Failure of U.S. Narcotics Policy*, ed. Alfred W. McCoy and Alan A. Block (Boulder, Colo: Westview Press, 1992), pp. 27-34; Bruce M. Bagley and Juan G. Tokatian, "Dope and Dogma: Explaining the Failure of U.S.-Latin American Drug Policies," in *The United States and Latin American Relations in the 1990s: Beyond the Inter-American System*, ed. Jonathan Hartlyn, et al. (Chapel Hill: Univ. of North Carolina Press, 1993), pp. 214-33; and Kevin Dougherty, "The Role of the U.S. Military in Interdicting the Latin American Drug Traffic: How the Latin Americans See It," unpublished paper, Troy State Univ. at Ft. Benning, March 1994.

22. Diego Ascencio, "Immigration and Economic Development for the 21st Century," in Kjonnerwood, pp. 147-53.

23. Naval Ministry, *Gazetta de Noticias* (Rio de Janeiro), 12 October 1923, trans. US Dept. of State Serials File on Brazil, 1910-29, State Dept. Archive code no. 823.20/34; and Armin K. Ludwig, "Two Decades of Brazilian Geopolitical Initiatives and Military Growth," *Air University Review*, 37 (July-August 1986), 56-64.

24. In 1915, Captain Edward L. Beach, US Navy, was commended by the Navy Department for averting great bloodshed in Haiti. He negotiated a truce between the armed forces of the principal rivals during a violent overthrow of the government, at great risk to his own life. See also Lars Schoultz, *National Security and United States Policy towards Latin America* (Princeton, N.J. Princeton Univ. Press, 1987), pp. 199-215.

25. Paul G. Havel, "The Role of Latin American Air Forces in Modernizing Society," unpublished paper, Troy State Univ. at Ft. Benning, March 1994; and Jorge A. del Carpio Tejeda, "La Policía Nacional en la Guerra Anti-Narcotraficante en Perú," US Army School of the Americas, July 1993.

26. Michael L. Connif, *Panama and the United States: The Forced Alliance* (Athens: Univ. of Georgia Press, 1992), pp. 169-71. A positive dimension of US policy in Panamá is the training of the new Panamanian National Police by the International Criminal Investigative and Training Assistance Program, a US Department of Justice operation. The program is strictly concentrated upon law enforcement, not national defense. This policy represents an alternative national security training paradigm of great potential for other countries.

27. Russell W. Ramsey, "The Colombian Battalion in Korea and Suez," *Journal of Inter-American Studies*, 9 (October 1967), 541-60.

28. Robert A. Pastor, *Whirlpool: U.S. Foreign Policy Toward Latin America and the Caribbean* (Princeton, N.J.: Princeton Univ. Press, 1992), pp. 287-89.

29. H. H. Fischer, "Contribucion de las Fuerzas Armadas en el Desarrollo Economico-Social de los Paises," Inter-American Defense Board, Washington, D.C., 1 June 1961.
30. Russell W. Ramsey, "Defensa Interna en los Años 80: El Modelo Colombiano," *Military Review*, Spanish edition, 67 (July 1987), 62-77.
31. Jaime González Parra, "Gracias, Capitán," *El Tiempo*, Bogotá, 27 April 1970, p. 2; and *Caretas* (Lima), 9 September 1992, p. 87.
32. Ecuadorian Correspondent, "The Army Learns of Human Rights," *The Economist* (London), 16 October 1993, p. 49; and Jennifer M. Taw, "The Effectiveness of Training International Military Students in Internal Defense and Development," National Defense Research Institute (Santa Monica, Calif.: RAND, 1993), pp. 15-22.
33. Charles Coll and Rachel Neild, "Issues in Human Rights," Paper #3 (Washington: Washington Office on Latin America, 1992), pp. 28-34. This analysis by a leading NGO sums up the pros and cons of training foreign military forces on moral topics.
34. Kenneth Anderson and Stephen D. Goose, *Landmines: A Deadly Legacy* (New York: The Arms Project of Human Rights Watch, and Physicians for Human Rights, 1993), pp. 216-20.
35. Richard L. Millett, "Central America's Enduring Conflicts," *Current History*, 93 (March 1994), 124-28.
36. Pamela Constable, "Haiti: A Nation in Despair, a Policy Adrift," *Current History*, 93 (March 1994), 108-11. For the idea that Latin America's predisposition to place sovereignty above all other diplomatic values may be declining, see Richard J. Bloomfield, "Suppressing the Interventionist Impulse," in Richard J. Bloomfield and Gregory F. Treverton, *Alternative to Intervention: A New U.S.-Latin American Security Relationship* (Boulder, Colo.: Lynn Reinner, 1990), pp. 132-33.
37. The most rational and compatible strategy to date appears in Gillian Gunn, *Cuba in Transition: Options for U.S. Policy* (Washington: Brookings Institution, 1993).
38. Robert B. Toplin, "Many Latin Americanists Continue to Wear Ideological Blinders," *Chronicle of Higher Education*, 30 March 1994, p. A48.
39. For indications that the Colombian public has long held their army in highest esteem, see Centro de Investigacion y Action Social (CIAS), *Estructuras Políticas de Colombia*, Colección "Monografías y Documentos," #3 (Bogotá: CIAS, 1969), p. 5; and "Encuesta Nacional," *Semana* (Bogotá), 11 January 1994, p. 55.
40. The School of the Americas instituted a Resources Management Course in 1993, with curriculum given at the Defense Resources Management Institute in Monterey, California, but tailored for Latin American application.

Review of: *Eisenhower: The Foreign Policy of Anti-Communism and Latin America*, by Stephen G. Rabe, Chapel Hill, N.C.: University of North Carolina Press, 1988. Reviewed in: *Military Intelligence*, April-June, 1989.

Stephen G. Rabe has set forth a revisionist alternative about the presidency of Dwight D. Eisenhower. Until recently, U.S. historians of Latin America have often accepted the notion of a languid World War II figurehead in the White House from 1953 to 1961. Ike's grandson David, and scholars such as Stephen E. Ambrose, Robert A. Divine, Fred I. Greenstein, Steve Neal and Herbert S. Parmet have changed this interpretation to reveal Eisenhower as a strong figure who shaped policy himself.

Rabe, however, is offended that Ike is made out be a humane statesman. Not so, he says, Eisenhower did not merely play golf while his anti-communist Secretary of State, John Foster Dulles, went red witch hunting in Latin America. According to Rabe, Eisenhower personally led the charge to put anti-communism before economic aid programs for Latin America. He advances that the military dictators who governed the nations south of the Río Grande in 1957 were a direct result of these policies.

In order to stress his point, Rabe mentions five times the misguided award of the Legion of Merit to military tyrants Manual Odria in Perú and Marcos Pérez Jiménez in Venezuela. Whether or not the U.S. Congress would have even considered a humanitarian aid program for Latin America just after the Korean Conflict, had Eisenhower recommended it, is never mentioned. There is no evaluation of worldwide communist military expansion between 1953 and 1961, so that, by omission of rationale, Eisenhower is made to look like a fool as he dogmatically demanded anti-communism in an area plagued by economic underdevelopment.

Yet this book is a milestone in U.S.-Latin American diplomatic history. Rabe did extensive research in the Eisenhower Library and among recently declassified National Security Council documents. He has given Latin American history its first book written in the language of international relations. He cites National Security Council documents by number and traces foreign policy to its actual source within the executive branch. Greater detail is now required by anyone who would analyze the Eisenhower years and their impact upon Latin America. With attention to detail will come the heightened East-West awareness that is lacking among U.S. scholars.

Rabe's book contains two chapters on the Cuban revolution of 1957-1959 and that critical period in Cuban foreign relations. These chapters may be the best short treatment to date on that vital subject. He also traces Harry Truman's Latin America policy. Even though he curiously omits Secretary of State George C. Marshall's strongly anti-communist position at the Bogotá IXth Inter-American Conference in 1948, he still shows that it was Truman, not Eisenhower, who extended the U.S. policy of containment to Latin America.

Russell W. Ramsey, Ph.D., D.Min.

    The author portrays the Colombian Battalion that fought for the United Nations Command in Korea as a token. This is a historical inaccuracy that raises questions in the reader's mind. Is the author deliberately omitting evidence which shows that Latin Americans, at the grass roots level, often thought and showed that the military expansion of communism in the 1950s was a danger to be opposed? A related criticism lies in a cause-and-effect assertion about the Central Intelligence Agency role in helping to overthrow the leftist Arbenz administration in Guatemala. What could have been a step forward in scholarly understanding about a U.S. foreign policy over-reaction disappears in the murky assertion that 100,000 Guatemalan citizens died as a direct result of U.S. intervention.

    Rabe is really reasserting Edwin Lieuwen's 1960 thesis that all U.S. military training and arms transfers to Latin America in the Truman-Eisenhower years were window dressing for a U.S. scheme to build a network of anti-communist strongmen throughout Latin America. Subsequent research on Third World arms transfers and on comparative military regimes in developing nations all combine to render the Lieuwen thesis invalid. Rabe researched more than enough evidence to see past Lieuwen's work.

    Eisenhower: The Foreign Policy of Anti-Communism and Latin America raises the stakes in the writing of U.S.-Latin American history to a new high. Stephen G. Rabe has done a vital piece of original scholarship. He has also opened the door for U.S. scholars of Latin America to abandon some of their comfortable guilt myths about their own country's role in Latin America.

Reviews of: *Sharing the Secrets: Open Intelligence and the War on Drugs*, by J.F. Holden-Rhodes, Westport, CT: Praeger Publishers, 1997; and *Drugs And Security in the Caribbean: Sovereignty Under Siege*, by Ivelaw Lloyd Griffith, University Park, PA: Pennsylvania State University Press, 1997. Reviewed in: *Strategic Review*, Spring, 1998.

Two excellent current books on the Western Hemisphere drug war open possibilities for viewing the phenomenon differently, and consequently for deriving a more effective counter-narcotics strategy both in the United States and in the Latin American countries affected by the narcotics plague.

Sharing the Secrets gives the initial impression of being an argumentative plea for vindicating the author's intelligence gathering concept. Author J. R. Holden-Rhodes was a U.S. Marine Corps combat intelligence officer, and later a U.S. Army intelligence analyst working on drug war issues in U.S. Southern Command. Now pursuing a second career as an academician, he makes the case for the use of "open source intelligence" (OSINT), as opposed to the traditionally compartmentalized and classified intelligence program, on matters relating to the Drug War.

Drugs and Security in the Caribbean is the first comprehensive survey of the drug war in that sub-region of Latin America. Author Ivelaw Lloyd Griffith is a political science professor at Florida International University (Miami), and is arguably the most authoritative and certainly the most comprehensively published scholar on Caribbean regional security issues. He grew up in Guyana.

Holden-Rhodes traces the history of U.S. Cold War strategic intelligence from its architects, George S. Pettee and Sherman Kent, to the post-Cold War thinking of Joseph Markowitz. Holden-Rhodes believes that OSINT, in contrast to closeted and classified intelligence gathering and processing, draws a broader community of interests into the drug war. OSINT reduces parochialism within the intelligence community and its accompanying tunnel vision, and instead focuses upon home and hearth issues like personal safety and the cost of government. Thus, while OSINT broadens the base of domestic support for the drug war, it is nevertheless "an art that is best practiced by that small group of people who have the gift of discerning substance and direction from information that others simply offer up in shopping list form."

Holden-Rhodes then traces the development of counter-drug intelligence efforts, leading to the founding of the National Drug Intelligence Center at Johnstown, Pennsylvania in 1988. He concludes that drug intelligence products have never been employed correctly because intelligence production has been functionally linked to the discovery of short-term interdiction targets. This discussion flows into the quest for a counter-drug strategy. Failing to unshackle counter-drug strategy from national security strategy has crippled the effort, he shows. Holden-Rhodes argues that this structural error dates from 1973, when President Richard Nixon put his quest for a drug war strategy into the hands of the

Watergate "plumbers": Egil Krogh, Gordon Liddy, E. Howard Hunt, and John Erlichman. The growing drug industry in Colombia is the base for Holden-Rhodes' analysis of an essentially flawed search to define the "drug threat," and his subsequent chapter on militarizing the war on drugs portrays a well-intentioned effort derailed by a distorted intelligence process that operates on the Cold War national security model. His chart linking military responses to identified narcotics syndicate threats would improve any textbook surveying U.S. national security policy.

Holden-Rhodes' description of the drug interdiction effort at the U.S. border with Mexico should be read in conjunction with Timothy J. Dunn's *The Militarization of the US-Mexico Border, 1978-1992* (University of Texas at Austin, 1995). While both are critical of U.S. strategy Holden-Rhodes blames flawed intelligence perception, while Dunn blames racist, imperialist prejudices in the national security community. Holden-Rhodes' last chapter, "Getting It Right," should have been made into two chapters, one containing his superb country-by-country analysis of the Western Hemisphere narco-industry threat, and one showing how his plan for employing OSINT would strengthen the U.S. national anti-drug effort.

In a candid portrayal of U.S. drug czar Barry McCaffrey, the highly decorated retired general who was Commander-in-Chief, U.S. Southern Command from 1994 to 1996, Holden-Rhodes believes that McCaffrey's forceful personality and high integrity will unite the U.S. national security community to wage the drug war, something the first three czars failed to do.

The Archbishop Colloredo desired sacred music of a certain style at Salzburg and, in 1777, sacked Wolfgang Amadeus Mozart, the composer whose music most nearly touched the heavens, for failing to produce the desired product. The archbishops of intelligence at the CIA, DIA, DEA, NSA, and DEA may not even hire J. R. Holden-Rhodes. Indeed, his final chapter barely touches upon the ways that his OSINT concept could be used to alter an essentially fragmented and reactive U.S. anti-drug strategy. Yet his music touches the heavens in the sense that OSINT, applied at a coordinated national level, might become the vehicle to awaken the body politic to the fact that the drug war is both real and devastating, and that rationally based interdiction measures could achieve success.

In my article "Reading Up on the Drug War," *Parameters* (Fall 1995), I lamented the absence of serious strategic literature about the drug war. That complaint is now inoperative. Ivelaw Lloyd Griffith's *Drugs and Security in the Caribbean* is a meticulous description of the phenomenon, written in the precise idiom of national security calculus. Professors teaching courses that in any way touch upon the narcotics plague would do well to prescribe Griffith's first chapter for student reading. Griffith covers the waterfront by relating hallucinogenic drug use to politics, economics, geography, the natural environment, national security, and finally to sovereignty. His chart called "Conflict Interactions in the Geonarcotics Milieu" is a sophisticated contribution to scholarship, supported structurally by another chart called "Geonarcotics, a Framework."

Griffith relates the demand side to the supply side by sketching geographic locales and human motivations for narcotics consumption. The portraits are highly credible, and they close the door on the usual criticism about books on the drug war which portray supply side or demand side without showing the connection. The next section mixes data with humanistic anecdotes on how drugs are actually transported through the Caribbean regional security systems. And these are followed by a highly readable explanation of how the narcotics trade distorts economic flow and especially economic development in the Caribbean region.

In a chapter called "Crime, Justice, and Public Order;" author Griffith shows the weakness of emerging criminal justice systems to cope with the narcotics plague, yet he also warns against the dangers of militarizing the effort. He opines that the Caribbean might be at "the dawn of Colombianization," a reference to the universally corrupting influence of narcotics abuse pitted against criminal justice systems. Griffith's final section on countermeasures in the Caribbean region reveals a better balance between supply side and demand side issues than is normally seen in books on this melancholy topic. His inventory of agencies and groups involved in the narcotics war is comprehensive and renders previous books on the Caribbean drug war obsolete. Declining to prescribe a unitary solution, he invites the people and leaders of the Caribbean region to "a long war" that must be waged on a "highly cooperative" basis.

Griffith's book has already been nominated for three awards: the Gordon K. Lewis Prize in Caribbean politics, the Bryce Wood Award in Latin American studies, and the Woodrow Wilson Foundation Award in social sciences analysis. This book may win or lose as a literary endeavor in three categories, but the reader can only win, for this is the best regional treatment of the narcotics plague yet written.

What can the Western Hemisphere gain from these works by Holden-Rhodes and Griffith? First, Holden-Rhodes offers a perceptual process by which to understand who and what is the enemy, and how best to employ society's resources against targets better selected. He does not want to discard existing intelligence mechanisms, but wishes to add his OSINT concept as the interpretive lens through which the American public and its elected leaders would view the drug war. Second, Griffith offers a precise regional portrait of the problem, emphasizing both supply side and demand side in prose that invites the reader to turn pages. Because he summarizes the threats presented by the Caribbean drug war in strategic terms as well as social impacts that ordinary citizens can visualize, his book tends to build support for solutions instead of frustrating or infuriating the reader. Third, both authors offer a model of excellent scholarship badly needed in a field which has often produced sloppily researched works portraying "great problems" with "no solutions."

Here are two views of the Western Hemisphere drug war, written in terms that national security planners and strategists can respect. Holden-Rhodes' OSINT concept may broaden the base of public support through a better understanding of the narcotics threat. Griffith meticulously links military and law enforcement threats to the quality of daily life in a region where millions of Americans work and take their vacations.

I recall when the spate of "what to do about guerrilla warfare" books in the 1960s clearly suggested that there was a neat solution attainable through the application of low intensity armed force and economic assistance. This giddy simplicity led to the quagmire in Vietnam, with shallow roots in public support. Holden-Rhodes and Griffith offer a way for the United States not to have a "narco-Vietnam" by gaining a truer understanding of the narcotics threat.

Both books would serve well as course texts, and both have already appeared on important desks within the Washington, DC beltway. To those who despair of rational solutions to the drug war; here, at least, are two intellectually strong gateways.

Essays on Latin American Security
The Collected Writing of a Scholar-Implementer

"Reading Up On the Drug War," Review Essay, *Parameters, Journal of the U.S. Army War College*, Autumn, 1995.

Readers can profit from a spate of books and articles about the world's struggle against narcotics. This literature can be grouped topically into investigative reporting, ideological cannon shots, and policy critiques. Some of the investigative reporting is so realistic that the reader feels drawn into the nether world of the narcotics culture. Some of the ideologically-driven authors disguise their rapier thrusts with footnotes, quotations, and other scholarly apparatus, thereby giving the impression of an objective policy critique. And the more scientifically written policy studies pull the reader into columns of data and pithy little annotations about what CHI2 really means in this case. One needs to be very focused to assess these books, for among them there is fascinating reading on a morbid, gripping, and sadly enduring topic.

María Jimena Duzan is a journalist with *El Espectador* (The Spectator) of Bogotá, a splendid newspaper aligned generally with the Liberal Party. Her *Death Beat*, translated from the Spanish in 1994 by Peter Eisner, is simply the best book of our times on crime reporting. With hair follicles tingling, the reader wonders how an attractive, well-educated woman got close enough to the murderous subjects she investigated – Colombia's infamous cartel lords – with her objectivity and her life intact. In 1989, Guy Gugliotta and Jeff Leon of the *Miami Herald* staff produced the still relevant *Kings of Cocaine: Inside the Medellín Cartel*, focusing upon druglord Carlos Lehder. Again, the odor of exploding dynamite, the grins of the payoff goons, and the screams of the syndicate's torture victims all come alive, with lots of facts that stand up to later discovery. Max Mermelstein was the evil brain behind the Medellín cartel during that era. He spilled his guts about the infamous Ochoa brothers, Juan David and Fabio, to adventure author Robin Moore, who published the tale in 1990 as *The Man Who Made It Snow*. Arturo Carrillo Strong was a narcotics agent in the southwestern United States during the 1970s, when hard drugs of Latin American origin were becoming a plague. His memoir, *Corrido de Cocaína: Inside Stories of Hard Drugs, Big Money, and Short Lives*, appeared in 1990 and gives the reader a chilling longitudinal awareness of the street drug culture in the United States.

The value of reading these accounts lies in comprehending the milieu and the strength of the challenge before plunging into the policy critiques, where the clinical language somehow bypasses the wretched lives that are under discussion. And, let it be said, there are many other bestseller paperback gut spillers by drug culture participants of dubious veracity. The volumes mentioned above are marked by plausibility and good writing.

Jaime Malamud-Goti produced *Smoke and Mirrors: The Paradox of the Drug Wars* in 1992. While the US Drug Enforcement Administration indeed made mistakes during its pioneer Andean operations, both the DEA and the Bolivian armed forces and National Police learned from their mistakes. Malamud-Goti became so emotionally involved in defaming the supply side anti-drug policy of

Russell W. Ramsey, Ph.D., D.Min.

President George Bush that his account is unbalanced. Kevin Jack Riley, a scholar of demonstrated talent, also lost perspective while indicting the Colombian armed forces and police in his 1993 volume called *The Implications of Colombian Drug Industry and Death Squad Political Violence for U.S. Counternacotics Policy*. He was partially duped by the syndicate propaganda machines; some of his villains are actually heroes of the anti-narcotics war.

Peter Dale Scott and Jonathan Marshall, an English professor and a newspaper staff financial analyst, wrote *Cocaine Politics: Drugs, Armies, and the CIA in Central America* in 1991. Already convinced that the 1980s conflicts in Nicaragua and El Salvador were contrived mercenary struggles initiated by President Ronald Reagan, these two apologists for the Nicaraguan Sandinistas and the El Salvadoran FMLN communist guerrillas indicted the drug war on similar lines. They discovered that there actually were no drug cartels in Latin America, nor even significant drug traffic save that being done by Reagan's "Contra" mercenaries in Nicaragua, General Manuel Noriega's Panamanian Defense Force, and the pro-US armies of Honduras and El Salvador. When this reviewer was a doctoral student in Latin American history, the University of California Press at Berkeley produced the leading scholarly works in the field. But their editorial decision to float this volume suggests a triumph of crudely ideological spin doctoring. Scott B. MacDonald's 1988 book, *Dancing on a Volcano*, for example, names most hemispheric druglords and is quite critical of US Andean drug policy; but it also shows clearly that Fidel Castro and his Sandinista allies en Nicaragua were selling drugs for cash to support their regimes in the 1980s.

There is plenty of room for scholarly writing that concludes US Andean drug enforcement policy to be a failure. The best short item on this theme is Bruce M. Bagley's and Juan G. Tokatlian's, "Dope and Dogma: Explaining the Failure of U.S.-Latin American Drug Policies," in Jonathan Hartlyn's, Lars Schoultz', and Augusto Varas's 1992 edited volume, *The United States and Latin America in the 1990s: Beyond the Cold War*. The weak spot in Professor Bagley's thesis – that enforcement on the supply side is ineffective – is that no alternative is presented beyond a generic plea for a coordinated approach. Michael Kennedy, Peter Reuter, and Kevin Jack Riley show statistically in their 1994 study, *A Simple Economic Model of Cocaine Production*, that alternative cropping, often recommended as a better choice than crop eradication among traditional Andean cocaine growers, is economically unfeasible. Kevin Jack Riley's 1993 RAND Corporation study, *Snow Job? The Efficiency of Source Country Cocaine Politics*, shows convincingly that in-country interdiction alone cannot win.

Alfred W. McCoy and Alan A. Block draw upon worldwide examples from Asia, the Middle East, Africa, and Latin America in their 1992 volume of essays, *War on Drugs: Studies in the Failure of U.S. Policy*. But they offer no specific alternative, and their definition of failure is not always consistent. In 1993, veteran Pentagon policy analyst Carl H. Builder found in his book *Measuring the Leverage: Assessing Military Contributions to Drug Interdiction*, that the problems of precise measurement and assessment were virtually insurmountable. Michael Childress would disagree, for he did a series of RAND Corporation studies which measure the drug trade with apparent precision. His 1994 work, *A System Description of the Cocaine Trade*, plus his 1993 studies with similar titles on heroin and marijuana should be read in conjunction with Builder's analysis. What emerges is the late Professor Hans Zetterbourg's oft-forgotten theory of the mid-range value in the social sciences. Global measurement yields statistical futility, and micro measurement produces precision about nothing that matters, so one picks the theory of the mid-range value. Childress' measurement parameters appear to be a healthy compromise between policy relevance and statistical precision.

Since a number of the studies concentrate heavily on the futility of fighting the drug war militarily in the Andes, through surrogate armies and police, one searches hopefully for some kind of study suggesting that the balanced approach – supply side interdiction at all levels, full court press against demand – may be working. The best exposition for the balanced attack is by Professor William O. Walker III, in a 1989 volume called *Drug Control in the Americas*. The Ohio Wesleyan University historian draws upon his research on little-known drug enforcement programs during the 1930s to make parallels with events in the 1980s. Professor Rensselaer W. Lee III argues in his 1991 book, *The White Labyrinth*, for the long-term, balanced approach. He examines bravely the case for legalization of addictive narcotics, concluding that such a policy would relieve some short-term problems at the expense of creating long-term social disasters.

Raphael F. Perl's 1994 study, *Drugs and Foreign Policy: A Critical Review*, may be the best single volume on how the illegal narcotics trade affects the US role in the world. It is complete, balanced, and much more objective than the earlier policy-bashing books, some of which are reviewed here. C. Peter Rydell and Susan S. Everingham carefully examined both supply side and demand side programs in their 1994 analysis, *Controlling Cocaine: Supply Versus Demand Programs*. A good analysis of US-Andean drug strategy appeared in Peter H. Smith's 1992 collection of essays, *Drug Policy in the Americas*. Professor Smith shows clearly the policy conflicts that occur when the United States, a global military power whose own citizens are a major cause of the drug problem, attempts to fight a supply side war through a foreign army and police apparatus. But his essays also show signs of progress, and, more important, ways to form regional anti-narcotics partnerships.

Readers who find the drug policy literature depressing will want to check out the annual *National Drug Control Strategy of the United States*. Public Law 100-690 has required the production of this statement by the Office of National Drug Control Policy annually since 1989. Concise yet comprehensive, this document reduces the labyrinth of statistics, government agencies, legal jurisdictions, human rights in conflict, public health challenges, and the rest of the drug war maze to understandable detail. Drug strategies involve many issues which people simply do not want to face. Some of these are curtailment of civil liberties, acknowledging drug abuse in one's own family, hiring foreign armies and police to kill their own citizens, charges of moral hypocrisy by hemispheric neighbors, raising taxes to fund an unpopular program in an era of runaway national deficit, and dragging the armed forces into law enforcement just when the *posse comitatus* principle – armies for foreign defense only – is coming into acceptance worldwide.

In 1990, the word "coke" meant white addictive powder to some, and a crispy brown drink in a familiar bottle to others. In 1990, US citizens spent $1.2 billion for "coke" (cocaine) produced in Colombia; the Coca-Cola Corporation International earned $1.2 billion worldwide for its soft drink. The Colombian army and National Police have lost more personnel in the drug war since 1983 than the United States has lost in all combat operations since 1973. The challenges to national security in the post-Cold War era are, according to most experts, financial deficit and ethnic war in remote areas. Both of these challenges link strongly to the narcotics plague. Military professionals will find the books, studies, and essays reviewed here of considerable value in understanding the reality that the armed forces are deeply involved in fighting the world's seemingly insatiable habit.

BIBLIOGRAPHY

Bagley, Bruce M., and Juan G. Tokatlian, "Dope and Dogma: Explaining the Failure of U.S.-Latin American Drug Policies," in Jonathan Hartlyn, Lars Schoultz, and Augusto Varas, eds., *The United States and Latin America in the 1990s: Beyond the Cold War.* Chapel Hill: Univ. of North Carolina Press, 1992.

Builder, Carl H. *Measuring the Leverage: Assessing Military Contributions to Drug Interdiction.* Santa Monica, Calif.: RAND, 1993.

Childress, Michael, Bonnie Dombey-Moore, and Susan Resetar. *A System Description of the Cocaine Trade.* Santa Monica, Calif.: RAND, 1994.

Childress, Michael. *A System Description of the Heroin Trade.* Santa Monica, Calif.: RAND, 1993.

— *A System Description of the Marijuana Trade.* Santa Monica, Calif.: RAND, 1993.

Duzan, María Jimena. *Death Beat*, trans. Peter Eisner. New York: Harper Collins, 1994.

Griffith, Ivelaw Lloyd. *Drugs and Security in the Caribbean: Sovereignty Under Siege.* University Park, PA: Pennsylvania State University Press, 1997.

Gugliotta, Guy, and Jeff Leon. *Kings of Cocaine: Inside the Medellín Cartel.* New York: Simon & Schuster, 1989.

Kennedy, Michael, Peter Reuter, and Kevin Jack Riley. *A Simple Economic Model of Cocaine Production.* Washington: National Defense Research Institute, 1994.

Lee, Rensselaer W., III. *The White Labyrinth.* New Brunswick, N.J.: Transaction, 1991.

MacDonald, Scott B. *Dancing on a Volcano.* Westport, Conn.: Praeger, 1988.

Malamud-Goti, Jaime. *Smoke and Mirrors: The Paradox of the Drug Wars.* Boulder, Colo.: Westview Press, 1992.

McCoy, Alfred W., and Alan A. Block, eds. *War on Drugs: Studies in the Failure of U.S. Policy.* Boulder, Colo.: Westview Press, 1992.

Mermelstein, Max, as told to Robin Moore and Richard Smitten. *The Man Who Made It Snow.* New York: Simon & Schuster, 1990.

Perl, Raphael F. *Drugs and Foreign Policy: A Critical Review.* Boulder, Colo.: Westview Press, 1994.

Riley, Kevin Jack. *The Implications of Colombian Drug Industry and Death Squad Political Violence for U.S. Counternarcotics Policy.* Washington: National Defense Research Institute, 1993.

Riley, Kevin Jack. *Snow Job? The Efficiency of Source Country Cocaine Politics.* Santa Monica, Calif.: RAND, 1993.

Rydell, C. Peter, and Susan S. Everingham. *Controlling Cocaine: Supply Versus Demand Programs.* Santa Monica, Calif.: RAND, 1994.

Scott, Peter Dale, and Jonathan Marshall. *Cocaine Politics: Drugs, Armies, and the CIA in Central America.* Berkeley: Univ. of California Press, 1991.

Smith, Peter H., ed. *Drug Policy in the Americas.* Boulder, Colo.: Westview Press, 1992.

Strong, Arturo Carrillo. *Corrido de Cocaína: Inside Stories of Hard Drugs, Big Money, and Short Lives.* Tucson, Ariz.: Harbinger House, 1990.

US Office of National Drug Control Policy. *National Drug Control Strategy.* Washington: GPO, 1989-1994.

Walker, William O., III. *Drug Control in the Americas.* 2d ed.; Albuquerque: Univ. of New Mexico Press, 1989.

Russell W. Ramsey, Ph.D., D.Min.

Review of: *Cocaine Politics: Drugs, Armies and the CIA in Central America*, by Peter Dale Scott and Jonathan Marshall, Berkeley, CA: The University of California Press, 1991. Reviewed in: *Military Review*, April, 1992.

The US national security establishment emerged victorious over fascism in 1945, then erected the threat called "Soviet communism" to maintain its control. When this exaggerated menace was discovered to be toothless in the 1980s, the "narcoterror" menace was invented to "keep the national security apparatus powerful and well funded." This is the thesis of the latest *j'accuse* in US-Latin American diplomatic relations, written by Pete Dale Scott, an English professor at the University of California at Berkeley, and Jonathan Marshall, editor of the financial analysis page of the *San Francisco Chronicle*.

This book will be considered respectfully by scholars because of its prestigious publisher, its footnote-laden format, and the fact that its authors, while not Latin America specialists, are serious researchers. In fact, Scott and Marshall use footnotes showing events that were incomplete, and they ignore critical events that happened between 1987 and the book's publication. The Senate Subcommittee on Terrorism, chaired by Senator John F. Kerry (D-MA) issued a 1989 "Report on Drugs, Law Enforcement, and Foreign Policy" that also figures heavily in the thinking of Scott and Marshall.

The authors lead one to believe that all Latin American narcoterrorists appear to be still at large, protected by former President Ronald Reagan's national security leaders. However, when checking off the roster of villains with a pencil, one notices that the Latin American rascals in the story are all dead or in jail. As for Reagan's own former team, National Security Adviser Admiral John M. Poindexter; his assistant, Lieutenant Colonel Oliver North; Assistant Secretary of State for Inter-American Affairs Elliott Abrams; Iran-Contra middleman, Major General Richard Secord; and several more of the national security policy men have been prosecuted and punished.

Nor do the visually voluminous sources in *Cocaine Politics* make a convincing case that Latin America's government leaders in Colombia, Panamá, Honduras and El Salvador, who were involved in the narcotics industry, were truly under the "protective aegis of US national security leaders." Especially cruel is the assertion by Scott and Marshall that Colombian military commanders virtually sponsored the narcoterrorists there. The record of Colombian military and law enforcement deaths in battle against the heavily armed *narcotraficantes* and the Colombian armed forces' policy of bringing to courts-martial those who sullied the military profession by connivance with the drug producers is well known.

While indicting the United States' highest leaders for inventing and then sponsoring the narcotics menace, they also exonerate Fidel Castro and the former Sandinistas in Nicaragua of any connection. Yet, it was in 1989 that Castro executed his African Campaign war hero, General Arnaldo Ochoa, and three others for allegedly dealing in drugs. Leftist writers have stated for two years in such journals as *The Progressive* that Ochoa was a scapegoat by which Castro hoped to distance himself from association with a drug-selling policy.

Professor John N. Moore in his *The Secret War in Central America* made irrefutable linkage between the Sandinista government in Nicaragua, Castro's Cuban regime and the active selling of narcotics to raise cash. Daniel Ortega, then president of Nicaragua, gave well-publicized speeches flaunting his drug-selling policy, bragging about how it would "finance his revolution within, and bring down the Yankee war machine as a by-product."

Scott and Marshall's thesis is glib. When one examines the entire story of what was known from nonclassified sources by the authors' final press date, their villain theory collapses.

Russell W. Ramsey, Ph.D., D.Min.

"The U.S. Andean Counter-Narcotics Initiative," *Military Review*, Hispanic Edition, May-June, 1991.

Narcotics abuse is a problem originating in the United States, where available cash combines with the public craving for dangerous, illegal, and addictive psychoactive drugs to create a world market. The major victim of U.S. craving for cocaine is the Andean region, where favorable agricultural conditions, remote spaces, and Constitutionally guaranteed legal rights have combined to attract the drug cartels. These cartels are virtually independent nation-states with production, packaging, transportation, and distribution systems all defended by an elaborate legal apparatus and high-technology war fighting systems. Further, they are linked to dangerous leftist revolutionary organizations which destabilize governments and murder citizens.

In 1989, world profits of Coca-Cola International – the legitimate "Coke Empire" – were $1.2 billion. In 1989, U.S. drug users funneled the same sum – $1.2 billion – into Colombia, alone, in support of the other "Coke Empire," the evil cocaine cartels.

Europeans buy heroin out of Asia's "Golden Triangle" at a comparable rate, creating the same ugly threats to regional security. But President George Bush has recognized that the U.S. has moral responsibilities in the Andean region, Mexico, and the Caribbean for the creation of the drug cartels. After all, in the past five years, they have killed over 300 soldiers and police each in Colombia and Mexico; have assassinated Colombian judges, Congressmen, and newspaper editors; and have significantly damaged the economy and the legal system of their unwilling host countries.

President Bush introduced the third National Drug Control Strategy to the Congress in January 31, 1991. "Our strategy," he stated, "is comprehensive... Our strategy works. And the thrust of our strategy remains the same: cutting down the supply and then suppressing the demand." The Presidential strategy is linked to other initiatives which increase hemispheric trade, improve control mechanisms for money laundering, and launch drug demand efforts in countries afflicted by the drug cartels.

President Bush's national Drug Control Strategy follows an intensive study of what has happened since the Cartagena Accords of February, 1990. One year before, at Cartagena, Colombia, the four Presidents of Bolivia, Colombia, Perú, and the U.S. met to face the mounting realization that drugs were not just a problem for those countries that consumed them nor the responsibility of those countries that supplied them. Tragically, addiction, crime, violence, and corruption had become ties that bound our nations together.

Common problems demanded common solutions, and the four "Cartagena Accord" nations have taken steps in the past year that produced results previously unattainable by going it alone. Here is a summary of U.S. anti-drug policy that has worked well in the post-Cartagena environment:

- Strengthen the political will of the Andean nations to fight the drug cartels,
- Increase effectiveness of the military and law enforcement agencies in the Andean region,
- Inflict significant damage on the trafficking organizations – U.S. budgetary commitment for post-Cartagena Year 1 took this form in the Andean region:

	FY90 program dollars (millions)			
	Colombia	Bolivia	Perú	Total
Economic support, law enforcement, intelligence:	29.9	56.6	33.4	119.9
Military assistance:	*60.5*	*40.9*	*39.9*	*140.3*
Total assistance:	**$90.4**	**$97.5**	**$73.3**	**$260.2**

With positive evidence of success in hand, measured in less cocaine delivered, higher street prices for drugs, more arrests of major distributors, and reduced mayhem inflicted by the cartels, the Bush administration now proceeds with its Andean initiative. In Fiscal Year 1991, the U.S. will provide about $370 million in resources and equipment to the Andean countries. For Fiscal Year 1992, the intention is to raise this funding to nearly $500 million, with some $285 million earmarked for economic assistance and the rest in police and military training and equipment. The goals remain the same as in 1990, with the addition of an initiative to create new jobs and new forms of agricultural success that will decrease the attractiveness of growing cocaine and cooperating with the cartels in the Andean backlands.

Latin American security professionals want to know, of course, what is being done about drug smuggling from Mexico and the Caribbean; after all, the Andean region is only part of the complex narcotics traffic. The U.S. Fiscal Year 1992 budget includes $2.1 billion for equipment and systems that essentially try to screen out illegal narcotics at the U.S. borders. This process, of course, includes illegal smuggling of Asian heroin, control of terrorists and their illegal weapons, and a broader picture than merely the Andean cocaine problem. Included within this package are initiatives for innovative detection technologies, stiffer penalties for pilots who transport narcotics, interdiction of precursor (preparation) chemicals, and beefed up border patrol on the U.S.-Mexican frontier.

Since the Cartagena Accords, U.S. politicians no longer bemoan "Latin America's drug problem." President Bush has laid its origins in the U.S., and he has stated often that the drug war must be won in every (North) American neighborhood before it can be won on a national scale. Latin American leaders are still sensitive about sovereignty, about the appearance created if U.S. military personnel operate in their backlands; and U.S. leaders fear the process of drawing

Russell W. Ramsey, Ph.D., D.Min.

the U.S. into Andean struggles against guerrilla forces through their connection with the narcotics cartels. Latin Americans and U.S. leaders both hope for larger economic solutions, such as a tariff-free Western Hemisphere, in which the appeal of the drug cartels would be lessened. But the narcotics scourge is a war, and military professionals throughout the Western Hemisphere must participate and comprehend the goals.

CARIBBEAN AND CENTRAL AMERICA

Review of: *Conflict, Peace, and Development In The Caribbean*, by Jorge Rodríguez Beruff, J. Peter Figueroa, and J. Edward Greene, Eds, St. Martin's Press, New York, 1991. Reviewed in: *Marine Corps Gazette*, December, 1993.

This volume of essays on Caribbean security issues can be viewed as a sequel to Dion E. Phillips and Alma H. Young, eds., *Militarization in the Non-Hispanic Caribbean* (Boulder, Colorado: Lynne Reiner, 1986). Several of the contributing scholars are the same, and they visit the same island republics to analyze force development against security challenges. This book is the outcome of a "Peace and Development in the Caribbean" conference held in 1988 at the University of the West Indies, Mona Campus, in Jamaica.

The individual essays on security forces in the Dominican Republic and Barbados are the best single country entries. Pablo A. Martínez, in the fourth essay, finds a disturbing tendency among Dominican military officers to express U.S. foreign policy views as their own (*entreguismo*, Spanish), but acknowledges increased military professionalism. In the sixth essay, Dion E. Phillips describes in careful terms the rise of a professional Army in Barbados – a departure from earlier dependency upon militia and police. Phillips has somewhat mollified the shrill, anti-U.S. view seen in the earlier 1986 book that he edited, probably reflecting the reduction in Cold War regional activity.

Raúl Bonitos Manaut, in the eighth essay, offers the best assessment of Caribbean-Central American security issue linkage ever written by a regional scholar. He shows why President Ronald Reagan viewed the combination of Cuban and Nicaraguan Sandinista military power as a legitimate threat to the region, not just to the United States.

There are two unifying theses in this work. First, the Caribbean island republics are converting their security forces from police and coastal patrol units into small, professional armies, with supporting sea and air assets. Second, the United States is playing a stronger role in this process, replacing earlier British, French, and Dutch military security influence. One only wishes that this distinguished collection of scholars would have acknowledged more strongly the fact that the narcotics kingpins offer genuine military security challenges to the region.

Russell W. Ramsey, Ph.D., D.Min.

"Analysis of the US-Mexican Border: A Strategic Literature Yet to Come," *Parameters, Journal of the US Army War College,* Autumn, 1997.

The US national security community bases its policies and strategies on the legitimacy of sovereignty, the philosophical centerpiece of the nation-state since the 1648 Treaty of Westphalia. The national security planner and the strategist who would visualize the massive flow of illegal immigration and the related narcotrafficking problem at the US border with Mexico through the eyes of the contemporary strategic literature are in for a rude surprise. The US-Mexican border literature is not strategic in nature; it is little more than an inventory of problems.

Ambassador George Kennan's 1947 "Mr. *'X'*" article in *Foreign Affairs* sounded the national security tocsin, to the satisfaction of most thinking people in the Judeo-Christian West, producing a robust, legitimate, and ultimately winning defense against the neo-barbarians of the communist East. Central to the policy of containment and the strategy of deterrence against communism were the value and legitimacy of the nation-state. By viewing the US-Mexican border as a giant social problem instead of a legitimate national security issue, the scholarly community is simply not producing a serious analysis of what is, essentially, a strategic set of issues involving sovereignty, borders, and the future of two huge nation-states.

Caspar Weinberger, Secretary of Defense from 1981 to 1987, has penned a novel with an obvious political message. Called *The Next War,* his 1996 chiller depicts five scenarios that project the United States into large-scale armed conflict. In one scenario, the United States invades Mexico in response to runaway illegal immigration, the northward flow of illegal drugs, rampant corruption, and seemingly uncontrollable political terrorism. The Mexican government is presented as completely incompetent to operate a stable political democracy, a veritable band of thugs in complicity with the worst criminal elements. If Weinberger's book was meant to be a caveat to Mexican government officials, the effect is unfortunate, for the scenario played out in the book fuels the ultraconservative myth that there are no functional strategic solutions to the problem short of outright invasion. Mexicans in 1997 have not forgotten the US occupation of Veracruz harbor in 1914 and the Pershing invasion expedition two years later.

If the Weinberger book reaches too fast for the trigger on the US-Mexican border problem, one might consult Timothy J. Dunn's 1996 study, *The Militarization of the U.S-Mexico Border, 1978-1992.* Dunn offers an important inventory of cooperation among local, state, and federal law enforcement agencies across the southwestern United States in their efforts to check the flow of illegal northward immigration. Then he creates a theory by summing up four national security issues affecting Latin America in the recent past: cooperative security measures on the US-Mexican border; the drug war, which he considers fictitious or pretextual; US policy in Central America during the 1980s, central to today's wave of democratization; and opposition to Fidel Castro's military adventurism. For

Dunn, these prove the existence of a militaristic Anglo-Saxon conspiracy against Latin America.

Professor Wayne A. Cornelius of the University of California at San Diego has assembled an unusually comprehensive set of essays on immigration policy. His 1994 edited volume *Controlling Immigration: A Global Perspective* discovers a "convergence hypothesis" among the industrially-developed countries who import cheap labor from developing nations. But he also validates a "gap hypothesis," meaning that, as these converging policies continue in place, they increasingly fail to accomplish their stated purpose, namely, to impose limits on an unwanted flood of economic immigrants. Professor Cornelius' conclusions were presented in his superb essay called "Economics, Culture, and the Politics of Restricting Immigration" in the 15 November 1996 issue of the *Chronicle of Higher Education.* He calls for the nation-states affected by economic immigration to establish some fundamental parameters, to decide what it is that they really want to do when they invite cheap foreign labor to immigrate and then take measures to restrict the ensuing ethnic flood.

The literature on illegal economic immigration, then, is either highly politicized on the liberal-conservative spectrum or narrow in scope. One suspects that professors in fields like agricultural economics and international finance will seize the torch on such critical issues as illegal immigration across the border between the United States and Mexico, given that these specialists are already creating a good literature on privatization and democratization in Latin America. The 1996 Index issue of the *Latin American Research Review,* which is the nation's prime source of research interest by scholars specializing in Latin America, shows only six articles dedicated to the Mexican border problem in 25 years. Scholars of international relations, national security policy, and military strategy need to revitalize the meaning of sovereignty in the milieu of massively penetrated borders.

Russell W. Ramsey, Ph.D., D.Min.

Reviews of: *Cien Biografias de Militares Distinguidos*, by Brig. Gen. Mario Perez Torres, Mexican Government Press, 1988; *Generals in The Palacio: The Military in Modern Mexico*, by Roderic Ai Camp, Oxford University Press, 1992; and *Cuban Leadership After Castro: Biographies of Cuba's Top Commanders*, by Rafael Fermoselle, U. of Miami North-South Centre, 1992. Reviewed in: *(*British) *Army Quarterly & Defence Journal*, April, 1994.

Cuba's generals from 1898 to 1959 were operating an internal security army and several police forces. These organizations were always corrupt and often incompetent, despite a considerable US investment of professional military and police training. Cuba's flag officers after 1959 evolved steadily from the fictitious romance of guerilla *comandantes* to fully professional status as commanders in a force that became Latin America's top military power in the mid-1980s. What these officers will now do as Premier Castro's political style wanes is a matter for study.

Mexico's flag officers, after 1910, are usually portrayed in books on Latin America as "good generals" because they were politically less deliberate than their counterparts in other Latin American countries. Their biographies, in a recent two-volume work by Brigadier General Mario Pérez Torres, are presently available in Spanish only; the title is *Cien Biografias de Militares Distinguidos (A Hundred Biographies of Distinguished Military Officers)*. These 100 thumbnail sketches of Mexico's senior generals and admirals give an inside view of the country's military history and of Mexican military leadership, which is usually absent from most Mexican histories. An analysis of Cold War era Mexican Army and Air Force generals has recently been published in Roderic Ai Camp's *Generals in the Palacio; The Military in Modern Mexico*.

At the beginning of this year, Mexico's military leaders faced two opponents, the violent but poorly armed peasants of the south and the much better armed drug barons.

Throughout the Cold War, Mexico's political leaders opposed the United States' efforts to overthrow Fidel Castro's pro-Soviet regime. Leading military commanders, however, privately told opposite numbers of their sympathy with the American view of Castro.

Cuba's military commanders, during the same period, were portrayed as potential enemies of the United States. They showed their ability to destabilize a number of non-communist governments in South America. Cuban formations were able to defeat some of the Republic of South Africa's best forces in Angola.

Rafael Fermoselle's *Cuban Leadership After Castro: Biographies of Cuba's Top Commanders* offers a brief military history of Cuba, a description of Cuban military structure since the 1959 revolution, and 100 pages of trenchant biographical material on Premier Fidel Castro's generals and admirals. These officers will weigh heavily in any calculus of Castro's and Cuba's future.

"The Bolivian Diary of Ernesto Che Guevara," *Hispanic American Historical Review*, November, 1996.

A team of Cuban scholars has worked for a decade on an edited set of Ernesto "Che" Guevara's memoirs on the Cuban Revolutionary War, published as *Pasajes de la Guerra Revolucionaria* (Havana: Editorial Politica, 1996). Mary-Alice Waters, a writer and longtime champion of the Cuban Revolution, worked simultaneously to prepare an English version, the *Episodes of the Cuban Revolutionary War, 1956-58*. Waters and the Cuban editing team started earlier on the other Che Guevara memoirs, the less complete account of his fatal expedition in Bolivia. These essays emerged as *El Diario del Che en Bolivia* (Havana: Editora Politica, 1987); they were refined and translated into English as *The Bolivian Diary*.

Che Guevara belongs to an exclusive fraternity of revolutionary theoreticians who were also force commanders in the field. His first literary effort, *La Guerra de Guerrillas*, was really a long essay, part theory and part application. A quick translation by the Central Intelligence Agency went to the desk of Robert F. Kennedy, soon to be attorney general and Cold War adviser extraordinaire to President-elect John F. Kennedy. The Kennedy brothers, hoping to build support for the forthcoming Alliance for Progress, perceived Guevara's piece as the expression of a serious threat to their hemispheric view. Consequently, a month before JFK's inauguration, orders were given to the U.S. Army to begin training the Latin American armies and security forces in counterinsurgency and nation-building programs.

In the early 1960s, English translations of Che Guevara's "On Guerrilla Warfare" came out in *Evergreen, Ramparts, and Monthly Review*; other Guevara essays followed. Gathered mostly from Cuba's *Verde Olivo* magazine, they were translated into English by Victoria Ortiz and published as *Reminiscences of the Cuban Revolutionary War* (1968). The same year, John Gerassi edited Guevara's essays and published them as *Venceremos! The Speeches and Writings of Ernesto Che Guevara* (1968). The Gerassi volume contains the essays on the battles against the Fulgencio Batista government, Guevara's political and economic theories, and the original "On Guerrilla Warfare."

The present work edited by Waters, *Episodes*, corrects hundreds of little errors that have crept into the Che Guevara essays; it also fully identifies figures alluded to or previously identified only by *noms de guerre*. Photographs, a glossary of terms, an order-of-battle chart, and rosters of names with minibiographies make this work mandatory reading for students of the Cuban Revolution.

Che Guevara organized a team of Cuban internationalist volunteers to fight alongside followers of Patrice Lumumba in Zaire, then called Congo. Guevara's work and message were a major force at the January 1966 Tricontinental Conference in Havana. In November of that year, he joined the guerrilla cadre he had inserted into the Bolivian altiplano, and he kept a diary during the ten-month effort to implant a revolution. Betrayed in the field, captured, and executed in October 1967 by the Bolivian administration of Rene Barrientos, he was immediately enshrined in the Valhalla of fallen revolutionaries. Aleida March obtained the diary – actually in two separate segments – and arranged for its publication under Cuban government auspices.

Daniel James translated and edited Guevara's field memoirs as *The Complete Bolivian Diaries of Che Guevara and Other Captured Documents* (1968). Until now, the James volume has stood as the definitive Guevara memoir on the Bolivia episode, just as the Ortiz and Gerassi volumes have been the sources for Guevara's revolutionary theories and his field command role in Cuba. Recently, however, Bolivian government officials have cooperated with Cuban authorities to release and validate more documents. Michael Taber and Michael Baumann worked with Waters to render the present version, *The Bolivian Diary*. Newly translated, it contains field notes by Inti Peredo and other field commanders who corroborate Guevara's notes and also fill in gaps.

Waters' meticulously edited pair of volumes is now the best original source for English-speaking scholars. Her attention to detail and her precision do not overcome the rough eloquence that was Guevara's style; the transcendental message of a new moral order bites through the prose with deceptive simplicity.

The Uruguayan poet Jose Rodo created, in the early 1900s, a Latin American metaphorical persona called Ariel, a romantic yet legitimate Icarus whose wings always melted in the heat of competition with the North American giant. Ernesto "Che" Guevara became Latin America's Ariel incarnate during the Cold War. He blended Marxist political and economic constructs of another time and culture with the essential spirituality of Latin America. Waters' meticulous volumes do for Guevara's work and writing what Arrian of Cappadocia did for Alexander the Great: preserve the thought and work of a tempestuous, controversial figure with honesty and artistic grace.

Essays on Latin American Security
The Collected Writing of a Scholar-Implementer

"On Castro and Cuba: Rethinking the Three Gs," Review Essay, *Parameters, Journal of the US Army War College*, Winter, 1994-1995.

Emperor Charles I of Spain sent his bold *conquistadores* (conquerors) to the Americas in the early 16th century. Hernán Cortéz subdued the Aztecs of Mexico, Francisco Pizarro wreaked havoc on the Incas of Perú, Gonzalo Jiménez de Quesada outfought the Chibchas of Colombia, and Pedro de Valdivia hounded the Araucanians of Chile, all in pursuit of the "three Gs:" gold, glory, and God.

Four centuries later, the newly imperial-minded United States sent its troops to Cuba, which the previous generation of North Americans had just helped liberate from the threadbare remnants of Spain's dying empire. These new-breed *conquistadores* were men of a different genre: novelist and adventurer Ernest Hemingway, Olympic superswimmer and Tarzan film star Johnny Weissmuller, over-the-hill Hollywood swashbuckler Errol Flynn, and the mobster casino chieftain Meyer Lansky. These men turned Cuba into North America's offshore playground and brothel, in the years before the sexual revolution in the United States made expensively scummy entertainment domestically accessible. Driven by new motivations in a different age, they redefined the "three Gs:" gambling, girls, and glitz.

Monarchs Charles I and Philip II of Spain went on, after their conquest of Indo-America, to transform the region culturally into a giant Catholic empire with an army of priests and friars. Their Iberian-Catholic handiwork lasted politically for three centuries of relatively peaceful empire, held together by remarkably few soldiers. Creole-led revolutions for independence between 1810 and 1830 produced modern Latin America, the world's largest and oldest block of independent, constitutional nations, leaving Spain in control of Puerto Rico and Cuba. US forces liberated Cuba in 1898, during a thunderous moment of naive idealism about exporting democracy. Cuba's reoccupation by the US neo-*conquistadores*, those proponents of the 20th century's "three Gs," created the conditions that allowed the illegitimate son of a wealthy Spanish immigrant to Cuba – one Fidel Castro – to become the primary thorn under the US national security blanket for 30 years. Never in his life a *campesino* (peasant), he became a global symbol of liberation, a romanticized champion of the poor. He overthrew a corrupt, inefficient army and replaced it with a revolutionary machine that challenged world powers on four continents. He outwitted US Presidents and Soviet Premiers with infuriating durability.

Ten important new works in the national security studies field examine the Cuban-US milieu during the Castro era. They are central to scholarship on the evolution of the US national security policy and strategy process between 1956 and 1991. But there is more at stake here than merely refighting the Cold War in the Caribbean. Fidel Castro virtually wrote the book on how a small power could play the superpowers against each other. While the world may not again organize itself into two militarily bristling supercamps, these books are excellent entries in a field often useful in the post-Cold War 1990s for US policy on Haití, Panamá, El Salvador, and Nicaragua; and they hold applications less geographically proximate for possible US roles in Bosnia, Cambodia, Iraq, North Korea, Rwanda, and Somalia.

Dozens of books purport to describe or explain the victory of Fidel Castro and his M-26 forces over Fulgencio Batista's regime in the late 1950s. The masterpiece in this genre is now Professor Thomas G. Paterson's, *Contesting Castro: The United States and the Triumph of the Cuban Revolution*. Sparkling style and objectivity combine with sophisticated interpretation to answer satisfactorily, for the first time, the apparently unanswerable question: How did Castro win? Paterson's answer: Castro correctly identified the unseen legacy of shame and anti-US feeling among Cubans about the moral cesspool that sprang forth from the 20th-century version of the "three Gs." Then, while the US national security establishment, the Batista dictatorship, and the urban resistance to Batista conducted business during the period 1957-1959 with the organizational efficiency of the stars in a Three Stooges film, Castro built a disciplined power machine papered over with romantic liberationist innocence.

Professor Paterson's meticulous description of armed and violent challenges within Cuba, and the confused, clumsy responses to those challenges by Batista's forces and the US national security system is simply the best ever written. And this book emerged in 1994 when the US national security apparatus, supposedly 30 years more mature and sophisticated, was struggling desperately for solutions to comparable challenges in Bosnia, Haití, Israel, Rwanda, and Somalia. There is no more Soviet Empire to swallow up revolutions gone awry in unstable developing countries, but the Three Stooges efficiency scenario seems to have peeked out from behind the US national security curtain again.

Once victorious, Fidel Castro led his revolution into the Soviet Union's camp, pounding the last coffin nails into the Monroe Doctrine. Triumphant at the botched 1961 Bay of Pigs invasion attempt by US-sponsored Cuban exiles, he was less clearly triumphant the following year after the 1962 missile crisis. Two new books now lay bare those chilling days when President John F. Kennedy directed his national security machinery personally, with mixed effectiveness.

Dino A. Brugioni was the chief electronic intelligence officer for the Central Intelligence Agency who unmasked the smuggling of strategic nuclear missiles and warheads into Cuba aboard Soviet cargo ships. His *Eyeball to Eyeball: The Inside Story of the Cuban Missile Crisis* is easily the best volume yet written on the complex world of technological intelligence and its interplay with the national security community. He offers the best insider description to date of what really occurred in the Kennedy White House while the United States and the Soviet Union teetered at the brink of a global nuclear holocaust for a week. The book has obvious meaning for those charged with monitoring nuclear warhead development in Iraq and North Korea, and for those who track the inventory of Russia's still massive nuclear rocket array. It has even stronger meaning for those who receive technical intelligence estimates and convert them into national security decisions.

Scoffers at the notion that a nuclear war machine can be exported by clandestine means should study Anatoli I. Gribkov's and William Y. Smith's, *Operation ANADYR: U.S. and Soviet Generals Recount the Cuban Missile Crisis*. Here, with sincerity and objectivity, the Soviet general (Gribkov) in charge of smuggling nearly a hundred strategic nuclear missiles into Cuba in the summer of 1962, reveals how it was done. A US Air Force general (Smith) responds with the military side of the national security decision process in 1962. And one ponders: if the Soviet Union almost succeeded in setting up a deliverable inventory of nuclear rockets in Cuba, 90 miles from US soil in a small country having a US base within it, what pariah regime in the 1990s is reading the same book with the purpose of avoiding the Soviets' mistakes that led to detection?

For a Soviet view of Fidel Castro's place in international relations, the new standard is Yuri Pavlov's *Soviet-Cuban Alliance: 1959-1991*. Ambassador Pavlov served the former USSR as senior diplomatic representative in Cuba, Costa Rica, and Chile; as a Latin American specialist in the Foreign Ministry, he played a key role during the Cuban missile crisis. He and his colleagues in the Soviet national security community sincerely believed that Fidel Castro was implementing a new and authentic form of socialism in Cuba and abroad. However, he also suggests that Castro became a "communist of convenience" in 1960 to bolster his regime against US invasion. In the epilogue, he shows his disillusionment with revolutionary socialism as evidence of violent repression and mass terror mounted in Cuba. Pavlov's final words of warning about the inherently anti-democratic nature of radical revolutionaries would not be out of place as required reading in US political science and history classrooms.

What of Fidel Castro, the man, and his place in world history? Jules Dubois (1959), Manuel Urrutia Lleo (1964), Herbert L. Matthews (1969), Ernest Halperin (1972), Carlos Franqui (1984), and Tad Szulc (1986) are some of the better-known biographers of Fidel Castro. In the apparent twilight of Castro's reign comes Robert E. Quirk's *Castro, A Biography*, a volume which eclipses all the others in objectivity, research, and scope; it is likely to stand as the definitive work until Fidel Castro no longer rules Cuba. With meticulous documentation, Professor Quirk captures the color of his subject while weaving a sophisticated fabric of the key events; and he avoids the crippling tendency of most Castro analysts to position his book somewhere on the liberal-conservative spectrum of US opinion. This volume, coupled with the Paterson study, opens avenues for conceptualizing and assessing Fidel Castro's enormous effect on US national security policy since late 1958.

And what is to be done as *fidelismo* (political credence in Fidel) wanes in Cuba? Georgetown University Professor Gillian Gunn has published the most specific answer in her 1993 work, *Cuba in Transition: Options for U.S. Policy*. Easily the best analyst of Cuban military operations in Africa during the 1980s, she now offers a rational agenda of carrots and sticks by which to bring the Cuban people out of the revised "three Gs" syndrome, so well explained by Professor Paterson, and into the range of possibilities in *Latin America in a New World* edited by Professor Abraham F. Lowenthal and Gregory F. Treverton. The Cuba policy entry in the latter is "Cuba in a New World" by Professor Jorge I. Domínguez. For a range of views on currents Cuba topics, Professor Donald E. Schulz offers another book called *Cuba and the Future*. The papers in the Schulz volume are the outcome of a January 1992 symposium at the Strategic Studies Institute of the Army War College, and the essay called "The Cuban Armed Forces in Transition" by Phyllis Greene Walker is a gem in the national security studies field.

For an independent yet complementary evaluation of the Cuban revolution and its recent adaptations to a changing world, Susan E. Eckstein's *Back From the Future: Cuba Under Castro* has balance and detail not found in other books. Her splendid 1994 analysis finds a Cuba not presented in political studies, a society that has evolved in ways that may reduce the passing of Fidel Castro to something non-catastrophic. Good but less unique is the eighth edition of Irving Louis Horowitz's interdisciplinary collection of essays, *Cuban Communism*. José Alonso's essay on the scapegoat execution of General Arnaldo Ochoa is strong, as is "The Politics of Psychiatry in Cuba" by Charles Brown and Armando Lago.

The US Army carried the institutional burden of working face-to-face with the Latin American military forces throughout the Cold War. Always there was the delicate balance to strike between fostering yet another repressive military regime and releasing a country to the Soviet Union's orbit. US Army leaders learned quickly from the mistakes committed in Fulgencio Batista's Cuba and moved on to a policy of selective equipping and quality training in the Spanish language. Despite the malignant and usually uninformed liberal-conservative dichotomy on US policy in Latin America, the region produced only one solid and enduring Marxist-Leninist regime during the Cold War, and that was Cuba. The books reviewed here suggest strongly that Fidel Castro's personal leadership coupled with the anti-US emotions rising from the revised "three Gs" agenda have more to say about Cold War Cuba than did Karl Marx.

"Strategic Writing on Cuba," Review Essay, *Parameters, Journal of the US Army War College*, Winter, 2001-2002.

Seven years have passed since this reviewer's essay "On Castro and Cuba: Rethinking the 'Three G's'" appeared in *Parameters*, and policy lines on US-Cuban relations have hardened in both Washington, D.C. and Havana since then. Yet there are important signals of impending policy changes emanating from both countries, and we explore here several works which set the tone for understanding the issues, followed by a more detailed examination of three new books which are significant contributions to the massive literature on this topic.

In 1994, Premier Fidel Castro carried out his sweeping policy adjustments occasioned by the collapse of the Soviet Union and its previous mentorship of Cuba. Politically, these adjustments included the authorization of a massive economic emigration from Cuba to Florida and the lifting of state censorship and other tight security rules affecting Cuban relationships with foreigners visiting or living in Cuba. Economically, Castro opened the Cuban socialist economy to allow about one-third of his population to live "outside the revolution," which means holding a job in a growing free-market sector created primarily by European investment and using the US dollar as primary currency. At the time of my earlier review, most Cuba analysts concluded that the demise of Fidel Castro as Premier and of *fidelismo* (passionate belief in Fidel's revolution) was imminent. Those analysts were wrong, and the works reviewed below show why.

To appreciate what has happened in Cuba since the demise of the Soviet Union, one should read Robert T. Buckman's chapter on Cuba in the Stryker-Post volume *Latin America 2001*. Buckman shows, dispassionately, that *fidelismo* may seem to be an illogical, failed policy to the outsider, but that Fidel Castro and his revolution are deeply meaningful to the seven million or so Cubans who live within it. Their basic necessities of life (food, first-line medical care, education, and shelter) are taken care of in exchange for a drab economic existence in old houses with leaky roofs and utilities that function with increasing irregularity. This judgment is corroborated by lectures delivered by Dr. Gilberto Fleitus, a Cuban oncologist, on 7 January 2000, and from Dr. Juan Valdez Paz, a Cuban historian, on 14 January 2000, both at the Felix Varela Institute in Havana. For an overview of where scholarship is moving on Cuba and its tumultuous history, Robert Whitney's "History or Teleology?" in *Latin American Research Review* is the best short summary. The books reviewed by Professor Whitner point clearly to a growing emphasis on the "mambi" theme, a reference to Cuba's non-white eastern population who have always been excluded to some degree from the island's political system and among whom all revolutions have either started or at least had an important strand. This view was further confirmed by Dr. Herbert Perez, another Cuban historian at the Oriente (Eastern) University in Santiago, on 10 January 2000.

Professor Thomas C. Wright's revised (2001) edition of *Latin America in the Era of the Cuban Revolution* reflects the somewhat chastened writing of the neo-Marxist left in the United States. Gone are the romantic interpretations of Castro's

Russell W. Ramsey, Ph.D., D.Min.

role in the Cuban struggle of 1956-1959, and of Ernesto "Che" Guevara's ill-fated filibuster in Bolivia in 1967. Professor Wright accurately portrays the limited neo-Marxist dimensions seen in Colombia's recent years of domestic mayhem. He continues to laud the Salvador Allende administration of Chile and judges the Augusto Pinochet dictatorship to have been all bad, an externally imposed pawn of the US Central Intelligence Agency. Yet I have heard prominent Chilean Marxist scholars who suffered at the hands of General Pinochet's terror apparatus, the DINA, state that the Allende government was ineffective, and that the system imposed by Pinochet now calls on Chilean leftists to become social democrats working to achieve and economic safety network for the poor. Further, Professor Wright insists that the Nicaraguan people genuinely wanted the continuance of the Sandinista government in 1990, while dozens of former Sandinistas state that their government was venal, needlessly militarized, and economically counterproductive. While chastened in tone, some US neo-Marxists within academia still cling to a governmental philosophy that was shown by Professor Timothy Wickham-Crowley's 1992 study, *Guerrillas and Revolution in Latin America*, to have little authenticity within Latin America, and appearing to succeed (Cuba and Nicaragua) only as a result of external financial support now vanished with the collapse of the USSR.

The book *Cuba: The Contours of Change*, edited by Susan Kaufman Purcell and David Rothkopf, is the one reviewed here which will attract most readers, for it addresses the fundamental policy questions extant between the two bad neighbors. This slim volume is a set of essays presented at a conference series entitled "Cuba: Preparing for the Future" conducted from April to June 2000 by the Council of the Americas, a think-tank group often sought-after by US political leaders for advice and endorsement of their Cuba policies. Professor Purcell is a vice-president of the Americas Society and Council of the Americas, with a long record of influential policy writing on Cuba, and she concludes in this book that the US economic embargo of Cuba is unfortunate but necessary. She cites the demonstrated durability of Fidel Castro's regime as evidence that his 1994 policy adjustments are not a transition to free-market economics and political democracy, but are, in fact, a shrewd scheme for maintaining his personalistic revolution in power. This view is opposed by Professors Andrew Zimbalist and Manuel Pastor, Jr., who see the 1994 reforms as stop-gap measures which are economically unsustainable within the greater environment of NAFTA and the Caribbean Economic Community (CARICOM). Rabid opponents of Fidel, however, will not take much comfort here, for Zimbalist and Pastor merely conclude that the reforms are unstable and unsustainable, but do not see them as soon to be replaced by sweeping neo-liberal policies in Cuba. The facts behind both of these viewpoints were clearly sustained in lectures by the Cuban economist Dr. Julio Carranza on 7 January 2000, and by diplomatic history specialist Dr. Carlos Alzugaray on 13 January 2000, both at the Varela Institute in Havana.

Politics of Illusion: The Bay of Pigs Invasion Reexamined, edited by James G. Blight and Peter Kornbluh, revisits the Bay of Pigs fiasco of April 1961. It does for the failed invasion by an exile force what Dino A. Brugioni's 1991 book *Eyeball to*

Eyeball, and Anatoli I. Gribkov's and William Y. Smith's 1994 book *Operation ANADYR* did for the November 1962 Cuban Missile Crisis. *Politics of Illusion* uses actual participants' accounts to establish what happened, at a time when major documents have just been declassified. This book too will draw much blood, like the Brugioni book and the Gribkov and Smith work, for both liberals and conservatives among the US inventory of policymakers on Cuba love to throw ideological bombshells at one another. What emerges from a careful reading of *Politics of Illusion* is a sad realization of three points. The United States, with all its massive resources and strategic advantages, developed very few workable options to the ill-conceived invasion. Each bureaucratic entity of the US government protected its own interests and image. No one, until President John F. Kennedy's final announcement of the tragic failure, took overall responsibility for conceiving and guaranteeing a coordinated strategy. So, as the book concludes, all parties indulged themselves in the politics of illusion and rendered flawed judgments. That appraisal squares with my own exposure to the planners of the era as well.

A book to love in this cluster is the photo-rich *Cuban Miami*, by Robert M. Levine and Moises Asis. Here we see the superbly energetic and creative side of the Cuban character, bound together by the tragedy of losing their homeland, but free to achieve in the country that still applauds Jacksonian Democracy. They are all represented here: the baseball stars, the dancers, the cartoonists, the architects, the housewives, and the domino players. Because the news media have presented the Cuban exile community as an orchestrated mob of howling anti-Castro right-wingers, this book is a charming, refreshing, and long-overdue antidote. Furthermore, it contains many well-written pages of sociologically-precise detail to accompany the superb photography. With this book, one sees the glory and the shame of the Cuban Revolution – the glory of what Cuba could now be under a climate of genuine democratic freedom, and the shame of having its talented people driven from their homes while those who remained built a dysfunctional welfare state on pillars of mythology.

The books reviewed here lead me to the same conclusions of my essay seven years ago – namely, that Fidel Castro has dug in for the long haul, and that the Cuban economy can stumble along for a few more years, sustained by a loyal leadership that glories more in the revolution than in the joys of neo-liberal economics. But one new conclusion also occurs: The time is nigh to apply the US policy of engagement. An exchange of diplomatic, cultural, economic, police, and military figures between the two countries, with careful attention to the nominations of the Cuban exile community, would create multiple links through which a gloriously endowed Caribbean island could reach its potential as a significant and respected nation.

BIBLIOGRAPHY

Blight, James G., and Peter Kornblug, eds. *Politics of Illusion: The Bay of Pigs Invasion Reexamined*. Boulder, Colo: Lynne Rienner, 1998.

Buckman, Robert T. "The Socialist Republic of Cuba." *Latin America 2001*. 34th ed. Harpers Ferry, W.VA.: Stryker-Post Publications, 2001.

Carranza, Julio (economics), Havana, 7 January 2000; Dr. Herbert Perez (history), Santiago, 10 January 2000; Dr. Jorge Herrera Ochoa (education), Havana, 10 January 2000; Dr. Carlos Alsugaray (international relations), Havana, 13 January 2000; Dr. Mayra Espina (sociology), 13 January 2000; and Dr. Juan Valdez Paz (historiography), 13 January 2000.

Levine, Robert M., and Moises Asis. *Cuban Miami*. New Brunswick, N.J.: Rutgers Univ. Press, 2000.

Purcell, Susan Kaufman, and David Rothkopf, eds. *Cuba: The Contours of Change*. Boulder, Colo: Lynne Rienner, 2000.

Ramsey, Russell W. "On Castro and Cuba: Rethinking the 'Three G's.'" *Parameters*, 24 (Winter 1994-95). Reprinted in *Strategic Reading on Latin America*. 3rd ed. Bloomington, Ind: 1st Books, 2001.

Whitney, Robert. "History or Teleology? Recent Scholarship on Cuba before 1959." *Latin American Research Review*, 36 (No. 2, 2001).

Wickham-Crowley, Timothy P. *Guerrillas and Revolution in Latin America*. Princeton, N.J.: Princeton Univ. Press, 1992.

Wright, Thomas C. *Latin America in the Era of the Cuban Revolution*. Westport, Conn.: Praeger, 2001.

Review of: *Fidel Castro*, by Robert E. Quirk, New York: Norton Publisher, 1993. Reviewed in: *North-South*, February-March, 1994.

The two last great *caudillos* of Latin American history, as seen in mid-21st century history books, will be Cuba's Fidel Castro and Chile's Augusto Pinochet. Quirk's biography of Castro appears at the same time as the English translation of Pinochet's autobiography and, while the books are vastly different, the two subjects are comparable.

Latin America was dragged into the Cold War as an accidental afterthought, when *Comandante* Fidel Castro invited in the Soviet Union's war machine, in 1961, to protect and strengthen his revolutionary regime in Cuba. Belatedly, the Soviets perceived the possibility of a southern encirclement strategy against its arch enemy the United States, but their ally Castro was always a little tainted, politically. He was too much the caudillo, the quintessential Latino strongman who swept into power when the Batista regime collapsed, and whose revolution always seemed more based on the persona of *número uno* than on scientifically correct Marxist-Leninist principles.

When Castro visited Chile in 1971, Pinochet headed security forces protecting him. Less than two years later, Pinochet seized power in Chile, and for the next 16 years the two caudillos not only squared off against each other but also symbolized and polarized Cold War politics in Latin America.

While giving a lavish account of his supporters and achievements, Pinochet fails to answer great questions surrounding his presidency, giving few details and only vague facts about which communists were carrying out specific acts of violence, the threats that had to be overcome by force, and the conduct of the repressions by state mechanisms under his control. Nonetheless, there is much detail not previously seen.

Perhaps by the year 2050 some enterprising historians may discover whether Fidel Castro was really a communist before 1961, and whether or not Chile would have become another shoddy Marxist-Leninist state in the 1970s had not Augusto Pinochet led the military overthrow of the government. These two books on the last and most symbolically visible of the Latin American caudillos will not answer those questions, but hundreds of other fascinating events are illuminated. Reading them together makes an interesting way to evaluate the interaction of the two regimes that espoused the strongest pro-communist and anti-communist policies during much of the Cold War in Latin America.

Russell W. Ramsey, Ph.D., D.Min.

Review of: *Operation ANADYR: U.S. and Soviet Generals Recount the Cuban Missile Crisis,* by Gen. Anatoli I. Gribkov and Gen. William Y. Smith. Edition q, Inc., NY, 1992. Reviewed in: *Army,* September, 1994.

Forty Caribbean-bound U.S. Navy ships in line threw up huge swells along the shores of the Panama Canal while people cheered on the banks. Thousands of U.S. soldiers flooded southern Florida's ports as they had in 1898 war of Cuban liberation. All the electronic surveillance and intelligence-gathering systems of the Cold War adversaries bristled as heads of state called for the latest information. It was the Cuban missile crisis of October 1962, and the military insiders now reveal the nuclear holocaust and the bloody invasion of Cuba that could easily have happened.

Gen. Anatoli I. Gribkov was a highly decorated tank commander in World War II. Promoted to major general, he was tasked in May 1962 to carry out the clandestine insertion of 40,000 Soviet military personnel – bombers, missiles, dozens of nuclear warheads, logistical support and a ground defense force – into Cuba. Prime Minister Nikita Khrushchev had become convinced that this alteration in the East-West correlation of forces, located in Premier Fidel Castro's newly communist Cuba, would open great strategic opportunities for the USSR. Gen. Gribkov commanded Operation ANADYR – the name of a remote river in Russia – with great skill, inserting a huge, high-technology military force right under the nose of the United States' most sophisticated intelligence apparatus.

Gen. William Y. Smith was a major working for the U.S. Joint Chiefs of Staff during the 1962 Cuban missile crisis. Many times decorated for his role in the air war over Korea, this highly educated officer became chief of staff and deputy U.S. commander of NATO forces in Europe during the late 1980s; his Soviet counterpart within the Warsaw Pact structure was Gen. Gribkov.

Background work for the book included five conferences held at Brown University between 1987 and 1992, and a Havana conference held in January 1992. Henno Lohmeyer of Edition q Inc., a German publishing house, produced Gen. Gribkov's memoirs in German before linking up the two former adversaries to produce *Operation ANADYR*.

This unusual book is crammed with revelations, corroborations and surprises. For military and diplomatic professionals, for scholars, for all who care about public affairs, this book is vital reading. Gen. Smith shows how the Cuban missile crisis conditioned subsequent Cold War military decisions and processes. He also reduces confusing intelligence and weapons jargon to the language of national security analysis, thus providing a vital case study in the evolution of the National Security Council. Gen. Gribkov shows how a significant number of Soviet military professionals genuinely believed in the extension of socialism through the use of clandestine military operations. In the language of the professional soldier, he reveals the heroism and the sacrifices called forth from his mixed force of technicians and combat troops. Delicate civil-military relationships are revealed, relationships that were once only a matter of highly subjective U.S. intelligence estimate. Gribkov also makes the startling revelation that Soviet generals often performed their arduous duties during the Cold War without any pocket money for routine travel expenses. He sketches the seminal steps by which the Cuban military forces were Sovietized in form and elevated to the status of the only world-rated, strategically projectable military force in Latin America.

This book does for the military side of the Cuban missile crisis what Dino A. Brugioni's 1991 book *Eyeball to Eyeball: The Inside Story of the Cuban Missile Crisis* did for the intelligence community.

Operation ANADYR could be the first of literary genre in which the Cold War players lay down all their cards.

Russell W. Ramsey, Ph.D., D.Min.

Review of: *Eyeball to Eyeball: The Inside Story of the Cuban Missile Crisis*, by Dino A. Brugioni, New York: Random House, 1992. Reviewed in: *Army*, November, 1992.

In the summer of 1962, the former USSR was engaged in the forward positioning of defensive and conventional military equipment in its new ally, Fidel Castro's Cuba. U.S. photographic intelligence had revealed for some time the presence of SA-2 (SAM-surface-to-air missile) antiaircraft defense missiles with non-nuclear warheads, and now, in the fall of 1962, the wizardry of clandestine photographic evidence revealed the presence of SS-4 (Sandal) offensive ballistic missiles.

Nuclear warheads were also discovered, a fact recently validated beyond dispute through the release of documents since the demise of the USSR, and a U.S. Air Force pilot, Maj. Rudolph Anderson Jr., was shot down and killed while piloting a U-2 surveillance aircraft for the Central Intelligence Agency.

The young President John F. Kennedy was reeling from criticism by Republicans and conservative Democrats for his handling of the 1961 Bay of Pigs fiasco in Cuba, and his mid-1962 response to the Soviet erection of the Berlin Wall. Facing a midterm congressional election (November 1962), President Kennedy carved out something in between the "nuke Cuba" group (Sen. Richard B. Russell and Air Force Gen. Curtis E. LeMay), and the "negotiate again" group (Ambassador to the United Nations Adlai E. Stevenson); this compromise was the Cuban quarantine decision of 22 October, 1962.

President Kennedy's quarantine, plus a Byzantine diplomatic effort in which his brother, Attorney General Robert F. Kennedy, partially snookered Soviet Premier Nikita S. Khrushchev about trading "our Jupiter missiles in Turkey for your SS-4s in Cuba," actually gave the young American president the middle ground.

The author of *Eyeball to Eyeball* has rendered all other books on the Cuban Missile Crisis of 1962 incomplete with his magnum opus. A Central Intelligence Agency officer from 1948 to 1982, he specialized in Soviet industrial installations and became a pioneer in strategic satellite imagery.

In the mid-1950s, the Eisenhower Administration formed the National Photographic Interpretation Center under Arthur C. Lundahl. Mr. Brugioni was one of the charter members and chief of the unit that actually prepared the crucial photographs for the White House during the Cuban Missile Crisis.

Following his retirement in 1982, he devoted a decade to researching every known detail about the international confrontation that former Secretary of State Dean Rusk termed "the most dangerous crisis the world has ever seen" and the only time when the two superpowers of the Cold War came "eyeball to eyeball."

Mr. Brugioni was indeed an eyewitness to much of this story, and he has painstakingly reconstructed the rest. The strongest feature of his book is the case for electronic intelligence as an absolute necessity in the making of national security decisions. National security specialists will shake their heads over the primitive functioning of the National Security Council and the Joint Chiefs of Staff in 1962.

Military logisticians will note with interest that south Florida was overwhelmed by the arrival of troops poised for the potential invasion of Cuba, an apparently unheeded lesson that most campaign studies of the 1898 Spanish-American War for Cuban Independence stress. Naval readers will discover the fine line between war and peace that exists when a naval quarantine (an act of war in international law) is being enforced.

Eyeball to Eyeball moves so far ahead of other books on the topic that one is tempted to accept Brugioni's conclusions uncritically. He shows how electronic intelligence, correctly used, can prevent the accidental launching of strategic forces by one side when it misreads the other side's capabilities or intentions. This is one of the specific caveats in Robert Kennedy's *Thirteen Days: A Memoir of the Cuban Missile Crisis*. Brugioni reveals the weakness in absolute dependency upon superiority in strategic weapons, advocated by then-Secretary of the Treasury Douglas Dillon in 1962, still accepted as gospel by Reagan-era arms superiority advocates.

Eyeball to Eyeball is robbed of being the once-and-always classic on its topic for two related reasons. The author is so steeped in the wonders of electronic eavesdropping and its link to national security processes that he barely considers guerrilla warfare and other forms of low-intensity conflict.

By President Kennedy's focus on withdrawing only the offensive missile threat (SS-4s, possibly SS-5s, all nuclear warheads) and his subsequent success in obtaining that concession, public opinion in the United States was diverted from the Soviet forces that remained in Cuba after October 1962.

By the mid-1980s, this force consisted of a 2,800-man combat brigade, more than 3,000 military advisers (working in Cuba and Nicaragua), and more than 2,000 military electronics technicians operating the Lourdes intelligence collection facility with over-watch capabilities across the continental United States. This is the array that trained and elevated Cuba's military capabilities, in the mid-1980s, to at least parity with Brazil and Canada.

While the author itemizes these troops and assets, he evidently sees them as less than strategic threats in their time. He also seems unaware that former U.S. Ambassador to the Soviet Union Llewellyn E. Thompson Jr., was the only one who had serious knowledge of how top Soviet power figures would think during an international crisis. Two decades later, Richard N. Lebow wrote that studies of Soviet intentions during the Cuban Missile Crisis "are, at best, clever speculations about Soviet behavior consistent with the few established facts."

Save, then, for some lack of historiographical balance, *Eyeball to Eyeball* is the volume that makes previous works on the Cuban Missile Crisis of 1962 appear incomplete, ideologically driven, or merely naive. As former Soviet officials continue to reveal their secrets, our knowledge of the affair should increase steadily until the year 2002, when the statutory floodgates of declassification will open still new vistas. Until then, no serious study of Cuban-U.S.-USSR affairs in the Cold War will be complete without taking stock of this careful and honest book.

Russell W. Ramsey, Ph.D., D.Min.

"Castro's Cuba: Insular Immutability Amid Winds of Change,"
Journal of Defense and Diplomacy, April, 1990.

"We do not know where they (FMLN communist guerrillas in El Salvador) obtained the weapons," President Mikhail Gorbachev told President George Bush on December 2, 1989. "We completed our weapons deliveries there (Central America and the Caribbean) early in the year."

The site was the Soviet luxury liner Maxim Gorky, anchored serenely at Malta harbor while Mediterranean seas raged and gale winds howled outside, symbolizing changes in the USSR and its East European sphere of influence. The topic was Communist military power in Central America, specifically, the Farabundo Martí guerrillas in El Salvador, who wrecked the Central American peace accords in a spectacular assault on the capital in the very week when the USSR and East Europe's big four were becoming more democratic and less militarily belligerent.

"Why," President Bush asked President Gorbachev, "are you still arming the rebels in Central America?" Recent events in El Salvador showed that the FMLN forces had been heavily rearmed with escalated levels of weaponry, all of it from the Soviet bloc. News analysts immediately reduced the exchange between Gorbachev and Bush on this topic to two ideas: Gorbachev was lying (deemed unlikely), or, Nicaragua's Sandinistas, who also deny complicity in the bloody El Salvador uprising of late November 1989 were lying (deemed likely).

President Gorbachev was not lying. The USSR carried out multi-billion-dollar arms deliveries to the Central American/Caribbean region in January-March 1989, then turned off the spigot. The Sandinistas did arm the FMLN in El Salvador, but the logistical source, the stimulus, the infrastructure, the expertise and the strategic deniability factor all attribute to one island. That island is not Malta, where the issue attained rare high-level visibility, but Cuba, where Castro rules as dictatorially as Stalin once ruled the USSR.

What threat does Premier Fidel Castro's Cuba present to the United States in the 1990s, expressed in credible war fighting scenarios? Many studies warn U.S. policy makers that Cuba is a danger, while others inventory Cuban military power. This analysis examines the actual military responses that Cuba is both capable of doing, and likely to do, in five scenarios.

Two premises underline this inquiry. The first is that Cuba is the second-highest ranking military power in the Western hemisphere, superior even to Brazil and Canada so long as Soviet military sustainment continues. The second is that, since the early 1970s, Premier Castro has acted out a sophisticated role as a perceived independent among the world's Marxist-Leninist states, when, in fact, his nation is the Soviet Union's primary agent of politico-military power in Latin America and Africa.

SCENARIO #1. *Glasnost-Era Rapprochement*:

Soviet interests in this scenario call for expanding the USSR's influence in Latin America at minimum financial cost, while appearing to present a low profile, non-threatening posture towards the United States. Ideologically, the USSR recognizes many national roads to socialism; diplomatically, Moscow's officials will work for a widening agenda of trade and cultural agreements. Visible arms sales are useful to the Soviets, but the sub-rosa arming of Latin American revolutionaries will be done on a low level of visibility. An increasing Soviet goal is the strengthening of relationships with Latin America's economically expanding Pacific coastal sector.

Cuba, in this milieu, remains a continuous low-grade threat to the United States. Castro can pipe in the weapons to Nicaragua, El Salvador, and Panamá, while Moscow feigns distance. Castro can advocate that Brazil, Argentina, Mexico, and the mid-sized debtors refuse repayment, and that they form a cartel that will replace the Organization of American States with an anti-U.S. political alliance. This ruse was acted out grandly on April 6, 1989, at the Palace of Conventions in Havana, when Castro advocated non-repayment of debt for the non-communist nations, then asserted, in Gorbachev's presence, that there simply was no problem with Soviet renewal and continuance of Cuba's $6 to $8 billion indebtedness to the USSR.

In Africa, Cuban troop withdrawal is only symbolic and could easily be reversed. Under the East-West rapprochement scenario, Cuban troops will maintain the Angolan government's shaky control over two-thirds of the national territory, and back the South West Africa People's Organization (SWAPO) in a drive to bring newly independent Namibia into the Soviet orbit.

Much smaller Cuban detachments will keep the socialist regimes in power in Ethiopia and Mozambique, permitting each of them to govern about half of the national territory. Without the Cuban troops, these pro-Soviet regimes would be overthrown, or the nations would just break up into warring districts within two to five years.

Most effective and least perceived of the Castro threats to the United States, under the rapprochement scenario, is the disinformation machine. Castro will continue to play off liberals against conservatives, Congress against the White House, the Pentagon against the State Department and Florida against Washington, D.C. As he has done well since the mid-1960s, he will divide U.S. opinion and policy, leading toward a continuing loss of stability and of U.S. influence in Latin America and Africa.

Some of the power void created will be filled directly by Cuba and the USSR, some by rising European and Asian powers, and some by local governments whose policies will often incline towards the USSR.

Russell W. Ramsey, Ph.D., D.Min.

SCENARIO #2. *Low-Intensity Conflict*:

Soviet policy in this scenario will call for feeding likely Marxist-Leninist winners through the specialized task assignments of its satellite nations. This creates deniability plus the illusion of multinational support. Cuba's main role in this scenario is to provide thousands of on-site, well-trained revolutionary managers, mostly disguised as teachers, technicians and medical personnel, who actually perform the deceptive roles. This task assignment achieves near perfect symmetry with Castro's own perceived role as Robin Hood to the world's developing nations. Cuban techno-revolutionaries peaked at 16,000 in 1985 and could be easily beefed up to 50,000 with little additional expense to the Soviet sponsors.

Should there be a breakdown in the Central American peace accords of 1988, a combat resurgence by the Contras in Nicaragua, unexpected successes by the Farabundo Martí Liberation Front in El Salvador, or an anti-U.S. call to arms by Manuel Noriega in Panamá, Castro will be the Soviet's man of the hour. He will coordinate the communist seizure of government while the United States stands by in helpless rage, liberals preach "understanding," conservatives egg on the Pentagon, and the Soviet block nations pour in diplomatic, military, economic and logistical support.

As new Castro look-alike figures emerge, Castro will welcome them into the club of virulent U.S. haters, taking care to preserve his senior status. A Cuban weakness in this scenario would be managing a Marxist-Leninist revolution on the Pacific side of Latin America, where Cubans are not admired, logistical support is tough, and local governments have better control.

The African segment of this scenario is specific, not general. Cuba can seriously threaten the anti-communist Union for the Total Independence of Angola (UNITA) guerrilla army in southeast Angola, and it can intimidate non-communist elements in Namibia, but it cannot do much more for the weak governments of Mozambique and Ethiopia.

SCENARIO #3. *Regional Non-Nuclear War, United States Involved:*

This scenario has different dynamics, depending upon the location of the conflict. Given a non-nuclear conflict, with U.S. forces engaged in Asia or the Middle East, the Cuban threat becomes a wild card. Castro can maintain the illusion of independence from Moscow, while playing out a number of options. He can step up low-intensity conflict operations in Latin America and Africa. He can act as an international figurehead to line up support for whatever nation or nations oppose the United States. He can stir up anti-war sentiment in the United States by the usual tactic of portraying the U.S. opponent as a nationalist-reformist government, thereby undermining support for U.S. military action.

SCENARIO #4. *United States and Soviet Union in Non-Nuclear Conflict:*

This is the first scenario on a rising intensity scale in which the Cuban war machine would directly confront the United States. Paramilitary and clandestine Cuban forces would lead the Nicaraguan Sandinistas in an overt invasion of Honduras and El Salvador. A major effort would be made to bring Panama into the communist orbit.

But U.S. citizens would discover, right in the homeland, that Cuba is a mid-range, conventional military power. Elite *spetznaz* troops would carry out attacks on shipping, electric and nuclear power stations, dams and airports in southern Florida, arriving in a variety of clandestine smallcraft. Several dozen MiG-23s (Floggers) would take on U.S. industrial and military targets of opportunity within the Caribbean Sea lines of communication. Larger numbers of less capable MiG-21s would support this effort and thereby divert scarce U.S. air assets. Foxtrot class Cuban submarines would attack U.S. shipping in coordination with fast surface patrol boats and formidable Soviet undersea assets. Cuban-based electronic warfare centers would jam U.S. communications and transmit intelligence data to Moscow.

While the United States would neutralize most offensive Cuban military assets within two weeks, the island would remain a forward Soviet military base, capable of sustainment by transport aircraft, useful for the landing and reloading of bombers. U.S. counter-air and antisubmarine warfare units would find their task made difficult by the ability of the Soviets to disperse their air and undersea assets between Nicaragua and Cuba. In this scenario, the United States would lack the combat power to invade and occupy Cuba, since the primary effort would be in Europe, the Middle East, Africa, or Asia. Still, significant quantities of U.S. air, sea, and undersea assets would be diverted from the primary war zone, and losses would be significant. Further, some forces would have to be retained in the Western Hemisphere to quarantine Cuba against mounting new strikes in Florida and Central America.

Cuban forces in Africa, in this scenario, would suddenly find themselves dependent upon a Soviet decision about strategic priorities. Should the USSR decide to cease delivery of military supplies and financial credits to sustain the Cuban troops in Angola, it is likely that the Republic of South Africa and UNITA would unite to cripple them severely. Cuban forces might also be overwhelmed by anti-government and secessionist elements in Ethiopia and Mozambique. A Soviet decision toward sustainment of the Cubans in Africa, in this scenario, would weaken its war-fighting effort in the primary theater.

SCENARIO #5. *Nuclear War, United States and Soviet Union:*

Cuba's military forces would have all the capabilities stated in the non-nuclear scenario (#4), but with some important differences. If Florida and the Caribbean air/sea lines of communication received nuclear strikes, Cuba, a non-nuclear power, would have to cope with fallout drift. Castro might send a conventional invasion force to Florida while the United States coped with nuclear fallout and damage zones, but more likely he would simply invade other Caribbean and Central American countries, making himself a regional power while the United States writhed and contended with the Soviet Union for national survival.

A summary of Cuban capabilities suggests that disinformation, clandestine conflict management, and tactical conventional interdiction are Cuba's three strongest playing cards. Experience shows that it has the will to use the first two against the United States, and those two plus the third capability against non-communist forces in Africa. The idea that Castro's foreign policy vis-à-vis the USSR is a brilliantly masked illusion of independence is central to the question of whether or not Cuba would actually use its military assets against the United States. The conclusion is that Cuba would, indeed, fight the United States in the scenarios set forth, and that, under these conditions, Cuba is a serious military threat.

Essays on Latin American Security
The Collected Writing of a Scholar-Implementer

Review of: *Cuba's Foreign Policy in The Middle East*, by Damian J. Fernández, Boulder: Westview Press, 1988. Reviewed in: *Naval War College Review*, Spring, 1990.

Premier Fidel Castro long ago expanded his original notions of sponsoring liberationist guerrilla wars into a full spectrum of politico-military services. Where once his peripatetic revolutionists schemed romantically – and unsuccessfully – at implanting *Maoist focos*, he later built a diplomatic and military array of overt and clandestine forces aimed at creating a Marxist-Leninist world.

Professor Damian J. Fernández, political science professor at Colorado College, traces Castro's efforts to become a significant player in the world's hottest region, the Middle East. His study was performed in the archives of the Cuban Information System at the University of Miami Graduate School of International Studies and in the Hispanic Division of the Library of Congress. The book is written primarily for Latin Americanists, and most of the Middle Eastern scholarly source materials appear to be secondary.

The first chapter is a summary of Cuban foreign policy from 1960-1985. It is easily the best of its kind in print.

Next, is a survey chapter on Cuban policies in the Middle East, as a region, followed by a chapter containing a country-by-country implementation of those policies. These two chapters form the centerpiece of the book. A special case study on Cuban-Libyan relations follows, and it contains some surprises. Where the casual observer might expect Muammar el-Qaddafi and Fidel Castro to find common ground as leading scourges of the industrial West, Qaddafi, while sharing Castro's anti-Zionist and anti-U.S. enthusiasm, in fact, finds Castro to be too faithful a Soviet ally.

The summary chapter develops some interesting conjectures on how and why Cuba is even a player in the Middle Eastern cauldron. After all, Cuba needs Middle Eastern petroleum but is financially bankrupt, totally beholden to Soviet largesse for significant purchases. The Middle East hardly lacks for glinty-eyed revolutionists who know the fine points of the AK-47 or the radio-detonated car bomb. Yet Fidel Castro has indeed multi-regionalized Middle Eastern turbulence with his presence, despite an overwhelming lack of assets and logical reasons.

Professor Fernández relies strongly on Foreign Broadcast Information Service bulletins for Cuban actions; more credibility would be attained through analysis of what Middle Eastern leaders think of Cuba. Michael Stuhrenberg wrote recently in the liberal weekly *Die Zeit* of Hamburg that "Cuba is considered by many of the poorest nations to be an international super-power... They view Castro not as Moscow's representative but as its successor." Professor Fernández does not go quite so far.

Pointing to the glittering opportunities which first attracted Castro to interpose his country in Middle Eastern affairs, Fernández concludes that the region is tough for any outsider to manipulate and that, even if he is not simply a stooge of the Kremlin, Castro still has to accept Soviet guidelines.

Russell W. Ramsey, Ph.D., D.Min.

"The Middle East might well be Fidel Castro's, and revolutionary Cuba's last international frontier," he says. Yet the chart on page 56 shows an impressive array of regional penetrations by a regime ruling a small country that U.S. patriots used to tell me, in 1960, could be "cleaned out by a squad of well-trained Marines with baseball bats."

Review of: *The Secret War in Central America: Sandinista Assault on World Order,* by John Norton Moore, Frederick, MD: University Publications of America, 1987. Reviewed in: *The Friday Review of Defense Literature*, March 11, 1988.

In 1979 and 1980, the United States provided the Nicaraguan Sandinista government with many times the humanitarian aid money ever extended to the overthrown Somoza regime. During that same time, the Cuban government was organizing in Nicaragua a proxy war to overthrow the government of El Salvador and lesser violence against Honduras and Costa Rica. The Sandinista government cooperated totally, using US aid money, Soviet arms, and Cuban advisors to create a Marxist-Leninist dictatorship, completely contrary to the spirit of the 1979 anti-Somoza front. They went on to build the largest per-capita military force in mainland western hemispheric history, months before disgruntled members of their own revolutionary coalition sought aid from the United States to create a democratic resistance. This is the thesis of John Norton Moore's *The Secret War in Central America*. The case is documented from pluralistic sources and is made in a neutral, nonpolemic way.

The corollary to Moore's thesis is that the Sandinistas' clandestine aggression, managed by Cubans with Soviet arms and support, has gutted two centerpieces of western hemispheric international relations. These are the prohibition of aggressive attacks and the response to such attacks with proportional force.

Moore's second chapter is a meticulously documented legal defense that he never was able to use. Charged with having the Central Intelligence Agency mine the Corinto Harbor, the United States government refused to submit to final jurisdiction by the World Court. Moore offers a reasoned defense based upon evidence of Nicaragua's exportation of weapons and personnel to the communist Faribundo Marti Liberation Front in El Salvador. He does not deny that the US CIA carried out the mining operations and other actions as well. His point is that those operations were a proportional force response by the United States and El Salvador against a much larger war of aggression being waged by the Nicaraguan Sandinistas.

The third chapter, again almost a stand-alone essay, is an expose. Moore takes a dozen popularly held views in the United States about events in Central America and shows how mainstream America is susceptible to disinformation techniques. These include the idea that the United States did not sincerely try to work with the 1979 victorious Sandinistas, the notion that it was the United States who militarized Central America, and the belief that the Nicaraguan Democratic Resistance (the "Contras") is a disreputable gang of displaced Somoza National Guardsmen. With considerable self-restraint, Moore offers the evidence to show that these and other perceptions widely believed in the United States about recent events in Central America are brilliantly cultivated falsehoods. Moore's self-restraint, ironically, has the practical effect of downplaying the pervasive hand of the Soviet Union's KGB, the Cuban Ministry of Information, and Nicaraguan Commandant Tomas Borge's information apparatus, all acting in concert to whipsaw US and European public opinion in their favor.

Moore's summation is a plea for the western hemisphere, at least, and hopefully the larger hemisphere as well to return to the central principle of the United Nations Charter. "Aggressive attack, whether covert or overt, is illegal and must be vigorously condemned by the world community. That same community," adds Moore, "must join in assisting defense against such attack."

Professor Moore has done battle in print over Central America with the polemical leftist Professor Noam Chomsky. Consequently, the academic community may characterize Moore's work on the topic as equal and opposite polemics of the far right, or at least as vintage Reagan administration apologia. The reader who holds sacred an independent opinion might first read Shirley Christian's 1985 *Nicaragua: Revolution in the Family*, David Nolan's *The Ideology of the Sandinistas and the Nicaraguan Revolution* (Coral Gables, 1985), and Thomas W. Walker's edited collection entitled *Nicaragua: The First Five Years* (Praeger, 1985). Jiri and Virginia Valenta's essay "Sandinistas in Power" (*Problems of Communism*, XXXIV, Sept-Oct, 1985) is packed with detail from multiple sources.

If Professor Moore's little book is indeed the politically neutral, central ground, then the question may fairly be asked: How have so many US intellectuals, ministers, politicians, entertainers, and journalists been fused so thoroughly that they form a coalition termed contemptuously by Commandante Tomas Borge as his "army of useful fools?" Here, Moore's book gives the substance but not the method. He details the explicitly wrong notions on who was aggressor and who was a victim that the Sandinistas have passed off on the floor of the US Congress, from the pulpits of mainline US churches, and through a dozen or more television specials of a supposedly neutral character. He omits description of the active measures and disinformation apparatus that the USSR, Cuba, and Nicaragua have operated with great success inside the arena of America's own foreign policy.

John Norton Moore writes international law in the grand manner of such American luminaries as Manley O. Hudson and John Bassett Moore (no relation), and Israel's Shabtai Rosenne. For fuller credibility, he should have mentioned that the United States damaged his two central legal theses in 1954 over the Guatemalan Castillo Armas affair and in 1961 over the Cuban Bay of Pigs counter-revolutionary attempt. In both cases, the United States acted unilaterally, without consulting the Organization of American States (OAS). The continuing lack of Latin American support for the US position that Nicaragua and Cuba are the true aggressors in Central America may derive strongly from perceived US support for the United Kingdom against Argentina in the 1982 Falklands/Malvinas War, and from the Reagan administration's refusal to give OAS machinery in Central America a chance through the Contadora Group (Mexico, Costa Rica, Panama, Colombia) Peace Plan of 1983.

University Publications of America has produced some vital books that fill a scholarly void, especially the Foreign Intelligence Book Series edited by Thomas F. Troy. One wishes that a publisher so careful with facts had included a bibliography, beyond the massive footnotes, with John Norton Moore's work on the Sandinistas.

Many of these sources are listed in the bibliography of Robert F. Turner's *Nicaragua v. The United States: A Look at the Facts* (McLean: Pergamon-Brassey, 1987). Turner is a colleague of Professor Moore, and his book is a political exegesis on ground that Moore visited through juridical language.

Clearly, not all the villainy in false perceptions of Nicaraguan Sandinista aggression is a triumph of the communist disinformation and active measures apparatus. Yet Moore's little book is the factual, central ground on the topic. Further writings on "Sandinista self-defense," "Contras as reactionaries," and "Reagan's militarization policy" will now stand revealed as polemics.

(Note: Moore holds the Walter L. Brown Chair of Law at the University of Virginia. He is also Director of Graduate Studies in the Law School, Director of the Center for Oceans Law and Policy, a frequent consultant to the US Department of State, and author of prestigious volumes of legal questions in Asia, the Middle East, and Africa.)

Russell W. Ramsey, Ph.D., D.Min.

"Cuba and Mexico: Profiles in 1994," (British) *Army Quarterly & Defence Journal*, April, 1994.

Against a background of change, Cuba and Mexico have now emerged with fairly stable governments. In both cases, however, there has been a price to pay. Fidel Castro, Head of State as well as Commander-in-Chief of the Army, has led a military-based society in Cuba since 1959. There is a two-year compulsory military service, and most heads of the public sector hold military rank. Mexico, by contrast, despite problems in January and February, is more democratic than her neighbors.

During the years following revolution, political stability had grown until very recently. The government has been dominated by the PRI – *Partido Revolucionario Institucional* – which since being formed in 1929 has been consistently re-elected, making Mexico basically a one-party guided democracy.

This apparent stability was rudely shaken by a New Year's Day rebellion by Indian peasants in southern Chiapas state. The resulting crisis deepened on Wednesday, March 23, 1994, when Mexico's leading presidential candidate for the election due on August 21st – Luis Donaldo Colosio, 44 – was assassinated during Colosio's presidential campaign.

In December 1898, after the war between Spain and the US, the sovereignty of Cuba passed to the USA. For four years the island was treated as a protectorate, but US interest did not end with independence in 1902. Cuba's army remained small and ill-equipped but had no real need for expansion because of her special relationship with the United States.

In 1933, Fulgencio Batista seized power in a sergeant's revolt with the support of the US. He was to rule until 1944 and again between 1952 and 1959. The army was now to increase in size, but in the event it did not have the ability nor the motivation to resist the new guerrilla tactics of Castro's Revolutionary Armed Forces (FAR).

Castro was therefore able to take power in 1959 against a collapsing army; the new communist regime was established. Against the background of the Cold War, the arrival of a communist government on her doorstep was to cause grave concern to the US. Within a few months Castro had abolished the old armed services set up by the dictator, Batista, and had begun to expand the FAR in response to what he perceived as the American threat. In May 1960, Cuba joined the Soviet bloc. An invasion by Cuban exiles, backed by the US government, at the Bay of Pigs in April 1961, was easily defeated.

Then in October 1962, photographs taken by the US Air Force showed that Russian bases were being built in Cuba. It was the first time the US had seen a visible threat so close to their territory. President Kennedy went on television on October 22nd to state "a series of offensive missile sites is now in preparation in Cuba" that could threaten most of the major cities of the United States. He said that Russian bombers capable of carrying nuclear weapons were being uncrated and ordered a naval and air blockade of Cuba, under UN supervision. He declared that the launching of any nuclear missile from Cuba against any Western nation would be considered as an attack on the US "requiring a full retaliatory response on the Soviet Union." US forces were placed on alert.

Between October 24th and 29th, there were secret negotiations between the two superpowers which ended with the then Russian dictator, Khrushchev, agreeing to halt the construction of bases in Cuba. He promised to dismantle and remove Soviet missiles already there. President Kennedy agreed to lift the blockade and promised the US would not invade Cuba. Tacitly, the US backed away from installing offensive missiles in NATO member Turkey. In early January 1963, both countries reported to the UN Secretary General U Thant that the crisis was ended.

Even so, on 9 May 1963 the US Defense Department estimated that 17,500 Russians were still in Cuba, including 5,000 troops. Thus, the Monroe Doctrine principle was breached, and Cuba became the USSR's forward base on the other hemisphere.

In return for Castro's support, the Soviet Union continued to give the Cuban armed forces modern equipment. Moscow also helped when Cuba began to intervene militarily in the affairs of far away countries such as Angola and Ethiopia. Cuban Army *"internacionalistas"* reached a peak strength of 60,000 in 1987, as Angola fought the UNITA anti-communist revolutionaries. By now, Cuba had large armed forces and, in time, the presence of her standing army was even to provide a cheap supply of agricultural labor. Discipline was brought into the lives of Cuban youth. Today, Cuba has one of the most modern armies for a country of her size.

However, the government has now become less popular and it is difficult to distinguish the work of the soldier from that of the civilian: 6 percent of the GNP is presently spent on defense. It is estimated that the total armed forces number 180,500: the Army have 145,000 men, the Navy some 13,500, and the Air Force 22,000.

Cuba faces several problems as Russian aid has gone. Because of her earlier dependence on the Soviet Union for technology and support, Cuba has no arms industry. Major rifts are developing within the services; several senior officers have defected. An early example was the Air Force Chief, General Rafael de Piño, who left in 1987. The economy is in a poor state, weakened because until a few years ago, almost 85% of Cuba's trade was with other communist nations. There are frequent shortages of consumer goods and discontent on the island over government support for such former friends as Ethiopia. Gradually, Cuban forces have backed away from overseas commitments.

As yet, there are no clear successors to Fidel Castro. His brother Raúl, lacks his charisma and authority. Cuba will have to moderate both her foreign and domestic policies.

What has happened in Mexico since the Spanish were finally defeated in 1821? The first real revolt against Spanish rule was in 1810, led by Miguel Hidalgo y Costilla; he was a priest interested in social reform but was captured and executed by the Spanish. However, he had already started the chain of events leading to the Spanish decline in Mexico which was to end with the 1821 rebellion. This time their leader was a soldier, General Agustín de Iturbide. Crowned Emperor, he, in turn, was forced from the throne in March 1823 by a republican revolt. The 50 years that followed saw 30 different presidents come and go, war with the United States, and the loss of Texas. There was even a brief period of French rule which ended with the execution of yet another Emperor, Maximilian. He had been Archduke of Austria and was installed and briefly supported by Napoleon III. Mexico seemed unable to move forward until the harsh military dictatorship of Porfirio Díaz in 1876. Whilst he brought economic progress, Mexico's masses remained in abject poverty.

In 1910, the peasants finally rebelled against the injustices of the system. Their great leader was Venustiano Carranza. The popular nature of this revolution was to ensure a more democratic way of government but took many years of bloody fighting – mostly without direction – to achieve. Díaz fled Mexico in 1911 but was replaced by a weak liberal, Francisco Madero.

Madero was murdered by General Victoriano Huerta, whose government was in fact a return to the hated system the peasants had fought to destroy: 1914 brought new uprisings and the revolutionary elders Emilio Zapata and Pancho Villa joined forces with Carranza. Huerta was removed and Carranza was proclaimed President in 1915.

The 1917 Constitution was based on the reasons behind and the aims of the Revolution but unrest continued. When the promised reforms were not forthcoming, Carranza was overthrown in a military-led revolt in 1920. This placed General Alvaro Obregon in power. Mexico's first three post-revolutionary presidents were former generals.

It was not until 1934 that the country began to stabilize under the reforming presidency of Lázaro Cardenas. His party, the PRI, has dominated politics since then and has been constantly re-elected. Throughout the 1920s, the army was adopting new methods and a clear distinction was to be made between the role of the army and that of the state. Cardenas continued this policy. Yet today's President Salinas still holds the rank of Commander-in-Chief of the armed forces. A separate sector for the military within the ruling party was created but abolished in the 1940s. Most observers credit Mexico with a constitutionally obedient military profession.

In 1941, military training for all 18-year-old males was made compulsory. This was in preparation for Mexico's part in World War II when 6,000 Mexicans served in the US army. A Mexican Air Force squadron flew P-38s against the Japanese and took part in the re-capture of the Philippines. Even after the war, US influence on the army was strong, and it was eventually reorganized on the US model.

From the late 1970s to 1982, the development of major petroleum reserves led to a period of industrial and economic growth. Mexico began to demand a larger role in world politics, and plans were made to modernize the poorly paid and equipped army and revitalize the defense industry. Severe economic and social difficulties after 1982, during the presidency of Miguel de la Madrid, meant the reform programme had to be scaled down.

Defense remains an important matter. The total armed forces are now 175,000: 130,000 are in the Army, 37,000 in the Navy, and 8,000 in the Air Force. Mexico's one-year national conscription is by lottery. The army was involved in anti-drug activities and national security planning, and there was the earlier fear of nearby guerrilla actions in Guatemala, El Salvador and Nicaragua spreading into Mexico.

She has, however, maintained good relations with her neighbors and has always refused to adopt sanctions against Cuba. Relations with the United States since World War II have also remained friendly, improving further in the 1990s with both governments seeking closer economic ties. They are both members of NAFTA, the North Atlantic Free Trade Agreement. Following last month's assassination of Luis Donaldo Colosio, see above, the United States Government loaned $US6,000mn to support the Mexican Government.

Within Mexico, the position is less secure and the army could be utilized and moved into the political arena once more. Their present role is largely domestic and, as noted, the army was used to restore order in January when a rebel peasant force gained control of several towns in Chiapas for a short while. The rebels were demanding political reform.

Mexico progresses along a shaky path to democracy: reform is still needed. As President Carlos Salinas de Gortarihas has discovered, the people are ready to fight for it, as they were in 1910.

Russell W. Ramsey, Ph.D., D.Min.

"Invasion: A Small Step in a Long Process," *Army Times*, November 12, 1994.

Knocking out the illegal regime of Gen. Raoul Cedras in Haití is a three-day operation for a division-sized maritime task force. However, restoring the legally elected president, Jean-Bertrand Arístide, to office and keeping him there to govern, would require a two-year peacekeeper task force of 10,000 military personnel. And creating a stable political democracy in Haití would require a foreign-operated tutorial regime, well-armed, for 25 years, and even such a multi billion-dollar, multinational effort might still fail.

Haití poses five zones of legitimate national security concern to the United States:

1. Haitian refugees require massive health assistance, are a public health menace to themselves, and do not integrate well anywhere. They pose a security and serious socio-economic threat to Dade County/Miami, and a moderate budgetary threat to Florida. Even under a negotiated, controlled regional diaspora, Haitian refugee resettlement and care will cost $350 million per year for two to five years.
2. Andean drug lords have bought up a haven within Haití's corrupt, brutal military government. Cocaine valued in excess of $250 million a year is distributed from remote sites on the jungle-clad seacoast and from Port-au-Prince harbor itself under regime protection. Drug profits now exceed looting to keep the Cedras machine afloat and go far to bypass the effectiveness of the partial economic embargo in place.
3. U.S.-Latin American political relationships are in a new era of cordiality. Regional trade pacts promise economic development with mass participation. U.S. leadership is weakened by the appearance of doing nothing to foment democracy in Haití, yet Latin American public opinion strongly opposed both a unilateral U.S. invasion and an inter-American invasion. Latin America places absolute national sovereignty on a higher plane than military interference for humanitarian purposes. The threat is the sudden loss of rising Latin American trust in the United States as a partner instead of the traditional role as regional policeman.
4. Beyond restoring Arístide, the price of building a democracy in an occupied Haití could easily cost a billion dollars annually.
5. No direct military threat to the United States is posed by Haití, but U.S. inability or unwillingness to oust the Cedras government carries a global cost. Abusive regimes and rogue-armed groups alike are emboldened at times by the failure of U.S. power to act decisively against repression or aggression, either alone or as leader of a coalition.

Supported from Guantanamo Naval Base in Cuba and by U.S. Atlantic Command elements in the Caribbean, the first phase would be the seizure of the harbor facilities to secure a maritime foothold through which to pass one or two additional mobile brigades with the task of securing key centers of resistance and communication. This second phase would complete the regime-toppling mission, leading to the long-term third phase where residual force levels would be determined by amounts of terrorist resistance. However, unexpected pockets of organized opposition at Fort Liberte or Jacmel, for example, could delay the second phase and even commingle it with phase three.

Sea Stallion and Sea Knight helicopters would carry the assault marines for the first two phases, supported by Supper Bell Cobra gun ships, carrier-based jet fighters, and naval gunfire from destroyers and frigates. SEAL teams would secure docking while dock-landing ships would off-load combat vehicles and combat support, and one or two amphibious assault ships would ferry in assault waves of troops by helicopter. The small but competent Dominican Republic Army would block a mass exodus of Cedras supporters along the rugged interior border, but some would trickle through.

The 7,000-man Haitian Army would employ strong-points with ambushes, human hostages, and demolition of key facilities to delay their inevitable defeat. Their small armor and artillery assets are ineffective and would be quickly neutralized. Key power centers would be secured within three days, minus isolated holdouts. The full panoply of tricks to deceive the news media would be employed, for Raoul Cedras watches CNN as faithfully as Saddam Hussein does. Staged atrocities, emotionalistic denunciations of the invasion force, and allegations of human rights violations would be exploited fully.

Keys to success

Keys to a successful invasion are to secure population centers with minimum casualties, focus on quick reduction of organized combat power, and prevent the melting away of the Haitian Army into a thousand terrorist squads clad in civilian clothes. Capturing Raoul Cedras and a few of his henchmen does not have the importance of nailing Manuel Noriega during Operation Just Cause in Panamá in December 1989, even though the news media would taunt invasion commanders about this issue.

The third phase calls for long-term occupation, restoration of law and order, gradual empowerment of the Canadian-trained Haitian National Police, and incremental expansion of a constitutional political system. The previous U.S. occupation of Haití, 1915-1934, offers a few useful lessons on the geography and sociology of resistance. But phase three itself calls into question a whole series of foreign policy issues beyond the scope of military operations, such as the conflict between sovereignty and regime incompetence.

A unilateral U.S. invasion of Haití would wreck recent hopes for a new day in Western Hemisphere relationships. A multinational invasion under the banner of the Organization of American States (OAS) or the United Nations is marginally justified if a significant number of member nation-states strongly support the measure with forces and money. At present, such support is not even close to a reality. The compromise package – a U.S. invasion followed by an inter-American force to do the third phase occupation and nation-building task – is tempting. There is a big difference between third-phase participation by the armies of two or three willing Latin American countries with U.S. forces to rebuild post-invasion Haití, and a genuine groundswell of popular opinion in Latin America to reoccupy Haití and convert it into a democracy. The compromise package – a U.S. invasion followed by an inter-American occupation force – carries an economic and political price tag far in excess of its value.

While the Haitian invasion scenario would initially be a Navy-Marine Corps action for U.S. forces, the need for U.S. Army and Air Force support would arise quickly at the end of phase two. Construction engineers, civil affairs units, medical units, military police, plus harbor and airfield operators would be needed in quantities far in excess of active army resources, necessitating a big bite into reserve component assets. All of this must be balanced, of course, against the rising Cuban problem in the same region, plus U.S. commitments to Asia, Africa, the Middle East, NATO, and Eastern Europe.

Coercive diplomacy, applied longitudinally by a large coalition of American and global powers, is the best solution. The armed forces will have a role, of course: Refugee operations, drug enforcement, and regional security. When Cedras falls, as all Haitian dictators eventually do, there may be a window of opportunity. The U.S. Marine Corps did a splendid job in building up national security institutions within Haití during the U.S. occupation. The Haitian Army and civil service they created were light years ahead of the body politic and consequently failed.

Haití is a French-African colony that accidentally occurred in the Americas. It is neither North American nor Latin American and does not fit into the inter-American System's democratic principles. Sadly, it may have to serve for years as little more than a measuring stick against which other American nation-states look quite good indeed by world standards. It is humane, not cynical, to avoid squandering lives and treasure in a vain effort to bypass a millennium of historical development.

Essays on Latin American Security
The Collected Writing of a Scholar-Implementer

Review of: *Learning from Conflict: The US Military in Vietnam, El Salvador, and the Drug War*, by Richard Duncan Downie, Westport, CT: Praeger Publishers, 1998. Reviewed in: *Military Review*, January, 2000.

Richard D. Downie was a US Army Lieutenant Colonel serving as Chief of the North and Central American Branch, Office of the Joint Chiefs of Staff, Directorate of Strategy, Policy, and Plans at the time of writing this important book. He traces the central core of Counterinsurgency (COIN) doctrine from the era of President John F. Kennedy, 1961-1963, through its application in Vietnam, its evolution into Internal Defense and Development (IDAD) doctrine in the 1970s, and onward to the Low Intensity Conflict (LIC) doctrine of the 1980s. He builds in carefully the application of these doctrines in El Salvador, 1981-1989, and in the Andean Drug War.

Downie's exposition on the genesis of the Kennedy-era COIN doctrine is nearly definitive. Chapter 2 should be a standalone mandatory reading for the professional military education centers. In subsequent chapters, Downie shows how certain civilian-military tensions pushed the US Army to recast COIN as IDAD. His exposition on IDAD is an important but less comprehensive discussion. As Downie moves inexorably to the advent of LIC, he is etiologically less definitive but intellectually consistent. He calls into question repeatedly his central thesis: Did or did not the US Army maintain a corporate memory of previous small war doctrines, evaluate these doctrines in past applications, adjust them to current small war challenges, and send out a force totally aware of the refined or altered doctrine? Further, he adheres to a syllogistic format developed in Golden Age Greece and much in vogue today with social scientists.

Downie states a series of propositions unified by the subject of each chapter. To each topic, he asks the question: Is this true, or did it succeed? If so, why? And if not, why not? The methodology is relentless, but the outcomes are no more than a series of educated judgments. Nevertheless, your reviewer can certify the historical strength of Downie's book as an insider participant in the three schools of small war doctrine, and in the three applications he describes. Downie gives a chart of each phase which links doctrine with lessons learned.

There are two aspects of this valuable book which make it more controversial than definitive. The first is that the search for the correct strategic theory does not equate to victory in small wars. The United States has committed money, troops, and arms in the 20th century to dozens of pro-guerrilla and anti-guerrilla environments. Further, by comparing doctrines used in Vietnam, El Salvador, and the Andean Drug War, Downie compares a war where the US Army was a major combatant and local force advisor with two more where the US Army was only an advisor and sponsor. Differences in geography, social structure, and technological environment suggest that there needs to be a particular US Army strategy for each small war campaign drawn from a common data base of historical experience. The second problem is that Downie's concern about doctrinal analysis, transmission, and

Russell W. Ramsey, Ph.D., D.Min.

corporate memory implies that the US Army is the sole doctrinal force operant. Reality suggests that any small war doctrine of the US Army will be carried out under political parameters defined by civilians, with resources allocated by civilians, and in conjunction with other US military forces, police agencies, and a complicated mix of friendly, neutral, and hostile foreign armed forces and police.

    The historical and analytical effort makes this book a head scratching read of importance to military, political, and national security professionals. The implicit non-existence of a correct doctrine in the corporate memory bank overlooks the military principle of flexibility, and the nature of armies in wealthy democratic countries.

Review of: *Nicaragua v. United States: A Look at the Facts*, by Robert F. Turner, McLean, VA: Pergamon-Brassey's, 1987. Reviewed in: *Naval War College Review*, Autumn, 1988.

"...If the US Congress decides once again to deny support to groups in Central America who wish to resist the Sandinistas, Nicaragua – with the continued support of Cuba and the Soviet Union – can be expected to succeed in its efforts to overthrow neighboring democratic governments." On 3 February 1988, four weeks after the book containing this warning became available, the U.S. House of Representatives defeated modest funding request that was 90 percent humanitarian and 10 percent military assistance.

If persuading the U.S. Congress to identify Nicaragua as the military aggressor in Central America is the norm by which Robert F. Turner's book must be judged, the verdict is in and he has failed. Yet, the case is rationally argued, assembled with balance, and meticulously documented.

Turner's "Background to Conflict" chapter describes the legacy of the two U.S. military occupations of Nicaragua, the broad-based Sandinista revolution of 1977-1979, and two years of U.S. economic support for the new regime. Next, the "Marxism-Leninism" chapter details the long-term process, 1961-1979, by which a dedicated minority manipulated the revolution and seized control in the hour of victory. That margin of control, Turner demonstrates, was Cuban support carried out within Managua by expert conflict managers.

The strongest chapter is "Nicaraguan Aggression Against El Salvador," which outlines the steps by which Cuba's government used Nicaragua as a staging base for arming and assembling a revolutionary coalition in El Salvador. Some attention is devoted to the brilliant steps by which disinformation and active measures were employed to deceive members of the U.S. Congress, the press, and the celebrity world. Succeeding chapters reveal a surprisingly well-documented pattern of Sandinista aggression against Honduras and Costa Rica.

The final chapter is a moral and legal argument for U.S. aid to the democratic resistance (Contras). Turner, once a U.S. Army Officer and later a State Department official in South Vietnam, offers no melancholy domino theory, just a warning that the United States will be forced to pay a higher military price to neutralize Soviet surrogate military power in Central America later.

Turner clears up many common misconceptions about recent turmoil in Nicaragua and El Salvador. The Sandinistas militarized to a level ten times higher than the Somoza regime they overthrew two years before the United States carried out modest regional defenses and support for the democratic resistance. For twenty months, the United States gave the victorious Sandinistas their largest aid package, greater than the sum provided to all the rest of Central America.

How then could anyone read this book and still hesitate to quarantine the Sandinistas, militarily, through force of their own people who saw them steal the revolution? Robert F. Turner, eminent international legal scholar of East-West surrogate conflicts, omitted a key chapter on the Soviet Union's role in Central

Russell W. Ramsey, Ph.D., D.Min.

America from this otherwise superb book. He does not seem to comprehend that the USSR uses first party (Cuba) and second party (Nicaragua) military surrogates because the United States lives in dread of being branded what it is – the ultimate military force in preserving Western civilization.

"Civil-Military Relations in Guatemala: What the Literature Reveals," *Military Review (Hispanic Edition)*, March-April, 2002.

Guatemala was an important political, economic, and military headquarters of the Mayan civilization, overwhelmed by the Spaniards in the early 15th century. The region was an important administrative center for Spain's Central American colonies, and the Native Americans were converted to Christianity but left in various stages of partial political and economic integration. Following the independence from Spain in the 1820s, Guatemala remained important in Central American affairs. It was a semi-feudal state with ultimate power vested in a small and generally light-handed military establishment that made and broke administrations.

Efforts at democratization included the controversial administration of Jacobo Arbenz Guzman in the early 1950s, overthrown by the CIA-backed *coup d'etat* staged by Col. Carlos Castillo Armas. Cold War dynamics impeded the growth of democracy thereafter, and by the early 1980s a poisonous situation had developed between leftist guerrillas lodged among indigenous Guatemalans in the north, and the populous *mestizo* Guatemalans in the south who had the support of the Army. Charged with human rights violations, the Army was cut off from US security assistance programs, 1983-1985, during which period occurred the bloodiest reprisal campaign against selected indigenous villages in the country's history. With the resumption of US military-to-military programs in 1986, violence declined and military professionalism improved. There were more lapses in democracy to be sure, but by 1996 a peace treaty was signed, and in 1999 the Guatemalan Truth Commission sorted out truth from accusation, and the government effected significant reforms in civil-military relations.

Here is a review of literature by which we may assess the validity of democratically acceptable civil-military relations in Guatemala today. *The Journal of Inter-American Studies & World Affairs* recently changed its name to *Latin American Politics & Society*, retaining the volume and issue sequence numbers. It is altogether fitting that the final issue carrying the previous name (Volume 42, Number 4) was entitled *Special Issue: Globalization and Democratization in Guatemala*, edited by Prof. John A Booth. The articles approach the subject from the political, economic, and structural aspects, but the conclusion is clear that participation in the worldwide neo-liberal economic process is mostly an impetus for democratization. *The Central Intelligence Agency World Factbook 2000*, available on the internet, contains an excellent thumbnail sketch of political, economic, military, and social factors. Guatemalan graduates of the Democratic Sustainment Course at the now defunct US Army School of the Americas collaborated to augment this web site with "Guatemalan Armed Forces," [http://www.mdngt.org/af/], arguably the best publicly available site in existence on the military forces of a small country.

Russell W. Ramsey, Ph.D., D.Min.

Professor Jennifer Schirmer's work entitled *Las Intimidades del Proyecto Politico de de los Militares en Guatemala,* used comprehensive and meticulously documented interviews with a broad spectrum of Guatemalan figures to assess the degree to which the Guatemalan Armed Forces are Constitutionally obedient. Published by the distinguished social science network FLACSO (Facultad Latinoamericana de Ciencias Sociales) in 1999, her book shows great progress in civilian control of the military, with structural weaknesses in the judicial realm. Less optimistic is a 1997 publication of the Myrna Mack Foundation in Guatemala called *Justicia Militar.* This volume, by a team of legal scholars, concludes that while the military forces are greatly reduced in size and role, there are still loopholes by which military personnel can function as a state within the state in certain areas. A different team of legal scholars, working also in 1997 under the Myrna Mack Foundation, published *Independencia Judicial.* This work concludes that the civilian judicial system is less than comprehensive, with functional gaps both for civilian litigants and for military personnel whose actions touch the area of civilian jurisdiction.

A 1998 publication of the Myrna Mack Foundation, again by a team of legal scholars, is *Cuatro Anos de Vigencia del Acuerdo Global Sobre Derechos Humanos: Cumplimiento y/o Transgresion?* This is a documented case study of actual human rights violations, and the institutional mechanisms set up to deal with them. The 1983 work *I, Rigoberta Menchu* won its author a Nobel Peace Prize as a supposedly valid testimony about military abuse against the peasants in a Guatemalan village. That book has now been challenged as largely fiction designed to support a neo-Marxist philosophical view. (*US News & World Report*, January 25, 1999, p. 17) Great controversy swirls around the killing of Bishop Juan Giraldi, who was leading the effort to identify and quantify military human rights abuses when murdered in April 1998. Miss Caludia Agreda, Bishop Giraldi's staff assistant for this project, was sitting as a student in the Democratic Sustainment Class at the US Army School of the Americas along with Guatemalan Army Lt. Col. Edgar Mendez, who was coordinating the release of names and records for Bishop Giraldi's investigation. In June, 2001, a Guatemalan court pronounced three army persons guilty of the murder, and a priest guilty as an accomplice (Reuters News Agency, Guatemala City, June 13, 2001). Whether this fortifies the case for the Army as an abuser, or for the strengthening of democracy via the fortifying of civilian court jurisdiction, remains to be seen.

Meanwhile, the Myrna Mack Foundation, well respected by current Guatemalan Army personnel, continues to publish excellent pamphlets for citizen education about their basic political and legal rights. *Los Partidos Politicos en Guatemala* (April, 1999), *Deberes y Derechos Civicos y Politicos de los Guatemaltecos* (December 1999), *Derechos Humanos* (January, 2000), *Los Promotores de Derechos Humanos* (1995), and *Las Autoridades en la Comunidad* (December, 1999) are all splendid examples of community education literature, the realm of action from which any genuine and lasting reform must come. Each book is laid out with caricatures and workbook format entries so that the reader my make notes, return to the booklet as a reference, and learn how the system actually works.

The path to democracy is slow and irregular, but the conclusion one obtains from the literature here reviewed is that Guatemala has moved far from the bleak, authoritarian and brutal times of the mid 1980s, when murder in the name of national security was acceptable, and guerrilla violence was seen as the path to democracy. Much activity in Guatemala resembles the United States in the age of President Andrew Jackson.

The Guatemalan experience tends to strengthen the conclusion that US Cold War measures in Latin America extended the reign of authoritarian regimes in several cases, and also that US policy blocked out the seizure of control by ruinous communist revolutionary forces. The case is also strengthened for US military-to-military diplomacy. US leftists who claim that Latin American contacts with the US military cause militarism should notice that Guatemala's worst human rights abuses occurred in the period 1983–1985, when the US Congress foolishly discontinued US security assistance to Guatemala under the dogmatic and wrong notion that "no more Vietnams" would be the outcome. Further, Guatemalan military cooperation with Catholic church officials seeking to create democratic and humane civil-military relations comes entirely as a by-product of Guatemalan participation in courses at the US Army School of the Americas (USARSA). This process is now being continued by the sending of Guatemalan students and guest faculty to the Western Hemisphere Institute for Security Cooperation (WHINSEC), the expanded educational facility which replaced USARSA.

The final question is whether the Guatemalan political structure will allow these democratically oriented military officers to operate the delicate balance required by civilian control of the military. And it appears that political and economic forces requiring adherence to World Trade Organization economic standards and United Nations political standards will indeed allow Guatemala to heal its civil-military wounds and become a democratic nation with a unique multi-cultural population.

Russell W. Ramsey, Ph.D., D.Min.

Review of: *We Answer Only to God: Politics and the Military in Panama, 1903-1947*, by Thomas L. Pearcy, Albuquerque, NM: Univ. of New Mexico Press, 1998. Reviewed in: *Hispanic American Historical Review*, August, 1999.

Much of Latin American history portrays Panamanian national life as a by-product of Spanish, Colombian, French, and United States hegemonic policy. In the early 1980s, geographic determinism – the isthmus as a convenient commercial terminus, or as a site for a good dig – gave way to Panamanian nationalisms as the focal theme. By the late 1980s, revisionism had moved onward to focus upon militarized isthmian politics, culminating in Operation Just Cause in 1989.

In *We Answer Only to God*, Thomas L. Pearcy connects, as he states, "the social history literature with the institutional literature," thus seeking "to situate the military more fully within the broader context of a sovereign, independent republic." Between 1960 and 1962, this reviewer was a United States Army Officer in the old Panama Canal Zone, and was privileged to hear the young Captain Omar Torrijos and other officers of the Panamanian Guardia Nacional articulate their dreams for an authentic nation state. Pearcy here shines his interpretive light on subsequent events that might be called a politics of police praetorianism, but he also derives a theory showing that Panamanian police praetorianism from 1967 to 1989 had authentic roots that dated from earlier times.

The section on colonial history is a survey. In it the author argues that incipient Panamanian nationalism was thwarted by Spanish colonial policy. This trend, he states, continued when Colombian efforts to create a constitutional republic with a capital at Bogotá translated into military control over independence-minded Panamanians. This section also evaluates United States security measures in Colombian Panama that were instituted between the Bidlack-Mallarino Treaty of 1846 and the 1903 treaty that produced both rights to the canal and the U.S.-friendly client-state known as the Republic of Panama.

Pearcy then shows that after 1903, the efforts by United States leaders to create a legitimate police institution constituted an alternative to the Caribbean and Central American revolving-door *golptismo* so prevalent in that era. The stage is set for an original thesis, the emergence of the police institution as the legitimate vehicle for Panamanian nationalism between 1931 and the advent of World War II security measures from 1940 to 1942.

Police commanders José Remon and Bolivar Vallarino were thus part of an established political and economic vehicle in the post World War II era, praetorians who made and unmade politicians. But they were also guardians of a Panamanian nationalism that did not fit the United States regional paradigm for Panama as a tranquil place from which to operate a neutral and vital Waterway. As Pearcy suggests, Omar Torrijos' rising star came from this tradition and was in no way idiosyncratic.

The historian who would evaluate Manuel Noriega as a powerful, nationalist, corrupt megalomaniac, or as a Cold War opportunist, can employ Pearcy's revisionist paradigm to good stead. Pearcy's linking of isthmian social forces in the 1930s to the police institution as spear-carrier for authentic Panamanian nationalism between 1967 and 1989 is a splendid and welcome contribution to Latin American history. This book is a model for the analysis of civil-military relations within developing nations in general, and within client-state nations in particular.

Russell W. Ramsey, Ph.D., D.Min.

Review of: *Panamá and the United States: The Forced Alliance*, by Michael L. Conniff, Athens, GA: The Univ. of Georgia Press, 1992. Reviewed in: *Military Review*, March, 1993.

Take out the scholarly apparatus and you have left about 150 pages, into which seven trenchant chapters detailing the history of US-Panamanian relations have been packed. The topic is emotional, and views on it are polarized.

Conniff begins his story as Hispanic Creoles in Panama City are deciding between independence or affiliation with Simón Bolívar's Gran Colombia (choosing membership after 1832). Michael L. Conniff, director of the Latin American Studies Center at Auburn University, clearly shows that the membership was halfhearted with Panamanian merchants always willing to talk about money and alliance possibilities with British, French, and US representatives, both governmental and commercial. The Panamá Railroad venture of the 1850s gets a splendid treatment, and the two French canal-building disasters are told with precision.

The author is again fair to all parties, while showing how President Theodore Roosevelt intervened in Colombian affairs during a time of internal weakness, to foment and crystallize the 3 November 1903 revolt in Panama City and Colón. He created a US War Department overseas colony in the Canal Zone – with the Republic of Panama's sovereignty always being secondary to this political stability and public sanitation – a package wrapped as a US national security concept called "Panama Canal neutrality." Conniff is meticulously fair when dealing with such sensitive topics as political corruption by Panamanian leaders, racism among US Canal Zone staff, Latino-West Indian racial tension among Panamanians, and those US security measures that were genuinely necessary.

The post-World War II era is presented as Panama's search for a national identity juxtaposed against the US Cold War security policies in this region that never saw a Soviet soldier in action. Conniff's explanation of US military support for the Panama Defense Force (PDF), which spun out of control under Manuel Noriega's dictatorship, is fair and factual. He sets *Operation Just Cause* of December 1989 in credible historical context. Because he does so well with all these explosive issues, one wishes Conniff had probed more deeply into the problems arising from the Cold War-era decision to place US Southern Command in Panamá, which added regional security controversies to an already supercharged menu.

This book should be used in the national security curricula at the US Army War College, Carlisle Barracks, Pennsylvania, and the US Army Command and General Staff College, Fort Leavenworth, Kansas. Its brevity and balance carry it beyond the regional study level, for it probes universal issues. The age of imperialism is still untangling in Africa, Latin America, Asia, Africa, and Eastern Europe. How does a wealthy, powerful democracy create and defend a humane endeavor in an overseas setting? How can industrialized nations use engineering miracles, like the

Panama Canal, to the world's benefit without creating extended political thorns under the national security saddle? What should be the definition of "neutrality and freedom of access" in the 21st century, be it the Panama Canal, the Bab al-Mandab Strait between the Red Sea and the Gulf of Aden, a natural gas pipeline across Europe, or a vet not built rail-ship-pipe-container system across any land barrier? Conniff opens a door to such study with precision, balance and brevity.

Russell W. Ramsey, Ph.D., D.Min.

Review of: *Operation Just Cause: The Storming of Panamá*, by Thomas Donnelly, Margaret Roth and Caleb Baker, New York: Lexington Books, 1992. Reviewed in: *Army*, July, 1992.

In 1907, the impatient President Theodore Roosevelt named an Army Engineer Corps lieutenant colonel, George Washington Goethals, in charge of completing the Panama Canal. Since that day, no single component of U.S. national security has been so closely entwined with the U.S. Army, even though a joint U.S.-Panamanian team of civilians has governed the water-way since 1979, and the U.S. military forces in the region are under U.S. Southern Command, a joint command answering to the Chairman of the Joint Chiefs of Staff.

From its independence in 1903, Panamá was governed by a series of oligarchic democratic administrations – the "12 families" – until the late 1960s, when the *Guardia Nacional*, trained by the U.S. Army to give Panamá a stability force, engaged in a populist *coup d'etat* under the charismatic Gen. Omar Torrijos.

A Torrijos contemporary – Col. Rubén Paredes (now retired) – and I were young lieutenants together in 1960. During a sopping wet, all-night military training exercise in the Ft. Sherman jungle, Paredes said, "Ramsey, Panamá is not a real democracy. The civilians who govern my country are pirates, and we *Guardia* [later PDF, for Panamanian Defense Force] officers are going to do something about it before Castro's supporters take over."

When Gen. Torrijos's cousin, Manuel Noriega, an intelligence officer, seized power in the early 1980s, the military government switched from populism to drug dealing, abusing the Panamanian democratic opposition and taunting the U.S. security forces in the region. To paraphrase Rubén Paredes, the pirate watchers became the pirates.

Just before Christmas 1989, President George Bush did what his predecessor Theodore Roosevelt had done 82 years before – he sent in the U.S. Army. The tasks were to protect American lives, guarantee the neutrality and security of the Panama Canal, empower the democratically elected administration of President Guillermo Endara to assume office from the usurper Manuel Noriega, and to bring Noriega to justice.

Thousands of U.S. and foreign civilians live in the metropolitan area surrounding the Panama Canal, and most Panamanian civilians were anti-Noriega and wanted him out. The Panama Canal, while an aging asset perhaps less valuable than in the era before super-tankers and super-carriers, is still a mighty but fragile prize. Installing a democracy amid the street thug minions of a rampantly xenophobic dictatorship is no easy chore. Doing this quickly, efficiently, with low military and civilian casualties, no damage to the canal, and minimal damage to civilian structures was a Promethean task. That the U.S. Army, working well in harness with the other services, to be sure, did it so well is a task of historical significance equal to the construction of the canal itself; yet, the Vietnam legacy still drove journalists and self-appointed moral critics to condemn the excess use of force, to trumpet atrocities by individual soldiers, and to allege lies by the military brass – all aimed, of course, at discrediting President Bush's decision to intervene.

This book hit the bookstores just as former strongman Manuel Noriega was convicted on eight of ten narcotics felony charges for which he was indicted in Miami, Fla., a visible signal that the last of the stated U.S. national security objectives was, indeed, carried out. The authors have done their homework, and their book is the best single volume on Operation Just Cause to date in terms of accuracy, objectivity and completeness.

History, political science, and national security affairs professors will want to order this book for their courses on contemporary defense issues and events. Readers will find every negative allegation made against U.S. forces mentioned frontally and addressed factually, with no attempt to excuse wrongful acts where they occurred.

Vital to academic growth in this arena of appraising wars in the short range is the citing of all sources, complete with name and organization. Where interaction between top civilian figures and military brass is discussed, two high journalistic standards are visible: source accountability and the impact of the relationship upon events.

In 1984, retired Maj. Gen. Winant Sidle chaired a committee to review Pentagon-press relationships, in the wake of news media anger over their treatment during Operation Urgent Fury, the 1983 Grenada Rescue. "The optimum solution to ensure proper media coverage of military operations," concluded Gen. Sidle's report, "will be to have the military – represented by competent, professional public affairs personnel and commanders who understand media problems – working with the media in a non-antagonistic atmosphere." The authors actually criticize Army handling of the press during Operation Just Cause, but their book is living tribute to what can be done when military and media share a like-minded commitment to truth in their operations.

Russell W. Ramsey, Ph.D., D.Min.

"Keeping Peace with the Panama Canal," *Journal of Defense & Diplomacy*, December, 1986.

"Something old, something new," advises the matrimonial tradition, "something borrowed, something blue." Either a wedding or a divorce will happen in 1999 when the United States must renegotiate base rights with Panama or remove its military forces adjacent to the canal. If marriage is the better option, U.S. and Panamanian leaders should pay heed to the ditty.

"Something old" is Simon Bolivar's metaphoric statement about the 1826 Congress of Panama. The spirit of this first Pan-American conference was to "shine upon a fraternity of American states, bound together by common hopes and ideals," wrote the liberator, making Panama *"el faro (the lighthouse) de las Americas."*

"Something new" would be the recognition by leaders in Washington, D.C., and Panama City that past thinking and behavior in both capitals will, by 1999, serve the interests of Moscow better than their own. U.S. delegates did not even show up for Bolivar's visionary meeting of 1626 and, since then, have turned their backs on legitimate national interests south of the Rio Grande. Panamanian leaders have used the United States as the villain by which to explain all their national failures for so long that yanqui-baiting is the only unifying national dogma.

"Something borrowed" is the ideal of a multinational peacekeeping force, utilized with great success in the vastly more combative Middle East. Authorized by the charters of both the United Nations and the Organization of American States, the concept of a peacekeeping force does an end-run around Latin American hypersensitivity over national sovereignty and North American skepticism over sharing the hemispheric defense burden with 60 percent of its people.

"Something blue" is the solid maritime strategy of Alfred T. Mahan, articulator and teaching mainstay of Progressive Era aggressive "blue-waterism." Control of critical maritime choke points, said Mahan, guaranteed freedom of the seas. Industrial nations must trade, and their navies must maintain interior lines to enforce the freedom to do so. The Panama Canal, of course, was the tangible embodiment of Mahanism.

Bolivar's strategic ideas were mostly terrestrial, while Mahan's were maritime, but both have a common moral base: the fostering and defense of a hemisphere where democratic governments could provide a system of economic opportunity in a climate of personal freedom.

The class warfare doctrines born in the Eastern Hemisphere, imported to the Americas under the guise of liberation systems and turned loose in practice by networks of blue-chip fanatics, are equally antithetical to Bolivarism and Mahanism.

Bolivar's Pan-Americanism ("something old") and Mahan's maritime strategy ("something blue") are compatible and, if logic governed the making of good strategy, would come together at Panama in 1999. The idea of turning over the defense of the Panama Canal when U.S. troop-basing rights expire to an Inter-

American Defense Force is one of those notions so obviously sensible that only human intractability can eschew it. Thus, "something new" (statesmanlike thinking between United States and Panamanian leaders) and "something borrowed" (peacekeeping forces) merit attention.

Politics vs. Practicality

The Remon-Eisenhower Treaty of 1933 removed the United States from direct peacekeeping roles within the Republic of Panama but continued basing rights in the Canal Zone. The Torrijos-Carter treaties of 1977 eliminated the zone, itself, with mandatory renegotiation of basing rights in 1999. The nationalistic scenario for 1999 – one which Soviet and Cuban strategists dare to dream about – is the head-to-head confrontation on traditional issues. In this nightmare, U.S. military-diplomatic negotiators will seek to lease X troop billets at Y dollars per year, for a specific time with renewal options. Panamanian military-diplomatic negotiators will portray the offer of X dollars to their public as a miserly return from the huge profits that the United States allegedly reaps from the canal. Ultranationalists in the United States will warn, darkly, that communist legions will seize the canal at the first East-West confrontation when U.S. soldiers are not stationed in close proximity. Their intransigence will give genuine assistance to the Kremlin by pushing the Panamanian middle class beyond acceptable limits. Panamanian ultranationalists, far right and far left, will use that wonderful Spanish epithet *entreguista,* one who hands over his country to its enemies for personal gain, upon its own negotiators. No offer of dollars per U.S. troop slot will be adequate, and any request for land-based troops beyond the marines at the U.S. Embassy will, regardless of generosity, be hailed as a North American invasion.

Ultranationalists in Panama City and Washington have, fortunately, been out-distanced by two simple facts. First, the Panama Canal is militarily indefensible beyond the deterrent level. Second, the Western Hemisphere is very defensible, so much so that the bankrupt Soviet client states in Cuba and Nicaragua could be disestablished and evicted. The solution to these two facts of life lies in the acceptance of Pan-American defense thinking and an Inter-American Defense Force.

Spadework Done

The 1947 Rio Pact provides for the mutual defense of the Western Hemisphere. Years of successful low-key U.S. military security training and assistance in Latin America, coupled with the creative thinking of military-statesmen like Colombia's Gen. Alvaro Valencia Tovar, have laid the groundwork. By linking the physically impossible defense of the canal to the creation of an Inter-American Defense Force at Panama in 1999, the Western Hemisphere will begin to enact Boliva's and Mahan's ideas.

The Inter-American Defense Force has many precursors: the Brazilian Infantry Brigade and the Mexican Fighter Squadron in World War II; the Colombian U.N. Battalion in Korea (1951 to 1953) and Suez (1956 to 1938); and in the Sinai Multinational Force (1982 to present); the East Caribbean Alliance in the Grenada Rescue (1983); bi-national and multinational naval maneuvers in both oceans and multinational maneuvers to contain Sandinista aggressive posturing from Nicaragua since 1981.

Its detractors say that Panama certainly would not allow soldiers from many counties on its soil when they already resent the US military presence. Some even say that Mexico and Brazil would allow communist revolutionaries to take over their countries and ally with the Soviet Union before putting the first soldier under extranational control.

The truth is that no top-level leader in Washington has ever dared advocate the Inter-American Defense Force. The U.S. liberal left would, perhaps, turn such an idea into a derisive media circus, while the U.S. conservative right would, perhaps, howl derisively over the Latin American military forces' ability to deter aggression collectively.

It is doubtful if Washington's foreign policy liberals will ever admit that Sovietization of Western Hemispheric countries has meant militarization at a level far in excess of the regimes they detest so vocally now. It is equally doubtful if Washington's foreign policy conservatives will ever admit that two well-trained high school boys can take out the Panama Canal, regardless of the U.S. security force, or that ratcheting up the nuclear arsenal did not prevent the USSR's takeover of Cuba in 1959 and of Nicaragua in 1979.

Possible Structure

So it is long past time for the United States to ask its Western Hemisphere partners to set the wheels in motion for the Inter-American Defense Force. It may consist of a six-nation brigade in Panama, several multinational coastal patrol fleets and three or four multinational air defense systems in the year 2000. It may not look like the North Atlantic Treaty Organization forces in Europe, and it may not-function smoothly, but opponents should consider the alternative.

They should call to mind the Soviet strategist, writing the best-case scenario, with the United States and Panama hopelessly deadlocked in a shouting match over base rights versus dollars per slot in 1999, while Cuban-trained revolutionary activists overturn the Panamanian government. Then, perhaps, these opponents and skeptics will give thought to combining the vision of Simon Bolivar and Alfred T. Mahan.

Panama in 1999 would be a very good place for the lighthouse from which that vision could shine.

"Panama Today: The West Should Help," (British) *Army Quarterly & Defence Journal*, July, 1989.

The crisis in Panamá came to a head with the election on Sunday 7 May 1989. Through various fraudulent practices General Manuel Antonio Noriega ensured that Carlos Duque and his party – the Coalition of National Liberation (Colina) – won the election, the first since 1984. They claim more than 50% of the vote. According to the US Observer Group, which included former President Jimmy Carter, there was widespread multiple voting by members of the Panama Defence Forces (PDF), violent intimidation of the population and fraud at the electoral count with ballot papers being burnt. In response to all this, the US Government sent 1,500 Marines to their bases in Panamá on Wednesday 10 May 1989. A further 2,000 Marines, at the time of writing, are on standby at Pendleton in California. Troops and assets for various Panamá reinforcement scenarios will come from the continental USA.

General Noriega, a former PDF intelligence chief, took power in 1981 when General Omar Torrijos was killed in an air crash. His rise to power came after he graduated from three courses at the US Army School of the Americas, formerly in Panamá. In 1966, when General Torrijos overthrew the elected government, the Panamanian economy was weak. General Torrijos' main achievement was to diversify the economy although this did leave a mountain of debt. There is even an 'offshore' financial centre – a sort of 'Caribbean Liechtenstein' operating in US dollars. Largely because of General Torrijos' promise of support in the crucial area of Central America, the US Government was prepared to turn a blind eye to its undemocratic 'system' of government. Besides, they, the US, were able to keep their military facilities. By 1984 General Noriega and the Americans were getting on so well that the US endorsed Colina's candidate in the election that year. In 1983 over 10,000 US and Panamanian troops took part in Exercise Kindle Liberty.

What then makes Panamá quite so crucial? The US Government bought the digging rights from France and completed the canal in August 1914; it was not just for the easier movement of shipping but as an instrument of grand strategy. The US Government sliced the Panamá isthmus off Colombia to form a republic which then granted the USA sovereignty over a ten mile wide zone along the 50 miles of the canal 'in perpetuity.' This zone, minus several military bases, has already been handed back to Panamá in carefully agreed stages under the 1977 treaty between President Carter and General Torrijos. The treaty states that all will be completed by December 31, 1999. In 1977 even some Democrats saw the folly of President Carter's canal treaty and felt that as a symbol of a new relationship with Latin America it would damage US interests in the long run.

However, the strategic importance of the military bases in Panamá cannot be ignored. They are the largest complex of US military and intelligence facilities on the Latin American mainland and are crucial to Washington's national security interest. These facilities cover over one quarter of the former US zone. Indeed, not just the military bases are strategically important. Should the canal ever be closed by an unfriendly Panamá, the Falkland Islands would then be the only 'Western' controlled passage from the Atlantic to the Pacific.

Since the 1984 election American public opinion and the Government have been divided over what policy to follow. Last year the State Department was issuing veiled threats to Noriega whilst the National Security Council was advising President Reagan and Vice-President Bush to be more subtle and take some concrete steps towards ousting General Noriega.

In February 1988, the US Government imposed economic sanctions on the Panamanian Government. Observers are now saying that this did more harm to the Opposition alliance – the Alliance of Civic Opposition led by Guillermo Endara – because General Noriega was and still is flush with drug money. The sanctions punished the middleclass who oppose Noriega. One of the most useful steps taken in the US over the last twelve months has been the grand jury charges of drug trafficking in Florida which have removed the last doubts about Noriega in the eyes of the rest of the world. Other steps such as $10m to help the opposition in Panamá failed. Indeed, the CIA's man in Panamá was arrested. The latest development, in June 1989, is said to be a plan by the Panamanian opposition to put £3.3m ($5m) on the head of General Noriega. The hope is that bounty hunters will turn him in for trial on charges of drug trafficking and money laundering.

So much for the recent past. Before looking further ahead to 1999 what happened during the early years of his tiny republic and what is likely to happen in the near future?

"Something old, something new" says the matrimonial bard, "something borrowed, something blue." Either a wedding or a divorce will happen in 1999. By the turn of the century the US must renegotiate base rights with Panamá or remove its military forces close to the Canal. If marriage is the better option, Panamanian and US leaders should take note of the bard.

"Something old" is Simón Bolívar's metaphoric statement about the 1826 Congress of Panamá. The spirit of this first pan-American conference was to 'shine upon a fraternity of American states, bound together by common hopes and ideals', wrote the Liberator, making Panamá "*el faro* (lighthouse) *de las Américas*."

"Something new" is the recognition by leaders in Washington DC and Panama City that past thinking and behavior in both capitals will, by 1999, serve the interests of Moscow better than their own. United States delegates did not even show up for Bolívar's visionary meeting in 1826 and, since then, have shown blindness to legitimate national interests south of the Río Grande. Panamanian leaders have used the US as the villain by which to explain all their national failures for so long that *yanqui* baiting is the only unifying national dogma.

"Something borrowed" is the multinational peacekeeping force concept, utilized with great success in the vastly more combative Mid East. One of its world architects is Colombia, from whose national territory, Panamá, was created as a US client state by President Theodore Roosevelt for the eminently worthy task of connecting the Atlantic to the Pacific by a canal (as mentioned above). Authorized by the Charters of both the United Nations and the Organization of American States, the blue helmet force concept does an end run around Latin American hypersensitivity over national sovereignty and North American skepticism over sharing the hemispheric defence burden with 60% of its people.

"Something blue" is the solid maritime strategy of Alfred T. Mahan, articulator and teaching mainstay of Progressive Era US domination. Control of crucial maritime passageways, advocated Mahan, guaranteed freedom of the seas. Industrial nations must trade, and maintenance of interior lines by their navies was the correct strategy by which to enforce it. The Panama Canal, of course, was Mahanism in action. Bolívar's *faro* and Mahan's lighthouse at Panamá are 88 years apart; Bolívar's strategic ideas were mostly terrestrial, while Mahan's were maritime. But both have a common moral base, the fostering and defence of a hemisphere where democratic government could provide a system of economic opportunity in a climate of personal freedom.

"Something old" (Bolívar's pan-Americanism) and "something blue" (Mahan's maritime strategy) are compatible. If logic governed the making of good strategy they would reach confluence at Panamá in 1999. The idea of turning over defence of the Panama Canal when US troop basing rights expire to an Inter-American Defence Force is one of those notions so obviously sensible that only human intractability can reject it. Thus, "something new" (statesmanlike thinking between US and Panamanian leaders) and "something borrowed" (blue helmet peacekeeping forces) merit attention.

The Remon-Eisenhower Treaty of 1955 removed the United States from direct peacekeeping roles within the Republic of Panama, but continued basing rights in the Canal Zone. The Torrijos-Carter Treaties of 1977 eliminated the Canal Zone itself, with mandatory renegotiation of basing rights in 1999. Panamanian Forces already guard the Canal's physical assets. Should Noriega turn pro-Castro, the USA would have to face the possibility that the Canal itself could not be retaken by force without damaging it beyond repair.

Nationalists in the United States will warn darkly that Communist legions will seize the Canal at the first East-West confrontation when US soldiers are not stationed there. If the US Government holds out it will give genuine assistance to the Kremlin by pushing the Panamanian middleclass beyond acceptable limits. Panamanian nationalists (far right and far left) will use that wonderful Spanish epithet *entreguista*, one who hands over his country to its enemies for personal gain, upon its own negotiators. No offer of dollars per US troop slot will be adequate. Furthermore, any request for land-based troops beyond the Marines at the Embassy will, regardless of generosity, be criticized as a North American invasion.

Nationalists in both Panama City and Washington DC have, fortunately, been out-distanced by two simple facts. First, the Panama Canal is militarily indefensible beyond deterrence. Or, in simple terms, an effective defence would certainly lead to damage and the closing of the Canal. Second, the economic strength of the West is such that the Soviet client states could be overturned. The solution of these two facts of life lies in the acceptance of "something new" (pan-American defence thinking) and "something borrowed" (an Inter-American Defence Force).

Russell W. Ramsey, Ph.D., D.Min.

There is still time for the United States to ask its Western Hemisphere partners to join in setting up an Inter-American Defence Force. This could be a six-nation brigade at Panamá, a multi-national coastal patrol fleet, and perhaps three or four multi-national air defence systems. All should be ready by the year 2000. An Inter-American Defence Force would have many precedents: the Brazilian Infantry Brigade and the Mexican fighter Squadron in World War II; the Colombian United Nations Battalion in Korea (1951-53) and Suez (1956-58); and in the Sinai Multi-national Force (1982-present); the East Caribbean Alliance in the Grenada Rescue (1983); bi-national and multi-national naval maneuvers in both oceans; and multi-national maneuvers to contain Sandinista aggressive posturing from Nicaragua since 1981.

Opponents should consider the alternative to an Inter-American Defence Force. They should remember the Soviet strategist hoping for the US and Panamá hopelessly deadlocked in a shouting match over base rights versus dollars per slot in 1999; while Cuban trained revolutionary activists overturn the Panamanian government. Let us give thought to combining the vision of Simón Bolívar and Alfred T. Mahan.

Panamá in 1999 would be a good place for the lighthouse from which that vision could shine.

"The Rough Rider Legacy: SUPERCOP in Panamá," *Journal of Defense and Diplomacy*, April, 1988.

Since 1982, Panama's Gen. Manuel Antonio Noriega has made and broken three civilian presidents. He commands the National Defense Force (FDN), and the strategic issues his presence creates are the explicit legacy of U.S. President Theodore Roosevelt's hasty creation of a convenient nation through which to join the Atlantic and the Pacific by constructing the Panama Canal.

Accused by a Miami Federal Grand Jury of enormous narcotics felonies, Noriega most probably will never stand trial in the United States. His predecessor as FDN commander, retired Gen. Reuben Paredes, is trying to persuade him to step down. So is former Panamanian diplomat José I. Blandon, long-time advisor to the FDN's intelligence staff (G-2), the sinecure from which for years Noriega influenced superiors, rivals, *narcotraficantes*, and foreign power figures.

But Noriega has resisted hostile street demonstrations with carefully restrained force, has elicited showy support from all levels of the FDN and still claims powerful friends within the U.S. and Soviet blocs. Viewing himself grandly as the agent of the state, ordained to carry Panamá through the final takeover of all Canal and former U.S. military assets, one reasonably asks if Noriega has any motive at all to step down. The corollary question then emerges. What damage to U.S. security can Noriega do by staying in power?

Newspaper, radio, and TV commentators have howled in rage that the United States is doing any business with a man who is possibly as corrupt as any of the worst developing nation potentates. Why, they ask, in the name of interdicting the *narcotraficantes* do we consort with this man whose FDN may be shielding the worst of the narcotics traffic from Perú and Colombia en route to the United States? During illegal drug transfers at Panama's National Airport, they argue, the FDN serves as the muscle, and Noriega as the kingpin. And why, in the name of fighting Nicaraguan communist aggression against El Salvador, Costa Rica and Honduras, it is asked, do we utilize an ally who possibly earns millions in drug sales and consorts visibly with communist bigwigs from Cuba, Nicaragua, and even the USSR?

Close U.S. association with Panamanian military and police officials goes back to 1848. When a treaty was signed with the Republic of Colombia that year for the United States to build a railroad across the Colombian Province of Panamá, railroad officials pointed out the lawlessness in the region. Tough U.S. policemen were sent down, first to be the police, then to train the local police.

In 1900 the rough-rider image from the Spanish-American War earned Teddy Roosevelt the vice presidency, and the assassination of President William McKinley propelled Roosevelt to the White House by September 1901. Needing a campaign issue for reelection in 1904, he portrayed ratification recalcitrance within the Colombian Senate as irresponsible obstructionism over his Panamá Canal project. Bribe money, several U.S. Navy cruisers, and hasty U.S. diplomatic recognition guaranteed the quick November 3, 1903, breakaway of Panamá from Colombia.

Russell W. Ramsey, Ph.D., D.Min.

The United States then had a weak client state in which to build the Canal, Roosevelt had his campaign issue, and Panamá tried to have an army.

Unfortunately, Panama's military independence leaders of 1903 overthrew the new civilian government three times in the first year. President Roosevelt had the army abolished, and created a U.S.-trained *Policía Nacional*, which would endure until 1954. And it was a tough police chief serving as president – Col. José Antonio Ramón – who brought U.S. President Dwight Eisenhower to the table for the Ramón-Eisenhower Treaty of 1955. Panama's share of Canal revenue was increased, and Panamanian co-sovereignty was acknowledged over the 10x44 mile glittering strip known as Panama Canal Zone.

In 1954 the *Policía Nacional* became the *Guardia Nacional*, and the commander of this essentially internal order force would never again be far removed from Panama's chief executive decisions. The nation's civilian *políticos* operate a collection of small parties that can seldom form a workable coalition in European style, and the political gentry from the world of banking and international commerce are not seen as truly authentic leaders by Panama's majority, the blue collar workers. While the political parties vied with one another to express xenophobic nationalism, always with Uncle Sam and his plush colonial bastion Canal Zone as target, the *Guardia Nacional* emerged as the perceived national champion of justice.

In the early 1960s, large numbers of Panamanian National Guardsmen – both officers and enlisted men – attended the U.S. Army School of the Americas at Ft. Gulick, in the Canal Zone, along with military men from 18 Spanish-speaking countries, and a few Brazilians and Haitians. Prominent among the students within the Counterinsurgency Operations Course, a Kennedy-era innovation, was a tall, serious young lieutenant, Reuben Paredes, who, in the early 1980s, became commanding general of the newly renamed Panamanian National Defense Force. Popular with the U.S. faculty was the dashing young Capt. Omar Torrijos Herrera, commander of the new *Orden Público* Company, a combat infantry unit based at the historic Spanish ruin *Panamá Vieja*. His soldiers dressed out like *barbudos* from Cuba and played the role of enemy guerrillas for the School of the Americas' counterinsurgency students on tough field training exercises.

By 1968 Omar Torrijos was a colonel, and he seized power after two *Guardia* colleagues chased a long-time *Guardia* foe – Arnulfo Arias – out of the presidency. Torrijos chose to walk the line between East and West. He borrowed some of Fidel Castro's nose-tweaking tactics in his dealings with the United States. He built up job opportunities and a place in the political system for the common worker. He kept Panamá solidly in the Western camp, despite extreme pressures from western hemisphere Communists to join them, and accusations from both Panamanian and U.S. conservatives that he was really a closet Castro.

Torrijos' great triumph was the Torrijos-Carter Treaty pair of 1977, under which Panamá got immediate occupancy of the former Canal Zone, increasing management over the Canal, and the power to renegotiate or sever U.S. military basing rights in Panamá by 1999. For four years Torrijos was a national hero. While he helped the non-communist revolutionary forces in Nicaragua during the

1977-1979 war there, the communist Sandinistas essentially discarded him in late 1979 in preference for Fidel Castro's military muscle. United States-Panamanian diplomacy seemed headed for a model relationship in the 1980s, but Omar Torrijos died mysteriously when his light plane crashed in 1981. His legacies were national control over the Canal Zone, conversion of the 2,000-man *Guardia Nacional* into the 8,500-man National Defense Force, control of the Canal itself by 1999, and a workable treaty that promised a U.S. military presence near the Panama Canal in the 21st century.

Torrijos' intelligence officer was a cousin, Col. Manuel Antonio Noriega. Born amid poverty in 1940, Noriega attended public school during the turbulent 1950s, then wrangled an appointment to the Peruvian *Escuela Militar de Cadetes*. He became a lieutenant in the *Guardia* during the exciting expansion years. In mid-1965, he attended the Jungle Operations course at the School of the Americas, and then discovered the power of being an intelligence officer in an internal security force. He spent all of 1967 at the School of the Americas, completing the Infantry Officer course, the Jungle Operations course (again), the Combat Intelligence Officer course and the Counterintelligence course. He returned to duty just as the *Guardia's* chieftains overthrew the government.

Noriega quickly worked his way to the top of the G-2 section. He was Torrijo's man in Nicaragua during the Sandinista revolution, and was visibly humiliated by the *9 Commandantes* in 1979 at a public display of their tough international allies. After Torrijos' death Noriega increasingly spent his time in FDN military politics, using his files on first one and then another rival to enhance his power. By 1984 his power was unchallenged. Cubans, Nicaraguans, and Soviets made deals with him to insert their revolutionary apparatus into Panamá. United States officials sounded him out about helping the democratic resistance (*contras*) in Nicaragua, and stopping the drug smuggling from Perú and Colombia through Panamá into Miami. The Miami Federal Grand Jury alleges that he and his FDN chieftains are the real linkage between the Andes Mountains drug producers and their Miami distributors.

Noriega has every reason to attempt to stay in power. Should he leave, he would have to go to a land having no extradition treaty with the United States. He would have to give up some of his money, and still defend himself against *narcotraficante* hit men who would want him silenced.

Unlike Omar Torrijos, who made a police force into a national army, Noriega has control of a force now numbering over 16,000 men. It is a personal army, like that of Fulgencio Batista in Cuba and Anastasio Somoza in Nicaragua. But personalistic armies have been the Communist bloc's best harvest, for they are easy to subvert, and once the *número uno* power figure is ousted, the communist revolutionary control apparatus is easy to impose.

Should Noriega hang in for the long haul, what will and can he do? He can play off the United States against Cuba, Nicaragua and the *narcotraficantes* on many issues. He can render the 1999 military base negotiations with the United States impossible, refusing all offers, whipping up street agitation, and offering useless crumbs to appease world opinion.

So why doesn't the United States get tough now and throw Noriega out? If he were to decide to join the Soviet camp, bring in Cuban and Nicaraguan weapons and advisors and bar the United States from using the Canal, what could Washington, D.C. do? Headquarters, U.S. Southern Command, is located near one of the world's most fragile transportation assets, the Pacific Locks to the Panama Canal. Noriega's FDN outnumbers the U.S. brigade in Panama, and U.S. weapons superiority, especially navy and air force air strikes, would be tough to utilize against the FDN without wrecking the Panama Canal itself. After all, guarding the Panama Canal is the FDN's official reason for existence as a combat army, but Noriega has cleverly made the protective force for the Canal into the force that maintains his regime.

Finally, should the United States select a combat operation to depose Noriega, he could play the equivalent of nuclear blackmail; he could take the Panama Canal hostage. He could hand Washington, D.C. a schedule for when the locks would be blown, one after another. Should a U.S. strike force threaten *Panamá Vieja* and his other military strongholds, he could play the trump card. He could blow the Madden Dam, discharging an 80-foot head of water, miles long, down the Canal, wrecking it forever with massive loss of life and shipping.

Would Noriega do such a monstrous thing? He stands accused by inner sanctum colleagues of arranging the death of Omar Torrijos. Others say they have watched him participate in grisly torture and political murder. No one really knows if he would wreck his country's original reason for existence to remain in power.

The nation of convenience created in haste by the rough-rider U.S. president now has a SUPERCOP at the top. Judging from past actions, Manuel Antonio Noriega is a much rougher rider than Teddy Roosevelt. Personal lord of a tough little army atop a fragile world asset, he may become a more serious strategic thorn in the United States' side than Castro's Cuba or Daniel Ortega's Nicaragua.

COLOMBIA: A CASE MODEL

"Insecurity and Violence in Colombia," *Military Review*, July – August, 1999.

Some would argue that the drug war in Colombia is the greatest national security challenge in the Western Hemisphere. General Alvaro Valencia Tovar's 1997 book *Inseguridad y Violencia en Colombia [Insecurity and Violence in Colombia]* is an effort to diagnose the problem and prescribe a solution. Had Tovar, considered to be Colombia's preeminent soldier-statesman, been born elsewhere, his career would have followed trajectories etched by such World War II figures as Generals Dwight D. Eisenhower, George C. Marshall and Douglas MacArthur, or diplomat-historian George F. Kennan. Tovar's long postmilitary career as historian, strategic analyst, and civil-military affairs commentator invites career comparisons to retired US Army General Colin Powell's public leadership role; historians Donald Kagan's, Martin van Creveld's and Paul Kennedy's literary works; and Charles Moskos' and Samuel P. Huntington's landmark studies in civil-military relations.

Having regularly reviewed other books and publications concerning the drug war and written articles for such journals as *Parameters, Strategic Review,* and the *Journal of Comparative Strategy,* I am aware that this melancholy literature can be divided etiologically into two categories: works whose authors identify the supply side – the makers and distributors of illegal narcotics – as the cause of the drug plague, and those whose authors point to the demand side – the drug consumers – as being the true villains. I expected Tovar to assign at least part of the blame – not with rancor but with his customary objectivity and candor – to the demand side (essentially the United States), which provides the shower of money that buys corruption, murder, economic convulsion, political havoc, and destruction of the family within Colombia.

US drug users sent $1.2 billion to Colombia in exchange for cocaine products in 1990 and over $6 billion in 1997. While this flood of cash corrupts Latin America's oldest two-party democracy in fundamental ways, the Colombian army and national police suffer 300 battle deaths per year, more in sum since 1985 than the US Army and police forces suffered during all post-Vietnam Cold War events. US Congressional discussions over the pittance of security assistance and drug-war training funds accorded to Colombia does little more than debate ways to shift the moral blame from Washington to Bogotá.

Given that Tovar has worked closely with the US Army throughout his long career, one might well expect him at least to discuss the US role in the Colombian drug war as at least part of his analysis. But just as Colombian historians refrain from Yankee-bashing in school texts that present the well-known US intervention into Colombian sovereignty to create the Republic of Panama in 1903, so too does

Tovar refrain from criticizing or even mentioning the incalculably destructive US role in causing the narcotics plague within Colombia.

In his book, Tovar shows Colombia as a divided country—simultaneously a modern political democracy and a narcotrafficking-driven society in near-anarchical condition. His linking of the second Colombia to the first is excellent. He traces Colombia's lamentable history of civic violence, which I described in the 1946-1965 section of the 1981 book *Guerrilleros y Soldados*[1] *[Guerrillas and Soldiers]*.

The Enemy Inside

Tovar shows how both domestic and Cuban-exported communism penetrated the Colombian culture erupting into rural violence during the Cold War and leaving structures in place that today are fully integrated with the narcotraffickers. Tovar gives a factual description of the armed subversive groups operating in Colombia since the 1970s and traces the diabolical union of communist guerrillas with rural bandit groups and their subsequent complete integration with criminal groups. The US news media regularly – and wrongly – portray these groups as narcotraffickers. In reality, narcoguerrillas consist of a loose coalition of murderous, pseudo-revolutionary criminals, who receive billions of illegal dollars from producing and selling drugs. They are armed with the best weapons and technology and hide under a deception cover that is so sophisticated most US journalists and even many scholars have not the slightest idea they are or have been deceived and "used."

There are three main strategic deceptions narcoguerrillas have imposed on most North American journalists and on many US drug-war policy analysts. First, there is no legitimate reason for armed guerrillas to exist in an open political democracy such as Colombia's. However, US writers regularly present the so-called Colombian Revolutionary Armed Forces (acronym FARC in Spanish) as an ideological group fighting for a cause that has some kind of moral justification. Second, so-called guerrillas – former bandits and now narcothugs – who are heavily armed, operate from a sanctuary "state-within-the-state" from which they kill, maim, intimidate, and control virtually every sector of Colombian public and private life. Third, within Colombia there is no network of government sponsored, right-wing paramilitaries whose existence creates a legitimate need for armed self-defense by citizen resistance groups. This entire idea is a strategic fantasy created by narcoguerrillas as a way of confusing US policy makers and weakening external support for the Colombian armed forces and police – the only organs narcoguerrillas can neither corrupt nor defeat in battle.

These three cruelly distorted ideas dominate virtually every story about Colombia in the US news media. Tovar clearly shows the evidence by which he concludes that these three ideas are the Western Hemisphere's most effective operation in strategic deception yet seen, but he mentions nothing of this almost universal distortion. He merely describes the structure by which the narcoguerrilla acts out events – complete with real killings and torture – capturing on videotape uniformed narcogoons in the process of pretending to be abusive soldiers or police and arranging delivery of polished "audience-ready" media packages through respectable intermediaries.

Tovar offers a summary of how the narcoguerrilla machine operates politically, militarily, and economically as a state-within-a-state, then launches into a prescriptive analysis suggesting a six-step approach to taking corrective measures:

- Colombians must understand the entire problem.
- Colombians must understand that multiple forces are producing a threat to their national existence.
- Colombians must admit that there is an ideological dimension – collectivist revolution – to the narcoguerrilla program, then fight it on a political level.
- The Colombian government must respond with timely, adequate force when force is required.
- Colombians must develop the political will to combat the narcoguerrilla on every level.
- After creating a national strategy for defeating the narcoguerrillas, Colombia must develop an implementing military strategy and carry it out.

Tovar also offers two great national choices: change the way Colombian society thinks or declare an all-out national war against the narcoguerrilla, fighting to win – however long it takes, however high the cost. He shows clearly the magnitude of these two choices. The educational approach seems more humane, but it is more difficult to orchestrate and could require 40 or more years to carry out. The politico-military choice carries a price tag of billions of dollars and thousands of lives. Neither choice is for the faint at heart. Tovar lays out a factual description of the threat sufficient to support the lamentable conclusion that there is no cheaper answer.

The Enemy Outside

For 30 years I have watched US news media and some – not all – of the US academic community wrongly portray the Colombian army as a human-rights abuser. Knowledgeable scholars, Colombian public opinion polls, and military experts portray the army as a world leader in humane backcountry operations and peacekeeping.2 The Colombian army is not only the victim of the murderous and cowardly narcoguerrilla in the field but of irresponsible US journalists who will not admit they are being deceived by a clever mix of radical leftists, political distortions, and drug profits that are doled out to people at all levels who will say anything for a price.

Municipal mayors in the Sinai region, policed by the multinational and observer forces, report the Colombian public opinion polls always show the army to be the most trusted national institution after the priesthood. Tovar clearly shows that so-called right-wing paramilitaries, which the US news media try to portray as a repetition of events in El Salvador in 1981, are in fact semi-trained groups of farmers living outside the army's protective influence – people trying to protect themselves from daily occurrences of extortion and murder.

Nearly a decade ago I showed how the narcoguerrilla was forming and destroying Colombian society in an article I wrote for the British Army *Quarterly & Defence Journal*.3 Since then, US political liberals have advocated decertifying the Colombian army from receiving security assistance and drug-war financial assistance based on falsified narcoguerrilla evidence created with paid killer-thug actors and supporting press interviews bought with money and intimidation. Many US conservatives have countered with such irresponsible proposals as spraying toxic chemicals and raining high-explosive bombs across the Colombian backlands. An alternative wrong solution proffered by US conservatives is to cancel Colombian security assistance as a budget reduction measure. This idea is a cruel hypocrisy, since American drug users created the Colombian drug problem and remain its principal financial bulwark.

I reviewed Tovar's autobiography in the November-December 1992 issue of *Military Review*.4 Summarizing Tovar's prescient analysis of several world crisis spots – recorded well before the events matured – I concluded the review with this sentence: "As events in the former Soviet Union and Yugoslavia now show, we should have been listening all along to military scholar-practitioners [like Tovar] who understood the Fulda Gap scenario and the Cold War paradigm, but who also knew the importance of coping with multifaceted conflict.5" Six years later Tovar prescribed two choices for rescuing his country: 40 years of suffering while Colombians learn to think differently or 10 years of bloody armed conflict while the narcoguerrilla is defeated.

An Ally for an Ally

When North Korea invaded South Korea in 1950, President Harry S. Truman sought allies, and Colombia was the only Latin American nation to send a fighting force, one that acquitted itself with great distinction. When the Arab-Israeli Conflict of 1956 posed a threat, President Dwight D. Eisenhower sought international allies, and the Colombian Battalion again was the only Latin American contingent.6 In 1981, the Soviet Union blocked UN peacekeeping efforts during the Arab-Israeli crisis. President Ronald Reagan again sent out the call for allies. The Colombian army once again responded, and it remains one of the few successful institutions keeping peace in that tortured region.

Of all Latin-American nations, Colombia most closely resembles the Untied States. Civilian control of the military and the *posse comitatus* principle – soldiers at the borders, police on the streets – came to Colombia in 1832. Civilian presidents have historically tried to select the best features of the US civil-military structure for application to Colombia's needs. Many analysts consider Colombia's army to be the best small war and peacekeeping force in the world.7

But, when Colombia asked her North American friend and mentor for help with the drug war – a war caused by mass US drug consumption – we replied by sending still more money to the narcoguerrilla, spouting moral lectures to the people doing the fighting and provided plenty of "news" stories useful to the narcoguerrilla in his scheme to neutralize the legitimate government and rule through narco-anarchy. Now Tovar advises his countrymen to go it alone; the old mentor up north finds it inconvenient to admit to being the cause of the cocaine problem.

Thus, this – the best book on the Colombian drug war ever written – is really a moral statement, however unintended it might be. The reader can conclude that the United States will take help if it is offered, but it will not provide reciprocal assistance even if the US drug consumer is responsible for the death of an ally.

Notes

1. Alvaro Valencia Tovar, *Inseguridad y Violencia en Colombia [Insecurity and Violence in Colombia]* (Bogotá: Universidad Sergio Arboleda, 1997).
2. Russell W. Ramsey in *Guerrilleros y Soldados [Guerrillas and Soldiers]*. Bogota: Tercer Mundo Edition, 1981.
3. Sanmiguel B. Miguel, "Human Rights Violations in Colombia: Colombian Government and Military Perspectives," *Journal of Low-Intensity Conflict and Law-Enforcement* (Autumn 1995).
4. Russell W. Ramsey, "US Narcotics Addiction Wrecks Colombian Democracy: The Facts About Her Army and Her Allies," *British Army Quarterly & Defence Journal* (January 1990).
5. Alvaro Valencia Tovar, *Testimonio de una Epoca [Testimony of an Epoch]*. Bogota: Editorial Planeta, 1992.
6. Russell W. Ramsey in book review in the November-December 1992 HispanoAmerican edition of *Military Review*, pages 96-97.
7. Russell W. Ramsey, "The Colombian Battalion in Korea and Suez," *Journal of Interamerican Studies* (October 1967).

Russell W. Ramsey, Ph.D., D.Min.

"U.S. Commits Money, Military to Drug War," *Columbus Ledger-Enquirer*, Sunday, November 19, 2000.

SOUTHCOM

Southern Command, the U.S. Department of Defense's Miami-based nerve center for Latin America and the Caribbean, is staffed by about 1,000 service members and civilians. SOUTHCOM has a permanent presence of 2,479 soldiers, sailors, and air force personnel, most in Puerto Rico, and relies on periodic training exercises of reservists and National Guard members to carry out medical and disaster recovery missions offered to host countries for emergencies.

SOUTHCOM is in charge of U.S. military activities across 12.5 million square miles stretching from Antarctica to the Florida Keys. It evolved out of U.S. construction of the Panama Canal, and moved to Miami in 1997 as part of the US' phased withdrawal from the Canal Zone.

(Source: Knight Ridder)

Even as activists protest United States' policy in Latin America, specifically, the U.S. Army School of the Americas at Fort Benning, U.S. involvement in the region is being redefined in Drug War, rather than Cold War, terms in this divided and volatile country

Plan Colombia

Congress this summer approved more than $1 billion in Colombia aid1, the bulk of it going to the Colombian military's battle against drug traffickers and the leftist rebels and right-wing paramilitaries who support them.

The aid package will help fund Plan Colombia, a three-year, $3.5 billion strategy proposed by Colombian President Andres Pastrana to halt the guerrilla conflict and terrorist violence, eliminate the drug trade and kick-start his country's flagging economy.

The aid represents the largest U.S. involvement with a Latin American military since the end of the Cold War, when Washington's support for anti-communist regimes ignited outcries over alleged U.S. complicity in coups, death squads, and human rights abuses.

American officials say that three Colombian counter-narcotics battalions being trained and armed by the United States have been thoroughly screened. None of their members have been involved in human rights abuses or have belonged to military units linked to right-wing paramilitary groups, officials say. U.S. officials will be permitted to review the use of American helicopters provided under the aid package to ensure that they are flown only on counter-narcotics operations.

The program marks a major shift in American policy. The United States previously awarded virtually all Colombian counter-narcotics assistance to the national police. The bulk now will go to the military. In addition to sending more American advisers to train the new counter-narcotics battalions, the United States will provide 18 Black-hawk and 42 Huey helicopters for ferrying the units into drug-growing regions and spraying herbicide on coca and poppy fields.

There are already 250 to 300 U.S. military personnel, most of them special forces, training Colombian personnel for counter-narcotics operations or engaged in drug detection, monitoring, and intelligence gathering missions. The Pentagon also operates five radar facilities in Colombia to detect drug smugglers.

Q&A

What is the primary force that drives the Colombian drug war?

In 1990, when it was becoming a national threat to Colombian democracy, $1.2 billion was sent to Colombia by U.S. citizens for the purchase of cocaine products. Several failed policies later, this figure approaches $7 billion per year in 2000.

Why is the problem so cruelly embedded in rural Colombian social structure?

Colombia's solutions to its rural violence in the 1970s were a world model of excellence in civil-military cooperation. Sadly, the economic development of the 1980s was allowed to bypass many rural zones, leaving these people as sitting ducks in an area where the narcotraffickers could organize their evil activities. Further, Colombia's booming new middle class does not exhibit the same sense of civic responsibility for the peasants that one saw in the 1960s.

Since we know that militarizing any drug war in a developing nation is ineffective, and that anti-democratic consequences can ensue, why did the U.S. Congress approve Plan Colombia?

The FARC guerrillas (FARC is an acronym for Revolutionary Armed Forces of Colombia, actually a mix of criminals and ideological rebels) have a war machine, a huge propaganda apparatus, and control over perhaps one-fifth of Colombia. For 10 years, they have killed an average of two soldiers or police per day and perhaps 10 civilians.

Further, the two political parties (Liberal and Conservative) are heavily corrupted by FARC and their narcothug allies. I recently visited a military hospital in Bogotá where 300 amputees, all victims of FARC attacks, are undergoing rehabilitation. The National Police have done good work and should be primary in the drug war, but FARC combat power requires a military response in a few limited areas.

How much is Plan Colombia costing, and what's in it?

Apparently it may total about $1.3 billion across three years, assuming that the uncertain political orientation of the United States does not change it. That sum is one-third of the dirty U.S. money sent annually to Colombia to buy drugs in 1990, and about 6 percent of the dirty money that U.S. drug users send annually to Colombia now.

Russell W. Ramsey, Ph.D., D.Min.

About eight percent of the total will be used for military units to operate in carefully controlled blows against the FARC infrastructure. The rest goes for infrastructure and civil assistance in the affected areas. Assistance to the Colombian National Police is smaller but separate from this sum and will continue. U.S. advisers and observers are on the ground in professionally sound relationships with Colombian officers. The situation is positive and in no way resembles the Vietnam conflict or El Salvador in 1981-1988.

Who are the paramilitaries and what do they do?

In the 1960s, the Colombian Army helped create self-defense units in the violence-torn areas, something like a state militia. I inspected these areas and saw good results. In the late 1980s, the Colombian Army tried once again to organize innocent peasants to protect themselves against intimidation and murder by the FARC. These self-defense units were quickly penetrated and subverted by the narcotraffickers, just as they captured the FARC, and became murderous drug pusher forces.

The Army quickly cut cords here and court-martialed several officers who compromised themselves with the paramilitaries. However, the so-called "Clearing House for Drug War Information" in Bogotá continues to push the line that the Army supports the paramilitaries and is guilty, both directly and by extension, of human rights violations. This is a vicious disinformation program designed to bring down the Colombian government.

Are other armed forces besides the Army involved?

For several years there have been small and effective programs carried out with modest U.S. security assistance by the Colombian Navy and Air Force. The biggest U.S. increment, until Plan Colombia, of security assistance went to the National Police, who have earned a reputation for efficient, corruption-free operations, headed by the now legendary and recently retired General Jose Serrano. He spoke at the U.S. Army School of the Americas on August 29, 2000 at the 10th Latin American Conference, and he is in great demand worldwide as a kind of "Elliott Ness" personality.

What is the relationship between the Colombian armed forces and the U.S. Army School of the Americas, especially in regard to the Drug War?

Colombian students (at the School of the Americas) from the Army, Navy, Air Force, Marines, and National Police have combat experience at home, plus peacekeeping experience in the Sinai Desert. This experience makes them valuable as guest instructors. The notion that the Colombian armed forces have some kind of problem in human rights is disproved by numerous studies on that subject, available to the public for inspection.

The U. S. Army School of the Americas is closing soon, and there are plans to open a new school with a broader mission under a higher level of command and civilian supervision. What relationship will exist between the Colombian armed forces and the soon-to-open Western Hemisphere Institute for Security Cooperation?

Again, while Colombian students probably will attend the Counter-Narcotics Operations Course, as do students from 16 other countries, there never has been any "special" relationship caused by the Drug War. Given that, as we go to press, there is no definite winner in the U.S. presidential election, it would be irresponsible on my part to forecast what either candidate, working with a closely divided Congress, might do.

What will be the outcome of the Colombian Drug War, and what is the greatest single problem stemming from it?

I predict that Colombia will gradually emerge from the horror of this narco-plague and that two-party democracy will survive. It will take 10 years. The greatest problem, for Colombian daily life, is the pervasive corruption that the plague has caused. But it will get better, for Colombia has been challenged before and democracy survived. They supported us in World War II with raw materials, in Korea and the Sinai with troops, and have always paid their debts. I believe we owe them whatever help they request that is reasonable, legal, and moral.

U.S. Army School of the Americas

The School of the Americas originated at Fort Amador, Republic of Panama, in 1946 as the Latin American Training Center – Ground Division. Four years later it was renamed the U.S. Army Caribbean School and was transferred across the isthmus to Fort Gulick, where Spanish became the official academic language.

In mid-1963, the school was renamed the U.S. Army School of the Americas to more accurately reflect its hemispheric orientation. Under the provisions of the 1977 Panama Canal Treaty, USARSA was relocated to Fort Benning, Georgia, in October 1984 and designated an official U.S. Army Training and Doctrine Command school.

Annual student enrollment is around 1,000 students, and since its inception the school has graduated more than 57,000 officers, cadets, noncommissioned officers and government civilians from 22 Latin American countries and the United States. Total budget for the U.S. Army School of the Americas at Fort Benning, GA, for 2000 is about $4.5 million, composed of two principal funding sources. (These figures do not include military salaries, which typically are not calculated in Army unit budgets):

- Operational & Maintenance, Army funds – $3.2 million
- Security Assistance funds – $1.25 million

The School of the Americas will close next month, to be reopened in early 2001 as the Western Hemisphere Institute for Security Cooperation.

Russell W. Ramsey, Ph.D., D.Min.

Review of: *Mayo del 68: Una Razon Historica*, by Jesus Antonio Rodriguez, Santafé de Bogotá: Oficina de Publicaciones Universidad Distrital, Francisco José de Caldas, 1995. Reviewed in: *Hispanic American Historical Review*, February, 1997.

Colombian social historian Jesus Antonio Rodriguez offers here the argument that the French leftist student uprising of May 1968 was central to neo-Marxist thought and manifestations occurring in Cuba, Bolivia, Vietnam, the United States, Czechoslovakia, and elsewhere. To test this hypothesis, we can examine the results of the May 1968 revolt in France itself, then test for forces and actors that radiated outward.

Student unrest against the Fifth Republic at the University of Nanterre spilled over to the Sorbonne, then generalized for several days throughout the Latin Quarter. President Charles De Gaulle and Prime Minister Georges Pompidou fought back with restrained force, and the revolt ended with two citizens killed, dozens injured, and millions of francs in property damage. A quick election was called, and De Gaulle won resoundingly, with the leftist parties losing half of their parliamentary seats. Ten months later, in April 1969, however, De Gaulle was unseated in a referendum that included many issues. (This synopsis is based on Wayne C. Thompson, "France," in *Western Europe,* World Today series, 1995, p. 168.)

Rodriguez posits these questions: What caused the uprising? Was it isolated? Why is it widely discussed today? Were the participants genuinely dedicated to Marxist revolution? And is the event historically powerful for its reality or for its mythology? His discussions are brief on each question, and all are based on secondary material easily available in standard references. The question of substance versus reality is so subjective that other authors do not discuss it.

The distinguished volume *Latin American Radicalism: A Documentary Report on Left and Nationalist Movements,* edited by Irving Louis Horowitz, José de Castro, and John Gerassi (1969), alludes only in passing to the Paris student uprising of 1968. The French Marxist Regis Debray has an essay in this volume; neither that essay nor his book *Revolution in the Revolution? Armed Struggle and Political Struggle in Latin America* (1967) credits the French student uprising with inspiring events in Latin America or elsewhere. Ernesto "Che" Guevara counseled his troops in Bolivia, in April 1967, that Debray (called Danton by the revolutionaries) would be more useful outside Bolivia than participating in the conflict (*The Bolivian Diary of Ernesto Che Guevara,* ed. Mary-Alice Waters, 1994, p. 364).

Jean-Paul Sartre was one of many intellectuals who praised Fidel Castro publicly in the early 1960s and went on to support student rebellion in Latin America later in the decade. Yet Colombia's "guerrilla priest," Camilo Torres Restrepo, never mentions French influence in what he terms the marginal influence of Latin American students in the Marxist struggle (Horowitz et al., pp. 496-98).

Brazilian revolutionary Carlos Marighella makes no mention whatsoever of the May 1968 Paris uprising in his June 1969 "Minimanual of the Urban Guerrilla."

Romanian social historians Michale Radu and Vladimir Tismaneanu devote their entire volume *Latin American Revolutionaries: Groups, Goals, Methods* (1990) to showing that Latin American neo-Marxism is a nonauthentic European import of the 1960s. One might therefore expect these two authors to credit the French radical students with inspiring their Latin American counterparts to revolutionary action. In early October 1968, thousands of Mexican students took advantage of the presence of the world press assembled to cover the Mexico City Olympic Games by staging huge riots and demonstrations. This student uprising was put down with much more violence than that used by the French security troops five months earlier. Yet the Radu and Tismaneanu volume makes little mention of the French model. Furthermore, T. B. Fehrenbach, in *Fire and Blood: A History of Mexico* (1995), does not mention the Paris uprising, and attributes the Mexican student revolt to the influence of visiting Cuban revolutionaries (p. 637).

French radicalism had much to do with inspiring the generation of Latin American creoles who led the revolutions for independence against Spain from 1810 to 1830. This reviewer suspects that there was some connection, probably more intellectual than physical, between the Paris revolt of May 1968 and leftist uprisings in Latin America during the late 1960s and early 1970s. But Rodriguez's book, *Mayo del 68*, makes no case at all beyond asserting its own title.

Russell W. Ramsey, Ph.D., D.Min.

Review of: *Testimonio de una Epoca Años Signados por el Conflicto en el que han Vivido Inmersos el Estado y la Sociedad Colombianos Bajo el Rotulo de la Violencia. [Testimony of an Epoch: Years Marked by the Conflict in Which the State and Colombian Society Have Lived Immersed under the Banner of 'The Violence'],* **by General Alvaro Valencia Tovar, Bogotá: Editorial Planeta, 1992. Reviewed in:** *Military Review Hispanic Edition,* **November-December, 1992.**

Alvaro Valencia Tovar was commissioned a lieutenant in the Colombian Army in 1942. He was nominated in 1975 for promotion from Commanding General of the Army, equivalent to Chief of Staff in the US Army, to Commanding General of the Armed Forces, a post equivalent to the US Chairman of the Joint Chiefs of Staff. Finding himself accused of a trumped-up coup plot, he retired rather than subject the Colombian government to controversy. In between, General Valencia had a military career that spans most levels of conflict and which links Latin American military currents to the larger milieu of the Cold War. Since retirement, he has run for President, taught history at three universities, and evolved from uniformed intellectual to world-class military historian.

General Valencia's newest book is rooted in his own historical view of Colombia – a somewhat remote and rural Andean nation that became industrialized, urbanized, and a regular player on the world stage during his career. The second theme is based upon the unique role of the Colombian Army since the Military Reforms of 1907, a small, highly professionalized army that has given substance to a Colombian political jingle:

> Colombia es una tierra de cosas muy singulares
> (Colombia is a land of very unusual things)
> Los civiles dan la guerra y la paz los militares.
> (The civilians make war and the soldiers bring peace).

In this context, then, of serving as an officer in an army of peacemakers who have the special trust of the people in a hurly-burly, often democratic, and sometimes violent society, General Valencia unfolds his first person account, starting with attendance at the U.S. Army Armor School, Ft. Knox, Kentucky during 1944. He commanded a company and served on the battalion staff of the "Colombia" Battalion in Korea, 1951-1953. He was Liaison Officer from the same "Colombia" Battalion to the United Nations Military Command while it served as peacekeepers in the Sinai, 1956-1958.

General Valencia commanded several battalions and brigades during the painful years of *"la violencia,"* the ugly rural political feuding that evolved into banditry and, ultimately, became caught up in Fidel Castro's machinery for exporting communist revolution onto the Andean mainland.

General Valencia was Commandant of the Army's Military Cadet School; Military Liaison Officer to the Inter-American Defense Board in Washington D.C.; and Chief of Operations on the Army General Staff. He authored and then implemented dozens of low violence, high impact systems by which small Army units could separate combatants, isolate bandit and guerrilla leadership elements, and expand the Colombian Army's unique role as protectors and peacekeepers. Ironically, and cruelly, he was made into the personal enemy of the Conservative Party clique, starting with his advocacy of sociological and historical curriculum being introduced into the Colombian Superior War College curriculum in the early 1960s.

President Alfonso Lopez Michelson wanted to promote his skillful and visibly humane Army Commander to be Commander of the Armed Forces in 1975, and the anti-Valencia elements in the Colombian Senate responded by gratuitously accusing the general of participating in a plot to seize power. General Valencia utilizes the present book to lay bare his complete innocence, to a degree of detail that makes heavy going for the general student of military affairs.

But the rest of the book is fascinating and unique reading, the personal account of a brilliant officer carrying out seemingly impossible military tasks with limited resources and a painfully correct adherence to Constitutional authority. General Valencia has previously published a novel *Uisheda* (1970) about *la violencia* which awaits only a willing film producer to achieve world acclaim; and five important volumes of military history and biography have emerged from his typewriter as he simultaneously has authored a popular syndicated newspaper column on public affairs since 1979. He has also just edited a six volume *History of the Colombian Armed Forces* (1992), writing the three volumes on the Army himself.

Testimonio de una Época is fundamental military reading and urgently needs to be translated into major world languages. It has the soldier-scholar-participant dimension of General Maxwell D. Taylor's 1972 *Swords and Ploughshares*, but it is also the doctrinal exposition of an innovator. General Valencia's creative ideas and actions in civil-military relations, international peacekeeping, and low intensity conflict make this book what Niccolo Machiavelli's 1532 exposition *The Prince* is to the art of kingship – a classic, enduring statement. As events in the former Soviet Union and Yugoslavia now show, we should have been listening all along to military-scholar practitioners who understood the Fulda Gap scenario and the Cold War paradigm, but who also knew the importance of coping with multi-faceted conflict.

Russell W. Ramsey, Ph.D., D.Min.

"US Narcotics Addiction Wrecks Colombian Democracy,"
(British) *Army Quarterly & Defence Journal,* January, 1990.

Colombia's first President, Francisco de Paula Santander, was an admirer of Thomas Jefferson, the third President of the USA. The nation became independent from Spanish rule in 1819; by 1826, Santander had established the Jeffersonian principle of civilian control over the military. His regard for the rule of law was known to his fellow countrymen and with the foundation laid down by Santander, Colombia entered into the 20th century as one of the world's new democracies.

By the middle of 1989, however, that heritage had all been wrecked by a shadow army of terrorists using the country's fertile and remote highlands plus guarantees under the Constitution as their refuge. Ironically, it is the United States' multimillion-dollar craze for drugs that funds the narcoterrorist threat to Colombia. Academics, journalists and politicians in the US rival each other in blaming Colombia. One day the Government is repressive; a week later the Government is too lame and permissive.

In 1961, I was Chief Instructor in the newly set up Counterinsurgency Course at the US Army School of the Americas, based in the now defunct Panama Canal Zone. All instruction was in Spanish and two Colombian Army captains were the star pupils in the pioneer class. Captains Rincón and Mejía knew the topic better than me, the US instructor.

Since then I have kept in close contact with the country and believe that much more should be known about Colombia's armed forces and the good example which they set in Latin America of constitutional obedience to the elected civilian authority. First the figures: the Army has 97,000 men drawn from a population now approaching 32 million. The National Police of 48,000 are divided into municipal and departmental detachments. They are not part of the nation's military establishment. The Navy and Air Force number 8,600 and 7,400 respectively. The Army is divided into ten Brigade Zones, administratively. The twenty-six Infantry battalions are supported by several artillery battalions, cavalry squadrons and engineer, signal and supply units of company size.

Constitutional obedience is easier to attain in a nation where there are no threats, but the Colombian soldier has served within his own country and in support of the Colombian Constitution in the face of challenges such as Liberal-Conservative Party feuding, left-wing guerrillas, bandits, and the narcotics industry.

The armed forces also have an honorable history of support for UN peacekeeping. Over 3,000 troops were sent to serve with a US Army division in Korea between 1951 and 1954. During these years the Colombian frigate *"Almirante Padilla"* served with the UN offshore support flotilla. From 1956 to 1958, 490 Colombian troops took part in a UN peacekeeping mission in Sinai, where they were particularly praised for their discipline. Since 1982, 400 Colombian troops on annual rotation serve with the Multi-National and Observer (MNO) Force in the same area and are highly praised.

In 1983 and 1984, Colombia offered troops along with other South American nations, to supervise a truce in the Nicaraguan civil war. Even now, at the height of the fight against the narcoterrorists Colombia plans to provide nine officers as part of the UN Observer Group in Central America, created by Security Council Resolution 637 in July 1989.

I toured Colombia in 1962, 1968, 1969, and later in the seventies viewing places disturbed by a process called simply *la violencia*. I wrote a history of the efforts by Colombia's two political parties (Liberal and Conservative) and the armed forces – especially the Army and National Police – to restore law and order to the troubled highland area between 1946 and 1965. In my view, the work of the Army vindicated the pacification methods of leaders like Dr. Alberto Lleras Camargo, President 1958-1962 and General Alvaro Valencia Tovar, Army Commandant in 1973. Today's Colombian national security leaders are likewise highly competent men and women.

However, since August 1989, Colombia has suffered from the escalating violence of the narcoterrorists. The Medellín narcotics cartel leaders in Colombia have lashed out against extradition of narcoterrorists to the United States for prosecution, begun haltingly in 1987 with the conviction of Carlos Lehder Rivas by a Jacksonville, Florida court.

In August 1989, narcoterrorists murdered Senator Luis Carlos Galán, who might well have won this year's Presidential election; a District Judge in Bogotá, the capital of Colombia; the National Police commander in the Department (State) of Antioquia; a dozen policemen; three mayors; five judges of lower courts; and seven soldiers. Murders continued in September and October, as bombs exploded in banks, automobiles, and mailboxes. Three more top narcotics dealers were extradited to the US, as President Virgilio Barco Vargas took his case to the United Nations.

Domestically, President Barco's attempt to use the State of Siege clause in the country's Constitution against the narcoterrorist area was overturned by the Colombian Supreme Court. Barco had wanted to use a sound method – temporary military mayors and courts – to restore order and civilian confidence. Colombia's judges went on strike to protest at their lack of personal security. President Barco received little help from overseas, although on Thursday, 28 September, President George Bush at the White House and in the company of President Barco expressed sympathy for Colombia's dilemma, which momentarily silenced the criticism directed at Colombia by US politicians and the press. Bush's aid package to Colombia, valued at $65 million (40 million pounds sterling), included five UN-IN Iroquois helicopters, two C-130B Hercules transport aircraft, eight DA-37 Dragonfly attack aircraft, some light trucks, infantry radios, hand-held weapons, and cases of bulletproof vests. Detachments of US Army personnel were provided for the in-country technical training of Colombian personnel.

Britain's help consists of training in explosives disposal, radio monitoring at bases in the United Kingdom, and a mobile training team from the Special Air Service (SAS) Regiment. Some years ago Sir Douglas Gordon of Scotland Yard reorganized and established the training programme for Colombia's National Police during the mid 1950s. France has offered high technology police training to combat the sophisticated electronics used by the narcoterrorists.

It was the triumph over *la violencia* that revitalized Colombian democracy in the early eighties.

What is *la violencia*? When did it start? It is the Spanish title for the period that started in 1946 when two Liberal candidates stood against each other for election, split the Liberal vote and enabled a Conservative Mariano Ospina Pérez to take office. The Conservatives, who had not been in power since 1930, started crude reprisals against their political enemies. Jorge Eliecer Gaitan, a leading left-wing Liberal, was assassinated in broad daylight in Bogotá during 1948. This led to the huge riot which became known as the *bogotazo*. The damage caused was said to be $570 million.

La violencia intensified under the rule of President Laureano Gómez (1950-53), who attempted to introduce an extreme right state. While this was going on, the Liberal Party backed the raising of large guerrilla formations in the Eastern Plains and the Central Highlands.

Gómez was succeeded by General Gustavo Rojas Pinilla, who halted the rural conflict but then initiated his own repression in the large cities and so, in turn, lost power in 1957. During Rojas' time, fighting, although on a smaller scale, continued between Government forces and left-wing guerrillas in the Central Highlands.

In 1957, the National Front, a coalition between the Liberals and Conservatives was formed. Under this agreement there were to be alternate Presidents from the two different parties. However, the unpopularity of the National Front led to only forty percent of the population voting in the 1964 congressional elections. By 1965, the left-wing and Liberal guerrillas, and savage rural bandit gangs had finally been dispersed by brilliant army tactics; by 1974, Colombia could again revert to peaceful political competition between the Liberals and the Conservatives. My study shows that 160,000 lost their lives during the 20 years of *la violencia*, although foreign academics usually offer unsubstantiated figures of 200,000-300,000.

It is in the areas only recently devastated by *la violencia* that the drug syndicates have now prospered.

Will this new US aid enable Colombia to defeat the drug threat? Sadly no. Indeed, faced in the 1980s by the narcoterrorists, Colombia's democracy may prove more threatened now than it was during *la violencia*. The 1.2 billion dollars spent annually by US narcotics users on drugs grown in and distributed from Colombia constitutes the threat. The newly announced US Military Aid is literally a drop in the bucket when compared to the size of the task faced by the Colombian authorities.

But US trade policy in this most important time has hit Colombia another blow. By refusing to participate in the London-based World Coffee Growers' Association price and quota agreement, the US has caused 150,000 rural Colombians to lose their jobs, in the center of narcoterrorist infested areas. The critical speeches by US politicians about "Colombia's" drug problem are ill-received by people who have had members of their family murdered by organizations that thrive on US drug money, as well as, by families now unemployed due to myopic US trade policy.

There is another problem for Colombia; this is the tendency of US academics who study South America to explain Colombia in neo-Marxist terms and to oppose almost all non-Communist governments and all non-Communist armies in Latin America. Thus, when the Colombian Army carries out an operation against the narcoterrorists, US academics inaccurately report military abuse of the population: their opinions are in turn reported by journalists in the media. Even the respected Amnesty International organization has been led astray on this issue. Yet, the narcoterrorist link with the left-wing is fundamental to Colombia's problem.

In 1975, Cuba's Fidel Castro sent in his clandestine DGI operatives to Colombia, selling drugs for the cash which Cuba lacks. The key figure in this undercover operation was Fernando Rovello, Cuba's Ambassador to Colombia, who set up connections with the narcoterrorists through the now-convicted criminal Johnny Crump. In 1981, Nicaragua's Sandinistas started to take a share of the drug profits. As is now well known, Colombian drugs passed through Panama, where, until the US Army action of 19 December, General Manuel Antonio Noriega sold protection. The link in Colombia was Captain Paul Atha, an agent of the Nicaraguan Interior Minister Tomas Borge. Nicaraguan President Daniel Ortega once boasted that he would "defeat the USA from within, with the little bullets that *yanqui* youth cannot resist (cocaine pellets)."

Inside Colombia, the narcoterrorist organizations pay the pro-Castro Revolutionary Armed Forces of Colombia (FARC is the Spanish acronym) to protect their operations. One Colombian left-winger, Jaime Pardo, was killed not long ago by narcoterrorist Gonzáles Rodríguez Gacha over internal policy and payoff disputes. Gacha, Pablo Escobar Gaviria, together with the three Ochoa brothers, and other top narcoterrorists remain hidden in the Central Highlands, protected by left-wing guerrillas, their own military units, and legal limits that restrict President Barco's use of his Army.

US intellectuals who accuse Colombia of being a repressive nation are wrong. Of all Latin America's governments, Colombia's political system is the closest to that of the United States in philosophy, function, and structure. Its solid two-party system pits a strong executive against a strong legislative body, with a complex and healthy two-party competition at the state and municipal levels. There is independent judicial review, equal to the executive and legislative bodies. Executive instability, a scourge in several other Latin American political systems, is not seen in Colombia. All this has continued amid an atmosphere of threats of violence and death from the narcoterrorists which is far in excess of that seen in Chicago during the years of US Prohibition.

Economically, Colombia suffers from too great a dependency upon her one export crop: coffee. Yet, faced with stiff worldwide competition in this market, Colombia's debt burden, $15 billion in 1988, is modest by the standards of other developed and developing nations. Colombia's leaders have resisted, like no other Latin American nation, pressure to engage in huge and unwise foreign borrowing. Where other nations have squandered their borrowed millions on corrupt operations,

Colombia has demanded a carefully supervised percentage of primary investment from each foreign capital investment. The mass printing of an inflated currency to satisfy public demand has been resisted. As a result, there has been a sustained economic growth of five percent and a remarkably – for South America – low annual inflation rate of twenty-five percent. These policies have carried the nation through the difficult economic times of the 1980s.

Colombia deserves three major kinds of assistance from the US. Firstly, the US should provide $500 million in security assistance. Secondly, the US should participate in the World Coffee Growers' Association price and quota norms. Thirdly, American political leaders should tell their own public that the narcotics problem now destroying Colombia is caused by the US.

Were he still alive, Thomas Jefferson might well point out that democracy in the United States itself is threatened by the present high level of narcotics abuse.

Perhaps Colombia, if it surmounts the present narcotics threat, will no longer look to Jefferson's country as the world's most attractive political system. If Colombia does surmount the present crisis, she will become the first nation to have solved narcoterrorism whilst operating under a Constitutional democracy.

Meanwhile, at the very least, the professional work of the Colombian armed forces should be recognized. Less than adequately equipped, faced with the daily threat of a wealthy and murderous terrorist foe motivated only by greed and working under the checks and balances of a democratic constitution, Colombia's Army is in the front line of the fight against the new enemy, the drug cartels.

"Internal Defense in the 1980s: The Colombian Model," *Journal of Comparative Strategy*, Winter, 1984.

Introduction

In 1946 Colombia had about twelve million people spread thinly across a huge, underdeveloped land. Most of them lived on the three great mountain chains in the western half of the nation. Five percent represented a rough-and-tumble cowboy culture in the vast Eastern Plains. The urban folk, a bare one-fourth, were scattered across ten major and two dozen minor cities, connected only by dirt roads, rickety railroads, and occasional air service.

The political system is a two-party republic, settled upon in the Constitution of 1886. Brief civil wars between the Liberal and Conservative Parties occurred about every ten to fifteen years in the nineteenth century. The national Army was small, and political leaders were more often gentlemen-lawyers than colonels or generals.

At the dawn of the twentieth century, Colombia was in the throes of a bloody civil war between the Conservatives, who were in power, and the Liberals, who were not. There were conventional campaigns by uniformed regiments, guerrilla fighting, and a general wave of social violence; about 50,000 people died in the fighting, now known as the "War of a Thousand Days.1"

When the mayhem ended, the Conservative Party regained control and stayed in power until 1930. During this era of stability, the *Reforma Militar* of 1907 put the Army on a codified, professional standard, the impetus stemming largely from the 1903 Root Reforms of the U.S. Army. The small and politically non-deliberative units were also employed in some public development projects, mostly in the remote areas and under full control of the elected civilian authorities.2

Significantly, the police remained small in numbers, decentralized, ineffective for internal order missions, and highly politicized. In 1928 there was Communist Party manipulation behind a strike by the banana workers of the Atlantic coastal area, where pay and living conditions were wretched. The local police were unable to control the rising tide of civil disorder, and Army units were sent in following a declaration of martial law. Despite two decades of professionalization, these units caused needless loss of life and provoked acts of retaliation before restoring order. Professional training in conventional tactics had improved the Army but had not produced successful doctrines for coping with civil disorder, especially with urban rioting.

In 1930 the Conservatives split their votes on two rival Presidential candidates and lost to the Liberals, who were credited with less than one-half of the ballots. With the Army guarding the polling places in the tense areas, an honest election was held. But, when the Liberals sent their appointees into the provinces to take control of police stations and hundreds of patronage jobs, Conservative incumbents decided to fight. Liberals retaliated with mob violence, and soon wild feuding erupted among dozens of villages in a classic Hatfield vs. McCoy pattern.3

Army units interceded in a few of these brawls but were hamstrung by lack of manpower and appropriate methods. Armed Peruvian elements seized Leticia, a Colombian river port; Colombia decided on national mobilization and sent its Army into the steaming Amazonian latitudes. Logistical support was poor, but the Army performed well as to conventional tactics, driving out the Peruvians and recapturing Leticia. The League of Nations vindicated Colombia, and the Leticia affair reunited the feuding political parties.4

The Liberals ruled for sixteen years. Army professionalization continued; a small but competent Navy was equipped for coastal and river patrol; and a small Air Force was formed. But the so-called National Police remained very political, very unprofessional, and structurally decentralized.

The 1946 Presidential election offered two Liberal candidates pitted against a single Conservative, who thereby won with less than one-half of the votes. The situation was an exact reversal of the 1930 election; again the minority party came into power through a fluke outcome made possible by the electoral system. This time, when Conservative police appointees and political patronage recipients tried to assume their posts, they met with fierce resistance from Liberal incumbents. Gang warfare followed, with Liberal stalwarts of one hamlet attacking Conservative diehards from the adjacent one, resurrecting the Hatfield-McCoy rivalries from the War of a Thousand Days and the 1930-1931 feuding. The Army rushed its thinly spread units from town to town; usually the soldiers were able to restore and maintain order with little bloodshed.

There was a dangerous social and economic imbalance in Colombia in the late 1940s, fueling Liberal-Conservative mob battles in the agricultural towns of the interior highlands. A strong Falangist element arose on the fringes of the Conservative Party, and the Colombian Communist Party made gains in the leftist sector of the Liberal Party, creating a climate of political extremism in the cities as well as in the hinterland. The only national institution capable of reducing the civil strife was the Army, which maintained a precarious political neutrality and had neither the resources nor a doctrine for coping simultaneously with dozens of little internal wars.5

By 1948 the death toll from the rural political feuding was in the thousands. Nevertheless, the Conservative administration prepared to host the IX Inter-American Conference in Bogotá. When the U.S. Secretary of State, General George C. Marshall, arrived with his delegation in March 1948, he found the situation to be very tense. The Conference, however, was uneventful until April 9, when a street hoodlum murdered a popular Liberal Party leader, Jorge Eliecer Gaitán, setting off shockwaves of violence.

Urban mobs began an orgy of looting, drinking, and killing. Conservatives and Liberals, Falangists and Communists, as well as several foreign political organizations, sent their goon squads into the streets, sacking each others' headquarters and inflaming the masses. A few key Army units fought heroically to save the Colombian government and the Inter-American delegations from certain murder at the hands of the mobs. The Colombian administration blamed the local Communist Party and instigators from the Soviet Embassy for the outbreak. The *bogotazo* was really a small social revolt, with extremist manipulation. Army performance was magnificent, inflicting remarkably few casualties; National Police behavior was disgraceful.

There were three important military consequences of the *bogotazo*. First, several hundred police deserters took their weapons into the hills to form an armed nucleus for pro-Liberal guerrilla bands. Second, hundreds of inmates were released from prisons all across the nation. Many of these, both hardened criminals and suspected political insurgents, joined rebel groups in the interior. Third, thousands of farmers and villagers who were previously not committed to the Hatfield-McCoy violence now saw their national and regional political leaders engaging in vicious verbal and physical attacks upon their rivals, providing a bad example to *campesinos* who needed little encouragement to exchange the hoe for the rifle or machete.6

The Army was an uneasy bystander as the Conservatives rigged the 1950 election and tried to quell armed revolt with police repression. Viciously counterproductive methods were used, such as reprisal killings against uninvolved Liberals and the masquerading of police in Army uniforms to fool the peasants.

By the early 1950s the Army had separated Liberal guerrillas from savage police elements in the mountainous interior, but Liberal guerrillas in the sparsely populated Eastern Plains took over virtual control of several regions. Gradually, the Army was pressured into abandoning low-violence methods. After more than two highly frustrating years with little success against the insurgents, the Army tried the scorched earth concept, burning villages and taking action against the people somewhat indiscriminately. The results were self-defeating, and the consciences of many officers were troubled. Out of this turmoil grew the Colombian Army's first steps toward a workable doctrine for the humanitarian maintenance of internal order.7

The Early Soldier Innovators

Major Eduardo Roman Bazurto drew up a plan in 1951 for the organization of self-defense militia units in the villages of the Eastern Plains. Colonel Gustavo Sierra Ochoa, brigade commander of the thinly spread troops in the Eastern Plains, formulated a new style of tactics. Published in 1954, his book *Las Guerrillas en los Llanos Orientales (The Guerrilla Battles in the Eastern Plains)* is a significant and generally unknown work in the development of unconventional warfare doctrine. Sierra Ochoa recommended that infantry brigades be reorganized into mobile, self-supporting battalions and companies. He emphasized that vigorous patrolling was necessary to establish contact with the peasants in order to identify the genuine leaders of the bandits and insurgents. Both officers stressed that the Army should capitalize upon its tradition as peacemaker among feuding elements, as protector of the peasants.

Two developments served to delay the adoption of new strategies and tactics for internal peacekeeping. First, the guerrilla resistance in the Eastern Plains collapsed for reasons more political and economic than military. An Army general,

Gustavo Rojas Pinilla, overthrew the Conservative administration in June 1953, with the support of national leaders from all sectors. Second, the Army had sent the crack "Colombia" Battalion to join the United Nations Command in Korea in 1951. This unit performed creditably against North Korean and Red Chinese units for two years, and the returning veterans were fed piecemeal into the infantry battalions deployed throughout the Colombian interior in order to upgrade the general standard of training. The result of this effort was to improve conventional tactics, rather than alter organizational structure and procedure. This outcome was unfortunate, for the Korean veterans raised the quality of military leadership and introduced such practices as night patrolling; two moves which would have facilitated a change to unconventional, low-violence peacekeeping tactics.8

After General Rojas Pinilla took over the government, he drew the Army into another unconventional role, namely, the use of its officer corps as peace negotiator and arranger of amnesties with insurgent groups. This practice rested upon a strong historical precedent from earlier civil disputes, which Colombian political pundits captured in a popular jingle:

> Colombia es una tierra de cosas muy singulars
> (Colombia is a land of very unusual things)
> Los civiles dan la guerra y la paz los militares 9
> (The civilians make war and the soldiers bring peace).

Army officers, including the President himself, in 1953 flew into remote areas in the Eastern Plains, arranging the *entrega*, a guarantee of personal safety and legal immunity in exchange for turning in one's weapons and going home. Many former guerrillas received tools, food, clothes, seed, and a small grant of money from the government. A few were betrayed and killed by former political enemies; some disliked working and took up banditry; and some hid their weapons and awaited the next opportunity to fight again.

Peace returned to most of the interior by the end of 1953. Across the Eastern Plains, Army units not only negotiated peace, but even helped the ranchers resume production. Eduardo Roman, by now a retired colonel and a rancher, put his earlier rejected theories into action by organizing local self-defense units, and by getting a mounted corps from the National Police stationed in the Eastern Plains.10

In the highlands the Army was successful in arranging the *entrega*, but the peasants were too numerous for the limited economic aid to do much good. In the Cunday triangle, sixty miles southwest of Bogotá, serious new troubles arose. Poverty was endemic, roads were nonexistent, wages bordered on slave labor levels, and the Colombian Communist Party had implanted a nucleus apparatus there in the 1930s. Several guerrillas and bandits, supposedly at peace since the *entrega*, infiltrated the area and set up an armed revolutionary enclave.

President Rojas, despite objections from Army unit commanders who now favored a low-violence methodology, ordered a tough conventional assault. In 1956 several battalions of infantry were concentrated in the Cunday triangle for a campaign, supported by jet fighter-bombers, half-tracks, and light tanks. Villages not even directly involved were flattened, little effort was made to discover the true ringleaders and isolate them, and no political pressure was brought to bear upon the feudal mentalities of the powerful landowners. In five months, the guerrillas were beaten as a military force, but hundreds of embittered young men now roamed the whole Toliman highlands area, forming bandit gangs and living off the vulnerable coffee plantations in classic Mafioso style. Again, a possibility for truly coping with back lands violence had been wasted in favor of the mailed fist.11

In 1955 the Colombian Army set up the Lancero School, which soon became one of the world's finest small-unit and unconventional-warfare combat training centers. The following year, the Army once again sent the elite "Colombia" Battalion to the United Nations force, this time based in Suez. The unit was given the thankless task of preventing clashes between Egyptian and Israeli units in the Gaza Strip; its performance was rated magnificent by observers from all sources.12 During this tedious but vital task, profound political changes which occurred in the Colombian homeland, finally allowed a humanitarian system of internal peacekeeping to be put into effect.

During 1956 President Rojas displayed an increasing inability to govern; neutrality changed to partisanship and ugly repression. The Army suffered the professional humiliation of having several officers become Presidential favorites and receive jump promotions to high military and civilian posts, without benefit of promotion boards. Once again the Army tried to maintain its apolitical stance, this time against one of its own career professionals who claimed to be using the Army's apolitical leanings for the good of the nation. President Rojas had done one other valuable service to Colombia, in addition to stopping the rural political warfare. Early in his Presidency he centralized, disciplined, reformed, and professionalized all law enforcement units in Colombia into a truly effective National Police.

But in late 1956, all military leaders recognized the damage President Rojas was doing to Colombia. In May 1957, with the full support of the political parties, the Church, and the unions, the four senior service chiefs ousted Rojas and formed a caretaker *Junta*, with a one-year limit to prevent civilian suspicion. The soldiers had once again brought peace, but this time they introduced into the Constitutional system some structural changes which facilitated democratic governance in a climate less charged with political excesses.13

The Alternation Plan: A Vehicle for Change

In early 1958 a widely participated-in National Plebiscite approved the Alternation Plan, according to which the two major political parties would take turns in filling the President's office, and all politically appointed jobs would be divided equally. A Presidentially appointed commission, with members from the armed forces, the universities, the Church, and both political parties, was empowered to gather facts and draw conclusions on the causes of *la violencia*, as the rural bloodshed was now called. Thieving bandit gangs committed all types of atrocities against the farmers in several regions, and two small guerrilla enclaves functioned with support from Moscow and Havana. The published study enlightened the nation but also provoked its own political uproar.

Alberto Lleras Camargo, first President under the Alternation Plan, gave a key statement on civil-military relationships shortly after his election:

> I am of the conviction that in the constant movement of politics, it is impossible to change, alter, modify, overcome, or reorganize everything; but there are institutions which cannot be replaced, which have been created by the ordered and patient action of thousands of humans, and whose structure is the fruit of mankind's technical experience and which require time to achieve maturity and efficiency. One of these institutions is the Armed Forces of a nation.
>
> *When an army is disorganized, when its human aspects are destroyed, we must wait ten to twenty years to re-establish the organization. No one can substitute for a highly specialized education, a life dedicated to a noble and difficult task, by calling on improvised or volunteer persons. And what a crime it would be to leave a nation defenseless, for whatever mean reason, whether partisanship, lack of confidence, or simple moral turpitude in the management of so delicate an instrument.*14

A philosophical basis for the armed forces' new strategy was a little known report by the French economist Father Louis J. Lebret. He applied to Colombia a French sociological theory drawn from the policies of Louis XIV. The armed forces would provide a trained, functional leadership institution to organize economic takeoff in the underdeveloped rural zones, while allowing democratic institutions to develop. Armed forces leaders set about to convert this theory into a workable plan. The commitment included bridge and road building, well drilling, health care, literacy instruction, and limited public housing construction, all guided by a civilian National Civic Action Council and subject to Congressional appropriations and audit. In 1963 the Colombian Army Commanding General, Alberto Ruiz Novoa, presented the annual Conference of the American Armies in the Panama Canal Zone with his report on the Colombian Civic Action program.15 Significantly, Central American senior officers expressed approval, but neither they nor their civilian political leaders accepted the spirit of the plan, or the self-discipline required to implement it sincerely.

Other changes in Colombia took place, starting in 1958 and paralleling the armed forces' commitment to civic action. Lightly equipped, self-sufficient infantry units were stationed in turbulent rural zones; experimental organizations were tested which could protect the peasants against the bandit gangs while simultaneously rendering public services. Colombian military journals became a fountainhead of articles on innovative, low-violence methods for internal peacekeeping. Much of the material was several years ahead of the thinking of both military and foreign affairs leaders in the United States, who were beginning to discover the seriousness of Soviet-sponsored guerrilla warfare in places like Cuba and South Vietnam. Lancero School graduates were placed throughout rural contact units; the Navy and

Air Force acquired light, rapid support systems for moving combat troops to threatened, isolated villages; and ingenious new forms of gathering intelligence were developed.16

Several civilian authors helped guide the armed forces in their doctrinal shift by publishing pioneer concepts. An attorney, Horacio Gomez Aristizabal, suggested in his *Teoria Gorgona* (1962) that rehabilitative colonies for captured rural criminals should be built and manned by the armed forces. These settlements would reform criminal behavior, protect the public, populate the remote regions for agricultural development, and cut the public cost of the prisons. Gonzalo Canal Ramirez, journalist, publisher, and later Colombian Ambassador to the Soviet Union, wrote in his 1966 *Estampas y Testimonios de La Violencia*, that the Army men were remarkable peacemakers, but *la violencia*, that was truly a moral and political issue for all Colombians to solve.

A Conservative political leader, and now President, Belisario Betancur, wrote a sociological portrait of the Colombian peasant in his 1961 *Colombia, cara a cara*. He advocated economic and educational development of the rural people, coupled with a grass-roots program of law enforcement. Orlando Fals Borda, Chairman of the Department of Sociology at the National University in Bogotá, brought out the first volume of *La Violencia en Colombia* in 1962, co-authored by a priest, Monsignor German Guzman Campos, and a lawyer, Eduardo Umaña Luna. While the book exposed many personalities, events, and documents to the literate urban public, much of the content was a political indictment of the Conservative Party as the prime cause of *la violencia*. The second volume appeared in 1964, with a less explosive effect on the public; by that time, three of the principal researchers were involved in the politics of the radical New Left movement.17

The interplay of pure banditry and left wing insurgency was accurately identified in a 1969 study by Fernando Landazabal Reyes, a colonel in the Army's artillery branch. His *Las Estrategias de la Subversion (Strategies of Subversion)* showed factually the process by which frustrated Colombian idealists were recruited by Cuban subversive agents at the precise time when Moscow was reopening diplomatic relations with Colombia in exchange for a tacit disavowal of sponsoring guerrilla operations in the hinterland. But the most articulate spokesman, activist, and symbol of the new Colombian military peacekeeping system is Alvaro Valencia Tovar, whose example and published works offer a genuine democratic choice to developing nations caught between Soviet-sponsored revolutionaries and U.S.-sponsored military regimes.

Alvaro Valencia Tovar

As a youngster at the Military Cadet School, Valencia wrote the "Oath of the Sword," a poetic pledge which bridges the troublesome gap between the medieval tradition of Spanish knighthood and the modern ideal of military obedience to legitimate civilian authority.18

Commissioned in 1942, he concentrated on the professional foundations of an officer's career. In 1944 he completed the Company Officer's Course at the U.S.

Army Armor School, Ft. Knox, Kentucky. As *la violencia* exploded in Colombia after the 1946 election, Valencia found himself commanding troops in a small army full of apolitical intentions but overwhelmed by the size of the problem and the lack of a conscious doctrine.

He was close enough to the savagery to develop a deep and lasting sympathy for the peasants, especially recognizing the frustration born of isolation and ignorance which made them easy recruits for the evangelists of political violence. He saw, as a junior officer, how the career of many a promising colonel was ruined by choosing sides among the civilian political opportunists.

In 1950 Valencia was promoted to captain, and the following year found him a company commander in the "Colombia" Battalion fighting in Korea. Achieving early promotion to major, he became a brigade operations officer during President Rojas's 1955 campaign against the insurgents of the Cunday triangle. While Valencia could see the professional improvements that the Korean War veterans brought to the Colombian Army, he also saw the senseless tragedy of high-firepower operations in the homeland.

He was next chosen for another international peacekeeping effort, this time as United Nations Command staff representative for the "Colombia" Battalion serving in the Gaza Strip. Witnessing his country's soldiers in the difficult task of controlling ancient vendettas between Israeli and Egyptian soldiers, he saw that such a situation was neither unique to Colombia nor totally without a humane solution.19

Valencia served in Washington D.C. as Colombian staff representative on the Inter-American Defense Board after the United Nations tour, and, in 1959, he returned to Colombia for early promotion to lieutenant colonel. When a Cuban-sponsored group attempted to set up a revolutionary base in a remote area of the Eastern Plains, Valencia was made battalion commander of the "Ayacucho" Battalion and was sent out to put his new theories into action.

Beginning with the premise that the social dimension was primary, and firepower and maneuver the secondary variables, Valencia immediately set his officers and sergeants to the task of face-to-face persuasion. Colombians were asked by fellow Colombians if they would prefer to solve their problems in cooperation with their own government, or risk having their futures controlled by foreign-sponsored revolutionaries. Contending factions were then brought into a state of dialogue. Schools were built, with their locations centered between feuding villages so as to require cooperation. Exiles were persuaded to return to their own land. Small bridges and roads were built, and a self-defense militia was created with National Police personnel as the front line of public order. The peacekeeping efforts took eighteen months and resulted in a battle death toll of zero. Peace has reigned since the work was completed in late 1960.

Following this achievement, Valencia attended the Colombian Superior War School and joined the Operations Division of the Army General Staff. He devised several plans for the new model operations and then took command of the "Colombian" Battalion in the remote Vichada Department of the Eastern Plains. This was the Army's finest battalion, and its mission was to defuse a well-financed

Cuban effort to start another revolutionary base. This was to be Premier Fidel Castro's "Sierra Maestra of the Andes," from which he would spread revolution throughout the South American continent.

Valencia's plans followed a carefully ordered doctrine: isolate the populace from the revolutionary organizers, fight the guerrilla units with continuous patrolling action, and consolidate the people by protecting legitimate leaders and building needed facilities. This operation was so successfully done during ten months of 1961 that the Cubans shifted their subversive efforts to the recruitment of radical college students, and sought a new area for rural operations.20

Valencia next became Commandant of the Infantry School. General Ruiz Novoa asked him to review Volume I of *La Violencia en Colombia*, the landmark sociological study just off the press. In a classified memorandum to his superior officer, Valencia concluded that the book had much merit because it legitimized the sociological approach to stopping the rural fighting, but that its liberal approach maligned unfairly the Conservative Party. A clerk leaked the memorandum to a Conservative Senator, whose ox had been gored by Valencia's successful work in the Vichada campaign. For Conservatives, any positive comment on *La Violencia en Colombia*, no matter how well balanced, was considered dangerous, and so Valencia became target of Conservative rage. Soon the Conservative newspapers demanded that Valencia be court-martialed, and that Ruiz Novoa, now Minister of Defense, be dismissed. Ruiz Novoa chose to fight with truth on his side; in an unforgettable appearance before the Congress, the highly respected Minister of Defense read off documentary proof that the Conservative Senator responsible for the attacks on Valencia had been meeting secretly with a murderous bandit, negotiating with him to intimidate opponents.21

In 1963, Valencia was promoted to Colonel and made Chief of Operations of the Colombian Army, from which post most of the plans were made that by 1965 finished off *la violencia* as a historical phenomenon. Early that year, Valencia was made brigade commander of the 5th Brigade Zone, where a mixed rural-urban Castro-sponsored group was setting up a guerrilla base in the Department of Norte de Santander. The group was called *Ejército de Liberación Nacional* (ELN). It received lavish Cuban financing; established a network of propagandists in Mexico, France, and the United States; and even trained some small combat units that could give Army patrols a serious fight. A defrocked priest, Camilo Torres Restrepo, once an Army chaplain and a researcher on the Presidential Commission on the Causes of *La Violencia*, had become a leftist revolutionary. Materials were published, attributed to his authorship, with claims that his doctrines could harmonize Christianity and revolutionary Marxism: ELN pressured its "guerrilla-priest" to prove himself in a combat action.

An ELN unit ambushed an Army supply patrol; as the guerillas, including Torres Restrepo, moved in to seize the weapons, the patrol leader, who had only feigned death, leaped up firing his automatic weapon. Torres Restrepo and the guerrillas were killed. Leftist revolutionary groups all through the Americas and Western Europe called for this action to signal the great revolution. They had a martyr, killed by the soldiers from whom he once had heard confession. But they failed utterly, because Colonel Valencia had a gritty reputation for telling the truth, and because he took quick steps to inform Torres Restrepo's family and responsible leaders with unimpeachable evidence.22

In 1968 Valencia was promoted to brigadier general, and by the middle of 1970 the much-publicized ELN was no longer a threat to public security. Valencia was made Commandant of the Cadet School in Bogotá, a post equivalent to the Superintendent of West Point. The author of the "Oath of the Sword" had come home. He set about upgrading the curriculum to be academically equal to that of four-year undergraduate colleges, and he instituted a genuine academic foundation in the social sciences. Appointed to a Presidential Commission on the condition of youth and education, he made a keynote speech on the campus of the National University, and was enthusiastically received in the rooms where Camilo Torres Restrepo had recently been a student folk hero. He wrote a classic novel about his experiences in the pacification of *la violencia*. Entitled *Uisheda*, a folk word invented by the author to mean "senseless violence for its own sake," the book is both accurate and socially sensitive.

In 1971, a gang of urban terrorists claiming to represent the defunct ELN ambushed Valencia's car on the streets of Bogotá; he and the driver survived serious wounds. Public outrage helped further discredit ELN, and in December 1971, Valencia was promoted to major general. He was sent to Washington, D.C., as Chief of the Colombian Delegation to the Inter-American Defense Board. Two years later he became Commandant of the Colombian War College.

The Alternation Plan ended in 1974 amid the usual gloomy predictions by the political scientists and journalists that the system would soon fall apart, and *la violencia* resume. In a free, remarkable nonviolent election, Liberal candidate Alfonso López Michelsen became President. Four months after assuming office he promised that peace would reign in the backhands of Colombia; Alvaro Valencia Tovar was promoted to Commanding General of the Army. The following year he was nominated for the office of Minister of Defense, the only military post in the Colombian cabinet. A clique of Conservative diehards who remembered how Valencia's honest actions in the Vichada, fifteen years before, had embarrassed their scheming colleague, now called in their debts to block the nomination.

Valencia made the final gesture for an honorable military man caught among the schemes of dishonorable civilian politicians: he retired. For two years his columns in *El Tiempo* delighted readers, and in 1978 he ran as a third-party candidate for the Presidency. Like efforts of this nature in the United States, his candidacy drew poorly at the polls, but his ideas were borrowed freely by the two major parties. Today he is in great demand as a writer, teacher, and lecturer.

Conclusions

The world would benefit greatly from an understanding of Colombia's solution to the rural violence. Men like Alvaro Valencia Tovar, and several dozen of his colleagues, could make tremendously beneficial contributions to world trouble zones like Central American and the Middle East. But leaders, both civilian and military, of the world powers exhibit difficulty in accepting that there are successful architects of peacekeeping systems from the smaller, less powerful nations. Fear of "another Vietnam" leaves many leaders in the United States blind to the fact that Colombians had all the classic problems of an outdated political system, radical demands for economic development, Soviet and Cuban-sponsored intervention, and rapid social change to confront. Their military budget and the percentage of men in uniform have consistently been well below the world average; foreign military aid was small and ended in the early 1970s.23 Most important, a democratic Constitution remains in force and operates well, with crime in the narcotics industry perhaps the top national problem.

What are the reasons behind Colombia's success? First, Colombian military thinking recognizes that civilian control of the military does not mean that military strategy, tactics, and operations can be neatly separated from political affairs, especially in a world threatened by Communist revolutionaries whose own societies are the most militarized of all. Second, military strategy to the Colombian officer has three dimensions: social structure, firepower, and maneuver. Third, isolation of criminals and foreign-sponsored revolutionary organizers is the first order of business; excellent tactics are the means for eliminating diehard criminals and armed insurgents, not for fighting the populace in an indiscriminate manner. Fourth, small and middle-sized nations can avoid the terrible expense and useless diversion of scarce resources devoted to a large, showy military establishment by joining in regional and international peacekeeping systems.24 The Colombians have done this three times with distinction, in two distant regions and in different political settings. Fifth, and most important, the Colombian strategy for peacekeeping offers, at minimal cost, a proven system that can be adapted to dozens of internal and multinational situations where violence costs lives and retards development.

The Colombian doctrines will not force the Kremlin to abandon its millenarian dream of exporting Communism by hiring its satellite clients to organize contrived revolutions in developing nation where democratic institutions are weak. They will, however, eliminate the environment in which such acts of international piracy can succeed, and they will improve the quality of internal law enforcement greatly. The Colombian doctrines will not force the United States and its North Atlantic Treaty Organization (NATO) allies to abandon firepower and maneuver as the classic variables of all military operations. They will, however, provide the third dimension – sociologically structured operations – so that the United States can better assist its network of allies among the developing nations, fostering local control and success at greatly reduced cost.

NOTES

1. Benjamin Latorre Chaves, "La Guerra de los mil dias," *Revista de las Fuerzas Armadas* (XIII: 37, March-April 1967), p. 55. Colombian National Histories Radically Exaggerate Battle Casualties Ever Since the

1. "War of a Thousand Days," a Phenomenon Recently Repeated By U.S. Journalists in El Salvador.
2. James V. Coniglio, "Nationalization of the Colombian Army: *La reforma militar*" (Master's thesis, University of Florida, 1970), p. 24.
3. Roberto Urdaneta Arbeláez, *El Materialismo Contra la dignidad del hombre* (Bogotá: Editorial Lucros, 1960), pp. 286-287. Perhaps 10,000 people were killed in the fighting.
4. Manley O. Hudson, *The Verdict of the League* (Boston: The World Peace Foundation, 1933), pp. 2-4.
5. Absalón Fernández Soto, *Memoria del Señor Ministro de Gobierno al Congreso Nacional de 1946* (Bogotá: Imprenta Nacional, 1946), pp. XIX-XX; and Russell W. Ramsey, *Revolución Campesina* (Bogotá: Editorial Cromos, 1970), pp. 90-91.
6. Russell W. Ramsey, *Soldados y Guerrilleros*, trans. & ed. Alvaro Valencia Tovar (Bogotá: Tercer Mundo, 1981), pp. 146-147.
7. Russell Ramsey, "*La Violencia*: Some Historical Perspectives," #S-139, Joint LASA-MALAS Conference. Bloomington, Indiana, October 19, 1980.
8. Russell W. Ramsey, "The Colombian Battalion in Korea and Suez," *Journal of Inter-American Studies*. October 1967, pp. 541-560: and Charles L. Steel, IV, *Colombian Experience in Korea and Perceived Impact on La Violencia, 1953-1956*. Gainesville, Florida, 1978: University of Florida master's thesis.
9. Jose Francisco Socarras. *El Tiempo* (Bogotá). June 13, 1964, pp. 4-5.
10. *Ejército* [Journal of the Colombian Army], No. 11. Jan 22, 1962, p. 2; and Cayo Jiménez Mendoza, "Autodefensa," *Revista de las Fuerzas Armadas* XII, (35), Nov.-Dec. 1965, pp. 177-184.
11. James D. Henderson, "Another Aspect of the *Violencia*," XXVI SECOLAS Conference, Tampa, April 20, 1979, pp. 20-22; and Russell W. Ramsey, "Critical Bibliography on *La Violencia* in Colombia, "*Latin American Research Review*; VIII:I, Spring, 1973, pp. 22-24.
12. Ramsey, "The Colombian Battalion," pp. 541-560.
13. Ramsey, *Soldados*, pp. 254-256.
14. "Historia y Antecedentes," *Revista Policía Nacional de Colombia*. No. 70. July-August 1958, pp. 109-116.
15. Despite the Kennedy Administration's commitment to Colombia as a showplace for democracy, this vital component was simply not understood by the New Frontiersmen.
16. Evelio Buitrago Salazar, *Zarpazo the Bandit*, trans. M. Murray Lasley, ed. Russell W. Ramsey (Tuscaloosa: University of Alabama Press, 1977), passim; and Russell W. Ramsey, "Colombian Infantry Faces Insurgency," *Infantry*, Nov.-Dec. 1964, pp. 4-8.
17. Professor Fals Borda and Monsignor Guzmán both became self-exiled in Mexico, claiming fear of governmental reprisal. Camilo Torres Restrepo,

another priest on the writing team, became an active revolutionary in the backhands.
18. Russell W. Ramsey, "The Spanish Military Orders: Alcántara, Calatrava, and Santiago," *The [United Kingdom] Army Quarterly and Defence Journal*, Summer 1983, passim.
19. When the Soviet Union attempted to frustrate the Camp David accords by blocking the creation of a United Nations Command to police the Gaza Strip in 1981, a Multi-National Force was established in 1982, with a battalion from Colombia.
20. There were once again few casualties. Valencia's doctrines appeared in *Revista de Infantería*, Dec. 1962 and July 1963.
21. Ruiz Novoa achieved a national following in the ensuing months, but chose early retirement over military opportunism.
22. Ramsey, *Soldados*, pp. 316-318; and Alvaro Valencia Tovar, *El Fin de Camilo [The End of Camilo]* (Bogotá, 1976).
23. Russell W. Ramsey, "Statistical Summary, Armed Forces in Latin America" (chart), *Civil-Military Relations in Colombia* (Gainesville, Florida: Regent Publishing Co., 1978), p. 64.
24. Alberto Lleras Camargo. "The War of the Wealthy," *El Tiempo*, trans. Russell W. Ramsey, *The Gainesville Sun*, Nov. 29, 1973.

Russell W. Ramsey, Ph.D., D.Min.

James D. Henderson's Review of: *Zarpazo de Bandit: Memoirs of an Undercover Agent of the Colombian Army*, by Evelio Buitrago Salazar, University of Alabama Press, 1977. Reviewed in: *Hispanic American Historical Review*, November, 1978.

Zarpazo de Bandit is the translated memoir of Evelio Buitrago Salazar, an enlisted man in the Colombian Army who specialized in infiltrating and liquidating bandit gangs during the later *violencia*. Written in diary fashion and containing sixty chapters of fewer than three pages each, the book relates with appropriate bravado its author's daring exploits. Even allowing for suspected exaggeration, there is little doubt that Buitrago was a remarkable soldier. The Colombian government recognized that fact when it awarded him the coveted Cross of Boyacá in 1965.

A chief virtue of this book lies in its character as a stat of middle-class protest against *violencia*. When Evelio Buitrago was impressed into the army on leaving a Cali movie house in 1956, he had already lost his father and a cousin in the bloodshed and had been forced to flee the family coffee *finca* located in upland Caldas department. For ten years he was, as he tells it, the bane of malefactors who roamed Colombia's central cordillera, one such being the infamous Zarpazo, whose guerrilla band the author single-handedly decimated. Buitrago has nothing but contempt for his adversaries, "monsters whose countless victims could not be avenged by society" (p. 4). Though his prose is choppy and at times stilted, and the text overly seasoned with praise to God, country, and the Colombian army, *Zarpazo the Bandit* stands as a useful and entertaining counterweight to the numerous sympathetic portrayals of *violentos*.

One cannot fault either the translation or format of this volume, though the inclusion of a glossary of Colombianisms would have enhanced it. The editor's short introduction is useful but misleading in its suggestion that there is a generally accepted taxonomy of *la violencia*, and the prologue by Colonel Guillermo Plazas is incorrect in its insistence that only the Colombian army kept the nation from "going Communist" during the upset of *la violencia*. These complaints aside, this reviewer commends the publisher, editor, and translator for making *Zarpazo* available to the North American reader.

"The Colombian Battalion in Korea and Suez," *Journal of Inter-American Studies*, October, 1967.

An international organization is only as effective as the degree of support which its sovereign members are willing to give it. This axiom would probably not be disputed, except for the fact that the word "degree" has the inherent property of evaluation hidden in its meaning. This evaluation, since it deals with the mainstream of a nation's political life, is not capable of purely quantitative analysis. A nation's ideas on sovereignty are involved in international cooperation. Its foreign policy, be it passive, neutral, or aggressive, is certainly involved. Its domestic status in terms of tranquility or violence, poverty or plenty, is deeply involved. A world power is tempted to preempt an undue share of the credit for the success of an international organization, especially in the field of conflict resolution. The contribution of a single weak nation is often overlooked, and yet the sum of the weak nations' contributions may conceivably be the balancing factor among irreconcilable giants.

The history of support for the United Nations, in its quest for mutual security, by the Republic of Colombia will be explored herein for its impact on the total picture of international security. To give an adequate evaluation of Colombia's participation in mutual security projects under the aegis of the United Nations requires more than an itemized accounting of the number of soldiers contributed.

An attempt will be made at total evaluation: first, by describing the factual events of the Colombian effort; then, by analyzing the impact of these efforts on Colombia's domestic affairs; and, finally, by studying the value of Colombian participation in the world political arena. Colombia, during the period under discussion, embraced a host of domestic problems which are typical of small-country disturbances in much of the world. Conclusions will therefore be drawn which seek to achieve some generic hypotheses about small-nation participation in international security affairs.

History of Colombian Participation

When the United Nations was being born at Dumbarton Oaks and San Francisco, the attending physicians were not overly anxious that midwives and surgical assistants be present in the delivery room. The specific reason for this attitude is found in the political setting of World War II, which saw victor nations preparing to preside over vanquished and non-participants. In simplified form, it was a question of giving the new organization the one quality which the League of Nations never had – the ability to act instantly with requisite military force in situations which threatened world peace. To the small nations, of which Colombia was just one of many, what such a concept provided for was not really an international organization but a Holy Alliance, capable, in their estimation, of becoming a very "Unholy" Alliance indeed should the big nations see fit to sacrifice small nations in the general pursuit of world harmony.1

Colombia was ably represented at the United Nations during the formative months in the person of Roberto Urdaneta Arbeláez. This man was a Conservative, Jesuit educated, and a militant anti-Communist. The fact that he was highly regarded in Colombia by leaders of both parties (Liberal and Conservative), made him a somewhat rare phenomenon in that nation's unhappy post-World War II partisan squabbles. He was an eminent international jurist and had held high posts, both in domestic and foreign affairs.2 Colombia's position at the San Francisco Conference as a member of the Latin American group which favored the supremacy of international juridical action over the more political concept of collective security was not without its historical background. Colombia had entrusted foreign disputes to the League of Nations or to international arbitration in the absence of an international organization on several previous occasions.3

On November 21, 1902, the ghastly War of a Thousand Days, which claimed over 100,000 lives, was negotiated to a peaceful settlement aboard the U.S.S. *Wisconsin* under the mediating auspices of President Theodore Roosevelt. For this service Colombia developed gratitude toward President Roosevelt and credence in the principle of arbitration.

Faith in both Roosevelt and arbitration was shaken somewhat following November 3, 1903, when a "spontaneous revolution" in Panama City suggested support from Washington, and an appeal to the Permanent Court of International Arbitration produced no immediate restitution.4 These issues resolved themselves through later negotiations, however, and Colombia's next international affair developed in its southernmost extremity, at a town called Leticia. Bands of Peruvian military and civilian personnel, officially disclaimed by the Peruvian government, seized Leticia and surrounding points by surprise in September of 1932.5

Colombia's Foreign Minister during this era was the young Roberto Urdaneta Arbeláez. He appealed to the League of Nations, which held an emergency session and sent a fact-finding commission. In the record time (for the League) of one month, Peru was declared the aggressor and enjoined to give up Colombia's territory. Peruvian troops were evacuated, and the lesser issues of the dispute were referred to a regional commission. The events of this peaceful resolution of a bellicose situation form an almost perfect model or case study in international organization. The effect of it was not lost upon Colombia. The Leticia affair also served to turn public attention away from growing violence in Colombia's backhands, a precedential specter which was to loom again.6

When World War II ended, Colombia, like the other Latin American countries, felt there was a necessity for both a world organization and a regional one. A tacit understanding was reached with U.S. planners: there would be a regional organization capable of more than idle conversation for the purpose of containing communism.7 But Colombia still favored the juridical approach to disputes rather than political settlement by the world powers. Indeed, Urdaneta Arbeláez participated in the writing of the statute for the International Court of Justice.8

Significantly, the Colombian delegation at San Francisco introduced a Charter amendment which reaffirmed, in more direct language than the basic instrument, the principle that all nations should fulfill the obligations they assumed under the Charter "in good faith." Although most small-nation proposals for a Charter amendment were defeated, this one was not.9 If those voting for it regarded their action as hollow verbiage to placate small-nation fears about big-nation recalcitrance, Colombia took the issue seriously.

Colombia was seated on the Security Council in the early days of the United Nations. Its delegation favored the bringing of all disputes, however irreconcilable, before the Council on the ground that there was, in every disagreement, some common ground if the parties would look for it. When Egypt brought before the Council on August 28, 1947, a dispute with Great Britain over bases in Suez, Alfonso López, Colombia's delegate, termed the matter a great opportunity to demonstrate the usefulness of the Security Council.10 It is noteworthy that during this period when the political parties of Colombia were feuding bitterly, its representatives in the United Nations – Urdaneta Arbeláez, a Conservative, in the General Assembly; and López, a Liberal, in the Security Council – pursued identical policies.

A minor social revolution took place on April 9, 1948, when the assassination of leftist-Liberal Jorge Eliecer Gaitán turned the city of Bogotá into a sea of tumult and bloodshed. Paradoxically, the Ninth Conference of American Ministers, which was going on in Bogotá at that time, ended in the establishment of the Organization of American States and a hemispheric treaty for pacific settlement of disputes. Another former Liberal president, Alberto Lleras Camargo, was elected first Secretary General of the new regional organization. During his tenure of office, the Organization of American States became a remarkably successful regional organization. It intervened time after time in the border disputes which plagued the Latin American countries and achieved an exceptional record in mediation. It should be recalled that Colombia has always regarded the Organization of American States as a complement to the United Nations and approaches the former as a regional adjunct to the latter.

In 1949 a long dispute arose with Peru over the question of Víctor Raúl Haya de la Torre, a leader of the Peruvian APRA, who sought protective exile in the Colombian Embassy in Lima. Finally resolved in 1954 after hearings by the International Court of Justice, this case dealt with a technicality of international law and never achieved the level of a threat to collective security.11 Also in 1949, the bloodshed and accompanying repressions arising out of the disturbance of April 9, 1948, had degenerated into something approaching guerrilla war, with the Conservative Party in the minority but politically dominant. Adherents of both the Liberal Party and the Conservative Party carried out armed raids against each other in the backhands. Both parties opposed communism categorically for its anti-Christian basis, but the Conservative Party was more vocal in its anti-Communist statements.

When rumblings from the Korean peninsula first reached the floor of the Security Council in mid-1950, most anti-Communist nations looked to the United

States for leadership.12 Once the die was cast to enter the conflict as a U.N. military command, countries favoring the proposal were solicited for contributions of troops.13 Secretary General Trygve Lie initially requested troops, especially infantry, from all United Nations members. Colombian Foreign Minister Evaristo Sourdis interpreted this request as addressed to all the members in general and stated that Colombia would meet its commitments to the United Nations in all forms when specifically asked.14 United States Ambassador Willard L. Beaulac expressed his thanks to those Colombians – more than 500 of them – who proffered their services, and *El Siglo*, voice of the Conservative regime, vied with *El Tiempo* in giving editorial support to the furnishing of Colombian troops.15

In late September, Colombia's finest naval vessel, the *Almirante Padilla* (a frigate displacing 1,430 tons), was offered to the U.N. Command. The newsmagazine *Semana* stated that the Director de la Armada, Captain Antonio J. Tanco, had suggested this plan, and dispatch of the ship was authorized on October 23, 1950, by Decree No. 3230. It seems self-evident that approval for the action came personally from Gómez. On November 1, 1950, the *Almirante Padilla* sailed from Cartagena and headed for the San Diego, California, Naval Base for combat refitting. Carrying a crew of ten officers and 180 men, this ship was destined for coastal patrol duty in Korean waters.16

Two weeks later, Colombian Ambassador Zuleta Angel offered the services of a battalion of infantry, consisting of 1,000 men and 83 officers; this matter was taken under advisement with appropriate gestures of appreciation by Edward G. Miller, U.S. Sub-Secretary of State.17 On February 5, 1951, intensive training for the nucleus of the battalion, some 40 officers and 250 noncommissioned officers, began at the Infantry School at Usaquén. Initial estimates called for a period of unit training in Puerto Rico, but this plan never materialized. The carefully selected volunteers comprising the leadership structure were presented their new rifles in a ceremony on the Bridge of Boyacá, highly significant in Colombian military history. Unit training then began for the entire battalion.18

In mid-February of 1951, Urdaneta Arbeláez informed the United Nations that Colombia was training a battalion of 1,083 men for the Korean conflict. He stated that if the United Nations so desired, Colombia would train an entire division and equip it with arms purchased *in the United States of Colombia*. The following week the *Almirante Padilla* sailed from San Diego to join the U.N. fleet operating off the Korean coast.19

With training completed and the men in a high state of combat readiness, the Colombian Battalion attended farewell Mass and ceremonies in the Plaza of Bolívar on May 12, 1951. Organized on the then-standard U.S. triangular model, the battalion sailed from Buenaventura on May 12, 1951, aboard the U.S. transport *Aiken Victory*, and arrived in Korea on June 16. After having been welcomed formally by both Mian Ziaud Din of Pakistan (Chairman of the U.N. Commission for the Unification and Rehabilitation of Korea) and Korean President Syngman Rhee, it was assigned as an integral battalion of the 21st Infantry Regiment, 24th U.S. Infantry Division.20 The Colombian Battalion fought as part of a U.S. division throughout the entire conflict. On February 12, 1952, it was transferred to the 31st Infantry Regiment, 7th U.S. Infantry Division. In July of that year the first commander of the battalion, Colonel Jaime Puyo, turned over command to Colonel Alberto Ruiz Novoa, who later became Minister of Defense and is presently retired.

On December 9, the battalion was presented the U.S. Presidential Unit Citation by General James Van Fleet, and on January 4, 1953, it received the U.N. Service Medal. In April it was transferred to the 17th Infantry Regiment, still part of the 7th Division, and the Panmunjom armistice negotiations in July 1953, terminated its combat service. During that month Colonel Ruiz Novoa turned over command to Colonel Carlos Ortíz Torres and went home to participate in the government of General Rojas Pinilla, who had overthrown the bloody administration of Laureano Gómez on June 13.21

The battalion's biggest combat actions were in the Kumsan offensive and the defense of Old Baldy. A total of 3,089 men participated in the action. Of these, 131 died in combat and ten from other causes. Combat wounds totaled 448, and noncombat injuries 162. There were 69 missing-in-action cases. A total of 18 U.S. Silver Star Medals (third highest combat decoration) were presented to Colombians and 25 Bronze Stars with V-device for valor (fourth highest combat medal). For meritorious service, two presentations were made of the U.S. Legion of Merit (second highest service award) and nine Bronze Stars.22 These decorations are in addition to those bestowed by Colombia's own government.

While the Colombian Battalion was in Korea, the nation maintained an embargo of all strategic materials to Communist China and North Korea. This embargo was particularly important with regard to petroleum, Colombia's second-ranking export commodity.23 The government announced on several occasions a willingness to train additional battalions if the United Nations would facilitate training and make armaments available.24 Significantly, on April 15, 1954, Colombia's delegation supported a New Zealand resolution in the General Assembly to note with "grave concern" that Egypt had not compiled with a Security Council resolution of September 1, 1951, calling upon that nation to cease discriminatory practices in the Suez Canal.25 The resolution was defeated, but it revealed Colombian interest in a different type of crisis in another part of the world. On November 25, 1954, the Colombian Battalion returned from Korea for a heroes' welcome in Bogotá.

The singing and shouting were short-lived, for Rojas Pinilla had stopped one guerrilla war, only to fall into authoritarian methods, corruption, and refusal to restore constitutional government. The battalion was sent into "public order" duty, which meant, in practical terms, the distasteful task of fighting fellow Colombians over a cause for which there was much popular sympathy. The disillusionment of some veterans was expressed by deserting to the guerrilla side, and by others in turning over their U.S.-made weapons to the guerrillas.26 A significant number of the veterans was, however, kept intact in the Colombian Battalion, which remained a kind of elite force for emergencies.

Just two years after the veterans of the Korean conflict returned, matters in the Mediterranean deteriorated into the situation commonly known as the Suez Crisis of 1956. When Israel refused to withdraw its forces from Egyptian soil and the Anglo-

Russell W. Ramsey, Ph.D., D.Min.

French task force stormed into the Port Said area, the General Assembly went into emergency session. In an all-night meeting on November 3-4, Canada, Colombia, and Norway sponsored a joint resolution to form a task force under United Nations auspices to supervise the "cessation of hostilities." Colombian Representative to the General Assembly Francisco Urrutia asserted, with the support of most Latin American nations, that he was "skeptical of assumption by the United Nations of an administrative role." He recommended a "kind of safety belt" around Gaza by stationing troops along the frontier.27 The furnishing of a unit by Colombia made little public impact. Three factors made it considerably less complex than the Korean episode: a military regime did not require a basis in popular support to send a military unit abroad; the Suez issue involved no ideological confrontations which could be related to Colombia's domestic scene; and support for the United Nations was one of the few issues on which most Colombians were in agreement in 1956.

On November 6, U.N. Secretary General Dag Hammarskjold announced that Canada, Colombia, Denmark, Finland, Norway, Pakistan and Sweden had all offered troops. By November 16, Ceylon, India, Czechoslovakia, Romania, Indonesia, New Zealand, Afghanistan, Chile, Burma, Brazil, Ethiopia, Iran, Ecuador, and Yugoslavia had extended the offer as well. On November 11, Canadian, Colombian, Norwegian, and Danish troops arrived at staging areas in Naples, Italy, and on November 15, units began arriving by air at Ismailia, Egypt. Dag Hammarskjold termed this force, under Canadian Brigadier General E. L. M. Burns, the "first truly international force," a reference to the fact that it eventually contained Communist, non-Communist, and neutralist forces. By December 11, Finnish, Indian, and Yugoslavia troops were also included in the task force, which was called the U.N. Emergency Force.28

After the Anglo-French assault force had withdrawn, the greatest potential trouble spot was the explosive Israeli-Egyptian border. The Colombian Battalion was assigned a patrolling role in the Khan Yunia zone of the Gaza Strip. During the last week in October, 1958, the battalion sailed for Colombia after nearly two years of tedious duty. The total troop participation in the action was 490 officers and men.29 Colombian leaders were well aware of the Judeo-Islamic blend in their own Hispanic background. This factor, combined with strong professionalism and long experience in handling explosive populations, made the Colombian Battalion's performance altogether noteworthy.

It was a very different nation to which the veterans returned. Rojas Pinilla, their former hero, had been ejected from office by a civilian coalition with support from the same army he once commanded. The armed forces chiefs had maintained a *junta* government from May 10, 1957, until the election of 1958, when Lleras Camargo became president. During this time, Colombia became, domestically, an orderly democratic nation. During the same period, its participation in international security activities also ended. The government since 1958 has repeatedly indicated a further willingness for such participation, but no occasion has arisen to accomplish it. Although Russia persisted, unsuccessfully, in demands that only African troops be used in the U.N. peacekeeping force in the Congo in 1960, a compromise was reached by employing only eastern hemisphere contingents. It is not known if Colombia will offer troops again if the United Nations should need then, but such an offer appears likely.

The Domestic Impact of Participation

In 1946 Colombia experienced a presidential election in which the majority party (Liberal) split over a moderate and an extremist candidate, permitting a minority candidate from the Conservative Party to win. Vigilance groups of Liberals and Conservatives commenced sporadic fighting in the backlands. Colombian Conservatives of this period favored a somewhat reactionary domestic policy and were violently anti-Communist. But Colombia was, at that time, desperately in need of programs of economic and social reforms, entities which were not likely to be forthcoming from a Conservative regime. When the Ninth Pan American Conference became the site of a bloody uprising, the Conservative administration laid the blame to a combination of Communist conspiracy and Liberal Party agitation. Strong-arm tactics were resorted to, and the Liberal opposition leaped willingly to the combat by forming a huge guerrilla movement.

Although Colombia's Conservative regime from 1946-1950 was accused of certain tinges of Spanish falangism, there were some powerful factors in the Colombian social fabric which made falangism impossible. Greatest of these differences between Colombia and Spain, which are often compared for their many resemblances, was the fact that the Colombian Army possessed a long heritage of noninterference in politics.30 The Conservative administration found it necessary, after 1948, to convert the National Police into a party power organ.31 Attempts were made to do this with the Army, and the promotion of certain officers believed to be Conservative in sympathy led foreign observers to announce that the Colombian Army, after 1948, was no longer apolitical.32 Closer examination reveals, however, that when the leaders of the frustrated Liberal Party and the guerrilla bands generally continued to think of the Army as a neutral.33 Colombian contact with U.S. military men began formally in 1939 as part of overall defense plans for the Panama Canal. In 1949 a U.S. Army and U.S. Air Force training mission were authorized for Colombia as part of the reoriented hemispheric defense program, and more than a decade of continuous exposure to their U.S. military counterparts had reinforced apoliticism in the minds of Colombian officers.

By the latter part of 1950, the guerrilla war in Colombia was reaching a peak in violence which was to continue until early 1953. The Conservative Party would not risk losing its hold on the nation, and the 1949 presidential election was rigged on the pretense of checking voter registrations. Faced with roughhouse tactics at the polling places, the Liberals withdrew from the election. Laureano Gómez, political boss of the Conservative Party and head of the intransigent faction which is often termed Falangist, won the election with only 15 opposing votes.34 From his election in early December of 1949 until his inauguration in August of 1950, Gómez actually ran Colombia by pulling strings behind the scenes.35 At his inauguration he announced a strongly pro-U.S. policy, and three months later he had decided to commit soldiers to the Korean action. But the Army was the one force inside

Colombia which tried not to take sides during the guerrilla fighting. Guerrillas would sometimes appeal to the Army for amnesty, and the government took advantage of public confidence in the Army to negotiate truce talks with the guerrillas.

In view of the great initial enthusiasm, both Liberal and Conservative, for the support of the Korean action by a Colombian force, a conclusion is asserted here that the Colombian Battalion went to Korea because both Gómez and broad segments of Colombia's politically conscious people honestly wanted it to go.36

The Colombian Communist Party had also formed an opinion about the Korean action. The small domestic organization was nearly shattered in government action following the *bogotazo* of April 9, 1948. Its small cadres were striving to penetrate the guerrilla movement, but the Liberal Party's democratic and Christian orientation and the Communists' weak leadership prevented widespread acceptance of Communist assistance. The Communists donated literature and organizational procedures to such an extent that the guerrilla movement was organized along classic lines developed by Mao Tse-tung. But the leaders were unquestionably idealistic and vigorous young Liberals. The Communist Party attempted to capitalize on the social division existing in Colombia and turn the war into a class struggle. But, to its dismay, much of the fighting consisted of traditional Liberal-Conservative mob battles and outright banditry. Ghastly acts of barbarity were daily occurrences, and outright bandits with notorious reputations could be found on both sides.

Thus, the party was caught on the horns of a dilemma. It needed to pose as the friend of the peasant in a just struggle, but the peasant was venting his spite on other peasants. Furthermore, the Army, generally a Communist target, was respected, perhaps by peasants more than by the intelligentsia. Nearly everyone hated the National Police, but paradoxically the organization was obtaining loyal service from hundreds of illiterate peasant recruits. The solution was to use the Korean participation as a propaganda outlet.37

Several countries around the world which sent troops to the U.N. Command in Korea were attacked by Communist propaganda. It was a relatively simple matter for the Colombian Communist Party to adapt worldwide slogans to the Colombian political situation. Volunteers for the Korean action, for example, tell of being called "cannon fodder" for an assault by "imperialist oligarchies" against the people of North Korea.38 A general propaganda assault was conducted by blending domestic injustices perpetrated by the regime with the decision to participate in Korea. Ironically, volunteers for Korean service were numerous, many Colombian men finding war in Asia more palatable than the heartbreaking civil conflict.39

There is one final motive which has been imputed to Gómez in deciding to send the Colombian Battalion to Korea. Units operating in Korea, unless they possessed first class armaments, were rearmed with standard U.S. military equipment. Gómez was therefore accused by some Liberals, and, at times, by the Communists, of sending the battalion in order to use the armament thus acquired against his political opponents. This accusation is highly improbable, for two reasons. First, negotiations had been under way for some time with most Latin American countries, including Colombia, for the United States to begin supplying arms for hemispheric defense. The Korean conflict had no direct bearing on the pacts, known as Mutual Defense Assistance Pacts, which were signed in late 1952 and 1953. Plans for hemispheric defense were seriously under way at the Ninth Pan American Conference at Bogotá in early 1948.40 Second, the Army strenuously resisted a partisan involvement in the guerrilla war of 1949-1953, and is not likely to have permitted its best weapons to be taken away and given to the National Police.

Urdaneta Arbeláez was recalled from the United Nations to serve as Minister of War during the Gómez administration. He did not have a realistic appraisal of the guerrilla war, and his tenure of office might generously be described as ineffective.41 In November of 1951, Gómez suffered a heart attack and turned over the active presidency to his first Designate, Urdaneta Arbeláez, who, it must be said in all justice, did make some conciliatory efforts with respect to the domestic situation.42

But it was during the administration of Urdaneta Arbeláez that the largest single impact of the Korean participation developed on the domestic scene. General Gustavo Rojas Pinilla, a man of Conservative sympathies, was sent to Korea to serve on the general staff of the U.N. Command. He did not actively command the Colombian Battalion in combat, but he was the idol of the men and of the Colombian Army at large. He consistently made accommodating statements which endeared him to Conservative leaders and also to U.S. policy makers. Gómez and Urdaneta Arbeláez failed to understand, however, the concept of public service which characterizes Colombian officers. Even if Rojas Pinilla favored the Conservative Party, he did not condone the abysmally ineffective measures against the guerrilla war being undertaken by the National Police under civilian direction. By leaving him in Korea, the government made a hero of him. An attempt was made at an honorable exile by assigning him for a time to the Inter-American Defense Board in Washington. When he returned to Colombia in early 1953, popular pressure was too great upon him to seize the reins of government.43

Too late, Gómez resumed active presidency and tried to get rid of Rojas Pinilla by sending him on inconsequential but remote missions. Although Rojas Pinilla tried sincerely to give the presidency to someone else, about ninety per cent of Colombia's politically conscious people demanded his personal assumption of the highest office. On June 13, 1953, he overthrow the government and became Colombia's first military dictator in several decades.44 He reduced the domestic violence dramatically in a few months but then fell under the influence of a sinister group of extremists who preyed upon his ego and his political naïveté for their own purposes. By early 1954, Colombia was plunged into a second guerrilla war, more localized but equally bloody. The National Police were taken out of the combat and the Army thrown in.45 The Colombian Battalion returned at this point from Korea and was used both as an elite unit and as a source of combat veterans to raise the general level of Army performance.

Veterans of the Korean conflict began to rise rapidly to positions of responsibility; gradually, these leaders lost confidence in their chief. When Rojas

Pinilla decided to furnish the Colombian Battalion again for the Suez action, his days were already numbered. He made it difficult for his military leaders to turn against him by increasing their material benefits, although not nearly as much as anti-military propagandists have since stated.46

In late 1956, Korean veterans were prominent in the foundation of the Lancero School, to provide a rugged training course in anti-guerrilla tactics.47 In May of 1957, the Army chiefs enlisted the support of the other armed forces to oust their graft-laden chief. Korean veterans were prominent among the group engineering this ouster. Germán Arciniegas has stated that the Army's restoration of democratic government (over its corrupted chief) was another demonstration of its public services, especially in view of the fact that it had only entered the political arena by popular mandate.48

When the Colombian Battalion returned from Suez, it became again an elite force of the Colombian Army. It was now serving a civilian chief who directed an anti-guerrilla campaign in accordance with universally accepted principles. Through a combination of wise political decisions by Lleras Camargo and excellent military operations by the Colombian Army, the second guerrilla was stopped and the entire problem of violence reduced to an annoying domestic problem of continuous rural crime.49 It is fortunate that these things were accomplished by 1958, for at that time a new problem associated with the name of Fidel Castro faced Colombia. The inability of Castro to turn the Colombian Andes into a giant Sierra Maestre, as the Cuban leader has often boasted he would do, is largely the result of high quality leadership in the Colombian Army.50 Many of the top leadership positions are occupied by men who fought with the U.S. Army in Korea.

The International Impact

Colombia at the birth of the United Nations was one of the more vocal among the small-nation group. The general tone of the small-nation demand was for juridical action instead of big-nation military action, and for a broadening of the humanitarian services of the organization. Few observers would deny that the total impact of the small-nation views in the formative days of the United Nations was considerably more than negligible. Insofar as Colombia was a pioneer and a spokesman among the small-nation group, it perhaps made an impression upon the entire organization.

There is no doubt that Colombia's participation in Korea made a big impact in Latin America and among small nations in general. Critics of U.S. military assistance have pointed out repeatedly that, when put to the test, all U.S. military aid to Latin America after World War II paid off with one battalion in Korea.51 Military missions were placed in several Latin American countries in the late 1940s for the purpose of imparting instruction to domestic forces, but there was no obligation on the part of the recipient nations to support U.S. military commitments on a worldwide basis. Therefore, when Colombia agreed to send troops to Korea, it became the only Latin American nation to fulfill that portion of its obligations to support the United Nations, not the United States.

Several Latin American countries actually desired to send contingents to fight in Korea. Infantry troops were probably the one commodity, aside from strategic raw materials, which many of these nations were capable of furnishing. But when General Douglas MacArthur, speaking for the United Nations with considerable authority, informed the U.N. Command that he would accept contingents in strengths of no less than one thousand, this ruled out plans made by the other Latin American countries.52 Thus, Colombia was the only country which lived up to the Charter amendment about meeting obligations in full measure, even though support for the amendment itself was enthusiastic in Latin America in 1945.

The diplomatic effect of being able to include a Latin American unit in the U.N. Command was of considerable value to the non-Communist world. It must be recalled that abstention from participation was universal among Communist nations and rather widespread among the so-called neutralists. Had the entire region of Latin America been excluded from the U.N. force, along with Afro-Asian neutrals, credence would have been established for the Communist claim that the Korean action was only an imperialist military invasion. In evaluating the overall situation of Latin America with respect to the Korean conflict, it should be remembered that the embargo of strategic commodities imposed by all the nations probably had as much practical effect as the sending of troops by all nations could have had.

At the conclusion to the Korean conflict there were protracted peace negotiations. As a result of having been one of the contributing or participating powers, Colombia's position as a voice in world affairs was considerably reinforced. The degree of Colombia's participation in numerical terms can be evaluated. Had the United States contributed the same number of troops to Korea in proportion to its population as Colombia did, the U.S. force there would have numbered only about 45,000 instead of about one-third of a million:

$$\frac{3{,}200 \text{ (No. Of Colombians)}}{12{,}500{.}000 \text{ (population)}} = \frac{X \text{ (No. Of U.S. troops)}}{170{,}000{,}000 \text{ (population)}}$$

Colombian participation in Korea and Suez? The first and obvious one is that small nations can play more than a negative role in world organization. Although this conclusion may seem too apparent to merit inclusion, it should be recalled that the role of small nations is generally considered inconsequential in the success or failure of international security. Second, it would appear that small, underdeveloped nations are fully capable of furnishing well-trained, responsible contingents for police actions. With the advent of the Congo action 1961 this conclusion became a *fait accompli*, but until the success of the Suez action there was no assurance at all that troops of several small countries could serve the U.N. banner effectively.

Third, the way in which Colombia's battalion fought in Korea demonstrates that the refitting of multinational contingents can be beneficial. In historical-retrospect, General MacArthur's decision not to accept units smaller than one thousand men appears to have been a mistake. Fourth, the Colombian experience demonstrated the desirability of having a body of men in an underdeveloped nation who have served in other lands in some sort of joint military endeavor in the pursuit of world harmony. The Korean veterans have been bloodied in the field against militant communism, and the Suez veterans, or those who went to Suez but not to Korea, have seen that other countries than their own can also have domestic injustices. Both bodies of men appear to be less likely to succumb to the lure of Communist insurgency or some other violent resolution of their social and economic problems.53

Fifth, the Colombian nation, partly from the presence of the veterans and partly from the diplomatic climate arising from the entire participation, appears to have gained a measure of national self-respect. The nation has participated in a unified endeavor before the eyes of the entire world and acquitted itself honorably. Closely related to this conclusion is another, the sixth, dealing with a comparison of the two endeavors. Colombian participation in Suez as well as Korea demonstrated support of the United Nations to achieve world harmony regardless of ideology. Communist propaganda could hardly attack the sending of Colombian troops to Suez when the Communist bloc itself supported the police action there.

Seventh, the international activities of Colombia during the period 1950-1958 helped improve the world's image of that nation. Eighth, and last, it appears not unreasonable that, if the majority of small nations could or would assume the active posture taken by Colombia in the United Nations, the small-nation power bloc would exert considerably more influence on international security. The small-nation power bloc is, by its very nature, a group possessing only ephemeral unity. But if most of the small nations would assume a willingness to furnish troops, and to back these measures with appropriate embargos and sanctions as Colombia has done, the failure of the large nations to reconcile their differences might be less destructive to international security. Despite tragic internal problems, Colombia has indeed met its obligations under the Charter of the United Nations "in good faith."

NOTES

1. John A. Houston, *Latin America in the United Nations* (New York: Martin Press, 1956), pp. 14-20; and Robert N. Burr & Roland D. Hussey, eds. *Documents on Inter-American Cooperation*. Philadelphia: University of Pennsylvania Press, 1955.
2. Ronald Hilton, ed. *Who's Who in Latin America*. Stanford: The Stanford U. Press, 1951, p. 66; and John D. Martz, *Colombia, A Contemporary Political Survey*. (Chapel Hill: The U. of North Carolina Press, 1962), pp. 116-126.
3. Ernesto Camacho-Leyva, *Factores Colombianos* (Bogotá: Editorial ARGRA, 1962), p. 300; and William O. Galbraith, *Colombia, A General Survey*, 2nd ed. (London: Oxford U. Press, 1966), pp. 135-36. Colombian Conservative Eduardo Zuleta Angel, later Ambassador to the United States, served as Chairman of the United Nations Preparatory Commission in London in 1946. Later that year, former President (Liberal) Alfonso

López became Colombia's representative on the Security Council. An original signatory of the Charter of the U.N., Colombia ratified on November 5, 1945.
4. Phanor J. Eder, *Colombia* (London: T.F. Urwin, 1913), pp. 38-46.
5. Manley O. Hudson, *The Verdict of the League* (Boston: The World Peace Foundation Press, 1933), p. 5.
6. Germán Cavelier, *La Política Internacional de Colombia* (Bogotá: Editorial Iqueima, 1960), Tomo III, pp. 196-203; and Special Operations Research Office, *U.S. Army Area Handbook for Colombia*, 2nd. ed. (Washington, D.C.: U.S. Government Printing Office, 1964), p. 386.
7. Houston, *Latin America*, vi-vii; Alberto Lleras Camargo explains how the Russians antagonized the Latin American block at San Francisco by offering to "liberate" them from the inter-American system. Alberto Lleras Camargo, *The Inter-American Way of Life* (Washington, D.C.: The Pan American Union, 1953), pp. 6-8.
8. Roberto Urdaneta Arbeláez, *El Materialismo Contra la Dignidad del Hombre* (Bogotá: Editorial Lucros, 1960), flyleaf.
9. Houston, *Latin America*, p. 22. See also *Charter of the United Nations*, Article 2, Paragraph 2: "All Members in order to ensure to all of them the rights and benefits resulting from membership, shall fulfill in good faith the obligations assumed by them in accordance with the present Charter."
Article 42: "Should the Security Council consider that measures provided for in Article 41 would be inadequate or have proved to be inadequate, it may take such action by air, sea, or land forces as may be necessary to maintain or restore international peace and security. Such action may include demostrations, blockade, and other operations by air, sea, or land forces of Members of the United Nations."
10. Houston, *Latin America*, p. 155.
11. Hubert A. Herring, *Latin America, A History From Beginning to Present* (New York: Alfred A. Knopf, 1961), p. 584. The case occupied large front page columns in Colombian newspapers during several periods when Colombia was also involved in international security activities. Faith in international arbitration never wavered, even when momentary events appeared unfavorable to Colombia.
12. *El Tiempo*, June 29, 1950, p. 4. Colombia's leading newspaper, voice of the out-of-power Liberal Party, editorialized under "The Impossible Neutrality" that the U.S. Army was fighting the world's battle for democracy, as it had in World War II, and that Colombians must render support.
13. *El Tiempo*, July 8, 1950, p. 1. Creation of the U.N. Command captured the banner headline, and accompanying articles characterized the North Korean occupation of South Korea as a "reign of terror."
14. *El Tiempo*, July 15, 1950, p. 1; and July 17, 1950, p. 8. A reserve captain of Colombian Navy (Pablo Emilio Nieto) offered to recruit several

thousand volunteers; estimates ran to 10,000 men who would serve if called.
15. *El Tiempo*, June 30, 1950, p. 4; and July 18, 1950, pp. 1, 27.
16. *El Tiempo*, November 1, 1950, p. 1; and *Semana*, September 30, 1950, p. 7.
17. *El Tiempo*, November 15, 1950, p. 1; and *U.S Department of State Bulletin*, November 27, 1950, p. 870.
18. *El Tiempo*, February 5, 1951, p. 1; February 20, 1951, p. 1; and February 24, 1951, p. 1.
19. *Time*, February 19, 1951, p. 36. Urdaneta Arbeláez was serving at that period as Minister of War, with primary attention devoted to the swelling guerrilla war in the eastern plains of Colombia.
20. *United Nations Bulletin*, July 1, 1951, p. 7; and *El Tiempo*, May 12, 1951, p. 1. News was received that month that the *Almirante Padilla* was doing coastal blockade duty on the Korean west coast in formation with the British cruisers HMS Ceylon and HMS Kenya, the Canadian destroyer, HMS Sioux, and the U.S. frigate USS Glendale. *El Tiempo*, May 17, 1951, p. 1.
21. Alberto Ruiz Novoa, *El Batallón "Colombia" en Corea* (Bogotá: Imprenta Nacional, 1956), pp. 1-15.
22. Ruiz Novoa, *El Batallón*, pp. 15-16; and Camacho Leyva, *Factores*, pp. 305. The casualty figures differ slightly but not significantly from those cited in Robert Leckie, *Conflict, The History of the Korean War, 1950-1953* (New York: Avon Book Co., 1962), p. 366.
23. *United Nations Bulletin*, August 1, 1951, p. 96; and August 15, 1951, p. 150. Colombia sold no strategic resources to any Communist nation during the Korean War era.
24. *United Nations Bulletin*, September 1, 1951, p. 245.
25. *United Nations Bulletin*, April 15, 1954, p. 305.
26. Eduardo Franco Isaza, *Las Guerrillas del Llano* (Bogotá: Librería Mundial, 1959), fly leaf; and SORO, *U.S. Army Area Handbook for Colombia*, p. 390. Available written sources on this point are sketchy and highly partisan, at best.
27. Gabriella Rosner, *The United Nations Emergency Force* (New York: The Columbia U. Press, 1963), p. 83.
28. *United Nations Review*, December 1956, 1; and *United Nations Review*, January 1957, p. 1
29. *United Nations Review*, April 1957, p. 8; and December 1958, p. 5.
30. J. Leon Helguera, "The Changing Role of the Military in Colombia," *Journal of Inter-American Studies*, July 1961, p. 351. In the 19th century military factionalism was generally capped off by civilian leaders; in the 20th century military professionalism generally cast the Army in a neutral role.
31. Germán Arciniegas, *The State of Latin America* (New York: Alfred A. Knopf, 1952), p. 161. An *El Tiempo* editorialist, Enrique Santos, jibed on

September 20, 1950, that the government should send 10,000 "wild beasts" (a reference to National Police called *chulavitas* in that era) to Korea, enhancing the war effort and hastening the pacification of rural Colombia simultaneously. "Caliban," *El Tiempo*, September 28, 1950, p. 4.

32. Edwin Lieuwen, *Arms and Politics in Latin America* (New York: Praeger, 1959), p. 87.
33. Germán Guzmán, Orlando Fals Borda, and Eduardo Umana Luna, *La Violencia en Colombia*, Tomo I (Bogotá: Imprenta de la Universidad Nacional, 1962), pp. 263-264; a note detailed discussion of this subject by a perceptive Liberal is found in Fidel Blandon Berrio, *Lo Que El Cielo No Perdona* (Bogotá: Editorial Minerva, 1955), pp. 279-291.
34. Camacho-Leyva, *Factores*, p. 54.
35. Vernoa L. Fluharty, *Dance of the Millions* (Pittsburgh: The University of Pittsburgh press, 1956) p. 112. The abnormally long "lame duck" period arose after the Congressional Liberal majority advanced the election six months in the vain hope of winning.
36. Herring, *Latin America*, pp. 518-519. This excellent textbook summarizes the impugnation of Gómez' motives but omits the popular support aspect.
37. Robert J. Alexander, *Communism in Latin America* (New Brunswick, New Jersey: The Rutgers University Press, 1957), pp. 251-252; and Gabriel Mejía, "Uno de los Bomberos Estuvo en la Guerra Contra Chinos Comunistas," *Revista Bomberos de Medellín*, p. 192.
38. Mejía, "Uno de los Bomberos," pp. 190-192.
39. Ruiz Novoa, El Batallón, pp. 1-5; and *El Tiempo*, February 4, 1951, p. 1.
40. The fact that hemispheric military defense plans pre-dated the Korean involvement is adequately covered in Adolf A. Berle, *Latin America, Diplomacy and Reality* (New York: Harper & Row, 1962), pp. 88-96; and John C. Dreier, *The Organization of American States and the Hemispheric Crisis* (New York: Harper & Row, 1962), pp. 26-31.
41. *The New York Times*, November 17, 1950, p. 13; and April 9, 1951, p. 24.
42. "Peace Pow-wows," *Newsweek*, October 1, 1951, p. 40; and *The New York Times*, November 7, 1951, p. 12.
43. Tad Szulc, *Twilight of the Tyrants* (New York: Henry Holt, 1959), p. 223.
44. Camacho-Leyva, *Factores*, p. 304.
45. Guzmán, Fals Borda, and Luna, *La Violencia*, pp. 263-264.
46. Szulc, *Twilight*, p. 234.
47. R. Puckett and J. Calvin, "Lancero," *Infantry*, July-Sept. 1959, p. 35.
48. Germán Arciniegas, "Arms and Latin America," *Americas*, January 1961, p. 39.
49. Martz, *Colombia*, pp. 276-277.
50. Russell W. Ramsey, "Colombian Infantry Faces Insurgency," *Infantry*, Nov.-Dec. 1964, pp. 4-7. This article develops the thesis that a combination of Korean War experience plus protracted anti-violence operations have made the Colombian Army one of the most progressive and combat-wise small armies in the world.

51. This idea is the thesis of a work called *Arms and Politics in Latin America* by Edwin Lieuwen of the University of New Mexico. He postulates that the hemispheric defense program was actually window dressing for a broader program of political unity. *The Struggle for Democracy in Latin America* by former U.S. Representative David O. Porter and Robert J. Alexander carries this thesis to the extreme by implying that U.S. policy intentionally fomented dictators to please certain domestic interest groups.
52. *Newsweek*, September 11, 1950, p. 40. "The Unified Command also insisted that minimum army contingents should be reinforced battalion strength with supporting artillery; and with engineer and ordnance units able to function as such. It also generally insisted that the contributing government should provide reinforcements adequate to maintain the initial strength of each unit. These requirements increased the efficiency of the military operation, but they undoubtedly discouraged broader participation by governments that were either unable or unwilling to contribute on this scale." Ruth B. Russell, *The U.N. Experience with Military Forces: Political and Legal Aspects*, (Washington: Institute for Defense Analysis, 1963), p. 35.
53. The apparent cohesion and potential weight of the veterans were observed in Bogotá in September, 1962, at which time a reunion of the veterans of Leticia and Korea drew several hundred men to the capital city.

"Colombian Infantry Faces Insurgency," *Infantry*, November-December, 1964.

The bandit group moved rapidly and silently through the mountains towards its objective – a rural hamlet. In the dim early morning light the group descended a towering Andean slope and spotted the target village nestled peacefully in a verdant mountain valley. The bandits, wearing captured Colombian Army fatigue uniforms and carrying a large assortment of excellent rifles and machine pistols, infiltrated silently into positions around the village. Their leader, who styled himself romantically as *El Matador*, swaggered to the rustic hut of the village mayor and presented the demand: food and drink, all the money in the village, horses, firearms and ammunition, and the handing over of certain "enemies" to be taken away as hostages. *El Matador* strolled back to his band.

As the dismayed villagers began to stumble out of their huts, he motioned his blood-thirsty men forward, their weapons at the ready, for the attack on the unarmed peasants. The deputy chieftain moved quietly to the rear of the narrowing circle of bandits, ostensibly to check on security. As the bandits closed up, some already reaching expectantly for machetes, a hail of rifle and machine gun fire cut them down from all sides. The frightened villagers fled, and *El Matador* ran for the hills screaming betrayal. Two Colombian soldiers charged from behind a bush and brought him down. As they led him away, the soldiers congratulated the "deputy bandit chief," who was actually a corporal in the Colombian Army, trained in penetrating bandit organizations.

This village was lucky, for the army saved its people from a horrible death.

In confronting the banditry, the Colombian soldier is faced with two very difficult questions. How does one distinguish the bandits, who are rural criminals motivated only by crime, from the Communist infiltrators? And when you have solved the detection problem, how do you track down these four or five thousand savages, organized into highly mobile bands of 15 to 30 men, in a nation which is 10 times the size of Pennsylvania? The final answers to these questions have not been found. The problem has been some 300 years in the making, and it will not be solved by a few bold, simple measures.

Today the U.S. Infantryman is required to understand insurgency problems embracing highly varied climates and cultural backgrounds. The Colombian problem is almost a casebook of counterinsurgency, for in its modern history alone Colombia has seen all phases of the spectrum from individual criminal action to open civil war, and from non-political "killing for killing's sake" to organized Communist conspiracy. The Colombian problem is deserving of our attention, not only because this nation is strategically located across the entrance to South America, but also because it has often demonstrated great friendship for the United States.

Colombia's interior contains vast, scarcely charted stretches of jungle and long ranges of dramatic mountains whose peaks are capped in eternal snow. Clearly a land of geographic contrasts, its interior was peopled in the mid-1500s by a hardy cross-strain of Chibcha Indians and Spanish adventures. Most of these rural dwellers clung to fertile mountain valleys and plateaus at the base of the crests, some working on coffee plantations but the majority resorting to subsistence agriculture. Banditry became an endemic problem among the peasants because they were cut off from the mainstream of the Colombian national life. Some of these rural people participated in the wars for independence from Spain (1810-1824) with little knowledge of what they were fighting for.

Since the time of Colombia's independence, the rural people have lived much as they lived three centuries ago. A "Hatfield and McCoy" tradition, much like that of the United States mountain people, grew up over the years, with the original cause of the dispute often long forgotten. Characteristic of the banditry was its utter senselessness, such as the killing of women and babies, as well as the intensity of its savagery, manifested in devilish cruelty.

In the midst of this scene the Colombian soldier fulfilled a role not unlike that of his North American counterpart on the Indian frontier during the settlement of the West. As Colombia's two major political parties, Liberal and Conservative, struggled with one another for the peasant's support, the nearest Colombian Army unit was often the only haven of justice and fair play. Perhaps the banditry, known as *la violencia*, would have passed quietly off the national scene in the post-World War II era if the two political parties had not resorted to armed conflict. Following the assassination of a Liberal idol in Bogotá in 1948, widespread rioting occurred in the cities, leaving some 30,000 people dead in an outburst known as the *bogotazo*. With the murder unsolved, the two parties began arming mobs of peasants. The Colombian Communist Party capitalized on the situation wherever possible, but the real tragedy was the arming and inciting of the bandit elements to fight for the two warring factions.

Virtual civil war prevailed from 1949 until 1953, when the political parties realized that the war had degenerated into "legalized" banditry and that the only winner might well be world communism. The Colombian Army was magnificently fulfilling its traditional role as pacificator and arbiter, managing to stay free of the political implications of the war. In 1951, although the army was desperately pressed to carry out its mission, it sent a battalion to the United Nations Command in Korea where, as the only Latin American contingent, it acquitted itself with great honor for two years.

In mid-1953, with the blessing of nearly all Colombians, Army Gen. Gustavus Rojas Pinilla took over the reins of government. The civil war ended, and thousands of combatants took advantage of an amnesty to resume normal pursuits. But General Rojas Pinilla could not solve the nation's political problems, and his government became harsh. Again, resistance groups took to the hills, although on a much smaller scale, and again the bandits found a good excuse for practicing their art. During the general's tenure of office, the Colombian Army founded a Ranger-type school known as *La Escuela de Lanceros* (literally, "Lancers' School;" see *Infantry*, July-September 1959). The 3,000 veterans of Korea were distributed among the Infantry units, and the army was placed in a posture of active counterinsurgency efforts. The Colombian soldier again remained a basis for stability and justice in the backlands while the political parties and the armed forces united in 1957 to eliminate General Rojas Pinilla as president and sponsored a democratic election.

When democracy returned to Colombia, a battalion of the Colombian Army was in Suez as part of the United Nations Command which supervised the separation of Egyptian and Israeli combatants in 1956. On the home front the army was given important new missions under the dynamic leadership of President Alberto Lleras Camargo. Aggressive counterinsurgency operations were undertaken against pockets of resistance. A few of these diehard groups turned out to be Communist led. Civic action programs were begun in the many disrupted areas where tools and farm stock were devastated and fields often reclaimed by nature. The civil government undertook far-reaching programs such as land reform, public assistance for rural areas, rehabilitation for hardened criminals, and educational radio programs.

By 1958 the fighting had subsided somewhat. About 5,000 bandits caused as many deaths annually, the victims usually innocent peasants.

How does the Colombian Infantry-man confront these bandit elements? He operates from small, widely distributed patrol bases, located within the seven brigade zones. To offset the lack of transportation, the soldiers rely on accurate, up-to-the-minute intelligence about bandit activities. Gradually, those peasants who have previously feared to "squeal" on the bandits because of terrorism are being won over by the Infantryman's demonstrated friendship plus his ability to defend them.

In an era when counterinsurgency suddenly holds the center of the stage in many regions of the world, it is surprising to learn how many of the techniques the Colombian Infantry-man has been using for several years.

German Shepherd dogs have demonstrated their ability to track down and pick out the bandits from an innocent looking group of peasants.

A system of colored discs, pinned to the soldiers' backs and changed frequently according to a secret schedule, has offset the identification problem caused by the bandits' possession of army uniforms. Until this technique was developed, more than one village turned out to welcome the protection of the "soldiers," only to learn that they were being invaded by uniformed bandits.

Helicopters have provided both a source of aerial observation as well as a means of transportation for quick reaction forces, but the supply is always limited.

In conjunction with the National Police, the Infantry units have gradually built up accurate files on known bandits. Photographs of village residents, combined with the use of identification cards and curfews, have enabled the soldiers to control the elusive bandits' nocturnal movements.

In the evenings and on Sundays, friendly Colombian Infantrymen help the villagers drain swamps, crown roads and learn their ABCs.

The result? Trust in the army, which is more or less traditional, and trust in the nation, which is entirely new to many of these demoralized people.

In any discussion of insurgency, the inevitable question must be asked: to what extent is the Colombian insurgency controlled or directed by the international

Communist apparatus? During the past two rural wars (1949-1953, 1954-1957), there was some evidence of penetration, although non-Communist leaders are generally conceded to have retained effective control over most of the combatants. However, the resolution of Colombia's political problems in 1958 coincided most unfortunately with the takeover of Cuba by Fidel Castro, who announced his intention of turning the entire Colombian Andes into a giant Sierra Maestre of South America. Ostensibly, the bandits would become the nucleus of the revolution, and the bearded Cuban would direct it himself. Attempts have been made to arm and train the bandits, and shipments of Cuban propaganda have been seized by Colombian authorities. Castro agents entering a bandit-ridden village in Colombia recently announced their plan for general insurgency leading to a national revolution. The bandit leader replied that he had run the village for several years and was not about to turn over his authority to "some Cuban" whom he had never seen, whereupon he killed the two agents.

This incident is significant, for it answers the fundamental question: if the Colombian Infantryman is so proficient at counterinsurgency, why does the banditry prevail? The answer is that the Colombian bandits neither have nor accept any real political direction. The soldier faces several hundred groups, all hating each other and the world they live in, all killing because they prefer killing to working. It was the way of their fathers before them, and it will be the way of their children until a re-education process is completed. But while the process is going on under the auspices of the government's social and economic programs, someone must protect the people. This the Colombian soldier does valiantly, often at the expense of his life. But he is not alone in his struggle. A U.S. Army Military Mission advises actively, often taking the field to view the latest bandit ravages. Colombian officers and enlisted men are trained at the U.S. Army School of the Americas in the Panama Canal Zone (see "CARIB COIN," *Infantry*, November-December 1962), where they can study anything from small arms repair to regimental tactics and where their personal experiences make valuable contributions to the Counterinsurgency Operations Course.

A typical week in the life of a Colombian Infantry company on public order duty shows why the troops are rotated frequently. Monday through Wednesday might find most of the troops out on long range reconnaissance patrols. The patrol bases, five or six per rifle company, are manned by security personnel. The patrols gather information on the terrain and bandit activities, visiting isolated villages to reassure the people. Logistical support is limited, and the soldiers supplement their diet by hunting while on the march. By Thursday, information may point to an impending bandit attack. A raid or ambush is planned, sometimes near the intended target village but preferably near the bandit hideout in the mountains. The company moves to the selected attack site, capitalizing on the information gleaned earlier in the week. If the bandits are not tipped off, the raid may yield several prisoners and enough bandit casualties to suppress operations in that particular zone for a few months. On Saturday, the company brings in its prisoners and conducts a critique on the combat action. Perhaps on Sunday an army surgeon will visit the company base, from which he will be escorted to the neediest villages by a combat patrol. As the doctor renders the first formal medical aid that some of the people have ever seen, the soldiers teach the people to read and write Spanish, assist in cleaning out drainage ditches or digging wells, and incidentally, convince the people that cooperation with the army is more sensible than collusion with the bandits.

The Colombian Infantryman is a first class fighting man. He traces his origins to the Battle of Ayacucho (1824), the "Yorktown" of the South American wars for independence, where, on a windswept plain a young Gen. Jose Maris Cordoba stepped forward and shouted, "Division forward, arms at discretion! Step of conquerors!" The tough, rag-tag volunteers closed on the Spanish regulars in a rush and drove them from the field in a fierce bayonet assault. The final three words of this unusual command, translated as *Paso de Vencedores*, are the motto of the Colombian Infantry. They have been bravely borne, through the wars for independence, through civil confusion bordering upon anarchy, against the Communist hordes in Korea, in an ugly political war where impartiality was difficult, under the glare of world opinion during the United Nations action in Suez, and finally in that most difficult and thankless of all Infantryman's tasks: counterinsurgency operations in his own country. The Colombian Infantryman's ability to control the banditry may well be the decisive factor which will enable his country to solve the difficult problems facing it, without abandoning the framework of democracy.

The annual death toll due to banditry has numbered in the thousands during the past 15 years. This year, for the first time, the incidence rate of bandit attacks has been reduced by half, and several famous bandit chiefs have been brought to heel. Recent articles in Time Magazine, verified by letters to the author form Colombian sources, have indicated that this is the first year in which the banditry has not been the largest political crisis facing the nation.

Russell W. Ramsey, Ph.D., D.Min.

EUROPEAN INFLUENCE

"The Spanish Military Orders," (British) *Army Quarterly & Defence Journal*, July 1983.

The Panamanian Guardia Nacional overthrew the civilian government in 1968 and, by 1979, had renegotiated the Panama Canal treaties with the United States. The Argentine Army seized power in 1976, curbed its worst abuses in late 1979, and then took on the United Kingdom in a losing war for the Falkland Islands in 1982. Elements of the Cuban Army overthrew a civilian dictator in 1933, and were in turn overthrown by militarized revolutionaries in 1959. The Cuban Army is now a major Communist power in the world arena. The El Salvadorian Army claims, since 1979, to be saving the country from Cuban revolutionaries, while others claim that the Army is itself a cause of popular resistance.

All of these are examples of the politically deliberative role played by the army in countries, which are supposedly Constitutional Republics. The mother country Spain is only in the eighth year of civilian rule, in her third attempt to function politically as a Republic. Western observers see in this apparently hypocritical process a pathology, rather than an ancient culture attempting to fit into a rationalistic political form. A whole sector of the western intelligentsia has even concocted an unscientific Marxist guilt theory, within whose convenient rhetoric the United States military forces are supposed to have created militarism in Latin Amana.

Curiously, the Whig-liberal guilt theory of the contemporary intelligentsia remembers knighthood in one of its forms – the Prussian Junker tradition – and projects it eclectically into the complex political milieu of Spain and her eighteen former colonies in America.

Completely ignored in etiological approaches to political management of Constitutional Republics by the armed forces of Spain and Hispanic America is the most important legacy of Spanish knighthood.

The Military Orders of Alcantara, Calatrava, and Santiago were vital forces in the formation of early modern Spain, and their mystique survives in the armies of Spain and the eighteen Hispanic American republics. They played a military role in driving the moors out of Spain, and an economic and social role in repopulating the land with Spaniards. Following three centuries as frontier combat forces and colonizers, they imparted their values and institutional forms to the men who conquered Spanish America. Knowledge of these processes is vital to an understanding of contemporary Spanish and Spanish American military attitudes.

Spain in the twelfth century consisted of three kingdoms: Leon, Castile, and Argon. Strong Islamic forces occupied the southern half of the country, and when Moorish leaders went over to the offensive, they imported crusading knights who consolidated southern Spain firmly under Moorish control between 1145 and 1150.

Alfonso VII of Leon determined to challenge the Moors and initiated a counterattack to the south.

The Spanish campaign depended upon retaining the Castle of Calatrava, south of Toledo in modern Spain. The Moors threatened to take it by storm, and Sancho III of Castile offered to award control of the castle to any Spanish force, which could defend it. Two monks organized an enthusiastic force of soldiers and colonizers in 1158. These forces held the castle, occupied the surrounding key terrain, and drove away the Moors. One of the leaders, Ramundo Sierra, then organized his forces permanently as a crusading colony of military friars, calling it the Order of Calatrava. By this act the first of the military orders was born, and a powerful new Spanish organization was actively fighting the Moors.

The Order of Alcantara was formed in 1218 as a frontier force on the Portuguese boarder. It was formed from a small, local order of military friars who were pledged to hold the Castle of Alcantara against the Moors, to the south. They were also supposed to colonize the Spanish border with Portugal. Thus, the Order of Alcantara, like Calatrava, was created out of necessity to hold a castle but ended up by becoming a military and social force on the Spanish frontier.

Most famous by far of the Spanish military orders was the Order of Santiago, founded in 1170 near the fortified town of Caseras in Leon. The order was established by a nucleus of thirteen crusading friars who already enjoyed military fame. They enlisted hundreds of young men under strict discipline and launched a campaign against Moorish strongholds south and west of Toledo. By 1172, the Order of Santiago had been awarded several castles and stewardship over vast lands on the Moorish frontier. Their missions were the same as those given to Calatrava and Alcantara namely to fight the Moors, guard the borders, and colonize.

The Military Orders developed a discipline, which was not seen among the crusading armies of the secular nobles. The friars lived under monastic vows of poverty and obedience, but also trained vigorously as soldiers. They wore a habit, which was modified for horseback riding and adorned with a cross and cockleshells or lilies. Mounted friars wore chain mail, under the habit, and a metal helmet. Most were armed with a metal-tipped wooden lance and a two-handed steel sword. Infantry friars carried a crossbow, a quiver of darts, and a short sword. Their bodies were protected by a leather vest with shoulder coverings.

While warfare of that era usually consisted of individual fights between opposing pairs of soldiers, the military orders developed effective organizational systems. Certain friars were trained to carry out logistical tasks. There were strict rules for the guarding of prisoners and the protection of non-combatants. The sick and wounded were cared for as wards of the order. Settlers were always brought into newly captured regions, and civil government was established. Thus, the orders added a civilizing dimension to their combat effectiveness.

By the middle of the thirteenth century, eighty years after the orders were established, Spanish forces had consolidated a frontier along the southern rim of modern Spain. In great battles like Las Navas de Tolosa (1212), Trujillo (1233), Cordoba (1236), Jaen (1246) and Seville (1248), the Moors were driven south to the Mediterranean shore. Their last political capital was at Granada. Legendary exploits by the friars of the three military orders gave the Spanish forces a distinct psychological advantage. Across Western Europe and within the cities of the northern Moslem world, tales circulated of the Santiago friars charging their enemies with the cry, "Santiago, *a ellos!*" (St. James, at them!).

For the next two centuries, the military orders functioned as armed landlords, collecting taxes, providing social services, and when needed, supplying armed forces to put clown Moorish rebellions. They also served as a stabilizing political force, since they held allegiance to the Pope. This minimized political friction between the three competing Spanish kingdoms. Then, near the middle of the fifteenth century, Spain was unified through the marriage of Ferdinand of Aragon and Isabella of Castile.

The three orders lived through one last era of military glory; this was followed by their passing as autonomous institutions. In 1474, Ferdinand and Isabella organized all their forces for the last campaign of the Reconquest and this culminated with the capture of Granada in 1492. Hundreds of friars in the red tunic of Santiago, the dark red of Calatrava, and the dark green of Alcantara, perished in this campaign. Ferdinand and Isabella, realizing that they could not govern a united Spain which contained autonomous religious armies with vast property now had – in 1493 – the orders converted to an honorary status. Their armed units were disbanded and their vast landholdings were turned over to officials of the monarchy.

As the years passed the spirit of Alcantara, Calatrava, and Santiago became embodied in legend, belief and behavior; all was sanctioned by splendid titles in the lodges, which bore their names. Most colonial officials of Spanish America were knights of officer rank in one of the three military orders and later, well after the Latin American revolutions for independence, military and civil officials obtained status through membership in one of the orders.

Most observers of the Hispanic military officer see the quest for individual and political glory, typified in the eleventh century legend of Rodrigo Diaz de Bivar, "El Cid." Closer observation reveals a sense of holy purpose, coupled with an easy assumption of civil duties by soldiers. These values are the legacy of the Military Orders of Alcantara, Calatrava, and Santiago, whose friars communicated directly with God on the field of battle, and guarded the social order humanely and constructively in times of peace. This is the perspective through which military officers of Spain and Hispanic America often view their role as guardians of the constitutional democracy.

Other aspects of the Spanish and Hispanic-American military forces are also ignored by the contemporary intelligentsia. Latin America and Spain are less militarized, whether expressed as a percentage of the population or of the gross national product, than any world region with a common cultural base. Their history of warfare, expressed in number of wars or number of deaths, is considerably lower than any major world region. There is even a positive and rational argument for the peacekeeping and civilizing role of the Hispanic-American armed forces, especially in remote, primitive areas. But any deep understanding of behavior by the military leaders in Spain and Latin America needs to be rooted in the ideology and actions of the Military Orders of Alcantara, Calatrava, and Santiago.

"The Defeat of Admiral Vernon at Cartagena in 1741," *The Southern Quarterly*, July, 1963.

"THE SPANISH PRIDE PULLED DOWN BY ADMIRAL VERNON" was the inscription over the kneeling figure of General Bias de Lezo on the bronze medal. On the reverse side appeared the words, *"WHO TOOK PORTO BELLO WITH SIX SHIPS ONLY."* The medals were cast by the overeager British when it appeared both the Spanish main seaport of Porto Bello and the British popular imagination in 1739, would do the same at Cartagena in 1741. The purpose for the discussion at hand is to explore the causes for the failure of a great amphibious assault, which was undertaken by a force under command of Vernon against the Spanish military bastion of Cartagena, presently the historic city of Cartagena, Colombia. There is no mystery about the outcome of the assault, for it was unsuccessful. The British forces were resoundingly defeated, causing a great and justly proud celebration among the defenders of Spain's weakening new world empire.

This battle, while it must be a study in failure, is significant for a number of reasons. First, although it was part of a larger war, it was an isolated battle in that war; it cannot, therefore, be given the classic military analysis in the setting of a larger campaign. Second, the invasion attempt was opposed by the faltering Walpole administration in England and was undertaken by popular demand against the better judgment of Vernon himself, sometime seadog, sometime member of Parliament, who had made good his boast that he could singe the power of Spain with minor forces at the less formidable fortress of Porto Bello. Third, the battle was hampered by virtue of its being a novel effort, an amphibious assault, while little doctrinal precedent. Where Winston Churchill's favorite Dardanelles project was to fail a century and a half later in 1915, so was this one doomed at the outset, and for many of the same reasons. That the same nation, which attempted it, was to fail again in the later venture is a classic illustration of failure to use the historical lesson.

There is a less obvious, somewhat sinister virulent behind this famous battle, which saw the champion of Protestantism pitted against the pillars of Catholicism, as indeed Cartagena was the very site of the Inquisition in New Granada. This undercurrent is found in the ancient hatred between Spaniard and Anglo-Saxon, stemming from the days of the many-sided rivalry between Elizabeth I and Phillip II. Spaniards, and modern day Colombians, can never forget that the British had victory medals struck in bronze before Vernon reached the main forts of Cartagena. Nor can they forget the frenzied preparations, which preoccupied for many years the coastal garrisons of the Spanish Main, preparations for the legendary *El Draque,* Sir Francis Drake, greatest of the British pirate-admirals. Although Drake was long dead and buried in a dramatic ceremony off the harbor at Porto Bello, *"El Draque"* was the cry of terror which accompanied the approach of every man-of-war bearing the British flag off the Spanish Main for decades. That Vernon should inherit the reputation and the title of pirate can hardly be blamed against the Spanish garrisons, who guarded what they legally claimed and undertook no aggression against England's American colonies. But from a legal point of view Vernon was no pirate, for a pirate is defined in maritime law as a robber of the high seas who neither owes allegiance to nor is sanctioned by any nation. Nor was he even a privateer, for he undertook this adventure, and all others of the period, in official vessels of the British Navy.

That Vernon was defeated is an interesting study in military history; that he undertook the assault in the first place is another brick in the immense wall of hate and prejudice which divides the worlds of Elizabeth I and Phillip II. Vernon's premature victory medal is displayed in the British Imperial War Museum with a typically restrained note to the effect that it was never issued because the attack suffered reverses. Columbians who maintain the restored fortifications at Cartagena have neatly underlined the words 'prematurely engraved medal' on the placard, which displays it.

The Political and Military Setting for the Battle

The attack upon Cartagena by Admiral Vernon was a battle between two European colonial giants over possessions of a particular colony; reduced to its simplest form, it was England's rejection of Spain's monopoly upon the Spanish Main. It was a little war within a larger worldwide struggle, which was going on between declining agrarian Spain and rising mercantile England. The struggle was complicated by the deeply seated religious, cultural, and national animosities, which existed between the two countries.

England was under the liberal administration of Sir Robert Walpole, the able but failing leader of the Whigs. George II reigned as limited monarch over a country, which was then in the throes of a nascent industrial revolution, the first in the world. British sea power was a mighty factor in world politics and also a powerful domestic issue. This sea power is loosely referred to in history as the British Navy, but it was actually a combination of an official navy, a gigantic merchant fleet, and various types of semi-official adventurers ranging from privateers to outright pirates. This dabbling in semi-official naval adventures led England into continuous disputes with Spain for a period of over two centuries and has given rise to a great and almost legendary epoch of naval seizures conducted by the Spanish authorities upon British shipping in the Caribbean.[1] The fact that these ships engaged in regular smuggling which violated both the spirit and the letter of numerous treaty arrangements between the two nations[2] did not dampen British nationalistic feeling; when a bellicose naval officer claimed that Spanish power in the Caribbean area was more apparent than real, he commanded an audience.

This officer was Admiral Sir Edward Vernon. Born in 1684, the second son of a cabinet minister, Vernon was educated well before his naval training.[3] He enjoyed a career of spectacular success, rising quickly from the ranks of the junior naval officers to the command of sixty-gun and seventy-gun ships-of-the-line. He served several terms as a member of Parliament during periods of relative naval tranquility and cleverly used a combination of his naval reputation and his violent oratorical style in the Parliament to promote aggressive action against Spain. Although other naval authorities saw clearly that the trouble between Spain and England in the Caribbean was the result of smuggling by English mercantile interests in Jamaica, Vernon pressed home the claim that Porto Bello, formerly the cornerstone of Spanish commercial defenses, could be taken with only six ships.[4] A number of forces combined in Vernon's favor to bring about the venture. Vernon was persuasive and was respected as a naval leader. Walpole was rapidly losing popularity, especially with the vested commercial interest, and virtually any issue to embarrass him was acceptable to the opposition, of which Vernon was a member. Porto Bello was an exceptionally fine choice for a target, as Vernon well knew, for in its harbor the Spanish *guardia costas* (coast guards or customs inspection vessels) were sheltered and fitted out for operations.[5] To these other factors favoring the decision to attack must be added the great intangible, the traditional hatred for the Spanish which produced a ceaseless desire to humiliate them at any opportunity.

Something of the intensity of this hatred can be gleaned from the wording of this portion of the king's message to the colonial governors about the situation:

> *Having been called upon by repeated provocations to declare war against Spain, we are determined by God's assistance in so just a Cause to vindicate the honor of our imperial crown to revenge the injuries done to our subjects... and by all possible means to attack, annoy, and distress a nation that has treated our people with such insolence and barbarity. We have therefore given orders for the equipping and setting forth an expedition against the territories of the Catholic King in the West Indies.*[6]

Thus, the apparent cause of conflict was the commercial rivalry, but the Puritan hatred for all things Catholic is rather transparent, especially when one considers that England was giving official sanction to her corsairs in the West Indies.

Vernon was raised to the rank of vice admiral on 9 July 1739 and instructed on 19 July to "destroy the Spanish settlements in the West Indies and to distress their shipping by every method whatever." [7] This fact is an interesting one, because war was not declared upon Spain until 19 October. [8] Prime Minister Walpole evidently had not forgotten Vernon's claim that he could take Porto Bello with six ships, for several units were detached from Vernon's command for another expedition, leaving Vernon exactly six ships-of-the-line. On 20 November 1739 Vernon led his small squadron into the harbor of Porto Bello, took the city and all its fortifications in one day, lost only seven me, and caused a national hysteria in England. Medals were struck showing Vernon's head with the inscription, *"HE TOOK PORTO BELLO WITH SIX SHIPS ONLY,"* likenesses of Vernon's head began to appear on taverns; Parliament voted him its thanks, and he was very much the man of the hour.[9] Today's visitor to Port Bello can still witness the devastation he brought upon that very old and historic city.

Although no one knew it at the time, Vernon's easy victory at Port Bello was probably the most fortunate thing, which happened to Spain for the remainder of the century. President of Panama, Don Dionisio Martinez de la Vega, had begged the mother country repeatedly to improve Porto Bello's defenses, it had not been done; thus, Vernon's victory was actually achieved over a mighty fortification whose defenses were in disrepair and most of whose artillery was not even placed for combat. Vernon probably recognized the actual dimension of what he had achieved, for he went on to recommend that England not engage in further attacks upon the mainland of the Spanish empire but rather concentrate upon naval warfare, which, he felt, would produce the greatest gains for the less effort.[10] But England was blinded with a wave of martial spirit, and unwise counsel prevailed over Walpole's protest[11] As a result, Vernon was reinforced not only with a tremendous naval squadron but also with a large detachment of marines and infantry, whose purpose was clearly a land battle. Attempting to pursue the course he deemed best, Vernon bombarded the city of Cartagena on 6 March 1740, causing a flurry of excitement but accomplishing little. Then he sailed up the coast to Chagre, a fortification on the Chagres River known historically as Fort San Lorenzo, and captured it on 24 March 1740.[12] Retiring to Port Royal, Jamaica, Vernon issued his famous order for the new rum commonly issued to British sailors to be diluted heavily with water, resulting in his nickname of "Old Grog" and placing the famous term "grog" in the English nautical vocabulary. This act had the practical effect of reducing the rampant drunkenness common among sailors of the period and greatly improving the efficiency of Vernon's fleet.[13]

On 7 January 1741, another large reinforcement for the purpose of the Cartagena attack was sent to Vernon in the form of twenty-five fighting ships under Rear Admiral Sir Chaloner Ogle and a force of 9,000 soldiers.[14] The commander of these soldiers was the excellent Major General Charles, Lord Cathcart, who unfortunately died while the expedition was still in the planning stages. The successor to command was a Brigadier General Wentworth, about whom little is known except that he was militarily incompetent.[15] A small but interesting component of the reinforcements sent to Vernon was a detachment of British colonials from both Jamaica and North America. The following is a portion of the royal decree, which went out to the colonial governors on 2 April 1740:

> The fleet to be commanded by our trusty and well-beloved Edward Vernon, Esquire, Vice Admiral of the Blue Squadron of our fleet... and the land forces by our right trusty and well-beloved Charles, Lord Cathcart whom we have appointed... Commander in Chief of the said expedition. We have also determined to raise a body of troops in our colonies on the continent of North America to join those to be sent from hence... And although we have not thought fit to fix any particular quota for our province... under your government... we doubt not in the least bit they will exert themselves upon this occasion as far as the circumstances of the colony will allow...[16]

One source indicates that a total of 2,763 colonial troops participated;[17] another states that 2,000 axemen were recruited in Jamaica along with some 400 Negroes.[18] The Virginia quota of 400 men was commanded by Governor William Gooch;

Laurence Washington, half-brother of George, became a captain in the unit, which had to be filled with convicts to meet the quota. The elder Washington participated only slightly in the fight, but his observation of it resulted in many war tales, which influenced the boy George, and in the naming of the Washington property after Vernon.[19]

As the rainy season on the Caribbean coast approached, a considerable amount of time was lost in quibbling over command and techniques; as a result, the combined amphibious expedition did not actually reach Cartagena until 3 March 1741. The fleet sailed in three elements under Vernon, Ogle, and Commodore Lestock. During the voyage several days were lost in searching for a potentially hostile French fleet known to be at large in the Caribbean. Although contact was not made with this fleet, a French frigate brought a full account of the invasion plans to Cartagena.[20] Notwithstanding the unpropitious beginning of the operation, the British force which arrived at Cartagena was a formidable one indeed. It contained eight seventy-gun ships, ten forty-gun ships, five thirty-gun ships, twelve twenty-gun frigates, twelve ten-gun corvettes, and four six-gun sloops, for sailors. This fleet escorted an amphibious force of one hundred thirty-six transports manned by fifty marines each. Thus, before the land forces were even included, the fleet strength was 13,590 men. Army elements consisted of about 9,000 soldiers who were distributed around the transports. This total strength of 22,590 men on hundred eighty-seven ships mounting a total 1,490 cannons was a powerful force for an expedition when more important encounters were taking place on the European battlefields of the War of the Austrian Succession.[21]

The Spanish setting for the battle was quite different, for the Spanish were faced with very different problems and entertained other ambitions. The policy of economic exploitation was being carried out in her American colonies as the economic base upon which Spain built her European schemes. Nevertheless, the military emphasis in Spain's American empire was primarily defensive whereas England's was aggressive. Salvador de Madariaga has pointed out that the Spanish garrisons in the new world sought no domination over other colonial areas and that England's aggressive naval policies were therefore unwarranted.[22] The question of colonial claims and the rights to those claims is a devious one with no definite end, but the fact remains that Spain's naval power was primarily designed for customs inspection of foreign traders in her colonial waters and for convoy duty of her cargo ships. Military power in the Spanish Main was concentrated along the coastal bastions for defensive employment against predatory naval attacks; the soldiers and their leaders were, at this time, mostly Spaniards, the day of the Creole military class being in the near future.

A temporary cessation of hostilities in the War of the Spanish Succession had brought an era of relative tranquility to the Spanish Main. However, an increase in predatory efforts, primarily British, put Spain back on her guard. The presidency of New Granada was raised to the status of a viceroyalty in 1739 by royal cedula, placing it on a par with the Viceroyalties of Peru and New Spain. The reasons for this action are not certain in Spanish history, but strong among the evidence is the fact that such a move was warranted by a desire to strengthen the region militarily and politically against British encroachments. The generally discredited Jenkins ear incident, used to whip up war fever in England, was most annoying to the Spaniards. Phillip V was further shocked by the capture of Porto Bello, which was not only a loss in prestige but which also was considered an act of betrayal. Stern measures were directed against England, to include the eviction of all Englishmen from Spain, termination of all legal trade with England, the dispatch of naval military forces against several English strongholds in Europe, and the outfitting of Spanish privateers to prey upon English shipping.[23]

Because the departure from England of Vernon's forces was accompanied by the equipping of Commodore George Anson with a rather motley fleet to prey upon the Pacific coastal ports of the Viceroyalty of Peru, the proposed attack upon Cartagena was a grave threat. If Cartagena should fall and a British force be lodged upon the Pacific coast as well, the Viceroyalties of Peru and New Granada might be cut in two; it was even conceivable that England might capture the entire continent of South America, which was lightly defended.[24] With the elevation of New Granada to the status of viceroyalty, and eminent Spanish military figure, Don Sebastian de Eslava, a lieutenant general in the royal army, was selected to be the new viceroy. He did not govern from Bogotá, normally the capital, for the reason that he had been chosen for the express purpose of leading the defense efforts at Cartagena.[25]

Eslava joined Don Melchor de Navarrete, Governor of the city of Cartagena and the adjacent district, and General Blas de Lezo, who commanded the local defense forces, in preparations for Vernon's onslaught. It was commonly believed that Vernon's success was practically inevitable;[26] Eslava immediately set about raising confidence and bettering the defenses of the city.[27] On the eve of battle the Spanish fortifications were almost as formidable to the attackers as Vernon's host must have seemed to the defenders. There was a small naval force of six ships-of-the line, each mounting forty guns and carrying a total crew of 1,300 sailors and marines. This force was augmented by an amphibious squadron of six galleons or troop transports, carrying an additional three hundred marines, and about one hundred smaller vessels not large enough to classify as warships. The thirty-gun French frigate, which had brought word of the invasion plans, was also present in the harbor. Spanish land forces included the Aragon Regiment of four hundred men, the Crown Regiment of 1,100 men, the Victory Regiment of six hundred men, two hundred veteran artillerymen formed into two batteries, two hundred local artillerymen (unseasoned) formed into two batteries, five hundred hired militiamen, and 1,500 Creole volunteers. These elements were in addition to the naval elements; by including a number of service troops, the total Spanish strength became 6,600 men, of whom 2,500 soldiers and 1,800 sailors were combat veterans, the rest being volunteers recruited locally for the emergency. This force was, of course, decidedly smaller than the attacking force.[28]

Eslava decided to command the defense forces in the main fort personally, choosing as his adjutant, which corresponded to executive officer, Melchor de Navarrete. The ships and smaller protective forts were placed under command of de Lezo, a grizzled veteran with one eye, one arm, and one leg.[29] Generally speaking, the fortifications consisted of one major fort, Castillo de San Felipe de Barajas, which mounted forty-four cannons, and five minor forts containing a total of one hundred six additional cannons. The entire system was protected by fortified trenches mounting a total of two hundred seventy-five more cannons of various calibers. Total firepower at Cartagena was four hundred twenty-five cannons, with a great supply of balls and powder. A protective boom was placed across the mouth of the harbor at Boca Chica.[30]

Aside from their tremendous desire to protect Spanish holdings in the new world, there was another factor motivating the Spanish garrison. Cartagena had been captured and ransomed by Sir Francis *Drake in 1585 and by the French*, to the tune of one million pounds of sterling, in 1697; the citizens had never forgotten the plundering and the indignities to which they had been subjected.[31] Thus, Cartagena was being defended by resolute and even desperate men who were defending Spanish possessions from the English, avenging Spanish military honor, and realizing well their fate if the British were successful.

Conduct of the Battle

The British fleet hove to off the coast of Cartagena on 3 March 1741. A sailing fleet of such size and variety of ships required some time to reassemble after a long sea voyage, and there was disagreement between Vernon and Wentworth over the question of where to land the troops. The fleet therefore spent the next few days reconnoitering the coastline while the commanders held councils of war.[32] A small Spanish sailing vessel from Havana had encountered the British upon their arrival at Cartagena, reported the size, direction, and several days after units of the fleet actually began assembling in the area. De Lezo informed Eslava of the report, and the Spanish garrison was put on full alert.[33]

On 13 March at 9:00 am, three British men-of-war were sighted off the main plaza of Cartagena. At noon, the larger two ships anchored near the Boca Chica entrance; the smaller one tacked up and down during the afternoon and anchored for the night with the other two. By 15 March, the British fleet completed its assembly some distance off Punta Canoa. Eslava sent four of his six warships out to the Boca Chica fortifications as a mobile reinforcement.[34] From 13 to 16 March, the British explored the marsh at Tesca, north of the main plaza, with the hope of finding deep water. There was, however, only one deep-water entrance to the bay, and that entrance was well protected. If a passage could be forced over the marsh at Tesca, about one-half of the fortification would have been bypassed without a shot being fired. But deep water could not be found, and sending the troops against the seawall from outside the harbor would have been suicidal. On 17 March Vernon abandoned the idea and transferred most of the fleet and all the transports down to Tierra Bomba Island, where preparations were begun for bombardment of the fortifications guarding Boca Chica.

At daylight on 18 March, an intense bombardment from both land and sea was initiated by the British against the outlying fortifications around Boca Chica. The garrisons responded enthusiastically, but the British were able to bring more cannons to bear and bomb many directions. After fierce bombardment for two days, thirty-one of the defenders' cannons had literally been blown off the mountings, and the parapets of the forts and trenches were reduced to rubble.[35] With these secondary fortifications (Santiago and San Felipe) reduced, Vernon was now free to land a much greater force on Tierra Bomba.[36] About five hundred cannons were set up for the reduction of the forts of San Luis and San Jose. Five days were consumed in preparing the batteries for firing, during which time Vernon became furious and urged Wentworth to make all possible haste. The wet season was beginning in earnest, making land movement, sea navigation and emplacement of artillery, observation, and health conditions very unsatisfactory. Time was very much on the side of the Spanish, but Wentworth blamed the delays on the slowness of his engineers and Vernon's failure to silence the Spanish secondary defenses.[37] Vernon retorted angrily that delay constituted treachery and that any engineer guilty of it should be court-martialed and shot.[38] A road was built through the woods to the north side of Fort San Luis, and elaborate fortifications were erected only three hundred meters from the fort. Finally, the bombardment began on 25 March.[39]

Fort San Luis was defended by about two hundred fifty men under command of a military engineer named Colonel Carlos Des Noux; it mounted twenty cannons. Fire was returned spiritedly from the fort and from the four warships supporting the Boca Chica defenses. On the first day Des Noux lost fifty men, and the walls of the fort threatened to crumble. Eslava and de Lezo paid the defenders a sudden visit during the bombardment and remained two full days. They were convinced that the fort was lost and instructed Des Noux to abandon it when further resistance was hopeless. Returning to the city, they dispatched some small ships for the evacuation of the garrison at Boca Chica.[40]

The British bombardment, in addition to more than five hundred land-based cannons, was supported throughout by a minimum of ten ships-of-the-line, all mounting at least fifty-guns. Nevertheless, the Spanish defenders were able to inflict numerous casualties among the attackers. On the night of 5 April, Des Noux led his battered survivors down to the small ships and evacuated the Boca Chica defenses. The four supporting ships were set afire and sunk in the main channel of the outer bay, but one fell into British hands in time to be saved. British naval elements cut the boom across the mouth of the harbor, and the British fleet sailed into the outer bay.[41]

Vernon felt that there was still every chance for success. He unwisely dispatched Captain Laws with the *Spence,* carrying the famous message which told of great success and imminent final victory; England went into new waves of hysteria.[42] The famous bronze medals were struck, showing General Blas de Lezo kneeling at the feet of Vernon in the act of handing over his sword; the Porto Bello triumph was alluded to on the reverse side.[43] Vernon had become convinced during his easy success at Porto Bello that the secret to overcoming the Spanish had been aroused and granted time to prepare, their defensive recalcitrance was legendary.[44] Therefore, Vernon urged Wentworth to mount an immediate assault against Fort San Lazaro, situated on commanding terrain above the city and accessible to troops by covered approaches.[45]

De Lezo, commanding the exterior fortifications still in Spanish hands, reinforced the garrisons at Fort Castillo Grande and Fort Manzanillo; the remaining two Spanish warships, together with the French frigate, were placed in the canal, which leads from the inner harbor to the small bay on the north side of the main plaza of the city. On 7 April Vernon anchored his ships near the mouth of the inner harbor and commenced a tremendous naval bombardment against the city and Fort Castillo Grande.[46] The entire artillery system of the defenses responded, and the cannon duel raged for eight days. Wentworth's infantry was largely aboard the transport ships in the bay during this bombardment. On 15 April, Eslava, de Lezo, Des Noux, and a Colonel Bernardo de Fuentes (commander of Fort Castillo Grande) held a conference aboard the Spanish warship *El Conquistador* and decided that Castillo Grande could hold out for only two more days. The cannons were therefore spiked, the parapets destroyed, and the troops evacuated on 16 April; a few hours later Vernon's marines stormed the fortification and took possession of it. The two Spanish ships which were blockading the canal *(El Conquistador* and *El Dragon),* the French frigate, and six galleons were stripped, burned, and sunk in the canal in such a way that passage was blocked.[47]

On 16 and 17 April Vernon concentrated upon reducing Fort Manzanillo, and still no troops had landed. On the night of 17 April this fort was abandoned by its defenders and occupied by the English. Vernon was now able to land the troops unresisted. The soldiers disembarked on the beach of Isla de Gracias at a point just north of Fort Manzanillo. A small advance over the road leading into the city was made against the Spanish infantry under de Lezo, who delayed as long as he could with the troops at his disposal and then retired. While this advance was taking place, Vernon sent naval elements over to the blocked canal for the purpose of clearing a passage; after two days of Herculean efforts the *El Conquistador* was raised and moved, partially opening the canal.[48]

Vernon had now done nearly all that the fleet could do in the way of support. He urged the irresolute Wentworth to mount an immediate attack against Fort San Felipe de Barajas and its surrounding fortifications. But relations between the two had broken down completely, and Wentworth seemed to place more importance at this time upon making his own decisions than on making correct ones. He also wanted Vernon to send a squadron through the canal to bombard the city from the tiny inner bay; a scheme, which Vernon correctly judged to be impossible.[49] As a result, Wentworth waited three more days before undertaking the main offensive. This gave the Spanish time to redistribute personnel from the fallen fortifications into the garrisons and to replenish supplies of ball and powder. Early in the morning of 20 April, Wentworth's attack finally began. He sent two columns to capture the monastery at La Popa and Fort Lazaro, both located on the high ground behind the city. For some reason he felt no confidence in the colonial regiments and left them largely aboard ships.[50] Thus he undertook his most critical action without using all his available strength. Lawrence Washington had found favor with Vernon and, although not permitted ashore by Wentworth, was made Captain of Marines aboard Vernon's flagship, from which post he observed the final phases of the attack.[51] Wentworth's attack was further weakened by the fact that yellow fever had set in among the troops during the long period of shipboard confinement; some of the men had not touched land since departing Jamaica, and others had been camped in swampland under the broiling tropical sun for days. They were hardly in condition for an attack through heavily wooded terrain up a very steep slope.

Early on the morning of 20 April the smaller force, numbering 2,000, succeeded in taking the convent at La Popa. The larger column, numbering over 3,000, had become separated during the long march upwards. The advance guard of 1,200 men under a Colonel J. Grant had acquired the services of a Portuguese deserter as a guide. This force approached Fort San Lazaro shortly after daybreak, although the plan had been to attack before sunrise. Colonel Grant hoped to deceive the Spaniards into thinking that his little force was reinforcement for one of the other forts marching out from the city. The deputy commander of San Lazaro, Captain Pedrol, watched while the British packed themselves into a narrow defile leading into the main gate of the fort. At the most appropriate moment, he gave the order to fire. The main batteries of the fort opened up on the British column, doing indescribable damage. Colonel Grant went down with the first volley, and no one was capable of taking over command. Confusion reigned supreme and was compounded by the discovery that the scaling ladders which the advance elements were carrying were too short to reach the tops of the walls. The force broke into fragments and ran back down the hill, leaving over four hundred dead, seventy-three wounded, and a large quantity of arms, ladders, and ammunition abandoned. As the advance guard pulled back in disorder, the main body of the force arrived. Failing to understand the cause of the initial disaster, its commander led it forward directly into the same defile. By this time adjacent fortifications had opened up from both flanks, and the British suffered over three hundred more dead and twenty-two wounded before extricating themselves.[52]

While Wentworth's infantry was suffering this reverse, Vernon's sailors and marines were giving a better account of themselves. The key fortification on the south side of the city at Pastelillo had been seized, although its garrison defended it to the last man. From this point a strong cannon fire was brought to bear directly on the city. In an effort to give Wentworth some artillery support, the salvaged Spanish warship *Galicia* (seized during the occupation of Boca Chica) was converted into a floating cannon platform and pulled through the canal to a point behind the city. Sixteen cannons mounted upon its deck bombarded Fort Getsemani from the north side, but Forts San Javier, Santa Isabel, San Lorenzo, and San Jose (all in the main plaza of the city) converged fire upon the hulk and killed most of the cannoneers. Vernon withdrew this experimental effort, which came to a dramatic end when the ship caught fire and drifted back across the harbor to the tip of Manzanillo Island, where it became a giant torch.[53]

On 21 April, Vernon asked for a truce to remove the dead and wounded, but Eslava only agreed to the first part of the request. The English wounded had already been collected by the Spaniards and taken to hospital areas within the city. At 6:00 that afternoon, the truce ended and the exchange of cannon fire began anew. On 22 April, Vernon asked Eslava to make an exchange of prisoners. Eslava said he would agree if Vernon would release the Spanish prisoners first, but Vernon refused to take such a chance.⁵⁴ The combination of battle and disease casualties had now reduced Wentworth's force to about one-half, and morale was extremely low. From 22 April to 28 April, a desultory exchange of artillery fires was maintained, and British troops and naval elements devoted themselves to completing the destruction of the forts already captured. The wet season was now unleashing its daily downpours upon the discouraged British, who were huddled into temporary camps or crowded into the diminishing number of ships. On 29 April the British troops began to re-embark, and by 1 May, the outer bay was cleared of the last Englishmen. Refitting and reloading for the battered fleet was accomplished at points near Boca Chica, and the last British vessel set sail for Port Royal, Jamaica, on 20 May 1741. The battle was over, and Cartagena was saved.⁵⁵

British losses totaled fifteen warships, thirty-six transport ships, and perhaps as many as 12,000 personnel, including all deaths and casualties from battle and disease, the latter taking as great a toll as the former. Spanish losses were about 1,500 man, nearly all battle deaths and wounds, and to this must be added the total destruction of over half of the fortifications protecting the city, as well as a large number of buildings and several ships.⁵⁶

The other British expedition under Commodore Anson had rounded the Straits of Magellan and sailed up the Pacific coast, preying on shipping and bringing back enormous loot. It was never able to attempt any type of landing operation. Thus, with England's major attention occupied in Europe, Anson incapable of invasion (which, in hindsight, was obvious from the beginning), and Vernon stopped in his attack; Spain's American empire was saved.

Vernon and Wentworth made two more attacks, one at Santiago de Cuba and the other through Port Bello towards Panama; both were lesser efforts than the Cartagena attack and were unsuccessful. By 1742, Vernon and Wentworth were both recalled to England, the former to rise to even higher rank in the British navy and the latter to pass into obscurity. These actions constituted the hugest part of the War of Jenkins Ear and contributed no small amount to the fall of the Walpole government.⁵⁷

Eslava and the Navarrete were both promoted, but Lezo had a falling out with the viceroy and received a posthumous castigation by court-martial shortly after his death in 1742.⁵⁸ There are hundreds of interesting anecdote about the attack on Cartagena, but the main purpose here is to examine the causes of Vernon's failure.

Analysis of the Causes of Failure

The attack upon Cartagena lends itself well to analysis because it was an isolated operation. There were no logistical systems or more senior commanders close enough to the operation to shed any impact upon the outcome of events. It was a clearly and neatly defined battle in which both commanders had absolute control of all their resources.

The selection of the objective was not in error, if one accepts the proposition that the attack should have been undertaken in the first place. Admitting that Vernon advised against it, we find that at no time did he voice objection once the plans were under way in earnest. The strong character of Vernon and his outspoken opinions expressed to the king, to the admiralty, and to fellow commanders make it doubtful that he felt his chances for success to be anything other than strong. The overall objective of cutting the Spanish colonies in two by landing Vernon's and Anson's forces at opposite ends is a bit ridiculous in view of the enormity of the task and the relatively diminutive size of the forces, especially Anson's. So there is doubt that had Vernon been successful, Spain would have lost much more than Cartagena with its defensive and commercial complex. Such a loss would have been a grievous and expensive one, but the British dream of seizing the entirety of Spain's' South American empire was simply not realistic.[59] Cartagena was, therefore, the correct tactical objective, but not an objective capable of delivering the desired strategic goal. Also Vernon and Wentworth chose the correct tactical objectives throughout the course of the battle, since Boca Chica was necessary to enter the harbor and San Lazaro was necessary to cut off the city and command the high ground.

The principle of the offensive was violated by General Wentworth on at least two critical occasions. After Vernon's ships had reduced the outlying fortifications around Boca Chica, an assault should have been attempted immediately upon Fort San Luis and Fort San Jose. The total number of cannons in both was small, and they could both be taken under direct cannon fire from two sides (the fleet across the front and the land-based artillery from the north). Such an assault would have given Wentworth's pent-up troops something to do and would have caught the Spanish in the process of redistributing defensive forces. Furthermore, it would have contributed to the general feeling of invincibility, which many Spaniards felt for the British attackers.

The principle of mass does not appear to have much bearing on the attack until the final efforts at the high ground above the city. All possible forces were brought to bear upon the Boca Chica area once it had been determined that reduction of the fortifications would be necessary. Certainly the critical terrain, once the harbor was entered, was the high ground above the city, and the major effort was made against these positions. But by failing to use the colonial troops, Wentworth did not achieve superiority at the critical point; thus, regardless of how well or poorly the attack was conducted, its chances of success were ruined beforehand.

The principle of economy of force had little bearing on the British effort but was beautifully adhered to by the Spanish, who used minimum troops in delaying actions again and again, often extricating them with such precision that they could be used at the next point of resistance after achieving maximum in delay. It was undoubtedly the Spaniards' ability to adhere to this principle, resisting the temptation to send major forces out to Boca Chica, which left them with enough troops to stop the British at San Lazaro.

The principle of surprise was lost when the British allowed the Cuban sailing vessel to escape. Better discipline within the fleet would have resulted in the placing of faster ships on the periphery of the formation in order to pursue and capture any passing vessel. Since the Cuban captain had time to count Vernon's vessels and identify them in some detail, it can be assumed that he passed fairly close to the fleet.[60] Surprise was not used effectively in reducing the Boca Chica fortifications.

A diversionary effort at Boca Grande might have been staged, followed by a lightning attack at Boca Chica. Artillery could have been put ashore farther north and pulled up through the woods for this effort; as the action was actually executed, the Spanish knew of the land-based artillery and were prepared to resist it.

Closely related to the lack of surprise is the almost complete lack of security throughout the operation. Vernon's early reconnaissance work along the coastline was augmented by careful study of harbor soundings and fortifications.[61] But the Spanish invariably knew where to put their forces for effective resistance or delaying action. The greatest security violation, indeed the greatest military fiasco of the operation, was the march up to San Lazaro by Colonel Grant. Attempting the rudest of deceptions in terrain adjacent to the garrison's own home city, he led his into the classic trap, that of facing the enemy's maximum firepower in column formation with the flanks blocked to dispersion. Even without the poor employment of terrain, the attack was doomed because the garrison was able to observe the attacking formation well before it took up the assault positions. Other violations of security included the failure to use the fine natural advantage of the heavily wooded approaches to the fortifications and the failure to employ the cloak of night to mask movements. Even the hated rains might have been turned to British advantage in masking movement, had there been some employed.

The principle of simplicity was violated after the British gained entrance into the harbor. When Vernon and Wentworth were unable to agree upon tactics, each pursued different courses of action. Thus, Vernon's marines were harassing the city at the very time when Wentworth's troops were being repulsed above the city. Other elements were being employed in reduction of fortifications already captured, even though the main objective had not yet been achieved. The British failed to arrive at a single plan of action and stick to it; a multiplicity of efforts caused the Spaniards annoyance but helped guarantee their eventual success.

The principle of maneuver was well used by the Spanish, who used small elements in successive delaying actions at critical points with great effectiveness. It was well used by Vernon in placing his warships at effective points for bombardment in support of the intended ground operations, but Wentworth did not seem to understand that his troops must move in order to seize ground. Long delays, slow movements of inadequate distance, and a total lack of imagination characterized all movements by the British ground elements and prevented their ever accomplishing a decisive action. It should not pass unobserved that all fortifications which were captured were simply reduced by a preponderance of artillery.

The final principle of war is unity of command, the failure of which was the key to British disaster at Cartagena. Had Vernon and Wentworth been able to agree beforehand on the point at which one would assume command from the other, the operation would almost undoubtedly have been successful. In the early stages, when rapid ground action was needed to take advantage of the tremendous shock value of Vernon's naval command from the other, the operation would almost undoubtedly have been successful. In the early stages, when rapid ground action was needed to take advantage of the tremendous shock value of Vernon's naval bombardment, Wentworth was following a cautious course assigned for a slow reduction of a fortification by classic means. Even this idea would have been successful if the strategy had been coordinated with the naval commander, but Vernon understood that the plan called for maximum speed in breaching Boca Chica. He was therefore concentrating a terrific artillery fire upon the fortifications and preparing an assault squadron to force an entrance. Thus, even though overwhelming force succeeded in forcing an entrance into the harbor, it was done through a compromise of two plans. Once inside, there was a complete absence of coordinated land sea strategy. Wentworth desired to keep the troops aboard the ships while the defenses were reduced through naval bombardment; Vernon was planning for naval artillery support in conjunction with a rapid ground assault. In this case, mere unity of command probably would not have guaranteed success, for had Wentworth had overall command, it appears doubtful that there would have been any success at all.

A major contributing factor to Vernon's defeat at Cartagena was the excellence of the fortifications. They were the result of years of careful study by the finest available military engineers in the world, and their excellence was quickly proved by the ability of an inferior number of stationary cannons to take heavy toll of a larger number of mobile-based guns. The design of the walls undoubtedly saved many Spanish lives and held off the British attackers, although there is no question that the walls could have been scaled or breached by a resolutely led force.

The attack on Cartagena was, then, a gigantic amphibious fiasco. In the ensuing recrimination between Vernon and Wentworth, the latter has undoubtedly suffered much from Vernon's colorful and forceful personality. But the accounts of the Spanish defenses were not written amid the rivalry between the British military and naval forces, and it is therefore an accepted fact that Wentworth's performance at Cartagena was extremely poor. But had he only been able to agree with Vernon on the specific point at which one or the other was in command, even the worst of tactics might have enabled the British to capture the city. The old notion that yellow fever actually defeated the British does not stand the test, for Wentworth was not even using all his available forces when he was defeated. Furthermore, if the attack had been carried out properly there would not have been time for yellow fever to make significant inroads on British strength.[62] The idea that Vernon did not support Wentworth with his ships once inside the harbor also does not stand up under examination.[63] Unity of command in amphibious operations is a principle whose mastery eluded the British in 1741; it was to elude them again in 1915 in the Dardanelle's debacle, and it remains today one of the most nebulous, elusive, and often violated principles of all combined operations.

NOTES

1. Archibald Wilberforce, *Spain and Her Colonies* (NY: Peter Fenedon Collier and Son, 1900), p. 232.
2. Martin A. S. Hume, *Spain, 1479-1788* (London: Cambridge Press, 1898), p. 374.

3. "Edward Vernon," *Dictionary of National Biography*, 1937-8, XX, 267.
4. Francis R. Hart, *Admirals of the Caribbean* (Cambridge: The Riverside Press, 1922), p. 132.
5. "Edward Vernon," *Dictionary*, p. 268.
6. Leonard W. Labaree, ed., *Royal Instructions to the British Colonial Governors*, (NY: Appleton-Century Co., 1935), II, 735-736. The italics here are mine.
7. "Edward Vernon," *Dictionary*, p. 268.
8. *Ibid*
9. Hart, *Admirals*, pp. 135-138.
10. Basil Williams, *The Whig Supremacy. 1 714-1 760*. (Oxford: The Claredon Press, 1952), p 223, and Hart, *Admirals*, p 151. During Vernon's hour of triumph in London he was granted a half hour audience with the king, at which time he advised that "the best advice I can think of giving is to lay aside all thoughts of... expensive land expeditions as all advantages may be better and cheaper procured by keeping a strong superiority at sea..." His Majesty listened absently and remarked presently that "soldiers were necessary," indicating that advocates of invasion had already prevailed upon his thinking.
11. C. Grant Robertson, *England Under the Hanoverians* (London: Methuen and Co., Ltd., 1949), p. 82.
12. "Edward Vernon," *Dictionary*, p. 269.
13. *Ibid.*, pp.269-270, and Douglas Ford, *Admiral Vernon and the Navy* (London: T. Fisher Unwin, 1907), p. 218. Vernon was a pioneer in obtaining better conditions for the British seamen. The word "grog" actually comes from the fact that Vernon customarily wore a grogram boat cloak; his sailors simply transferred the abbreviated form of his garment from his person to the diluted drink, and hence the word came into the English vocabulary.
14. Har, *Admirals*, pp. 139-140.
15. Ford, *Admiral Vernon*, pp. 150, 155-156.
16. Labaree, *Royal Instructions*, II, 736.
17. Jesus Maria Henao and Gerardo Arrubla, *History of Colombia*, trans. J. Fred Rippy, (Chapel Hill: University of North Carolina Press, 1938), p. 137.
18. Pedro Julio Dousdebes, *Cartagena de Indias, Plaza Fuerte* (Bogota: Prensa de la Fuerzas Armadas, 1948) p. 151.
19. Douglas S. Freeman, *George Washington* (New York: Charles Scribner's Sons, 1948), I, 65-69. The complete American contingents were as follows: Massachusettes, five companies; Rhode Island, two companies; Connecticut, two companies; Pennsylvania, eight companies; Maryland, three companies; Virginia, four companies; North Carolina, four companies; however, all sources admit that the size of these companies varied greatly and that their total effectiveness was small. Lawrence Washington stated that the men suffered greatly while training under

British army officers in the tropical heat of Jamaica; many of the colonial troops were bitter that they sacrificed so much and played so small a part in the final outcome of the attack.

20. Hart, *Admirals*, p. 143.
21. Dousdebes, *Cartagena*, pp. 150-151.
22. Salvador de Madriaga, *The Rise of the Spanish American Empire*, (New York: The Macmillan Co., 1947), pp. 124-126.
23. Rafael Altamira, *A History of Spain*, trans. Muna Lee (New York: D. Van Nostrand Co., 1952), p. 436.
24. Henao, *History*, p. 135; Hume, *Spain*, p. 375; and James A Williamson, *A Short History of British Expansion*, (London: Macmillan and Co., Ltd., 1922), pp.386-387.
25. Henao, *History*, pp. 135-137.
26. Hume, *Spain*, p. 375.
27. Henao, *History*, p. 136.
28. Dousdebes, *Cartagena*, p. 152.
29. *Ibid.*, pp. 151-152, and Henao, *History*, p. 136.
30. Dousdebes, *Cartagena*, p. 140-141.
31. Freeman, *George Washington*, I, 65.
32. Hart, *Admirals*, p. 143.
33. Dousdebes, *Cartagena*, p. 153.
34. *Ibid.*, p. 154.
35. Dousdebes, *Cartagena*, p. 154.
36. Hart, *Admirals*, p. 144.
37. *Ibid.*, p. 145.
38. "Edward Vernon," *Dictionary*, p. 270.
39. Dousdebes, *Cartagena*, p. 155.
40. Ibid
41. "Edward Vernon," *Dictionary*, p. 270.
42. Ford, *Vernon*, p. 155.
43. Henao, *History*, p. 136. A poem sung in England for the occasion went: "We did so cannonade, and such breaches we made, / And so many of their houses set in a flame, / They did submit to fate and the town surrender, / To Admiral Vernon, the scourge of Spain."
44. Freeman, *George Washington*, p. 68.
45. "Edward Vernon," *Dictionary*, p. 270.
46. Dousdebes, *Cartagena*, p. 156.
47. *Ibid.*, p. 157
48. *Ibid.*
49. Hart, *Admirals*, p. 148.
50. *Ibid.*, pp. 149-150.
51. Freeman, *George Washington*, I, 69.
52. Dousdebes, *Cartagena*, pp. 158-159, and Hart, *Admirals*, p. 150. Nearly all of the accounts of the attack on Cartagena carry mention of this action. Most of the writers apparently believe that it was fought literally at the

gates of the city. Most of the sources show evidence of flights of imagination and embellish the account with bayonet charges, last-ditch resistance, and even British prisoners chained to the walls as hostages. The Dousdebes account is based on eye-witness reports and has been checked on the actual terrain.
53. Dousdebes, *Cartagena*, p. 159.
54. *Ibid.*, p. 160, and Hart, *Admirals*, p. 151.
55. Dousdebes, *Cartagena*, p. 160.
56. *Ibid.*, p. 161, and Hart, *Admirals*, p. 152.
57. Williams, *The Whig*, p. 224.
58. Dousdebes, *Cartagena*, pp. 285-286. Dousdebes develops the mystery surrounding the downfall of Blas de Lezo in the light of two possibilities. The first, and most likely, is that the Spanish leaders had a falling out after t he victory, the result of which was that charges were pressed against de Lezo. The second possibility is that de Lezo's performance in the defense was not really as gallant as most accounts portray it. This seems unlikely because of de Lezo's previously demonstrated heroism, the British feeling that de Lezo was the enemy leader of significance (placing him on the premature victory medals, for example), and numerous accounts of his fine leadership in the defense. However, one of Eslava's official reports mentions de Lezo's unworthy action during the defense. A logical guess about the mystery would be that the first interpretation is valid and that Eslava's report, which was written well after the battle, was twisted to vindicate himself.
59. I am cognizant of the diametrically opposed conclusions reached in Charles E. Nowell's "The Defense of Cartagena," *Hispanic American Historical Review*, XLII (November-December, 1962), 477-501. I contend that British land strength was too weak and pro-Spanish settlement too strong for Vernon to have taken over the entire Panamanian Isthmus if he had captured Cartagena in 1741.
60. This failure is apparently not Vernon's for his battle order clearly indicated by name the speediest ships as security for the fleet. Signals for such contingencies were included in the sailing order issued at Port Royal. See Hart, *Admirals*, pp. 143-144.
61. *Ibid.*, p. 143.
62. Williamson, *A Short History*, p. 387.
63. The notion seems to have originated in Tobias Smollett's *Roderick Random*, an autobiographical novel based upon Smollett's naval adventures. All sources pointing to Vernon's guilt in not furnishing support were traced to this account, which sheds some interesting and colorful light on the battle but which is written in a semi-farcical vein. Also, the author is completely naïve about tactics, having been a minor surgeon during the Cartagena attack. Since his other military observations are easily invalidated by more reputable manuscripts, his opinion on the point may be rejected.

Russell W. Ramsey, Ph.D., D.Min.

"German Espionage in South America, 1939-45," (British) *Army Quarterly & Defence Journal*, January, 1988.

Obsessed with the power and prestige of Britain's MI6, Hitler, in an attempt to counter its influence, built up the military intelligence section of the German High Command, the *Abwehr*. Under the general Admiral Wilhelm Franz Canaris, who directed *Abwehr* activities from 1935 until 1944, it was the Third Reich's national intelligence and counter-intelligence organisation for almost a decade.

However, Hitler was also obsessed with loyalty, and as early as 1932 he had already created the *Sicherheitsdienst* (or SD) under SS Lieutenant General Reinhard Heydrich, a cashired naval officer. Heydrich's SD oversaw all Nazi party security operations, and SD *Ausland Amt VI* became the Nazi Party's own intelligence and counter-intelligence organisation.

As the Germans advanced through Europe and North Africa in 1939-41, Latin America assumed some importance in Hitler's mind. Mexico had already nationalised US petroleum operations in 1938 and before the outbreak of war over a million tons of Mexican petrol were shipped to Germany. Elsewhere, the Italian airline LATI was an important presence in Brazil; fascism was gaining ground in Argentina; the Chilean Army and Police had been trained by German officers since before the First World War; and the Colombian airline SCADTA – whose initials stood for 'Colombian-German Air Transport Company'-employed many reserve *Luftwaffe* pilots based within striking range of the Panama Canal. From 8,000 miles of Latin American coastline, German agents could screen commercial shipping, monitor Allied naval forces and convoys, and coordinate U-boat attacks from a network of secret radio sites.

Using several hundred professionals, a budget that seems modest in retrospect, a decentralized network of radio contacts and small amounts of military logistic support, Admiral Canaris' *Abwehr* carried out most of the Third Reich's intelligence and counter-intelligence operations during the war. There was, however, great rivalry with the SD, reflecting the vicious power struggle that Heydrich waged against his opponents until his assassination in 1942 by Czech partisans. *Abwehr* personnel were often military and naval men who had been detailed to intelligence work, although a host of "spy novel" characters were also employed – including business adventurers, society prostitutes, embittered technical geniuses and Nazi sympathizers abroad – as civilian mercenaries.

In countering German intelligence efforts in Latin America, the British MI6 displayed the professionalism recounted in Sir William Stevenson's *A Man Called Intrepid,* and a creative derring-do worthy of Ian Fleming's James Bond. British operations were characterized throughout by a tiny but expert staff and the use of electronic means of intelligence gathering. Protection of Allied shipping and the furtherance of British wartime political goals were MI6's main aims. The killing of SS General Heydrich, for example, was planned at a secret M16 camp on the Canadian shore of Lake Erie.

The US Army and Navy officers who mobilized their nations's huge war effort distrusted foreign intelligence agencies almost as much as they disliked Latin America's Byzantine history of politico-military scheming. Seeking to keep open a simplistic, all uniformed intelligence territory for their military and naval attaches, they were, however, dislodged by FBI Director J. Edgar Hoover. Hoover knew little about Latin America, but he brilliantly foresaw a way to increase his Bureaus's domain. By portraying those such as Mexico's oil expropriator and Argentina's Peronists as *latino* versions of the gangsters he had defeated in America's big cities, Hoover was able to move his agents south of the Rio Grande on no more authority than a telephone call from President Franklin D. Roosevelt.

Hoover's Special Intelligence Service (SIS) was the only American overseas apparatus ever created within a domestic police agency for clandestine operations in one theatre – Latin America. Even General William Donovan's Office of Strategic Services (OSS) was blocked from action in the Western Hemisphere by Presidential fiat. The SIS received grudging cooperation from the Army, Navy and State Departments, usually when any two of these three could agree long enough to gang up on Hoover. Like MI6, the SIS was also able to make use of the then-new electronic methods of countering enemy intelligence operations.

In December 1941, the US and Mexico signed a military pact that led, among other things, to the collapse of a scheme to divert Mexican crude petroleum to Germany in large quantities. Mexican nationalistic feeling against 'Yankee domination' was the Germans' main asset, but by 1943 democratic forces were firmly in control in Mexico. Franco's Spain, through the ubiquitous Military Intelligence Service (SIM, Spanish abbreviation), was also caught meddling in Mexican security affairs, though this was of little consequence. Mexico declared war on the Axis on 29 May 1942 and in 1944, a Mexican Air Force squadron aided in the liberation of the Philippines, which had once been governed from the Viceroyalty of New Spain when both were part of the Spanish Empire. Mexico emerged from World War II to become the respected host of the 1945 Chapultepec Conference on Western Hemispheric security.

The German aerial threat to the Panama Canal was minimized in June 1940, when the Colombian government removed all German employees of the SCADTA airline. But *Abwehr* radio operators continued to be responsible for putting many a U-boat commander on the track of cargo ships that were leaving the Panama Canal. One retired US Merchant Seaman recalled, in a 1980 interview, the day that three ships were torpedoed from under him in the space of ten hours!

Even before the war, US planners had considered that the most likely route for an attack on America would be via Brazil. The US Atlantic Fleet, in their 1939 exercise, practised the interception of a German invasion of north-eastern Brazil. American fears were heightened in June 1940 when British intelligence passed on a report that German troops were headed for Dakar in West Africa. US Army Deputy Chief of Staff, General George C. Marshall had ordered a secret study on defending Brazil from German attack two years earlier.

In the event an Axis invasion of Brazil was never a serious possibility, but the strategic location of the country drew the attention of Allies and Axis alike. Brazil lay close to the convoy routes around the Cape to the Far East and New Zealand, and Brazilian foodstuffs were an important contribution to the Allied war effort. For their part, the Germans entertained hopes of overturning Latin America's largest country through wooing the native fascist movement, which had already mounted an abortive coup in 1938. Using the Italian airline LATI, *Abwehr* sent agents and equipment to Brazil, from where they could also fan out to neighbouring countries across the lightly-policed borders.

British intelligence helped persuade Roosevelt of the threat to Brazil and from that awakening flowed the strengthening of US security operations and the beginnings of Lend-Lease programmes for Latin America. In 1941, a classic British disinformation campaign, recounted in H Montgomery Hyde's *Room 3603*, turned Brazilian dictator Getulio Vargas against the agreement under which LATI operated from Brazil. Pressure from the US State Department followed, and in December 1941, American fuel supplies to LATI were suspended. The airline was evicted from Brazil that same month, thus removing *Abwehr*'s largest single source of logistic support.

Pro-Allied sentiments then prevailed in Río. Brazil declared war on Germany and Italy in August 1942, and an excellent Brazilian Infantry Brigade and a fighter squadron fought with the Allies in Italy against the retreating Germans.

Chile was never a strong prospect for the Germans during World War II. German leaders had over-estimated the extent of pro-German feeling among the Chilean officer corps which, although they might have emulated their German tutors' military excellence, eschewed Nazism. Consequently, *Abwehr* operations were infiltrated almost as soon as they had begun and the entire network was eventually flushed out. Some of the German operations in Chile were amateurish, clumsy, even amusing.

Argentina, on the other hand, was the Nazis' big hope in Latin America. Berlin believed that Peronism would allow Argentina to mature into a huge replica of Franco's Falangist Spain. Yet there is evidence that even those Argentine officers who supported Peron had recognised as early as 1942 that the Axis could not win the war and that the best chance for Argentina lay in exploiting the stand-off between Russia and America that would follow. *Abwehr* officials were dumbfounded to see their cells identified and arrested by security forces acting with nationalistic fervour in a land that the Germans had thought sympathetic. On 12 February 1944, Hitler sacked Admiral Canaris, partly because of *Abwehr*'s failure in Argentina. The reality was, however, that most countries had already decided on who would win the war.

German clandestine operations in Latin America during World War II provide much of interest to the researcher. Panama, the Canal Zone, neighbouring Costa Rica and Venezuela and the Andean lands were also the subject of German attentions, and these areas await definitive study. However, Dr. Leslie B. Rout, Jr. and Dr. John F. Bratzell have made the first real study of *Abwehr* action in Mexico, Brazil, Chile and Argentina in their book *The Shadow War*.[1] They have compared recently declassified documents in all the countries concerned with interviews of surviving agents, and their meticulous research is blended with a style of writing that combines the best of modern history with spy-novel intrigue.

Nevertheless, a serious political re-interpretation of Latin America during World War II is long overdue. The prevailing view is that the Americas stood together against the inroads of the Nazis, save perhaps in Argentina where some of the evil influence was already present. Marxist interpretations, on the other hand, tend to ignore the German 'shadow war' whilst painting the United States as the power which introduced spies and political manipulation to Latin America in order to control governments from Washington.

An objective consideration of German activity in Latin America suggests several trends for further analysis. Where the Germans concentrated well-trained agents, provided adequate funding and maintained a consistent objective, they were sometimes able to achieve their objectives. American efforts to persuade South Americans to reject German advances were most successful when Washington was able to offer a candid *quid pro quo*. The futility of using linguistically and culturally ignorant personnel for the delicate work of intelligence and counter-intelligence was demonstrated by all parties. That the FBI was an inappropriate choice to undertake such operations is clear, even though individual FBI agents did excellent work in Latin America.

To those who believe the modern KGB to be incapable of installing a minority government by force, the evidence of German activity in Latin America offers a clear warning. Couple a programme of active subversion with a sympathetic local minority – as the Germans attempted to do in Argentina – and add the intriguing dimension of military aid after the incumbent government has been overthrown (which the Germans could not) and the result is a Soviet-controlled Cuba or Nicaragua.

Other less dramatic lessons can be learned from these German operations. Dictatorships are not immune from bureaucratic power struggles, nor do they draw any distinction between diplomatic and military intelligence. Developing nations that lack a professional internal security force are obvious targets for foreign subversion. The relationship between the press, particularly a free press, and foreign interference in domestic political affairs was highly important even in the 1940s; today it is multiplied in importance by electronic media. Finally, disinformation campaigns, often denounced as useless or impossible, appear to have worked well forty years ago under conditions not unlike those of today.

NOTE

1. *The Shadow War: German Espionage and United States Counterespionage in Latin America* by Dr Leslie B Rout and Dr John F Bratzel, University Press of America.

Russell W. Ramsey, Ph.D., D.Min.

"The Third Reich's Third Front," *Military Review*, December, 1987.

Forty years is a vital time lapse to those who would know the shadow world of spies, sabotage and subterranean diplomacy. Statutorily, the highest secrets of state become public province and, geriatrically, the gumshoe actors who made the secrets are often still alive to reminisce.

Adolf Hitler was obsessed with the powers of Britain's Military Intelligence Number 6 (MI-6) and created the *Abwehr* to counter its influence. Directed by the genteel naval officer, Admiral Whilhelm Franz Canaris, the *Abwehr* functioned for a decade as the Third Reich's national intelligence and counterintelligence organization.

But Hitler was also obsessed with loyalty and so he created the *Sicherheitsdienst* (SD). Schutz Staffel (SS) Lieutenant General Reinhard Heydrich, cashiered from the German navy essentially for being a thug, oversaw all Nazi Party security operations. His SD *Ausland Amt VI* was the Nazi Party's own intelligence and counterintelligence organization. [1]

As the *Wehrmacht* advanced into central Europe and then into the Low Countries, Latin America assumed some degree of importance in Hitler's mind. Mexico nationalized US petroleum operations during Hitler's lightning grab of his central European neighbors. In the same period, Italy's LATI airline became an important presence in Brazil and political Fascism was showing power in Argentina.

German military men had trained the Chilean Army and National Police (*Carabineros*) since before World War I. Colombia's SCADTA airline had plenty of reserve *Luftwaffe* pilots based within striking range of the Panama Canal. Perhaps 8,000 miles of Latin American coastline was available from which German agents might screen commercial shipping, monitor Allied naval forces and troopships, and coordinate U-boat attacks from clandestine radio sites.

Admiral Canaris' *Abwehr* carried out most of the Third Reich's intelligence and counterintelligence operations throughout the war, using several hundred professionals, a budget that sounds modest in retrospect, decentralized wireless equipment and small amounts of military logistical support. There was some rivalry with the SD apparatus, mirroring the vicious power struggle Heydrich waged against governmental and other party rivals.

Abwehr personnel were often *Wehrmacht*, *Luftwaffe* and naval officers detailed to intelligence work. The *Abwehr* employed a cast of spy novel characters – business entrepreneurs, society prostitutes, embittered technical geniuses, ideological zealots – as civilian mercenaries. It recruited some of its best agents for Latin America among pro-Nazi elements of Czechoslovakia. Latin American expatriates were found even in the United States and recruited by the *Abwehr*. [2]

Britain's MI-6 displayed the professionalism recounted in Sir William Stevenson's *A Man Called Intrepid*, and the creative derring-do of Ian Fleming's James Bond, in countering the German's clandestine thrust into Latin America.

British operations were characterized by tiny, but expert, staffs, employing the latest of electronic wizardry in close coordination with the Royal Navy. British goals in clandestine warfare, within Latin America, were protection of Allied shipping and denial of primary resources to the Axis.

The US Army and Navy officers who mobilized their nation's power for World War II disliked Latin America's history of Byzantine politico-military scheming, and distrusted overseas intelligence agencies. Seeking to retain a simplistic, all-uniformed intelligence territory open for their military and naval attachés, they were knocked out of the ring by the US Federal Bureau of Investigation (FBI) director, J. Edgar Hoover.

America's SUPERCOP knew little of Latin America, but he foresaw, brilliantly, a way to increase his agency's domain amid a wartime crisis. To President Franklin D. Roosevelt, Hoover portrayed such Latin American figures as Mexico's oil expropriator and Argentina's Peronists as *latino* versions of the gangsters he had defeated in America's big cities. Then, he boldly moved his operatives south of the Río Grande on no legal authority beyond a telephone call from Roosevelt.[3]

Hoover's Special Intelligence Service (SIS) was America's only overseas apparatus created within a domestic police agency to do clandestine work in one theater – Latin America. General William J. Donovan's flashy Office of Strategic Services (OSS) was blocked from action in the Western Hemisphere by presidential fiat. Hoover's SIS was characterized by electronic excellence and grudging cooperation with the Departments of Army, Navy and State, except when any two of those three could agree long enough on an issue to gang up on Hoover.

The State Department received copies of the *Abwehr*'s deciphered messages regularly by mid-1941, enabling the Federal Communications Commission (FCC), the FBI, and the US Coast Guard to coordinate countermeasures. *Abwehr* men in Río de Janeiro, Brazil; Quito, Ecuador; and Buenos Aires, Argentina, were placed under surveillance by Hoover's SIS and even, upon occasion, fed false bits of information.[4]

German operations in Mexico peaked in 1941, when a scheme to divert crude petroleum in large quantities to the Third Reich's military needs was squashed. Mexican nationalistic feeling against Yankee domination was the German's main asset in this affair. President Avila Camacho weathered traditional anti-US sentiment to bring his country into cooperation with the Allies. His security forces assisted the FBI's SIS in a big cleanup of *Abwehr* operations during June and July 1941. Domestic FBI agents caught many of the US-based links to this network.[5]

By early 1943, democratic forces were strongly in command in Mexico. An estimated 250,000 Mexicans served against the Axis as members of the US Armed Forces. A squadron of combat aircraft from the Mexican Air Force, with some 300 flying personnel, aided in the liberation of the Philippines, which were once governed from the old viceroyalty of Mexico as a component of the Spanish Empire.[6] Franco's Spain had been caught red-handed meddling in Mexican security affairs through the ubiquitous Military Intelligence Service (SIM-Spanish abbreviation). Mexico emerged from World War II as the respected host of the Chapultepec Conference on Western Hemispheric security.

The German aerial bombing threat to the Panama Canal was minimized when Colombia's government removed the *Luftwaffe* men from their jobs with the SCADTA airline. *Abwehr* agents near the Panama Canal Zone reported being unable to view the canal personally because of tight security, making it difficult to report ship traffic.[7]

But *Abwehr* radio operations in the western reaches of the Caribbean were responsible for putting many U-boat commanders on the trail of cargo ships. One retired US merchant seaman recalled, in a 1962 interview, the day three ships were torpedoed out from under him in 10 hours! *Abwehr* radio reports from the Caribbean Basin carried news of Japanese fleet maneuvers near Indonesia, and possible US naval responses, in early December 1941.[8]

Brazil drew Hitler's attention because of the possibility for an air-sea invasion across the 1,500 mile strip of the Atlantic Ocean that divides Africa from South America. Italy's LATI airline was a major logistical channel by which *Abwehr* sent its operatives and their equipment into Brazil. From there, the agents could fan out to the other countries of South America across the lightly guarded frontiers.

To Hitler, an additional attraction was Brazilian foodstuffs, important to the European Allies, and the possibility of overturning Latin America's largest country by wooing the native Fascist movement. As early as 1938, Winston Churchill had said, "...even in South America the Nazi regime... begins to undermine the fabric of German society."[9]

British intelligence operations, however, were effective in persuading the Roosevelt administration that the German cross-Atlantic operation to Brazil was a possibility to be taken seriously. From that awakening flowed the strengthening of US security activities and the incipient lend-lease programs for Latin America. In February 1939, the Army deputy chief of staff, General George C. Marshall, ordered the Army War College to do a study on making Brazil and Venezuela safe from German invasion.[10]

A classic British disinformation operation turned Brazilian President, Getulio D. Vargas, against the agreement under which LATI operated its planes in Brazil. US State Department pressure followed. The *Abwehr* reported mounting pro-Allied political sentiment in Brazil. LATI was evicted by the Brazilian authorities, cutting off the *Abwehr*'s largest single logistical system. Brazilian army and air force units replaced US security forces based in the northeast hump of Brazil.

Leaders in Río de Janeiro then made Brazil into Latin America's strongest pro-Allied nation. They dispatched the excellent Brazilian Infantry Division and the First Fighter Squadron to Italy, where they fought with the Allies against retreating German and Italian forces. The shutting down of the *Abwehr*'s operations in Brazil, coupled with its entry into the war as a strongly pro-Allied combatant, was Nazi Germany's greatest defeat in the Americas.[11]

Operations in Chile were never strong for the Germans during World War II. German political leaders overestimated pro-German sentiment among the Chilean officer corps, which tended to admire the military excellence of their German tutors but eschewed Nazi political ideology. Consequently, *Abwehr* operations were infiltrated almost at the outset, and eventually the entire network was flushed out. Some of the German clandestine operations in Chile were amateurish, even amusing.

Argentina was, of course, the big political hope of "Nazidom" for a future ideological clone on the South American continent. The belief in Berlin was that Peronism would mature into a huge replica of Franco's Falangist movement in Spain. The most careful study yet done of this possibility concludes that nothing short of an Allied blockade or overt military threat could have changed Argentina's pro-Axis stance in 1941.[12]

Yet, by late 1942, there is evidence that Argentine military officers were recognizing that the Axis powers simply could not win World War II and that the best chance for Argentina to realize its world power dream lay in exploiting the US-Soviet standoff that would follow. Consequently, *Abwehr* officials were dumbfounded to see their cells identified and arrested by security forces, acting with nationalistic fervor in the land they had thought to be sympathetic.

On 12 February 1944, Hitler sacked Canaris, putting the *Abwehr* under the SD. The reason given was the bungling of clandestine operations in Argentina and Turkey. The reality was that most countries had already decided on who would win the war.[13]

It is time for a serious political reinterpretation of Latin America in World War II. The prevailing view has been that all the Americans stood together like a family of good fellows against the inroads of the wicked Nazis, save in Argentina where some of the evil influence was already present. Neo-Marxist reinterpretation tends to ignore Nazi Germany's shadow war against Latin America and to paint the United States as the power which introduced spies, counter-spies and political manipulation to control governments from Washington, DC.

A cool consideration of the German shadow war suggests several trends for further analysis. Where the Germans focused well-trained saboteurs, adequate funding and a consistent strategic goal, they, several times, achieved a substantial objective. US successes in persuading Latin Americans to counter German manipulations were the most visible where a candid *quid pro quo* was offered by Washington. The uselessness of sending linguistically and culturally uninstructed personnel to do the delicate work of shadow war was demonstrated by all parties. The overall inappropriateness of having the FBI function as an overseas intelligence agency was revealed, even though the agents themselves did excellent work.[14]

To the dreamer who holds the Soviet's KGB (Committee of State Security) incapable of installing a minority government by force, the German experience on that point is instructive. Couple a capable program of active subversive measures with a sympathetic internal minority, which the Germans did in Argentina, and add the intriguing dimension of military protection after the incumbent government has been overthrown, which the Germans could not do. The result becomes a Soviet-controlled Cuba or Nicaragua. Facts assembled for writing *Wiping the Frost From the Window* showed clearly how the Soviet-Cuban clandestine warfare machine can overturn a government in the Western Hemisphere without an open declaration of conflict or intention, something the operatives of Nazi Germany's *Abwehr* could only dream of doing.[15]

Other lessons, less dramatic, are available from Germany's clandestine operations in Latin America. One is that dictatorial regimes, such as Hitler's Nazi government, are not immune from inter-agency bureaucratic power struggles. Furthermore, the notion, often expressed by clandestine operations planners in the Western democracies about the dictatorships having no problem with a gray zone between military and diplomatic operations, simply is false based upon the German experience.

Another lesson is that developing nations that lack a professional apparatus for internal security are sitting ducks for foreign subversion and manipulation of their fragile governments. The interplay of the free press and externally engineered political events was highly critical in the 1949s and has probably increased in severity in the age of the electronic media. Disinformation operations, so often dismissed by free speech advocates as philosophically impossible or politically inconsequential, appear to have worked well for all sides in the 1940s, under political dynamics not too different from the scenario of the 1980s.

Helping non-Communist republics of the Americas to remain independent of the Soviet-Cuban power projection apparatus is now a significant professional task of the US military officer. An understanding of German shadow warfare operations in that region during World War II is vital to US diplomatic and military leaders in the 1980s. For the evidence is clear that the Soviet-Cuban operatives have already done their historical homework and tightened up the weak spots in the clandestine warfare system.[16]

NOTES

1. Leslie B. Rout and John F. Bratzel, *The Shadow War* (Frederick, Maryland: University Publication of America, 1986), 7-12.
2. F.B.I. Report, *Totalitarian Activities – Brazil Today* (December 1942).
3. Rout and Bratzel, 37.
4. Stanley E. Hilton, *Hitler's Secret War in South America* (New Ballentine Books, 1982), 213-14.
5. Ladislas Farago, *The Game of the Foxes* (New York: David McKay, 1971), 455-66.
6. Hubert Herring, *A History of Latin America from Beginning to Present* 3d ed., (New York: Alfred A. Knopf, 1968), 368.
7. Donald A. Yerxa, "The Special Service Squadron and the Caribbean Squadron, 1920-1940," Naval War College Review (Autumn 1986): 61; and Hilton, 66.
8. Interview, the author with a merchant seaman, 1962; and Hilton, 77-78.
9. New York Times (17 October 1938).
10. Forest C. Pogue, *George C. Marshall, Education of a General* (New York: Viking Press, 1963), 337.

11. Hilton, 170-172; and Col. Ford G. Daab, "The Brazilian Air Force and World War II" *The Air University Review* (July-August, 1986): 68-69.
12. Herring, 750-51; and Rout and Bratzel, 363.
13. The scholarly, high-principled Admiral Wilhelm F. Canaris was hung naked on a meat hook by the Gestapo at Flossenburg as the penalty for his role in the 1944 assassination attempt against Hitler's life. The villainous General Reinhard Heydrich had already been executed two years earlier by a clandestine operation planned at Sir William Stephenson's mysterious Camp X, on the Canadian shore of Lake Ontario, and performed in Czechoslovakia! William Stevenson, *A Man Called Intrepid* (New York: Harcourt, Brace, and Janovich, 1976), 187-90; and Roger Manuel and Heinrich Fraenkel, *The Canaris Conspiracy* (New York: David McKay, 1969), 224-25.
14. Rout and Bratzel, 35-38, makes a clear distinction between the executive manipulations through which FBI Director J. Edgar Hoover expanded his operations into Latin America, and the superb work of individual agents who often took on these assignment with little professional background in that part of the world.
15. Russell W. Ramsey, *Wiping the Frost From the Window: Soviet-Cuban Active Measures and Disinformation in Central America* (US Department of State, Public Policy Division-Central America, April 1985). While German *Abwehr* operatives did many combinations of subrosa activities that became a partial model for later Soviet-Cuban destabilization operations, the Nazi government was never able to offer the potential architect of a coup d'etat, or staged revolution in Latin America, the certainty of military protection after the seizure of power.
16. There is fertile ground for the researcher on clandestine operations in Latin America during World War II, Panama, the Canal Zone, neighboring Costa Rica and Venezuela, and the Andean lands were subjected to German spy activities and these areas await definitive study. Dr. Leslie B. Rout Jr. and Dr. John F. Bratzel have done pioneer work on *Abwehr* action in Mexico, Brazil, Chile and Argentina in *The Shadow War*; Stanley E. Hilton's *Hitler's Secret War in South America, 1935-1945* (New York: Ballentine, 1985) contains more detail on operations in Brazil, but little at all on the other countries.

Russell W. Ramsey, Ph.D., D.Min.

REVOLUTION AND GUERRILLA WARFARE

Review of: *Guerrillas and Revolution in Latin America,* by Timothy P. Wickham-Crowley, Princeton, New Jersey: Princeton University Press, 1992. Reviewed in: (British) Army *Quarterly & Defence Journal*, July, 1994.

Here is a rigorous study of the guerrilla wars in Latin America during the Cold War era. Timothy Wickham-Crowley, Sociology Professor and Associate Director, Centre for Latin American Studies at Georgetown University, has examined six guerrilla conflicts in the period 1956 to 1970 on the basis of five variables. He then applies the refined methodology to 28 more guerrilla struggles which took place from 1970 until the late 1980s.

Professor Wickham-Crowley's six study models are guerrilla conflicts once active in Cuba, Venezuela, Guatemala, Colombia, Peru and Bolivia. He scrupulously investigated the following five variables.

Was a guerrilla organisation genuinely established during the conflict? How extensive was the support for that movement among peasants and workers? What were the comparative strengths of the armed guerrilla units and the nation's armed forces under challenge? To what extent did the United States give military support to the government under challenge? And was there a government of the patrimonial/praetorian type which the author calls a "Mafiacracy"?

His conclusions from the first part of his study contain surprises. Peasant and worker support did not automatically materialise in some cases; in others, when support did materialise, it was not decisive. More government troops and weapons, and the existence of US military assistance, again did not win the conflict.

Using the Boolean system of logic for reducing common sets of variables, Wickham-Crowley then applies his paradigm to 28 more cases where significant guerrilla activity was at least reported extensively. His results again validate statistically, resulting in a scientifically neutral, objective way to explain the triumph of revolutionary guerrilla forces in Cuba, in 1959; of comparable forces in Nicaragua, in 1977; and the failure of all the other guerrilla forces in the Latin American region to overthrow their national governments.

Wickham-Crowley's present book, when combined with the reading of Michael Radu and Vladimir Tismaneanu, *Latin American Revolutionaries: Groups, Goals, Methods,* Foreign Policy Institute Book (Washington DC: Pergamon Brassey, 1990) produces a scholarly analysis on the Latin American guerrilla warfare syndrome for the general student of history and revolutionary warfare. The Wickham-Crowley volume fills the same void for Latin American guerrilla conflicts that Crane Brinton's *Anatomy of a Revolution,* rev. ed. (New York: Vintage Books, 1965) filled for the study of national revolutions, namely, the achievement of scientific inquiry on a subject where intellectualised emotionalism has too often been accepted as academic writing.

For the specialised student of Latin American politics and conflict, two earlier volumes still have value in the wake of Professor Wickham-Crowley's cardinal study. These are Georges Fauriol, ed., *Latin American Insurgencies,* Georgetown University Centre for Strategic & International Studies (Washington DC: National Defence University Press, 1985), and Luis Mercier Vega, *Guerrillas in Latin America* trans. by Daniel Weissbort (New York: Frederick A Praeger, 1969). Other literature, now outdated, includes some titles whose scholarly objectivity should have been questioned at the time of their publication. These include Richard Gott, *Guerrilla Movements in Latin America* (New York: Doubleday & Co., 1972); Irving Louis Horowitz, Josué de Castro, and John Gerassi, eds., *Latin American Radicalism: A Documentary Report on Left and Nationalist Movements* (New York: Random House, 1969); John Gerassi, *The Great Fear in Latin America* (New York: Collier Books, 1966); and James Petras and Maurice Zeitlin, ed., *Latin America: Reform or Revolution?* (New York: Fawcett Publications, 1968).

The Wickham-Crowley volume is both the classic in the field, and the best methodological work yet seen on the analysis of guerrilla conflict.

Russell W. Ramsey, Ph.D., D.Min.

Review of: *Latin American Revolutionaries: Groups, Goals, Methods*, by Michale Radu and Vladimir Tismaneau, a Foreign Policy Institute Book, Washington D.C.: Pergamon-Brassey, 1990. Reviewed in: *Military Intelligence*, April-June, 1991.

Revolutions have become complicated in Latin America. That is one of the author's themes in the seven chapters which form the conceptual one-third of this book. The other two-thirds is organized into a descriptive directory of armed revolutionary groups throughout Central and South America.

The author's knowledge base and viewpoint establish a new level of sophistication among academic literature on this admittedly emotional topic. Revolution in contemporary Latin America is mostly of European intellectual origins, filtered into the Western Hemisphere since 1967 by Cuba and thereby rendered palatable. It is led, as Crane Brinton showed in his 1938 landmark *Anatomy of a Revolution*, not by the oppressed but by disaffected elements of the privileged class. The Catholic Church is heavily involved, in ways which will surprise many readers. Anti-leftist violence is on the rise. Its origins, say the authors, spring not from after-hours vigilantism by U.S.-influenced local armies, but from a spontaneous tide of a perceived need for self-defense.

While the definitional essays in the book are filled with insights, readers who do not specialize in Latin American revolutions will need the other two-thirds of the volume to understand the essays. Groups known by three Spanish initials abound in every sentence, as do obscure names. Thus, the directory portion is to the conceptual part what the periodic table of the elements is to the reader of a chemistry textbook: a necessary lexicon. The directory is impeccably accurate on organizational history, but has two curious dimensions.

The entry of Nicaragua is about the Sandinista National Liberation Front, the nation's legitimate government for 13 years. One would expect to see a directory of the Democratic Resistance ("Contras") instead. And Cuba's support role – financing, arming, training, role model – behind many Latin American guerrilla and terrorist groups is absent. The authors merely state that support for each group is domestic, external, or both.

This book belongs on the reference shelf of any scholar, journalist or policy maker who would deal intelligently with Latin American in the 1990s.

Review of: *Will It Liberate? Questions About Liberation Theology*, by Michael Novak, New York, NY: Paulist Press, 1986.
Reviewed in: *Journal of InterAmerican Studies and World Affairs*, Winter, 1987-1988.

Michael Novak begins his analysis of liberation theology with an economic conclusion about Latin American history. "North Americans caught the fundamental idea of economic liberation - that the way out of poverty is invention." By contrast, Latin America remained "relatively changeless, impressed with power (and especially the power of the state)... less concerned with material advance than with noble feelings and a sense of culture."

The first chapter establishes the author's respect for the principal architects of liberation theology: the Jesuit Father Juan Luis Segundo, former Brazilian priest Hugo Assman, the Peruvian professor Gustavo Gutiérrez, Mexico's José Miranda, and the US Jesuit Arthur F. McGovern. Their works are known in the United States largely through the Maryknoll (New York) Missionary Order's Orbis Press.

Novak gives his assessment of the seven tenets that form liberation theology, acknowledging that its advocates do not entirely agree. These are: (1) the new man, (2) utopian sensibility, (3) a naïve vision of the state, (4) no theory of wealth creation, (5) the abolition of private property, (6) the existence of class struggle, and (7) the evil of private property. He considers that hatred of political, economic, and military influence of the United States in Latin America helps to unify the movement.

Next comes a chapter on western economic history. Sin, creativity, and voluntary association, Novak says, form a liberal theology which bypassed Latin America. Consequently, the Latin American concept in general, and the liberation theology view of capitalism in particular, are flawed. Novak moves on to defend regulated capitalism. He shows how the recent "rim of Asia" miracles - booming economies in Japan, South Korea, Taiwan, Singapore, and Hong Kong - were produced by societies having vastly fewer natural resources and greater population densities than much of Latin America.

Novak defends Pope John Paul II for his 1985 condemnation of liberation theology and offers his own alternative: creation theology. Novak utilizes the question-and-answer form of disputation (characteristic of Catholic theology since its development by Bishop Ambrose of Milan in the 4th century) to analyze the central points of liberation theology in relentless fashion. The economic understanding of Karl Marx was flawed; both the Soviet Union and the People's Republic of China have long since moved away from Marx. Then what is dependency? Who are the poor? Do the advocates of liberation theology merely echo the political rhetoric of those Latin American politicians who find it more convenient to blame developmental failures on the Colossus of the North than to look in the mirror?

Novak indicts liberation theologians for refusing to identify fully their own economic prescription. Do they advocate democratic socialism? One-party socialism? Agrarian collectivism? Or Marxist-Leninist communism? He offers his own remedy: a regulated capitalism driven by individual inventiveness, which he holds to be truly revolutionary and truly Judeo-Christian. He does not rule out the possibility of democratic socialism in Latin America.

Novak's book is a meld of already published essays added to newly written chapters. While the ideas in each chapter are clear, the themes do not flow smoothly. Charts of Latin American economic indicators are included, but with little interpretation or commentary. Novak presents the tenets of liberation theology grouped in sets, each accompanied by his own critique; his arguments are consistent, but the presentation is not. The book would have greatly benefited from a biographical section, something to give background sketches of the main figures who have contributed to the advance and development of liberation theology. The endnotes which accompany each chapter appear comprehensive, but no bibliography is provided. All omissions could have been adequately provided in the space now taken up by the author's field research notes, which add little.

Despite structural flaws, Michael Novak's *Will It Liberate?* raises serious questions about the validity of liberation theology. Scholars who take a strong pro-liberation theology position will find themselves pressed to reply to Novak's logic in their pursuit of credibility, for he presents powerful arguments in support of his critique. Latin American history badly needs an updated version of John Lloyd Mecham's definitive 1966 study, *Church and State in Latin America*, a book, by the way, which Novak never mentions.

Review of: *Guerrillas: The Men and Women Fighting Today's Wars*, by Jon Lee Anderson, Times Books, 1993. Reviewed in: *Army*, August, 1993.

Jon Lee Anderson became fascinated with the revolutionary mystique projected by the Argentine revolutionary Ernesto (Che) Guevara and set out to discover what motivates such people. He visited and resided for several weeks each with five active guerrilla movements that were heavily engaged at the time. He dodged bullets, caught infectious hepatitis, made contacts on both sides of the lines and somehow survived with field notes intact.

His five guerrilla movements run the ideological gamut: El Salvador's pro-communist FMLN (Spanish abbreviation for *Farabundo Martí National Liberation Front*), the anti-Soviet *Mujahidin* coalition in Afghanistan, the *Karen* nationalist guerrillas of Burma, the *Polisario* movement of western Sahara, and a *Shabbub* combat group of the Palestinian *intifada* operating in Gaza.

The sections on the FMLN are the strongest; the author's material checks out factually with independent observers who know all five movements.

His book is topically organized, and so one visits guerrilla psychology, war financing, political grievances, legal issues and religious beliefs in slices that cut across each of the five movements chapter by chapter.

The author does not seem to have been influenced by the tedious body of social science literature on guerrilla movements, which is a blessing; his viewpoint is fresh.

Guerrillas, he finds, are the world's last romantics: they believe in their causes with an outrageous optimism that overcomes the misery of their environment.

His book is the statement of the individual guerrilla warrior, the complement to Ann Ruth Willner and Dorothy Willner's classic essay "The Rise and Role of Charismatic Leaders" in Karl von Vorsy's *New Nations: The Problem of Political Development.*

The author concludes that the guerrilla mystique transcends ideology and culture. His book is filled with the smell of campfires and horse dung, the crack of rifles and the screams of the wounded, and the millenarian dreams of disparate thousands who know nothing of Karl Marx nor of Thomas Jefferson.

Culture, not ideology, lights the psychological fires that drive guerrilla fighters, and from within their apocalyptic vision they fight on for the Utopia that never quite materializes.

Russell W. Ramsey, Ph.D., D.Min.

"Neo-Marxism Rides the Black Legend," *Journal of Low Intensity Conflict & Law Enforcement,* Winter, 1997.

Two cultural distortions of Christian doctrine have joined together in the 1990s to threaten relationships between North America and Latin America. The first is the Black Legend, an old British prejudice against Spain which crossed the Atlantic and expresses itself in a hypocritically pietistic North American condemnation of Latin American values and behaviors. The second distortion holds that Jesus of Nazareth was a political revolutionary, a heretical yet periodically popular reversion to the *heteroousious* concept by affirming that the Son is of a different substance from the Father.

Black Legend and Liberation Theology

In modern North American terms, the Black Legend paints all Latin American countries as socially regressive societies, ruled by an evil triumvirate of Roman Catholic prelates and clergy, plundering economic entrepreneurs, and viciously abusive armed forces. The Jesus-as-revolutionary heresy in contemporary North America proclaims that its followers must go into Latin America to educate the people about the evil exploitation which they do not perceive, then organize and arm their converts in the region to overthrow their governments by force. A one-party totalitarian regime is then to guarantee equitable distribution of all resources according to need.

Marriage of Two Distortions

Since the demise of the Cold War and its tangential exacerbation of Latin America's internal tensions, most Latin American experts have expressed a cautious yet optimistic view of the region's move toward neo-liberal economics and democratic political pluralization. Yet a small element within the US political fabric insists upon forcing revolutionary liberation theology upon the changing Latin American scene, using the crudest and most factually distorted elements from the Black Legend to buttress their case against the military and police. The real goal here is to destabilize the Latin American nation-states sufficiently that neo-Marxist armed cadres can seize control of genuine, multi-sectoral evolutions, or, with luck, seize control of any available revolution, as Fidel Castro's small "M-26" cadres did in January of 1959 in Cuba, and as the "9 Comandantes" did in Nicaragua during the 1979 consolidation phase of the broad-based Sandinista revolution. But the political milieu of Cuba in 1959 and Nicaragua in 1979 do not exist in Latin America today, except possibly in Cuba among democratic elements who are weary of Castro's personalistic, one-party dictatorship. Timothy P. Wickham-Crowley's meticulous 1992 study of guerrillas during the Cold War showed that there was never any mass support for neo-Marxist guerrilla forces, and that the neo-Marxists only succeeded in Cuba and Nicaragua because the governing regimes there were shabby, Mafioso dynasties.

Black Legend History

Bartolome de Las Casas accompanied Christopher Columbus, settled in Spanish America took orders of the priesthood, and took moral umbrage against the cruel treatment of indigenous peoples by the Spanish colonizers. In celebrated debates and in powerful treatises which he wrote, Las Casas became the 'Apostle of the Indies.' But his efforts at reform within the Spanish Empire were exploited by Britain's Henry VIII, Elizabeth I, Oliver Cromwell and others as a propagandistic weapon in a multi-century power struggle against Spain and her empire. The list of Black Legend proponents is long and distinctly unattractive.

Professor Charles Gibson has summarized these racial, religious, and characterological attacks against Hispanic society into six categories: authoritarianism, decadence, corruption, bigotry, indolence, and cruelty. Montaigne, Montesquieu, and Voltaire are some of the French *philosophes* who fortified the Black Legend. Karl Marx opined that Simon Bolivar, the Liberator of northern South America, was a tyrant and a buffoon. When the United States invaded Mexico, Marx expressed the hope that the Yankees would conquer all the way down to Panama, thus disempowering the 'corrupt, lazy Mexicans' forever.

George Washington Crichfield published a two volume history of US-Latin American relations in 1908, asserting without evidence or reference that Latin Americans were racially inferior across a broad spectrum. Theodore Roosevelt invoked the Black Legend to whip up combat fervor among his Rough Riders, and to stir the US Senate to support his 1903 armed interference in Colombia's Isthmian affairs so that canal digging could start in Panama during his administration. To defend his 'Roosevelt Corollary' to the Monroe Doctrine, authorizing US military action in the Caribbean and Central America to maintain political stability and forestall European interventionism, he referred to the people of the region as 'those wretched Dagos.'

In the twentieth century, expressions such as 'tin pot dictator' are commonly understood to mean a Latin American general holding presidential powers illegally and unrepentantly. Most US citizens since the, Vietnam War era were raised on the television show 'Zorro' (the Fox) on Saturday morning, a Walt Disney program based in nineteenth-century Mexico just across the US border. Sergeant Garcia is the resident buffoon. He is fat, lazy, cowardly, inept, deceitful, and stupid, making him the quintessential Black Legend prototype; and he is the only Latin American military figure ever seen by most US citizens. Latin Americans, by contrast, regularly see John Wayne and other Anglo-Saxons portrayed in uniform as hero figures by Hollywood film directors.

Marxism and neo-Marxism have a different but related history of coincidence with Latin America. Karl Marx revealed faint hope for peasants as revolutionaries, a fact well documented in David Mitrany's 1952 study, *Marx Against the Peasant.* [1]

Robert Alexander summed up early Cold War era Marxism within Latin America in his definitive 1957 study *Communism In Latin America* by showing it to be primarily an urban worker phenomenon.[2]

It was Mao Zedong's compilation *On Guerrilla Warfare*, translated by retired US Marine Corps General Samuel B. Griffith, that opened the door for revolutionaries to project Marxist ideas into under-developed rural world regions. It was the Argentine physician Ernesto 'Che' Guevara who distilled Mao Zedong's account of Asian peasant revolution and Karl Marx's notion of European proletarian revolution into a political formula also entitled *On Guerrilla Warfare* for uniting the peasants of Latin America into a giant class struggle. The fruition of armed neo-Marxist doctrine in Latin America coincided with protest against US anti-Communist policy in developing nations during the 1960s to alter fundamentally the perspective through which most US academic specialists on Latin America viewed the region.

The Marriage in Session

Professor Stanley Stein's keynote presidential address to the Conference on Latin American History in 1960 proclaimed an end to any hope for electoral democracy with regulated free enterprise systems in place. Revolutionary means of political and economic change were both necessary and inevitable, he assured the assembled scholars who had previously tended to interpret Latin America as a region developing along lines of Judeo-Christian constitutional democracies. Shortly afterwards, the US Congress authorized federal grants on a scale previously unknown. Jokingly known as the "Castro prevention money," the applied outcome of this effort was to produce an entire generation of Latin Americanists who for years supported the neo-Marxist view of the region to which their scholarly careers were dedicated. Much of this so-called scholarly literature was expressed in the symbols of the Black Legend. Dozens of books and articles proclaimed the Cuban and later the Nicaraguan revolution as the correct regional models; all US national security programs in the region as fascist repression; and dependency theory economics as the only valid paradigm.

The Jesus-as-revolutionary heresy was marketed by the Maryknoll Missionary Order, theologically interesting because this organization had more missionaries murdered during the communist takeover of China than any other comparable group. Their training school in New York, their Orbis Press, and their small but effective cadres became a major vehicle of liberation theology in the United States, making it more overtly political and more committed to violent revolution than indigenous liberation theology espoused within Latin America by such dedicated Catholic prelates as Gustavo Gutierrez in Peru.

Luis E. Aguilar edited *Marxism* in Latin America in 1968, a cardinal work which showed clearly the crossover between the Black Legend and Marxism.[3] After dependency theory became a mainstay in the neo-Marxist canon, it was nearly impossible in the United States to buy a book about Latin America, or to take an introductory college course, without learning that the Black Legend agenda was true, that neo-Marxists were soon to liberate the region, that all US policy in the region was repressive, and, of course, that US neo-Marxists were the ultimate opponents of racism and oppression.

Reality

Throughout the Cold War, Latin America maintained about two soldiers per thousand citizens and devoted about two percent of its gross domestic product on military programs. The two prominent exceptions here are Castro's Cuba, whose level of militarization towered at the top of the world scale with North Korea and Communist Romania, and Sandinista Nicaragua, whose force levels were massive between 1980 and 1989. In fact, even the Latin American military dictatorships during the Cold War era were supported by troop and weapon ratios less mighty than those of democratic Western (NATO) Europe, which were in turn much less armed than communist Eastern (Warsaw Pact) Europe. It is standard neo-Marxist fantasy to assert that Latin America was a region forcibly occupied by its own armed forces throughout the Cold War. It is a strategic reality to conclude that the only two countries having armed forces and weapons large enough to prevent overthrow of the regime by determined popular opposition were Castro's Cuba and Sandinista Nicaragua.

US graduate students were permitted by several prestigious institutions to spend a month or two in Cuba having a carefully managed tour Castro's showcase social programs, then receive a semester of academic credit for overseas studies. Mexico's famous philosopher-writer Octavio Paz denounced the process of bestowing academic credits and medals for propaganda trips to Cuba, following which he was pointedly ignored within neo-Marxist circles. Michael Novak showed clearly in *Will It Liberate? Questions About Liberation Theology* (1986) that US liberation theology pertaining to Latin America was a biblically disjointed disguise for secular revolution.[4] Novak further showed that the enthusiasm among US academics for dependency theory was based upon the totally erroneous conclusion that Argentine economist Raul Prebisch's statist and structuralist economics, widespread in Latin America during the 1960s and 1970s, were a nationalistic form of socialism.

In the 1980s, the Latin American Studies Association passed a number of resolutions condemning the Reagan administration's policies in Central America. While the resolutions may have had majority support, they were worded in bitter neo-Marxist rhetoric that was decidedly unscholarly. Then, in 1990, a team of Romanian-American scholars, Michale Radu and Vladimir Tismaneanu, published *Latin America Revolutionaries: Groups, Goals, and Methods*.[5] This study revealed most Marxist thought, actors, and action in Latin America to be an inauthentic European import. Two years later, Robert A. Packman's *The Dependency Movement: Scholarship and Politics in Developmental Studies*, revealed the fallacious reasoning behind the assumptions of leftist US scholars who prescribed revolutionary socialism for Latin America, believing the Latins too economically inept to work out their own future.[6] Robert Brent Toplin opined in his 1994 essay

Russell W. Ramsey, Ph.D., D.Min.

"Point of View: Many Latin Americanists Continue to Wear Ideological Blinders" that many US scholars of Latin America simply did not know that the region was already well along in a neo-liberal economic growth trajectory, and that neo-Marxist economic paradigms had already failed. Paul H. Lewis argued in his 1996 "Review Essay: Political Scholarship" that neo-Marxist posturing about Latin America by US scholars of the region was a spillover from the era of anti-Vietnam protest, and that the neo-Marxist regional paradigm did considerable injustice to the study of Latin America.

What Does It Mean?

The Black Legend pre-dates Marxism in Europe, North America, and Latin America. US scholars specializing in Latin America prior to 1960 weilded considerable influence in trying to overcome the Black Legend. The incomparable Professor Lewis Hanke traced the life and work of Bartolome Las Casas, thereby laying the groundwork for Latin America's own authentic human rights tradition. After 1960, it became *de rigueur* for the rising tide of newly minted Ph.D.s in Latin American studies to approach their region from the neo-Marxist position. Missing from their analyses was the fact that one must deprecate the native capacities of a region to develop its own authentic form of governance and economy in order to affirm that a foreign revolutionary concept, staffed by armed foreign cadres and ideologues, is the only route to freedom and justice.

The largest distortion of US neo-Marxists who study Latin America has always been that the United States is an enemy so militarized and so innately oppressive that the wicked Colossus of the North can invade at will, and control from afar by manipulating Latin America's own military forces. Despite some disgraceful excesses in the name of anti-communism on the part of several Cold War era Latin American regimes, it is a fact that about two percent of US military assistance dollars across the period 1947 to 1989 were devoted to the entire Latin American region. Wild exaggerations of US military power and intentions, coupled with the worst of the Black Legend slander about Latin America's own armies, bankers, business entrepreneurs, police, and elected officials have flowed from the pens of the neo-Marxist scholars. Yet Latin America's armed forces and police have more requests for United Nations peacekeeping missions than they can fill, and Latin America's progress with neo-liberal economics and democratization is truly impressive by comparative world standards, in the judgment of most qualified economists.

A Note of Caution

Is one to conclude that US political conservatives are innocent of using the Black Legend to derive policy in Latin America? The Congressional Record is replete, across the Cold War era, with conservative political opinions to the effect that the Latins know little of democracy, and therefore must be ruled by *caudillos* (strongmen) who will keep them in line. These displays of Black Legend racism are the specific cannon fodder out of which the neo-Marxists constructed their false liberation mythology. But this situation, equally ugly anti-*latino* racism from both sides of the US political spectrum does not apply to academia, where neo-Marxism was simply *de rigueur* for an entire generation.

A Note of Hope

Latin Americanists in the United States need to rediscover the fact that they are licensed to study a fascinating world region through the lenses of history, sociology, political science, anthropology, economics, linguistics, literature, law, or some other discipline having a body of reasoned evidence to sustain it. By the year 2010 or 2015, US trade with Latin America will exceed US trade with Germany and Japan combined. Exciting and innovative new forms of democratic governance will be in place, and some of these will not look like a photocopy of US or European institutions. Black Legend stereotypes will die away as the region takes on economic importance, just as demeaning anti-Japanese caricatures lost credibility when Japan became an economic super-power. And scholars will express wonder and amazement at a package of interpretive writings in the recent past that proclaimed the validity of the Black Legend agenda as a basis by which to advocate that Latin America's governments needed to be overthrown and replace by revolutionary socialist monoliths, manned by people who have never run a successful government nor a fruitful economy anywhere in the world.[7]

NOTES

1. David Mitrany, *Marx Against the Peasant*, (Chapel Hill, NC: University of North Carolina, 1952).
2. Robert J. Alexander, *Communism in Latin America* (New Brunswick, NJ: Rutgers University Press, 1957).
3. Luis E. Aguilar (ed.), *Marxism in Latin America* (New York: Alfred A. Knopf, 1968).
4. Michael Novak, *Will It Liberate? Questions About Liberation Theology* (New York: Paulist Press, 1986).
5. Michale Radu and Bladimir Tismaneanu, *Latin American Revolutionaries: Groups, Goals, and Methods* (Washington, DC: Pergamon-Brassey's, 1990).
6. Robert A. Packenham, *The Dependency Movement: Scholarship and Politics in Developmental Studies* (Cambridge, MA: Harvard University Press, 1992).
7. The author also recommends the following works which address a range of issues associated with the topic of this essay and which have been drawn upon in support of the arguments made: Charles Gibson, *The Black Legend: Anti-Spanish Attitudes in the Old World and the New* (New York:

Russell W. Ramsey, Ph.D., D.Min.

Alfred A. Knopf, 1971); Paul H. Lewis, "Review Essay: Political Scholarship," *Journal of Interamerican Studies and World Affairs* (Winter 1961); Russell W. Ramsey, *Guardians of the Other America's: Essays on the Military Forces of Latin America* (Lanham, MD: University Press of America, 1997); Russell W. Ramsey, "Hopeful Neoliberals, Derailed Collectivists: Emerging Paradigms on Latin America," *Journal of Comparative Strategy* (Winter 1996); Ruth Legur Sivard, *World Military and Social Expenditures*, 1997, 20th ed. (Washington, DC: World Priorities, Inc., 1997); Robert Brent Toplin, "Point of View: Many Latin Americanists Continue to Wear Ideological Blinders," *Chronicle of Higher Education*, March 30, 1994; and Timothy P. Wickham-Crowley, *Guerrillas and Revolution in Latin America: A Comparative Study of Insurgents and Regimes* (Princeton: Princeton University Press, 1992).

US - LATIN AMERICAN MILITARY RELATIONS

"The Role of Latin American Armed Forces in the 1990s," *Strategic Review*, Fall, 1992.

The Author: Dr. Ramsey is Distinguished Visiting Professor at the U.S. Army School of the Americas, Ft. Benning, GA. Dr. Ramsey graduated from West Point in 1957 and received his Ph.D. from the University of Florida in 1970. From 1960 to 1962, he was the first assigned instructor in counterinsurgency at the Spanish-language U.S. Army School of the Americas, then located in the Panama Canal Zone. From 1987 to 1992 he was Professor of National Security Affairs at the Air Force's Air Command and Staff College where he also directed the Latin America Symposium Series. He is the author of many books and journal articles on Latin American military and national security issues.[1]

In Brief: U.S. commentators have often portrayed Latin American militaries as obstacles to democracy in the region. But abuse of military power in Latin America was never as bad as in other parts of the developing world. In addition, "constitutionally obedient militaries" can make a major contribution to sustaining the current wave of democratization and the shift to free markets. U.S. policy should take "villain myths" about Latin American militaries with a grain of salt and support their roles as nation builders and agents for economic development.

"Gold, Glory, and God" are the famous (or infamous) "three Gs" taught by many historians as the motivation for the Spanish conquest and colonization in the Western Hemisphere in the early 1500s. The term is code language for the commonly accepted view of rapaciousness by the Spanish *Conquistadors*, implying that they came to get rich, at Latin America's expense; conquer new lands for the Crown; and gain millions of new Catholic believers for the Pope.[2] For the 1990s and beyond, the "three Gs" remain an easily memorized code for the roles that Latin America's much maligned armed forces need to play in the development of the region. The "three Gs" will, however, have different meanings than in the past.

If Latin America's current great wave of democratization is to endure, the region's booming shift to free market economics will have to pay off in jobs and decent living standards. There are urgent tasks that only the armed forces can accomplish to ensure such economic development. The armed forces will have to perform their altered task in a spirit of Constitutional obedience, with total awareness on the part of their leaders that each thing they do, or fail to do, has an economic impact. And U.S. policy in Latin America will have to support the concept of the Latin American military forces as nation builders and developers.[3]

If the recommended new policy works, the "three Gs" will mean that Latin America's armed forces will: plug yawning gaps in the drive to free enterprise development (gold); assist their governments toward self-perpetuating electoral democracy (glory); and protect vital civil liberties such as religious freedom under a Constitutional framework (God). To see how this concept might work, it is necessary to visit some academic myths about Latin America's armed forces, and to summarize briefly the economic theories which have governed Latin America in the past. Then, we can make the case for involvement by the armed forces of Latin America in economic development. Such roles, incidently, are not new.[4]

Villain Myths Versus a Factual View

U.S. academicians specializing in Latin America have vilified the region's armed forces in terms employed by no other group of regional experts.[5] Throughout the Cold War, many U.S. scholars portrayed Latin America as the victim of the East-West conflict which resulted in U.S. policies that used Pentagon dollars and weapons to prop up abusive, constitutionally disobedient regimes. The real enemy in Latin America, opined most U.S. scholars, was not Marxism-Leninism or Soviet-Cuban destabilization operations; it was Latin America's own military forces, and the U.S. military apparatus that sustained them.[6]

In reality, Latin America was ruled "gently" by Spain during the colonial era, certainly in comparison with other empires. Spain's Latin American empire, lasting nearly three centuries, was religious and economic in nature, and while there were few armed revolts during the colonial period, Latin Americans had to fight much longer and wage much bloodier battles to free themselves from Spain than their North American neighbors had to do to secure independence from Britain.[7]

When the Latin American Wars of Independence (1808-1830) ended, the region lay in ruins; only the generals had leadership experience, and only the armies could repair roads, deliver the mail, and, in short, govern the vast land expanses. This power vacuum was filled by the *caudillos*, men like Juan Manuel de Rosas of Argentina and Antonio López de Santa Anna of Mexico. They were rural political figures, not professional military officers, and they made and toppled governments in a hurly-burly process that paralleled the politics of late medieval Spain and England.[8] In the late 19th century, military missions on contract from Prussia and France laid the basis for professional armies in Latin America, and Britain's Royal Navy did the same with some of Latin America's sea services. Throughout the 19th century, Latin America had only two regional wars. Measured in number of wars, percentage of national budget for defense, percentage of military age males in uniform, and percentage of deaths resulting from war, Latin America was the least militarized region of the world.

In the 20th century, Latin America's armed forces remained small. Most South American armed forces professionalized on the European model and became internal security forces, with occasional departures into *coup d'etat*. Central American and Caribbean armed forces remained, by comparison, personalized militias, answering to a *caudillo* and his cronies.[9]

After World War II, the United States unwisely drew Latin America into the Cold War at a time when there was no really dangerous communist threat to the region. Early cold warriors in the United States lacked the sensitivity to distinguish between legitimate social protest and armed communist insurrection.[10] By crying "wolf" so often, the U.S. government had a difficult time making both U.S. voters and NATO governments alike believe that there really was an armed threat when Fidel Castro's Cuban Revolution did become the Soviet Union's power surrogate in the region.

Meanwhile, throughout the Cold War, Latin America's armed forces were maturing, for the most part, into the most advanced and most appropriately configured militaries of the world's developing regions. While U.S. scholars were publishing polemical articles and books about "Pentagon-sponsored militarism in Latin America," far more abusive militarism was rampant in many nations of Asia, the Middle East and Africa; and the Marxist-Leninist nations were the most militarized of them all.

In all the 20th century, Latin America had just one regional war that did not directly involve the United States as a combatant: the Chaco War, 1935-1938, between Bolivia and Paraguay. And many times, Latin American states submitted their border disputes to diplomatic, juridical, or multi-national arbitration, e.g., the Colombian-Peruvian conflict at Leticia, 1932, refereed successfully by the League of Nations. Often, the Latin Americans put their small forces at the service of international blue-helmet efforts in Korea, Suez, Africa, and even in Central America.[11]

Economic Policies

Colonial Latin America was governed by an imperial economic policy-mercantilism that consisted of two stable components. Valuable raw materials were taken from Latin America to the mother country: gold, silver, indigo, sugar, lumber, copper, and cotton; and Latin Americans had to buy their manufactured or processed goods from the mother country. In both cases, the mother country exploited the colonies and, of significance for the present, denied the Latin Americans any practical experience whatsoever in money borrowing and lending, operating corporations, manufacturing, shipping, market development, distribution, and sales.

In the era of the *caudillos* (circa 1830-1890), small numbers of entrepreneurs learned how to do business with Europe and the United States, often in ways which worked against Latin America's people. Entrepreneurship never became an important civic value, and Adam Smith's free enterprise philosophy never truly penetrated Latin America.[12]

Positivism - an economic derivation from the sociological theories of Auguste Comte - reigned in economic circles at the dawn of the 20th century; men like Porfirio Diaz of Mexico operated their statist economies on principles that they believed to parallel the Darwinian "survival of the fittest." Like the rest of the world, Latin America suffered badly during the Great Depression. When World War II ended, the United States halted its policy of paying artificially high prices to the Latin American countries for petroleum, ores, and strategic raw materials. As a result of such economic dislocations, the region was in deep economic trouble at the outset of the Cold War.

Nationalistic industrialization programs - known collectively as "structuralism" - were advocated by Argentine economist Raúl Prebisch for Latin American development after World War II. These concepts prevailed from the late 1940s into the late 1970s. However, the alluring promises of Marzism had already won over many Latin American intellectuals in the 1930s, and by the Cold War era there were just enough who advocated state ownership of the means of production to convince U.S. Cold War statesmen that Latin America had a serious domestic communist threat. When Cuba became militarily linked to the USSR after 1960, it lent credence to the notion of a communist threat south of the border.

Fidel Castro appeared to be making an economic success out of Marxism-Leninism after 1961. People did not know that his "socialist Utopia" was a militarized welfare operation financed as a showcase by Moscow. Consequently, some genuine Marxist-Leninist groups did spring up in Latin America, with Moscow and Havana exploiting this opportunity to the fullest. Gullible U.S. scholars wrote about the validity of Marxist economic theory in Latin America, confusing the region's historic statist economic policies with the totalitarian economic policies of the former Soviet Union. The term "neo-colonialism" was coined to explain how Latin America was still a subjugated region, owned and exploited by its own "ruling class." The word *entreguista* became the stylized hate symbol for a business or political leader who sells out his own country for *imperialismo yanqui* or "neo-colonialism." The Brazilian economist Fernando Enrique Cardoso created a highly intellectualized paradigm called "dependency theory," which influenced the thinking of many U.S. scholars of Latin America.

What the academic advocates of Marxist economic policies in Latin America failed to see was a significant economic maturation process in Latin America itself. On their own, and in spite of rival East-West ideological efforts to "educate the Latins," the region's leaders watched the miracle of Asian Rim economic development and the East European drive to political freedom. They discovered the truth of Simón Bolívar's claim that constitutional liberty and economic freedom really go together.

In the military sphere, subtle forces, invisible to most outside observers, were at work in Latin America throughout the Cold War, fostering the employment of the military not only for internal security, but also for civic action and economic development. Continuing and expanding this precedent could help to foster democracy, plug key gaps in the economic development process, open doors for new investment, protect existing markets, create new markets, and defend constitutional political behavior by all parties.

Uniformed Nation Builders

There is evidence that creole militia in colonial Latin America sometimes played small economic roles in the continuing war against smuggling, worker disputes against colonial authorities, and, occasionally, construction of roads and harbors, Latin America's earliest codes of military law are, in reality, trade union (gremio) codes.[13] There is evidence that after 1830 the armed forces played a significant role in the restoration of law and order, the renewal of government services, and, to a limited degree, the reconstruction of economic functions.

The era of professionalization between 1870 and 1940 worked against the use of the armed forces in economic roles, since wartime roles and capabilities were emphasized over ancillary and civil functions. Nevertheless, military forces still performed engineering functions in remote areas, protected (and sometimes abused), native populations, and performed temporary economic tasks during earthquakes and other natural disasters. Several hundred Latin American officers attended U.S. service schools during World War II; at Ft. Riley, Kansas, courses were taught about the employment of the U.S. Army Corps of Engineers in the economic development of the Mississippi River, the construction of the Panama Canal, and the opening to settlement of the U.S. western plains.[14]   U.S. policy makers could have capitalized upon such a scheme for Latin American officer-students; instead they insisted that Latin American military forces become a kind of "mini-NATO" in the Cold War milieu.[15]

But Latin America's own military officers picked up the idea of using the armed forces to develop the national economy, for both better and worse.[16] As an example of the latter, the Army of Juan Perón's Argentina established its own set of national factories, a trend further advanced by Brazil under the military regime of the late 1960s. This form of military-dominated economic development had three goals: to establish a tightly controlled domestic arms industry; to wave the national flag against foreign economic domination; and to provide a source of revenue for the armed forces independent of taxation. This approach was similar to Mussolini's fascist state paradigm. Unfortunately, these policies exacerbated existing militarism, created an unnecessary regional arms competition, and discouraged private sector investment in the manufacturing of ships, trucks, aircraft, bulldozers and other vital machinery.

On the other hand, Colombian military officers who were engaged in stopping the long, agonizing violence between partisan *campesinos* in the backlands, discovered the teachings of Father Louis Lebret. Fr. Lebret, who had commented extensively on the role of the French armed forces in the era of Louis XIV, offered in modern words both a philosophical rationale for using the military as a disciplined institution under democratic control to aid in economic development and a roster of functions.[17]   Between 1958 and 1965, the Colombian Armed Forces brought these functions to fruition with spectacular success,[18] the benefits of which are lost on journalists who now see only the impact of the narcotics industry on Colombia.[19]

Economic Roles for the Latin American Armed Forces

Military personnel in Latin America, as in all countries, receive continuing education. Mathematics and literacy instruction (*alfabetismo*) of military recruits is positive gain in countries where free, public education does not truly extend to all. Parallelling basic instruction is the technical training (*capacitacion*) provided to military personnel during their periods of service. The United States bases the argument of Congressional funding of such programs as the Civilian Conservation

Russell W. Ramsey, Ph.D., D.Min.

Corps in the Great Depression, and of Job Corps, since 1964, upon the linkage between literacy and technical training for the underclass, and heightened economic production by the labor force. Clearly, in countries where the lack of literate and technically qualified workers hinders economic development, the educational contribution of the Latin American armed forces is positive and quantifiable.[20]

Services provided by the armed forces in the remote regions of the nations help integrate these areas into the national economy. The armed forces provide transportation, field equipment, organizational discipline, and the ability to protect the populace in remote regions from armed criminals and rebels. The armed forces provide the field medical services which the public and private health systems cannot. They extend law and order to a population not accustomed to being protected by their own government. They build roads, health clinics, boat docks, airstrips, storage barns, and human shelters on a short-term basis while these regions are being incorporated into the national mainstream. In some cases, they can even operate public schools on a limited basis until the region is made safe and secure.

The armed forces protect natural resources. For example, they have competent, well-educated staff who function as a go-between among workers, companies in a hurry to exploit the environment for profit, and government officials who are afraid or unwilling to carry out their environmental policing functions in remote areas.

The armed forces can play a major role during natural disasters, such as floods, famine, earthquakes, hurricanes, tidal waves, and fires which demand disciplined planning and logistical capabilities. A model here is the close relationship between the U.S. armed forces and the American Red Cross. But several Latin American countries already have functional models in place which do the job for a lot less money than the U.S. counterpart military-civilian team. And only the armed forces can restore order in the face of widespread looting and violence that often accompany natural disasters.

Several positive, non-combat roles of the armed forces which have economic development functions already exist. One is fighting the *narcotraficantes*. The narcotics industry has an enormous, negative effect on economic growth in developing countries.

A second role is the protection and assistance of tourists. The protection of tourists is vital because so many Latin American countries depend upon tourism as a source of revenue. The maintenance of stability is also an economic role for the armed forces. Educated and disciplined armed forces acting under legitimate authority can prevent debilitating *coups d'etat* which are costly in terms of public damage, loss of life, broken trade treaties, and altered policies that disrupt production and discourage investment. The key here is, of course, that armed forces must not take advantage of an armed challenge to their governments.[21] Latin America's regional record on this delicate issue is far superior to that of Africa, mainland Asia, and much of the Middle East.

Finally, there are passive economic roles that the armed forces can play, and negative roles that they should not play. Armed forces must recognize that their own cost may itself be a national security issue; defending a bankrupt nation-state is a contradiction in terms.[22] As in the case of the United States, this involves a delicate interplay with the legislative branch, which approves the budgets in many Latin American countries. The outcome can be huge financial savings, or enormous wastage through deals with unscrupulous civilian politicians.

By analogy, in the United States there exist hundreds of unnecessary installations in which the military must acquiesce in order to obtain congressional support for weapons, personnel levels, and salaries. On this issue, the notion of a totally apolitical military hierarchy disappears; a better paradigm would be for Latin America to educate "politically aware" officers who are "obedient to elected administrations."[23] Scholars who categorically condemn the Latin American military forces for "military interference in civilian politics" are, for the most part, naively unaware of how civilian populations manipulate the national defense issue in all free societies to obtain local spending, whether for bases or contracts.

U.S. Policy Imperatives

Most analyses of U.S. policy toward Latin America are characterized by one of two simplistic, dangerously incorrect views.[24] On the one hand, "conservatives" have held since early in the 20th century that the United States should make deals with military, financial and political leaders of Latin America who will keep order. Research on authoritarian regimes demonstrates that, with the exception of the Pinochet dictatorship in Chile (1974-1989), they do not carry out their promises to provide for economic development. It was after all the authoritarian regimes of Fulgencio Batista in Cuba, and Anastasio Somoza in Nicaragua, that paved the way for communist revolution, the very outcome that U.S. supporters of the these dictatorships wanted to avoid.

On the other hand, "liberals" have fostered the notion that the armed forces of Latin America are the chief enemy of freedom, and that, if they could just be abolished, democracy and prosperity would both flourish. During the Cold War years, this often meant caving in to Castro-sponsored revolutionists, who lurked behind the scenes in many a reformist political group in Latin America. Had this view prevailed, several countries besides Cuba and Nicaragua would have suffered the misery of Marxist-Leninist rule.

If both these approaches have led to failure, what is the proper U.S. security policy for Latin America? What can the United States do to encourage the military forces of Latin America to promote economic development in a climate of Constitutional obedience? Continued attachment to both democracy and free enterprise is not a foregone conclusion in Latin America: Several of the region's armed forces do have a history of "saving the nation" via *coup d'etat* when things go wrong politically. Exacerbating the problem is the growing pressure for protectionist trade policies in the United States. Such policies do great economic damage to both the United States and Latin America. The political effect on Latin America would be to actually encourage some Latin American armed forces to engage in "praetorianism" again, posing as national defenders against the bullying northern oppressor.

U.S. liberals must recognize that Latin America is going to have military forces whether or not they like it. Since the 1648 Treaty of Westphalia, the military forces of a nation-state have constituted the purest expression of sovereignty. But U.S. conservatives who advocate backing *any* Latin American elements who promise to maintain order and stability must also recognize, now that the Cold War is over, that their concept is economically inverted. The exciting economic growth in Latin America today occurs in countries with democratically elected governments, not dictatorships. For example, returning to office the legally elected Haitian President, Jean-Bertrand Aristide, should be a high U.S. priority, even if it means disarming and jailing segments of Haiti's armed forces by Organization of American States or United Nations forces.

Assisting Latin American Militaries

There are several policies the United States can pursue to help Latin America's armed forces play constitutionally obedient roles that encourage economic development.[25] First, the United States should continue to support such installations as the U.S. Army School of the Americas at Ft. Benning, Georgia, where Latin American military officers can take U.S. courses in Spanish. The school is actually an inter-American center for the sharing of doctrine that works, and which fosters U.S. philosophical beliefs on civil-military relations.[26]

Second, Latin American military officers who have positive track records in creating economically useful roles that follow constitutional norms should be invited to participate in Hemispheric economic and political dialogue. Their didactic presence is worth many times the cost of making them available. Third, both public and private economic development projects in Latin America should be designed and carried out so that local military leaders can exercise a planning voice and discover useful roles.

Fourth, the United States needs to recognize that it is not the sole investor in Latin America. It needs to encourage other nations who do business in the Hemisphere to work with Latin America's military leaders. Investment in timber producing forests, development of off-shore fishery operations, and provision of commercial air service in remote areas are all examples of economic nation building that create and require ancillary military roles.

Fifth, while the United States now plays a greatly diminished role in selling and transferring arms to Latin America, the U.S., in conjunction with Latin American nations, should attempt to reduce the arms trade in the region. Latin American military officers should be made privy to U.S. expertise in weapons sales, limitation, and control in such arenas as Western Europe, Asia, and the Middle East.

Sixth, the United States should serve as an educational catalyst for helping Latin Americans discover the best roles for their military forces as their economies develop. U.S. universities offering courses in Western Hemispheric business, public administration, and economics should bring Latin America's top military intellectuals to their classrooms as consultants and instructors. Often overlooked in policy circles is the fact that many of Latin America's top business and government leaders hold U.S. post-graduate degrees.

Last, U.S. military assistance for Latin America should be designed to minimize the potential negative economic role of Latin American militaries. For example, U.S. policy should specifically prohibit assistance to Latin American armed forces that intend to engage in manufacturing that competes with the civilian sector. A nation receiving military assistance should be required to show how the funds will be used to foster economic development.

Now that the Cold War has ended, U.S. academics need to re-examine the role they played in forming opinions about Latin American militaries between 1947 and 1989. If they do this sincerely, they will see that they unfairly maligned Latin American armed forces in general, blaming the many for the sins of a few, and demanding that the Latin American military meet unrealistic standards. Following an honest re- appraisal, we can recognize the potential for development that Latin American armed forces provide. Latin American militaries have been playing positive roles in most of the countries for years and have a far better performance record than their counterparts in other world regions. They can now focus on economic development as an adjunct to democracy. In so doing, they will fulfill the highest dreams of Simón Bolívar and the other liberators who thought that political democracy and free economies, defended by constitutionally obedient soldiers, provided the best hope for peace and well-being.

NOTES

1. This article is based on a paper presented at the School of the Americas "Conference on the American Armies" in August 1992.
2. Gregory Cerio, "The Black Legend: Were the Spaniards That Cruel?" *Newsweek*, Special Issue, Fall/Winter 1991, pp. 48-51.
3. Gabriel Marcella, "Whither the Latin American Military?" *North-South: The Magazine of the Americas*, Vol. 1, No. 2, August-September 1991, pp. 34-37.
4. Rear Adm. Jerome Smith, USN, Vice Commander-in-Chief, U.S. Southern Command, "Banquet Address," *Proceedings, 8th Air Command & Staff College Latin America Symposium*, Maxwell Air Force Base, AL, October 1991, pp. 33-37.
5. See Lyle N. McAlister, "Recent Research and Writings on the Role of the Military in Latin America," *Latin American Research Review*, Vol. II, No. 1, Fall 1966, pp. 5-36; and David W. Dent, ed., *Handbook of Political Science Research on Latin America* (New York: Greenwood Press, 1990).
6. See Edwin Lieuwen, *Arms and Politics in Latin America* (New York: Frederick A. Praeger, 1961); and Edwin Lieuwen, *Generals vs. Presidents: Neo-Militarism in Latin America* (New York: Frederick A. Praeger, 1964).
7. Russell W. Ramsey, "The Spanish Military Orders," *Army Quarterly & Defence Journal*, (U.K.), Vol. 113, No. 3, July 1983, pp. 342-347.
8. Benjamin Keen, *A History of Latin America*, 4th ed., (Boston: Houghton Mifflin Co., 1992).
9. See John J. Johnson, *The Military and Society in Latin America* (Stanford, CA: Stanford University Press, 1964); and George Philip, *The Military and South American Politics* (London: Croom Helm, 1985).

10. Stephen G. Rabe, *Eisenhower: The Foreign Policy of Anticommunism and Latin America* (Chapel Hill, NC: University of North Carolina Press, 1988).
11. See Russell W. Ramsey, "Colombian Battalion in Korea and Suez," *Journal of Inter-American Studies*, Vol. IX, No. 4, October 1967. The trend has continued with Colombian troops in the Sinai Multi-National and Observer Force in the 1980s, and Argentine naval units in the 1991-1992 Persian Gulf War.
12. Michael Novak, *Will It Liberate? Questions About Liberation Theology* (New York: Paulist Press, 1986).
13. Lyle N. McAlister, *The "Fuero Militar" in New Spain* (Gainesville, FL: University of Florida Press, 1957).
14. Lt. Gen. Henry J. Hatch, USA, Chief, U.S. Army Corps of Engineers, "Beyond the Battlefield: The Other Dimension of Military Service," 1989 Kermit Roosevelt Lecture.
15. See Willard F. Barber and C. Neale Ronning, *Internal Security and Military Power: Counterinsurgency and Civic Action in Latin America* (Columbus, OH: Ohio State University Press, 1966). Also Maj. Gen. H. H. Fischer, USA, Chief, U.S. Delegation to the Inter-American Defense Board, "Memorandum for the President," May 24, 1961, Washington Dc. See No. 3, page 1: "Civil Action is the technique of efficiently utilizing the capabilities of the military and national security forces of a nation to help the local population in projects of economic and social development, in such areas as health, sanitation, well- being, education, and agriculture. . ."
16. Edward B. Glick, *Peaceful Conflict: The Non-Military Use of the Military* (Harrisburg, PA: Stackpole Books, 1967). This book was influential in triggering public assistance programs carried out by the U.S. and South Vietnamese armed forces in the former Republic of Vietnam; an inherently valid set of policies is denigrated by public disgust with the outcome of that conflict.
17. Louis J. Lebret, *Teaching Function of the Armed Forces; The Economic and Humanistic Missions*, reprinted in Spanish in *Study on the Condition of Development in Colombia* (Bogotá: Editorial Cromos, 1958).
18. Russell W. Ramsey, "Internal Defense in the 1980s: The Colombian Model," *Journal of Comparative Strategy*, Vol. IV, No. 4, 1984; and in Spanish, *Military Review* (Hispanic- American Edition), Vol. LXVII, No. 7, July 1987.
19. Jorge Gómez Lizarazo, "Colombian Blood, U.S. Guns," *New York Times*, January 28, 1992.
20. Roberta S. Ramsey and Russell Ramsey, "So Why Does Job Corps Work?" *College Student Journal*, Vol. 17, No. 1, Spring 1983.
21. Tim Padgett, "This is the Last Roar of Militarism," *Newsweek*, February 17, 1992, p. 34; and Carlos Salinas de Gortari, President of Mexico, "We Have Got to Get Together," *Newsweek*, February 3, 1992.
22. Maj. Gen. Bernard Loeffke, USA, President, Inter-American Defence Board, "Keys for Civilians Who Want to Understand and Work with the

Military," *North-South: The Magazine of the Americas*, Vol. 1, No. 5, February-March 1992, pp. 18-23.
23. Louis W. Goodman, Johanna S.R. Mendelson, and Juan Rials, eds., *The Military and Democracy: The Future of Civil Military Relations in Latin America* (Lexington, MA: D.C. Heath & Co., 1990).
24. Lars Schoultz, *National Security Policy of the United States Toward Latin America* (Princeton, NJ: Princeton University Press, 1987).
25. Gen. Colin L. Powell, USA, Chairman, Joint Chiefs of Staff, *National Security Strategy of the United States* (Washington, DC: U.S. Government Printing Office, 1992); and Georges Fauriol, ed., *Security in the Americas* (Washington, DC: National Defense University Press, 1989).
26. Russell W. Ramsey, "La Escuela de las Americas: 40 años y 50 mil Graduados," *Military Review* (Hispanic- American Edition), Vol. LXXVIII, No. 1, January 1988, pp. 2-7.

Russell W. Ramsey, Ph.D., D.Min.

"US Military Courses for Latin Americans are a Low-Budget Strategic Success," *North-South*, February-March, 1993.

The United States will spend about US $15.5 billion in foreign assistance programs during FY 1993, a little less than half of which (US $7.3 billion) is tagged for military security programs. Nearly two-thirds of US military security assistance funds (US $5.3 billion) end up in the contentious Middle East; Latin America, fully engaged in economic privatization and rapid democratization, gets about US $860 million of this money, mostly to help fight the drug war in the Andean Region.

A small component of military security assistance funds (US $47.5 million) is called International Military Education and Training (MET), and US $12.9 million (MET, Latin America) of this operates most of the Western Hemisphere's longtime bargain basement secret; military courses in Spanish for the armed forces of Latin America, plus Spanish-speaking US military personnel. Recent human rights abuses by El Salvador's armed forces, and earlier repressive actions by military governments in South America, now couple with a rising isolationist mood in US politics to put at risk a half-century old program that has produced more peace, regional security and constitutionally obedient military behavior per dollar than anything comparable in any world region.

The US armed forces have been quietly working with their Latin American counterparts since 1943 by operating a network of schools offering courses in land, sea and air warfare, in the Spanish language, for officers and enlisted soldiers, sailors, airmen and police. The total number of graduates in just under a half-century now reaches 85,000, a figure exclusive of perhaps 25,000 additional Latin American military personnel who have routinely attended schools operated in the English language within the United States.

In 1943, the US Army Air Force began training air crews in Spanish, at Peru's request, at Albrook Air Force Base, and the US Army installed radar and vehicular maintenance courses, also taught in Spanish, at nearby Ft. Clayton, both bases being on the Pacific side of the Canal Zone. Latin American military leaders asked for continuation at war's end, and the former US Army Caribbean Command responded by reopening a school for flight crews and flight support personnel, conducted in Spanish at the Albrook Base, and a similar one for ground support personnel at Ft. Clayton. The US Navy and Coast Guard operated no formal school but continued binational maneuvers, training, and limited logistical and material support with their Latin American counterparts.

The onset of the Cold War redefined Latin America's national security position in US policy eyes. In 1949, the US Army moved its training operation for Latin American personnel to Fr. Gulick on the Atlantic side of the Canal Zone, and by 1956 all English language courses had been eliminated. In 1950, the US Air Force made the school at Albrook Air Force Base a permanent institution, with Spanish language instruction focused on regional air power needs.

President John F. Kennedy's hemispheric security policy was designed to protect the humanitarian dimension, the Alliance for Progress, but its value was not fully understood due to US public confusion over the unhappy results of counterinsurgency doctrines in Vietnam, and the vastly different Latin American region. In 1961, the Army's school at Ft. Gulick added the Counterinsurgency Operations Course, thereby acknowledging Latin America as a regional Cold War player with a genuine threat: Fidel Castro's revolutionary exportation machine. The following year the school was renamed the US Army School of the Americas (USASOA). The counterpart school at Albrook Air Force Base, in that period, took the name US Air Force School for Latin America.

The US Coast Guard was chartered, in 1961, to field a Mobile Training Team for Small Craft Operations in Latin America as a public assistance and national security component of the Alliance for Progress. By 1969, this highly successful venture was handed across to the US Navy and rechristened the Naval Small Craft Instruction and Technical Training School (NAVSCIATTS) at Rodman Navy Base in the Canal Zone. The Inter-American Defense Board (IADB) matured in that era as an advisory body to the Organization of American States. In October 1962, the IADB opened the Inter-American Defense College (IADC), operated on the same post (Ft. McNair, Washington, D.C.) as the US National Defense University (NCU), and paralleling the North Atlantic Treaty Organization (NATO) Defense College in Rome. While increasing numbers of Latin American guest instructors were appearing on the rosters of the other three schools in the Canal Zone, and senior Latin American military advice was sought in the management of these schools, the IADC was, from the beginning, a truly Inter-American institution. It is a war college, in curriculum level, and its faculty work for the IADB, not the US Department of Defense.

The US Congress took on increasingly, after 1973, the "no more Vietnam" syndrome. The 1976 Arms Exportation Control Act, unlike the 1961 Foreign Military Assistance Act, was candidly intended to prevent the US military from having anything to do with the maintenance of internal security in selected foreign countries. Most proponents of the "no more Vietnam" concept were unaware that Latin America, since 1830, has had fewer wars, fewer battlefield deaths, a smaller percent of its men in military uniform, and a vastly smaller percent of its gross domestic product spent on military things than any other world region. Many political leaders of the "no more Vietnam" genre were also duped into acceptance of the neo-Marxist fantasy that Latin America was a feudal region occupied forcibly by its own soldiers, who were in turn "armed and trained by the Pentagon." As a result, enrollment at the four schools declined during the 1970s, and certain countries were barred from sending students.

The would-be military dictator Manuel Noriega of Panama, holder of three course diplomas from the US Army School of the Americas, deliberately provoked crises which forced the School of the Americas to move from Ft. Gulick, Canal Zone, to Ft. Benning, Georgia, in 1984, and the sister Air Force school to move to Homestead Air Force Base, Florida, in 1989. The Infantry School, at Ft. Benning, turned out to be a much superior locale for the School of the Americas, and enrollment flourished immediately. The Air Force school also flourished in Florida, under the new name Inter-American Air Force Academy (IAAFA). In the fall of 1992, Hurricane Andrew destroyed the IAAFA, along with most of Homestead Air

Force Base, and the school was moved quickly to Lackland Air Force Base in Texas. Fortuitously, a short time prior to Hurricane Andrew, the Air Force had turned over helicopter training to the US Army, which opened an aviation branch of the USASOA at nearby Ft. Rucker, Alabama. Only the US Navy's NAVSCIATTS, colloquially called the Small Craft Warfare School, remained in Panama by 1992.

Statistical analysis of graduates from the four schools, by country, shows some trends. Numbers parallel challenges. For example, Colombia needed aviation personnel desperately during World War II and sent more than 2,000 men through the US schools in the Panama Canal Zone. El Salvador, under assault in the 1980s from the Marxist-Leninist FMLN and simultaneously pressured by the White House, the Pentagon and the US Congress to cease military atrocities in the name of national defense, sent several thousand students to all the schools. Also, for numbers to be meaningful as an impact measurement tool, one must put graduates in the numerator and force size in the denominator. Remembering then, that only Castro's Marxist-Leninist Cuba (1960-present) and Sandinist Nicaragua (1979-1990) show high levels of militarization by world standards, a few dozen graduates of useful courses, conducted amid the US military way of life among students and faculty from several of the Americas at one time, would appear to be influential.

The comparative horizontal dimension is instructive. Thousands of foreign students attend English language courses under US military auspices, among them many Latin Americans. In these settings, they can compare situations and standards with colleagues from 50 or more countries simultaneously. At the four Spanish language schools, there is no way to compare daily life and military procedures with, way, an officer from the Middle East, Asia, Africa, or Europe. But there is ample opportunity to find and compare the dimensions of Latin American life. The fact that several dozen graduates of the four schools have risen to the highest ranks in their respective services translates into cultural and national security linkage, not just with the United States but between and among fellow Latin American countries.

In the 1980s, Latin America experienced two great waves; political democratization and economic privatization. At the dawn of the 1990s, it was difficult to find Latin American military personnel who approved even passively of human rights abuse, and most thought of the military *coup d'etat* as part of the past. As the Cold War ended, many Latin American military personnel believed that the United States was too quick to cheer; they still faced drug wars, the urban poverty crunch, the environmental threat, massive foreign debt, the pains of industrialization, Asian and European economic competition, and civilian political demagogues who taunt them and then blame them no matter what they do. Yet soaring costs of armed forces, perceived lack of national security threats, and budgetary competition for resources in a truly democratic atmosphere meant that they were all cutting the size of their military forces. What then is to be their future?

General Jose de San Martin already stated it in 1820. It is "to protect the innocent oppressed" (political democracy) and "help the unfortunate" (economic development). The Latin American military forces have valuable roles to play: disaster relief; maintenance of civil order during turmoil; combating the drug lords;

serving the population in the remote backlands; policing offshore seas, lakes, rivers, and airways; and, of course, serving as the ultimate symbol and substance of national sovereignty. US enthusiasts of democracy in Latin America have for too long villainized the Latin American military forces as the true hurdle to democratic development. This theory is little more than intellectualized emotionalism, playing upon an old "black legend" theme from 18th century British Whigs who held Spanish manhood to be inherently violent, cowardly and immoral. The record of the Latin American armed forces in helping their citizens, developing their economies and sustaining the unity and territorial integrity of their countries is consistently superior to that of comparable world regions since 1830.

The budget for the four US schools that train Latin American defense facilities would not make their operations more efficient and productive.

The Army (USASOA), Air Force (IAAFA), and Navy (NAVSCIATTS) schools should be combined under the Department of Defense into the Inter-American Defense University (IADU), staffed by all the US armed forces and their counterparts from Latin America. Consideration should be given to installing branch campuses throughout Latin America, operated administratively by host countries. After a transitional period, this combined set of schools could be merged with the IADC, and the entire operation placed under the IADB, making the IADU an OAS training and security institution at all levels.

Course offerings should parallel the military needs of the region, as they presently do, rather than seek to compete with military needs in Europe or Asia. Courses on international peacekeeping, international law, history, government, anti-narcotics operations, worldwide mercy missions, weapons disarmament and national security processes in such places as the former USSR and Yugoslavia need to be added or strengthened. The present emphasis on human rights is appropriate, not as a response to anti-military pundits and leftist radicals in search of a cause but because the subject is always important for people who bear arms and hold public trust. By these means, the armed forces of Latin America will be enhanced in their abilities to support economic development, with constitutionally obedient performance at all levels.

Russell W. Ramsey, Ph.D., D.Min.

"A Military Turn of Mind: Educating Latin American Officers," *Military Review*, August, 1993.

In his 1820 *Voyage to South America*, US observer Henry Brackenridge opined, "Excepting the entry of General (George) Washington into Philadelphia, or General (Andrew) Jackson at New Orleans, there is no instance in modern history, of respect paid to a mortal, equal to that shown to General (José Francisco de) San Martín, on his entry into Buenos Aires, after the Battle of Maipu." [1] On 8 September 1820, San Martín himself wrote, "My mission is to protect the innocent oppressed, to help the unfortunate, to restore their rights to the inhabitants of this region, and to promote their happiness;" a moral commitment quite distinct from that often ascribed to Latin America's military officers by Western academics and journalists, as they continue the "black legend" (*leyenda negra*) against people and things Hispanic by exaggerating and even inventing destructive attitudes and behavior among Latin America's military officer corps.[2]

The US Armed Forces have been quietly working with their Latin American counterparts since 1943 by operating a network of schools offering courses in land, sea and air warfare in the Spanish language, for officers and enlisted soldiers, sailors, airmen and police. The total number of graduates in just under a half century now reaches 82,990. An additional 25,000 Latin American military personnel have routinely attended schools operated in English within the United States by the US Armed Forces. Another several thousand Latin American military personnel have been influenced by US mobile training teams (MTTs), advisory missions and participants with US personnel in binational or multinational maneuvers.[3]

The Historical Origins

Latin America's commitment to foreign military education and training began in the wars of independence, when British and other European veterans of the Napoleonic Wars came to help the Creole leadership organize local armies to defeat Spanish royal military power.[4] Creole leaders such as Colombia's President Francisco de Paula Santander and US President Thomas Jefferson advocated the democratic development of independent nations in the Western Hemisphere after 1830, but the process was marred by the rise of the *caudillos* - regional strong men such as Argentina's Juan Manuel de Rosas; Paraguay's Francisco Solano López; and Mexico's Antonio López de Santa Anna. Lack of civic training in democratic processes and the massive devastation of the wars of independence coupled with a pre- Enlightenment Spanish military institution - the soldier-priest figure who exercises civil authority - caused the *caudillos* to give Latin America a bad name as a militaristic, semifeudal region.[5]

Chile opened the door to modern military professionalism in the Latin American region in 1886 with the invitation of a German military mission to train the army. Perú, a regional rival of some intensity in those days, responded with the importation of a French military mission. Britain's Royal navy dispatched officers to train Argentinian naval personnel as well. In the early 20th century, Chilean military and police training missions diffused professionalism throughout the Andean region, Mexico and Central America.[6] South America's armed forces became highly professionalized on the European model; Central America and the Caribbean retained *caudillos* backed by armed forces having personal identification with the strong men.[7]

During the age of gunboat diplomacy, the US Marine Corps trained the nucleus of a national security force during interventions in the Dominican Republic, Haiti and Nicaragua; and the US Army helped establish a National Guard for Panama.[8] During World War I, as British maritime power receded in the Western Hemisphere, US Navy officers conducted small binational maneuvers and training operations with the Atlantic South American navies.

In the late 1930s, native Fascist movements were operational in Mexico, Brazil, Argentina and Chile; and two networks of Nazi Germany's espionage systems set up bases to overwatch Allied shipping and guide U-boat skippers to their targets. German immigrant pilots worked for Colombia's SCADTA, a nationalized airline, and some had orders to watch for an opportunity to bomb the vital and vulnerable Panama Canal. Intensive diplomacy by Navy officers helped redirect Argentina toward the Allied camp, and President Franklin D. Roosevelt persuaded Brazil to place large army forces in the northeastern hump facing Africa to bar a potential German invasion.[9] Army Air Force, Navy and Coast Guard personnel co-manned radar sites with local counterpart servicemen on strategic overwatch sites such as the Galápagos Islands, and US regional leadership quietly Americanized the process of foreign military assistance and training within most of Latin America while the eyes of the world focused upon the battlefields of World War II.

Roots in World War II

In 1943, the Army Air Force began training air crews in Spanish, at Perú's request, at Albrook Air Force Base, and the Army installed radar and vehicular maintenance courses, also taught in Spanish, at nearby Fort Davis, on the Pacific side of the former Canal Zone. These two processes, when World War II ended, were momentarily shut down; Latin American military leaders asked for continuation and even expansion of the courses. The former Army Caribbean Command responded by reopening a school for flight crews and flight support personnel, conducted in Spanish at the Albrook Base and a similar one for army support personnel at Fort Davis. The Navy and Coast Guard retained no formal school but continued binational maneuvers, training and limited logistic and material support with their Latin American counterparts.[10]

The onset of the Cold War redefined Latin America's national security position in US policy eyes. In 1949, the Army moved its training operation for Latin American personnel to Fort Gulick, on the Atlantic side of the Canal Zone, using a beautiful complex of concrete buildings built during World War II as a hospital. By 1956, all English language courses had been eliminated. In 1947, when the Air Force became independent, Latin American security experts, wearing the new silver blue uniforms, made the school at Albrook Air Force Base a permanent institution, with Spanish language instruction focused upon regional air power needs.[11]

Russell W. Ramsey, Ph.D., D.Min.

The Cold War Heyday
President John F. Kennedy's administration sparked the heyday of the US schools for Latin America. Kennedy's hemispheric security policy was designed to protect the humanitarian dimension, the Alliance for Progress. The overall security process from that era may be seen in retrospect as unique, humane, inexpensive and strategically determinative, but its value was not fully understood at the time. Consequently, there is only a limited constituency within the national security community in the United States who understands the importance of the US Spanish language military schools now serving both US and Latin American personnel. The political opponents of those schools have succeeded in heaping ridicule upon them.[12]

In 1961, the Army's school at Fort Gulick added the Counterinsurgency Operations Course. Both substantively and symbolically important, it signaled a shift to the acknowledgment of Latin America as a regional Cold War player with a genuine threat - Fidel Castro's revolutionary exportation machine.[13] The next year, the school capitalized upon the themes of inter-American military brotherhood and professionalized officership, already seen in its motto "one for all, and all for one" (*uno para todos, y todos para uno*), by renaming the institution the US Army School of the Americas (USASOA). The counterpart school at Albrook Air Force Base took the name US Air Force School for Latin America, and for several years the two schools blended their students and faculty for occasional social contact.

In 1963, Colombian army officers highlighted the success of their civic action, psychological operations and counterinsurgency programs in putting to rest the hideous rural strife known in their country as *la violencia* before hemispheric national security leaders at the Conference of American armies.[14] The Kennedy era counterinsurgency doctrine, expanded tragically beyond its intended boundaries in Vietnam after 1965, was in its early pristine glory.[15] The Coast Guard was chartered in 1961, to field an MTT for Small craft Operations in Latin America as a public assistance and national security component of the Alliance for Progress. By 1969, this highly successful venture was handed across to the Navy and rechristened the Naval Small Craft Instruction and Technical Training School (NAVSCIATTS) at Rodman Naval Base in the former Canal Zone. Throughout the 1960s, enrollment flourished at the US-operated Spanish language land, sea and air warfare schools for Latin American personnel; and Inter-American Defense Board matured as an advisory body to the Organization of the American States. Increasing numbers of Latin American guest instructors were appearing on the rosters of the schools in the Canal Zone, and senior Latin American military advice was sought in the management of these schools.

Post-Vietnam Blues
Hard times fell upon the schools in Latin America during the 1970s. A wave of military regimes in Latin America during that era depended upon internal security forces to retain power, some of their personnel committed human rights violations and some of these personnel were graduates of the US-operated schools. The US

Congress increasingly took on the "no more Vietnam" syndrome, opposing anything that suggested extending the Cold War into developing regions. The 1976 Arms Exportation Control Act, unlike the positively worded 1961 Foreign Military Assistance Act, was candidly intended to prevent US military personnel from having anything to do with the maintenance of internal security in selected foreign countries.[16] While some Latin American military personnel were guilty of human rights abuses, and some generals participated in *coups d'état*, most uniformed professionals belonged to armed forces that had a constitutionally intended internal security role. Further, most of these personnel practiced a far higher level of human rights and military professionalism than their counterparts in comparable developing world regions.[17]

Most proponents of the "no more Vietnam" concept in Congress were tangibly ignorant that Latin America, since 1830, has had fewer wars, fewer battlefield deaths, a smaller percentage of its men in military uniform and a vastly smaller portion of its Gross Domestic Product spent on the military than any other world region.[18] Furthermore, these congressional leaders could not understand that US military training had a positive impact, not on national leaders, but on military individuals and units. Few wanted to hear that by prohibiting US arms sales, military assistance and training, they were forcing the more retrograde armed forces into the competitive world market, giving the former Soviet Union a free victory, allowing it the pretext, for example, to rush army tanks, MiG-23 fighters and schooling programs to the Peruvian army and air force. Many political leaders of the "no more Vietnam" genre were also duped into acceptance of the neo-Marxist fantasy that Latin America was a feudal region occupied forcibly by its own soldiers, who were in turn "armed and trained by the Pentagon."

Big Changes in the 1980s

Personnel from the Latin American police and security forces were barred from attendance at the US- operated schools in 1977. But the 1980s unleashed another unforeseen set of forces that have resulted in placing these schools on the threshold of realizing the dreams of San Martín, Santander and Jefferson- the existence of democracies where military forces protect the national boundaries, as well as human rights throughout the Western Hemisphere. Ironically, would-be military dictator Manuel Noriega of Panamá, holder of three course diplomas from the USASOA, forced his professional military alma matter to leave Panamá. For some years, observers had been saying that Panamá was not the best place for the US- operated military schools, despite Simón Bolívar's oft-quoted idea about the Isthmus as the "lighthouse of democracy." Larger countries, such as Argentina, complained that they were sending their officers to receive training as less-than-best training facilities, in what was essentially a US national security colony.

In 1984, Noriega manipulated the Panamanian government from behind the scenes to force a showdown, demanding that a Panamanian general be named commandant over the USASOAs at Fort Gulick, one of the military facilities not on President Jimmy Carter and General Omar Torrijos 1977 treaty's list for US retention until the end of 1999. US law has always prohibited command of US military personnel and assets by a foreign officer, as Noriega well knew, and the United States refused to buckle under.[19] The school was quickly moved to Fort Benning, Georgia, where the Infantry School provided facilities and training opportunities superior to those in Panamá, and on a more economical footing for the US taxpayer. In 1989, Noriega's hostile actions as illegal head of state in Panamá rendered Albrook Air Force Base unsafe for further instructional use. The Air Force school there, renamed the Inter-American Air Force Academy (IAAFA), moved to Homestead Air Force Base, Florida. Like the USASOAs farther north at Fort Benning and the US Navy's NAVSCIATTS, Spanish-speaking US personnel were allowed to attend the school to receive career development instruction in their own fields, and both US and guest Latin American instructors were on the faculty. In the fall of 1992, Hurricane Andrew destroyed the IAAFA, along with the most of Homestead Air Force Base, and the IAAFA was moved with great efficiency to Lackland Air Force Base, Texas. Fortuitously, a short time prior to Hurricane Andrew, the Air Force turned helicopter training over to the Army, which opened an aviation branch of the USASOA at Fort Rucker, Alabama.

Impact Analysis

Statistical analysis of graduates from the four schools, by country, shows some trends - and the numbers parallel challenges. For example, Colombia needed aviation personnel desperately during World War II to replace potentially disloyal German immigrants from the national airline, SCADTA, and to man radar stations, and sent over 2,000 men through the US schools in the Panama Canal Zone. El Salvador, under assault by the Marxist-Leninist FMLN and simultaneously pressured by the US Congress to cease military atrocities in the name of national defense, sent several thousand students to all the schools. Also, for numbers to be meaningful as an impact measurement tool, one must put graduates in the numerator and force size in the denominator. Remembering, then, that only Castro's Marxist-Leninist Cuba (1959-present) and Sandinista Nicaragua (1979-1990) have high levels of militarization by world standards, a few dozen graduates of a useful course, conducted amid the US military way of life among students and faculty from several Americas at one time, would appear influential.

The comparative horizontal dimension is instructive. Thousands of foreign students attend English language courses under US military auspices, among them many Latin Americans. In these settings, they can compare situations and standards with colleagues from 50 or more countries simultaneously and without the ideologically pressurized factors that the former Soviet Union employed to convert its guest military students into loyal communists. At the four Spanish language schools, there is no way to compare daily life and military procedures with, for example, an officer from the Middle East, Asia, Africa or Europe. But there is ample opportunity, thanks to the common bonds of language and religion, to find and compare the best in Hispanic American life. The fact that several dozen graduates of the four schools have risen to the highest ranks in their respective services translates into cultural linkage, not just with the United States but between and among fellow Latin American countries.

In the 1980s, Latin America experienced the two great waves: political democratization and economic privatization. At the dawn of the 1990s, it was difficult to find Latin American military personnel who approved even passively of human rights abuse, and most thought of the *military coup d'état* as part of the past. As the Cold War ended, many Latin American military personnel felt that the United States was too quick to cheer. They still faced the drug war, the urban poverty crunch, the environmental threat, massive foreign debt, the pains of industrialization, Asian and European economic competition and civilian political demagogues who taunt them and then blame them, no matter what they do. Yet, soaring costs of armed forces, perceived lack of national security threats and budgetary competition for resources in a truly democratic atmosphere meant that they were all cutting the size of their military forces. What then is to be their future?

San Martín already stated it in 1820; it is "to protect the innocent oppressed" and "help the unfortunate." The Latin American military forces have valuable roles to play in economic development under obedience to civilian authority: disaster relief; maintenance of civil order during turmoil; combating the drug lords; serving the population in the remote backlands; policing the offshore seas, the lakes, the rivers and the airways; and, of course, serving as the ultimate symbol and substance of national sovereignty. US enthusiasts of democracy in Latin America have for too long villainized the Latin American military forces as the true hurdle to democratic development. [20] This theory is little more than intellectualized emotionalism, playing upon an old "black legend" theme from 18th-century British Whigs, who held Spanish manhood to be inherently violent, cowardly and immoral. The record of the Latin American armed forces in helping their citizens, developing their economies and sustaining the unity and territorial integrity of their countries is consistently superior to that of comparable world regions since 1830. The budgets for the four US schools that train Latin American defense personnel are a scarcely perceivable blip on the computer screen of US defense costs, and they have repaid the cost of their existence many times over.

What Should Be Done

USASOA, IAAFA and NAVSCIATTS should be combined under the Department of Defense into the Inter-American Defense University, staffed by all the US armed forces and their counterparts from Latin America. Consideration should be given to installing branch campuses throughout Latin America operated administratively by host countries. Course offerings should parallel the military needs of the region, as the presently do, rather than seek to compete with military needs in Europe and Asia. But courses on international peacekeeping, international law, history, government, antinarcotics operations, worldwide mercy missions, weapons disarmament and national security processes in such places as the former Soviet Union and Yugoslavia need to be added. The present emphasis on human rights is appropriate, not as a response to antimilitary pundits and leftist radicals in search of a cause but because the subject is always important for people who bear arms and hold public trust.

Russell W. Ramsey, Ph.D., D.Min.

If Bolívar, San Martín and Santander were alive today, they would approve of the four schools and advocate their expansion and further development. Jefferson might remind us that he founded the US Military Academy at West Point in 1802 to teach moral character and military skills to fledgling career officers whose business was to defend democracy.

Graduates by Country

School/Country	USASOA	IAAFA	NAVSCIATTS	Total
Antigua	-	-	18	18
Argentina	625	368	-	993
Bahamas	-	-	45	45
Barbados	1	-	19	20
Belize	6	11	57	74
Bolivia	3,967	1,120	713	5,260
Brazil	351	244	-	595
Chile	2,268	1,438	-	3,706
Colombia	8,148	4,453	56	12,657
Costa Rica	2,352	100	219	2,671
Cuba*	291	263	-	554
Dominica	-	-	17	17
Dominican Rep.	2,269	1,104	263	3,636
Ecuador	3,315	2,977	62	6,354
El Salvador	6,670	1,757	491	8,918
Grenada	-	-	22	22
Guatemala	1,668	991	305	2,964
Guyana	-	21	28	49
Haiti	50	48	12	110
Honduras	3,591	1,933	591	6,115
Jamaica	-	4	16	20
Mexico	507	548	2	1,057
Nicaragua**	4,693	811	170	5,674
Panama	4,235	1,321	485	6,041
Paraguay	1,076	508	103	1,687
Perú	3,987	1,232	18	5,237
St. Christopher	-	-	17	17
St. Lucia	-	-	26	26
St. Vincent	-	-	14	14
Surinam	-	6	-	6
Trin. & Tobago	-	-	6	6
United States	1,464	46	-	1,510
Uruguay	927	604	22	1,553
Venezuela	3,241	2,042	81	5,362
Total	**55,702**	**23,950**	**3,338**	**82,990**
(Countries:)	(23)	(25)	(28)	

*Ended 1959   **Ended 1979

NOTES

1. Henry M. Brackenridge, *Voyage to South America* (London, 1820), 212-16.
2. José Francisco de San Martín, "Decree at Pisco," 8 September 1820 quoted in Christian García-Godoc, ed., *The San Martín Papers* (Washington DC, 1988), 108-109. For the genesis of this prejudice, see Oliver Cromwell, "Speech at the Opening of Parliament, 1656," reprinted in Wilbur C. Abbott, ed., *Writings and Speeches of Oliver Cromwell* (Cambridge, MA: Harvard University Press, 1947), Vol. IV, 260-64; for a moderate version of the "black legend" repackaged as contemporary neo-Marxist conspiracy theory, see Paul Johnson, "The Plundered Continent," in Paul M. Sweezy and Leo Huberman, eds., *Whither Latin America?* (New York, 1963), 25-40.
3. Cumulative numbers of graduates were obtained by the author from the commandant or commanding officer, U.S. Army School of the Americas (USASOA), Fort Benning, Georgia; Inter American Air Force Academy (IAAFA), Lackland Air Force Base, Texas; and Naval Small Craft Instruction and Technical Training Schools (NAVSCIATTS), Rodman Naval Base, Panamá, October, 1992. See the chart appearing with this article.
4. Hubert Herring, *A history of Latin America*, 3d ed. (New York: Alfred A. Knopf, 1968), 258.
5. George I. Blanksten, *Constitutions and Caudillos* (Berkeley, 1951), 34-37 and Russell W. Ramsey, "The Spanish Military Orders," (British) *Army Quarterly & Defence Journal* (Summer 1983).
6. John J. Johnson, *The Military and Society in Latin America* (Stanford, CA: Stanford University Press, 1965), 69-72.
7. George Philip, *The Military in South American Politics* (London: Croom Helm, 1985), passim (this idea is the thesis of the book).
8. For a rich bibliography of first-person memoirs on these topics see Ivan Musicant, *The Banana Wars: A History of United States Military Intervention in Latin America from the Spanish-American War to the Invasion of Panamá* (New York: Macmillan Publishing, 1990), 447-54.
9. LTC Russell W. Ramsey. "The Third Reich's Third Front," *Military Review*, (December 1987): 58-65.
10. Richard A. Gorell, *Annual Historical Review: U.S. Army School of the Americas* (Fort Benning, GA. 1990), 1-7; LTC Russell W. Ramsey, "La Escuela de Las Americas, 50,000 graduados en el transcurso de los 40 años." *Military Review*, Hispanic Edition (January 1988): 2-7; Mike Fitzgerald, "NAVSCIATTS," Full Mission Profile, 1990, 62-64; Staff, "IAAFA Mission and History," pamphlet, US Air Force IAAFA, Homestead Air Force Base, Florida, 1990, 1-3; and author's interviews with MG Bernard Loeffke, Chairman, Inter American Defense Board, 1990.
11. Author's interviews with COL Thomas Crystal, USAF, commandant, US Air Force School for Latin America, 1960-1962.

12. Author's interview with COL Robert Rhine, G-2 (director, Army Intelligence), US Army Caribbean, 1961. The only objective summaries of this issue are found in Lyle N. McAlister's "The Military," in John J. Johnson, ed., *Continuity and Change in Latin America* (Stanford, 1964), 136-60, and his "Recent Research and Writings on the Role of the Military in Latin America," *Latin America Research Review* (Fall 1966): 5-36. Not all opponents of US arms and military training for Latin American are neo-Marxists. A liberal view-probably subscribed to by most US academics who study Latin America-holds that any US military assistance in all its forms simply magnifies militarism in Latin America. The holes in the argument are: 1) Latin America's own valid historical civil- military relationships, democratic but not respectful of civilian authority over the military as an absolute; 2) A confusion between cognitive education-the realm of facts and effective education-the realm of the emotions that control behavior; 3) A naive view, during the Cold War, that militarism would go away if US military assistance were denied, overlooking the Soviet record in arming allies and training revolutionaries; 4)the historically untenable notion that the existence of armed forces is the starting point of war and dictatorship; 5) Massive ignorance among academics about relative military abusiveness in developing regions and the Marxist-Leninist states, in comparison with Latin America. A complementary theory is that most US academicians who study Latin America fell guilty about the age of gunboat diplomacy and opposed US Cold War security measures in the region as if they were an extension of the Roosevelt Corollary, an artificial linkage heavily stressed by Castro's Cuban propaganda effort.
13. Russell W. Ramsey, "Caribbean Counterinsurgency," *Infantry Magazine* (November-December 1962): 21-23.
14. LTC Russell Ramsey, "Internal Defense in the 1980s: The Colombian Model," *Journal of Comparative Strategy*, Vol. 4, No. 4 (1984): 349-67.
15. The author personally heard the Kennedy "brain trust" lecture on these topics at the first course ever offered in counterinsurgency at Fort Bragg, North Carolina, January 1961, and again during their spring 1961 visit to the USASOA. The author also personally saw notes form the White House in the president's handwriting saying, "How is the anti-guerrilla training program going down there?"
16. See Dick Cheney, secretary of Defense, *Annual Report to the President and the Congress* (Washington, DC, 1992), 17-19, for a recent summary of US security assistance programs. Training for Latin Americans at US professional schools is only a small line item under International Military Education and Training (a small component with $7.3 billion annually for all foreign military assistance), which serves over 5,000 foreign military personnel from 100 countries annually.
17. Lars Schoultz, *National Security and United States Policy Toward Latin America* (Princeton: NJ, 1987), 290-92. Here is the "Uncle Sam is guilty under all scenarios" paradigm. Exploit human rights abuses by Latin

American military forces-some of them since revealed to be hoaxes, none of them examined comparatively or contextually-are taken as a valid policy rationale for the withdrawal of all US military assistance programs in Latin America. Schoultz's thesis is that Latin America's military forces could make no real contribution to Western Hemispheric defense against a major attacker, and hence all other security arguments lack validity. That same denigration of US security policy was used by Edwin Lieuwin in his 1961 *Arms and Politics in Latin America*. Had Lieuwin's advice been followed in the 1960s, one can easily visualize that five or six countries other than Cuba and Nicaragua would have experienced the Marxist-Leninist nightmare during the Cold War.

18. One can screen the British Statesman's Yearbook from 1830 to the present, in five-year intervals, for military force levels, spending levels, and recent conflicts, tabularizing the countries of the world by geographic region. The factual basis for the present vendetta against the Latin American armed forces on the part of most US professors who specialize in the region is thus undercut. When they are confronted with this evidence, however, one finds them retreating to Alfred Vagt's *A History of Militarism* (New York, 1937), which deals with Prussian Junkerism and has no cultural relationship with Latin America.
19. Schoultz, 167-68.
20. Georges Fauriol, ed., *Security in the Americas* (Washington, DC: National Defense University Press, 1989), 359-69. Fauriol's book was edited well before it was certain that there would be democratic and peaceful outcomes to the several Central American conflicts of the 1980s. It is a much more balanced and rational statement than the Schoultz volume, which seems to have been written as a vehicle for ending the Reagan policy in Central America.

Russell W. Ramsey, Ph.D., D.Min.

Review of: *Hemispheric and U.S. Policy in Latin America*, Edited by August Varas, Boulder, Colorado: Westview Press, 1989. Reviewed in: *International Freedom Review*, Summer, 1990.

A summary of *Hemispheric Security and U.S. Policy in Latin America* is not difficult: the book does not seriously address the issues it raises. Massive foreign and internal debts south of the Río Grande are easily among the top security concerns on the minds of Latin American and U.S. leaders and policy makers. In addition, the money-gulping, democracy-wrecking problem of the *narcotraficantes* (criminal drug cartels) occupies top security planners' attention in Bolivia, Perú, Colombia, and the United States. Neither of these issues qualify for more than tangential mentions in this book, and even then not as real security threats. Moreover, Cuban on-site meddling and arming of Latin American revolutionaries is mentioned only a few times, and, indicatively, in a jocular vein calling into scorn the viewpoint that Cuba presents a genuine threat.

Somewhat redemptively, five of the eight essays are of some quality. Four deal with issues of military policy; one deals with the Contadora Plan for Central America. The coverage is interesting, occasionally original, but hardly adequate to give the full treatment to Latin American security issues which the book's title implies.

The other three essays are straightforwardly leftist polemics, with the usual array of symbolic terms, twisted quotes from the writings of U.S. security experts, and no mention of Soviet or Cuban military adventurism in the region. A sampling follows: Robert Scheer's leftist polemic, *With Enough Shovels* (1982), is the cited factual base for Regan era nuclear polciy; U.S. Caribbean policy, after 1980, is said to have been made by "ruling groups"; Cuban-sponsored or assisted revolutionary groups are called "popular movements"; governments friendly to the United States are "conservative neocolonial political forces"; and U.S. policy in Nicaragua becomes "theology" and ". . . facts are irrelevant," according to a 1985 interview with leftist ideologue Noam Chomsky. Meanwhile, valid issues - massive foreign debt, narcotics smuggling, emerging Latin American relationships with Asia and the Pacific, shifting patterns of arms sales, and emerging democratic trends - are scarcely mentioned.

The first essay, "U.S. Military Doctrines," is a superficial and sometimes inaccurate summation of U.S. security policy in Latin America since World War II. For example, the authors misuse the April 11, 1984 *New York Times* story about El Salvador's FMLN Communist guerrillas supposedly being armed with "U.S. weapons captured from the Salvadoran Army" by quoting the source for this article to be Pentagon spokespersons and not the *New York Times*. Robert Turner's 1988 book *Nicaragua v. United States: a Look at the Facts* exposed this story as a disinformation triumph of the Cuban- directed Sandinista Information Ministry. The weapons were, in fact, imported from Vietnam, having been captured from the defunct South Vietnamese Army in 1975.

Authors Thomas S. Bodenheimer and Robert Gould, two medical doctors engaged in leftist social action and writing, devote nearly half of the article describing the Reagan administration policy in Central America as part of a worldwide scheme to "rollback" the Soviet Union and fragment its territory. While there were early Reagan ideologues who talked of "dismembering" the U.S.S.R. itself, no serious analyst of Reagan-era Central America policy believes the Reagan Doctrine to be more than an effort to prevent forward Soviet military basing in Nicaragua, a concern for which there was hard evidence in the early 1980s.

The second essay is Varas' own. He argues with sound logic that the U.S. position in Latin America was less unified and less powerful in the 1980s than in the 1960s, a consequence of "post-Vietnam War breakdown in the United States on a domestic consensus for foreign policy and economic competition from Japan and Europe. . ." He then writes about "security regimes," utilizing this term to describe both the militarized governments of certain Latin American nations - of which he obviously disapproves - and a new international order of security policies among the nations of Latin America as a region. He defines this as "a set of implicit or explicit principles, norms, rules and decision-making procedures around which actors' expectations converge in a given area of international relations."

Why, one wonders, is Varas so vague on a potentially valuable concept? Latin American diplomats and generals have advocated these "specified zones of Inter-American military cohesion" in many contexts since the 1930s. One example was Colombia's agreement to provide "blue helmet" troops to the United Nations (Korea, 1951-53; Suez, 1956-58); the Sinai Multi-National and Observer Force (1990). Another is the several maritime accords on fishing naval maneuvers, drug enforcement, nuclear-free defense, and electronic intelligence between the "Southern Cone" nations of South America.

Varas' concepts are interesting, but he does not define them. He calls for "specific security regimes" emphasizing "particular dimensions of security" and "not ignoring the U.S. presence in the region." He offers only one specific concept, a "free naval transit" security regime that would be "nuclear free," although Professor Varas seems unaware of how much is already being done in this area. Many aspects of his essay may be explained by the fact that Varas is a political sociologist and international relations analyst at the Institute of Latin American Social Sciences in Santiago, Chile, an independent leftist think tank known by its Spanish abbreviation FLACSO.

Mark Falcoff, an analyst at the American Enterprise Institute, contributes a short, excellent piece called "Military Security and Strategic Issues." He examines "alignment, nonalignment, and realignment" among Latin American nations as three possible bases for future U.S. policy in Latin America. "Nonalignment," as described herein does not connote an anti-U.S. military policy, but rather the absence of a NATO-like military alliance, such as envisioned under the 1947 Río Pact. Perú, in 1990, opposed the United States' 1989 "Operation Just Cause" removal of Manuel Noriega from Panamá and yet contracted for U.S. mobile training teams to enhance its anti-narcotic forces. Discussing each of the three stances in terms of recent political changes, both hemispheric and worldwide, Falcoff concludes that "there will be no open support for the United States" in Latin America, and that many Latin American governments will seek nonalignment.

Russell W. Ramsey, Ph.D., D.Min.

Margaret Daly Hayes' article "Understanding U.S. Policy Toward Latin America" is balanced and reasoned, but limited in scope. An economist with the Inter-American Development Bank, she defines several realms of U.S. policy goals in Latin America: encouragement of democratic governments, economic development, freedom of commerce, and integrity of borders. She argues for consistency in U.S. policies, and for a "positive response in the societies toward which they are directed." The United States should define its interests in Latin America more carefully than it has in the past. Then it should apply its policies consistently, she says, with special sensitivity to positive signals in each country.

Jorge Rodríguez Beruff, Director of Strategic Studies at the University of Puerto Rico, contributes "U.S. Caribbean Policy and Regional Militarization." He believes that the Caribbean was well along toward embracing "popular movements" in the 1970s, but that the Reagan administration then "re-militarized" the region. Professor Rodríguez offers tables on military training and equipment delivered to Caribbean nations by the United States during the early 1980s, and a chart on Cuba's defense budget in support of his ominous thesis: "popular" movements are being crushed by "conservative neocolonial" forces armed and trained by the United States. The charts are partial and selective: Soviet arms to Cuban and clandestine Cuban arms to "popular movements" are not represented in the charts. Missing also is the fact that arms sales and grants to the Caribbean from several nations (Britain, France, the U.S.S.R., etc.) were larger than those from the United States during this era.

Raúl Benítez and Lilia Bermúdez, political scientists at the National (Autonomous) University of Mexico, attack the Reagan administration's Central America policy in an essay titled "Freedom Fighters and Low Intensity Conflict." They assail it as merely the edges of a scheme to destroy the U.S.S.R., through alliances with retrograde elements throughout the developing world. This central thesis is buttressed by a footnote citing an interview with Noam Chomsky, the MIT speech professor who writes polemical books and articles for the U.S. Far Left on most international arenas (Vietnam, Middle East, Central America, South Africa, nuclear weapons, etc.).

Carlos Portales, Varas' colleague at the FLASCO Institute in Chile, offers excellent insights in his essay, "South American Regional Security and the United States." He offers a 7-point agenda for a "Cooperative Security Regime," suggesting that subregional units of South America define common interests and form categorical security regimes. Unlike Professor Rodríguez, Professor Portales shows awareness that the United States gave up the leading role as Latin America's arms supplier in the mid- 1970s, and he advocates subregional peacekeeping[1] on a broad array of issues.

The last essay, "The Contadora Initiative," is a blue chip piece by Niña María Serafina of the U.S. Congressional Research Service. She demonstrates how regional peacekeeping in Central America would have worked in 1984 had the U.S. backed the Contadora Plan offered by Mexico, Panamá, Colombia, and Venezuela. On-site observers from the four sponsoring Latin American countries were to have supervised the withdrawal of all foreign military personnel. The Reagan administration opposed it on the grounds that the Cubans would evade detection by posing as Nicaraguan civilians, with Sandinista help. This essay reads like a prediction of the roles now being played by the Organization of American States and United Nations peacekeeping and observer forces in Central America, in 1990.

The book concludes without an editor's summary or bibliography. It is thus impossible to obtain full citations for some of the footnotes and seminal works which may have influenced the several contributors of the essays. For this book to have met the lofty sweep of its title, it would have to reach out to much broader issues: debt, narcotics, specific country security issues such as Haiti's inability to operate a democracy, European influence, Japanese investment and trade competition, and the growth of fledgling democratic institutions in countries like Guatemala and Paraguay.

Bashing U.S. military policy one more time, and its vulnerable handmaiden from past eras - the Latin American military forces - is twenty years out of date and completely inadequate in the scope of its analysis. Ignoring Cuban subversion and the fact that most socialist countries are eagerly rejecting[2] the kind of system that Cuba flaunts simply reveals the obvious: that several of these writers see Western Hemisphere security issues in the same light that Fidel Castro sees them. The contributions of the bona fide, even-handed essays somewhat balance the political orientation of the book, but do not begin to fill the voids in topical coverage. One also wonders if any of these writers know that the military apparatus of the United States in Latin America - its own hemisphere - accounts for .06 percent of the worldwide U.S. military assistance budget, and claims .01 percent of the United States' two million uniformed military personnel.

NOTES
1. Under Professor Portale's plan, for example, Argentina and Chile would join with other nations having interests in Antarctica to guarantee neutrality.
2. Chile, for example, voted for the return of democracy in 1989, and not for the socialism of the Allende regime which was ousted by General Pinochet in 1973. Nicaragua, especially its "revolutionary youth," voted out the socialist Sandinistas in early 1990, Panamanian voters chose in 1989 to reinstitute democracy, not "ultra-nationalist socialism." El Salvador voted the moderate democratic coalition down in favor of the politically conservative ARENA party.

Russell W. Ramsey, Ph.D., D.Min.

"Training Latin American Forces," *Journal of Defense and Diplomacy*, April, 1988.

"Ramsey, you see this milk carton?" the Panamanian Guardia Nacional lieutenant was asking me angrily. I peered through the 2 a.m. haze in the dense jungle beside the Chagres River, barely able to make out the letters: Lechería Estrella Azul (Blue Star Dairy). My colleague answered his own rhetorical question.

"Los dueños son piratas (the owners are pirates)," he hissed. "They sell milk that passes health inspection to Americans on the Canal Zone at a fair price. The milk that fails inspection, they sell to their own countrymen at double the price." He squashed the offending cardboard carton in his hand with silent fury.

"You are a political democracy," I replied, which was true in 1961 when the incident occurred. "Change the system. Sue Estrealla Azul in court. Patronize another dairy." This, I knew, was how U.S. military officers correctly influenced their Latin American counterparts on the fine points of constitutional civil-military relations. After all, I was leading these Latin American officers from 18 nations on a tactical counter-insurgency exercise, as a faculty member of the highly reputed U.S. Army School of the Americas.

"Ramsey, the owners of Estrella Azul are the president, a Supreme Court justice, and the president of the National Bank," my friend was saying. "We, los militares, must rescue the common people or Fidel Castro will do it for us."

The lieutenant is now a general in the Panamanian National Defense Force, which has run the country, directly or indirectly, since 1967. Could I or my U.S. Army colleagues have taught that officer to stay in the barracks politically, and still block pro-Castro insurrections from within and without? Can any foreign military presence change a nation's behavior? This question is exactly a century old in Latin America, and the answer is critical, for it is the key to whether or not Latin America will swing over to the Soviet bloc in the 21st century.

Latin American military officers in 1988 spend more of their active career years going to school than any comparable professional group in the world. A century ago they rarely had any real military training at all, nor much of a formal education. Their long, bloody revolutions for independence featured small creole militia and large campesino units, trained and melded by British veterans of the Napoleonic Wars, against Spanish Royal troops.

Throughout the 19th century, Central American and Caribbean military forces were directed by caudillos, pre-professional men who were really rural políticos. The small exceptions took place in Mexico, influenced briefly by French military trainers during the reign of Maximilian I, 1862-1867; Cuba and Puerto Rico, which had some exposure to U.S. military leadership after 1898; and Panama, where U.S. police trainers were a small presence along the route of the Panama Railroad after 1848.

South Americans imported European army expertise and British naval professionalism in the wake of its two 19th century wars. Argentina, Brazil, and Uruguay had great difficulty defeating Paraguay in the bloody War of the Triple

Alliance, 1864-1870. In the aftermath of the conflict, Argentina brought in German officers to train the army and Royal Navy officers to modernize the fleet. Rival Brazil did the same, but also imported French military officers for army training.

In the War of the Pacific, 1879-1883, Chile bested Perú and Bolivia for control of the coastal port of Arrica and a Pacific corridor. Chile then hired a German training mission that built an army and a constabulary that became, for 50 years, the model of all South American armies, and is still evident in uniforms and dress parade customs. Perú hired French military missions, and Royal Navy influence soon became visible in west coast fleets. Shortly after the turn of the century, contract missions from Chile to Colombia and Perú spread the German drill system, and reliance on German and French military rifles, through the northern Andean countries.

World War I ended most direct German influence in South American military training, and the period between the two world wars brought other important developments in foreign military influence within Latin America. In Central America, U.S. police and military training were strong social forces within Panamá, Nicaragua, Haití and Cuba during the early 20th century. This influence waned, however, during President Franklin Roosevelt's Good Neighbor Policy in the 1930s.

In South America, a new type of military force and a new threat radically altered the nature of foreign military influence. The new force was air power, and training missions from Italy and the United States were instrumental during the 1930s in Latin America's pioneer air forces. The new threat was the Axis Alliance, and both Hitler and Mussolini tried to capitalize on their South American military influence through their army and air force missions. By 1938, U.S. Army, Navy and Army Air Corps missions were setting up training relationships that endured into the mid-1970s. Italian and German military trainers and saboteurs alike were identified and sent home by the host governments.

From 1945 until the Vietnam Conflict era, U.S. military missions, school training allocations and arms supply comprised overwhelmingly the greatest foreign influence on Latin America's armed forces. Rarely has a world power, during the course of superpower rivalry, enjoyed so clear an opportunity for 30 years. That era ended in the mid-1970s. Patterns of influence in the 1980s are radically altered, partially in some directions seen a century ago, and partially towards direct institutional control by the Soviet Union through its military missions, surrogates and clandestine apparatus. Important U.S.- Latin American military ties remain, however, and an understanding of the issues that existed from 1946 to 1975 is vital to the prevention of several more Soviet takeovers before the year 2000.

First, training of a foreign military force is often misunderstood as a means of wielding foreign policy influence. The imparting of cognitive facts - how to write an operations order, how to preflight an aircraft - does not translate into military allegiance. The congruence of values lies in the affective education realm, and it may take generations of transnational military exposure to convince foreign officers that constitutions are to be obeyed, that peasant conscripts in uniform have human rights. In the short range, the military officers of several Latin American countries beyond Cuba and Nicaragua may actually prefer the Soviet model for its apparent (but unreal) freedom of military action.

Second, inculcating foreign military personnel with elaborate abstractions, such as civilian control of the military, is, at times, physically impossible. The military representatives of Soviet totalitarian systems, of theocratic states, of military dictatorships all may, upon occasion, find greater local acceptance for their version of how thing should be done.

Third, international arms sales today are so expensive and so tied to lengthy tailstreams of parts and repairs, that they may, in some ways, be the permanent form of peddling influence among foreign military forces. During the 1946-1975 era, this factor was apparently not as determinative as many strategists believed.

Fourth, from 1946 to 1975, U.S. political leaders, especially in the Congress, acted out the liberal-conservative game in the Latin American milieu as though it was an extension of U.S. domestic issues. Thus, liberals thought they were enhancing Latin American democracy by demanding reduced U.S. contact with Latin American military institutions, while conservatives thought that support for outdated dictators in uniform would forestall Soviet influence. Southern conservatives in the Senate thought that arming dictators like Fulgencio Batista in Cuba and the Somoza dynasty in Nicaragua was strategically sound, when the evidence suggests that extended U.S. support for these two anachronistic regimes set up the conditions for a pro-Soviet takeover. Pro-defense liberals of the Kennedy era advocated the counterinsurgency and nation building doctrines for the Latin American military, but Vietnam Conflict-era liberals were completely wrong in thinking that denial of arms and military training to Latin America would encourage democratic development.

The Reagan administration shows clearly its awareness that propping up discredited dictators does not prevent pro-Soviet takeovers, and that denying arms sales and military training south of the Río Grande River does not reduce militarization. Further, the 1980s have seen some earlier forms of institutional influence upon the Latin American armed forces validated, some new forms developed and some inappropriate forms abandoned.

From 1946 to 1975, U.S. influence was exerted within the Latin American military forces through five basic systems.

First, most countries had U.S. military, naval, and air training and advisory missions assigned in the national capital, but separate from the diplomatic attaché presence.

Second, most Latin American military equipment during the period was of U.S. origin, either bought or granted outright, and with the equipment came a variety of internal and external training mechanisms.

Third, there were special schools for Latin American military personnel: the U.S. Army School of the Americas, and the Air Force School for Latin America, both in the former Panamá Canal Zone.

Fourth, a regular slot or two was filled by several Latin American armed forces at U.S. service schools, ranging from the senior War College classes to the cadet or midshipman ranks of the service academies.

Fifth, joint maneuvers and staff exercises were conducted from time to time, much reduced from the NATO scale, but still militarily significant.

In the 1980s, the former Military Assistance/Advisory Groups (MAAGs) are mostly gone. Special advisory and training groups are present for a finite period in threatened countries like El Salvador and Honduras. Second, the United States is no longer the largest provider of military equipment and the technical training that accompanies such equipment. France, Israel, Sweden and the United Kingdom are all major providers of arms and small technical training missions.

Arms, Flow, Latin America, 1971-1986

COUNTRY	RECEIVED ARMS FROM:	SUPPLIED ARMS TO:
Argentina	Brazil, Austria, Belgium, Bulgaria, France, FRG, Israel, Italy, Perú, Spain, Sweden, Switzerland, UK, USA	Bolivia, Central African Republic, Jordan, Kuwait, Morocco, Uruguay
Bahamas	UK	None
Belize	UK	None
Bolivia	Argentina, Austria, Brazil, Canada, France, Israel, Italy, Netherlands, Spain, Switzerland, Taiwan, USA, Venezuela	None
Brazil	Australia, France, FRG, Israel, Italy, ROK, Sweden, UK, USA	Algeria, Argentina Bolivia, Burkina Faso, Chile, Colombia, Ecuador, Egypt, Gabon, Guyana, Honduras, Iraq, Iran, ROK, Libya, Morocco, Nigeria, Qatar, Saudi Arabia, Suriname, Thailand, Togo, Tunisia, United Arab Emirates, Uruguay, Venezuela, Zimbabwe
Chile	Brazil, Canada, France, FRG, Israel, Netherlands, Spain, Sweden, Switzerland, UK, USA	Uruguay
Colombia	Australia, Brazil, France,	None

	FRG, Israel, Italy, Netherlands, Spain, Switzerland, UK, USA	
Costa Rica	Panamá, Spain, USA	None
Cuba	Czechoslovakia, Poland, USSR	Angola, Colombia,*Congo, Nicaragua, El Salvador*
Dominican Republic	France, USA	None
Ecuador	Brazil, Canada, France, FRG, Israel, Italy, Netherlands, Portugal, Switzerland, UK, USA	None
El Salvador	France, Israel, USA, Yugoslavia	None
Guyana	Brazil, France, North Korea Netherlands, UK, USA, USSR	None
Haití	Canada, Italy, UK, USA	None
Honduras	Brazil, Israel, Morocco, Spain, UK, USA, Yugoslavia	None
Jamaica	UK, USA	None
Mexico	Canada, France, FRG, Israel, Singapore, Spain, Switzerland, UK, USA	None
Nicaragua	Algeria, Bulgaria, Cuba, France, Israel, North Korea, Libya, Poland, Spain, USA,* USSR	El Salvador*
Panamá	Argentina, Canada, France, Spain,UK, USA	Costa Rica
Paraguay	Argentina, Brazil, Chile,	None

	Israel, Spain, USA	
Perú	Argentina, Brazil, Canada, France, FRG, Italy, Netherlands, Portugal, Spain, Switzerland, UK, USA, USSR	Argentina
Suriname	Brazil, UK, USA	None
Trinidad and Tobago	France, Sweden, UK, USA	None
Uruguay	Argentina, Belgium, Brazil, Chile, France, FRG, ROK, Spain, USA	None
Venezuela	Brazil, Canada, France, FRG, Israel, Italy, ROK, Spain, UK, USA	Bolivia, Botswana

*Indicates arms supplied to a rebel group fighting against the government of the country stated.

In the 1980s the Soviet Union, Czechoslovakia, Poland, Libya and North Korea are major providers of weapons to Cuba and Nicaragua, with large training missions both visible and sub rosa. The Soviet Union has been, since the mid 1970s, a major arms and training provider for Perú, a melancholic condition caused entirely by the obstructionist action of a liberal element within the U.S. Congress that thought it was retarding militarism in South America by denying Perú the sale of U.S. F-5 aircraft (1974) and nine years later of F-16 fighters. By some estimates, the United States now provides only 12 percent of major arms sales, overall, to Latin America, with the Soviet Union, France and possibly Israel exceeding the United States as suppliers. The Soviet training apparatus that accompanies its arms sales is vastly larger than any comparable effort ever fielded by the United States, exclusive of clandestine pro-Soviet operatives proving arms and training for the overthrow of pro-Western governments (See chart 3).

The special U.S. military schools for Latin Americans are now gone from Panamá, which took over most of the former Canal Zone in 1979. Replacing them are the U.S. Army School of the Americas, re- opened at Fort Benning, GA; the Inter-American Defense College in Washington, D.C.; and several course configurations offered by the U.S. Navy and Air Force within their own service schools. Latin Americans are still visible in small numbers at all levels within the U.S. military education system, and several Latin American countries now accept

Russell W. Ramsey, Ph.D., D.Min.

U.S. military personnel within their own professional education systems. Finally, several Latin American countries conduct joint training with counterpart U.S. forces (See chart 4).

Where then is the principal erosion of U.S. influence within Latin American military profession since the era of hegemony? Who, if anyone, has filled the void?

Foreign Military Sales Agreements*
(FY 1986 - $ in thousands)

East Asia and Pacific	$1,988,106
Near East and South Asia	2,026,222
Europe and Canada	2,489,436
Africa	126,366
American Republics	317,845
Antigua & Barbuda	615
Argentina	219
Barbados	355
Belize	524
Brazil	6,022
Chile	673
Colombia	6,268
Costa Rica	5,962
Dominica	458
Dominican Republic	7,309
Ecuador	4,887
El Salvador	122,040
Grenada	591
Guatemala	5,133
Haiti	1,135
Honduras	79,329
Jamaica	9,079
Mexico	5,493
Panamá	3,605
Perú	8,883
St. Christopher-Nevis	388
St. Lucia	385
St. Vincent & Grenadines	4,632
Uruguay	1,003
Venezuela	42,360
International Organizations	**111,086**
WORLDWIDE	**7,059,137**

*A program through which DoD sells defense articles, defense services and training to foreign governments.

First, the Latin American nations have matured greatly since the 1960s and fill many of their own voids. Thus, Brazil and Argentina both produce and sell weapons, with Brazil boasting an impressive list of customers in most world regions. Second, there is a wholesome exchange of officer students among most South American nations, and among a few Central American and Caribbean nations. A few Latin American service colleges have exchange programs with counterpart institutions in Spain and Portugal.

Third, much of the former U.S. arms sales have passed quietly along to third party nations that do not seek to exert wholesale political influence with the customer. Thus, Israel sells arms in large quantities to Ecuador and Honduras, seeking no return beyond payment and support for Israel's Middle East policies within the United Nations. Australia, Sweden and the Netherlands all have Latin American arms customers, but exert little influence among them.

Fourth, the Soviet Union wields an unparalleled quantity of influence over the military forces of its two client states, Cuba and Nicaragua. Numbers of advisors sent to the host country, numbers of student slots for Cubans and Nicaraguans in the USSR, and quantities of arms supplied are vastly greater than the relationship that existed between the United States and all Latin American countries in past years. Further, the Soviets show considerable flexibility in dealing with Peruvian military officers, whose forces use large quantities of Soviet planes, tanks and antiaircraft equipment. While some Peruvians were shocked at the primitive, secretive nature of life in the USSR during their course of study there, the raw number of Peruvians exposed to Soviet thinking is greater that total Peruvian-U.S. exposure during the early 1960s.

Finally, France and the United Kingdom have taken up some of the void left by the decline of U.S. influence among the Latin American military forces. The overall effect here is ideologically positive, but the proliferation of arms supply guarantees a logistical nightmare in the event of future cooperative warfighting.

International Military Education & Training**
(FY 1986 - $ in Thousands)

	DELIVERIES ($)	STUDENTS TRAINED
East Asia and Pacific	9,700	1,356
Near East and South Asia	9,833	1,029
Europe and Canada	9,375	637
Africa	9,478	683
American Republics	8,310	2,669
Antigua & Barbados	45	10
Bahamas	46	29
Barbados	69	15
Belize	72	23
Bolivia	143	23
Colombia	1,005	881
Costa Rica	222	76

Dominica	46	10
Dominican Republic	688	132
Ecuador	709	150
El Salvador	1,441	370
Grenada	75	18
Guatemala	357	95
Haití	233	20
Honduras	1,047	350
Jamaica	295	59
Mexico	190	19
Panamá	507	170
Perú	611	67
St. Christopher-Nevis	27	8
St. Lucia	48	13
St. Vincent & Grenadines	51	13
Suriname	34	7
Trinidad-Tobago	50	10
Uruguay	100	19
Venezuela	100	63
General and Regional Costs	5,289	
WORLDWIDE	**51,985**	**6,374**

** A program that provides training and training support to foreign governments as grant assistance. Figures shown here include military assistance service funded and Section 506. The program is considered fully delivered when funded.

The image of Uncle Sam as gunslinger for Latin America is somewhat reduced by the multi-nationalization of arms sales, but this one small psychopolitical benefit scarcely offsets the loss of influence and western hemisphere arms standardization.

Influencing the Latin American military forces is a delicate task for the U.S. armed forces. Is it even worth the effort in a milieu where Senator Jesse Helms advocates for the Pinochet dictatorship in Chile, and former House speaker "Tip" O'Neal advocated for the Communist Sandinistas in Nicaragua? The USSR seems to think so.

Soviet geostrategic thinkers, influenced by Dr. Viktor Volski at the Moscow University's Institute for Latin American Studies, are highly sophisticated in their approach to the Latin American military institutions. Volski and his coterie have seen, correctly, that the Latin American military officer is part of the technocratic leadership element among whom successful Communist revolutions are made. Soviet propaganda portrays the Latin American military man as a bumbling, repressive caudillo through its U.S. fronts, while at the same time, making highly positive overtures to the Latin American officer in his own country.

Many U.S. academic analysts and journalists fall into a sophisticated trap, continuing to portray the Latino officer as an enemy of true democracy, and helping the Soviet Union to persuade that same officer that Soviet friendship is sincere. The

1977 Carter-Torrijos treaties contain no basing rights whatsoever for the United States in Panamá beyond the year 1999. Here is a major, watershed issue, both substantive and symbolic, of U.S. geostrategic power in the Americas. The Soviet Union will appeal directly to the nationalistic sentiments within Latin America's political and military leadership, offering large quantities of arms at low cost, with huge advisory structures, in exchange for not supporting a continuance of U.S. military basing rights in Panamá. It remains to be seen if the United States can acquire the political sophistication of the USSR's Dr. Viktor Volski in dealing with the Latin American military professional, or if the White House, and more often the Congress, will view the milieu as a legitimate extension of domestic liberal-conservative grandstanding.

United States military leaders are highly educated on the world power arena. They know how to field an apparatus capable of influencing the Latin American military officer in ways that are pro-constitutional, pro-economic development, and anti-Soviet bloc. The U.S. military leaders are themselves constitutionally subordinate to elected civilians whose ignorance of geostrategic issues in Latin America reflects longstanding public apathy toward U.S. military security in the western hemisphere. Thus, it seems likely that the Soviet Union's politico-military revolutionary exportation apparatus will take over at least two more Latin American countries by 1999. In the post mortem, someone may discover that influencing the target country's military men in the 1980s was the key dynamic behind their success.

Russell W. Ramsey, Ph.D., D.Min.

"World Needs School of the Americas," *The Albany Herald*, March 20, 1995.

In 1947 the U.S. Army made a few of its technical courses in the old Panamá Canal Zone available to the Latin American military and security forces. Courses in tactics, administration and support services were added over the years. Attorney General Robert Kennedy once deemed the school "an important part of the administration's Alliance for Progress." The School of the America's faculty gradually included officers and sergeants from most Latin American countries, using Army service school lesson plans that were translated into Spanish.

In 1984, one of the school's graduates - Manuel Noriega of Panamá - had gone sour. Acting as a policeman-dictator, he made an illegal demand for the school to have a Panamanian commandant, and the Army promptly moved the operation to Fort Benning, GA. Leftist political activists immediately targeted the school as a "training ground for dictators and human rights abusers," part of their bigger plan to reduce U.S. and democratic influence in Central America and impose heavily armed communist regimes within the region.

School of the Americas today is approaching its 50th anniversary. Its 56,000 graduates include a few foul balls, but the overall influence of the school in bringing professional standards to the armed forces and police of the Western Hemisphere is incalculable. Courses ranging from one month to one year and guest instructorships ranging from one to three years mix U.S. and Latin American military and police professionals.

All instruction and all support activities are conducted in the region's most universal language - Spanish - something that cannot be done for military training in other world regions due to linguistic disparity.

What good is the school, and what has it accomplished? The technical content of the courses is probably the least vital dimension, although the quality is good and contents are important. School of the Americas has trained, for example, more medics and more heavy engineering equipment operators than the entire school system of several small Latin American countries.

Officers from countries where military interference in government was once common have learned to submit to civilian political decision-making through their horizontal contact with U.S. and fellow Latin American military professionals. Personnel from countries whose armies once made war on their own populations have either changed or left the uniformed services.

School of the Americas is only one small component of these positive trends, of course, but the influence is measurable by tracing the rise to high positions of many of the graduates within their national forces.

School of the Americas today serves U.S. and regional interests in three ways. First, it creates a network of military and police professionals within the world's fastest growing economic region who can communicate and cooperate on challenges as disparate as Haitian refugees and the Andean drug war. Regional wars costing billions of dollars are thus averted.

Second, democracy and free enterprise are booming in Latin America, and enhanced military and police professionalism serves constitutional stability, something often missing in turbulent countries within Eastern Europe, Africa, Asia and the Middle East.

Third, the United States cannot afford to maintain a force large enough to police the world, and no one liked it very much when Uncle Sam policed northern Latin America in years past. By empowering the Latin American military and security forces to deal with the narco-traffickers, terrorism, natural disasters, service to remote populations, illicit arms trade, governmental plundering and regimental disputes, the United States avoids paying out billions of dollars.

School of the Americas costs annually about $3.5 million, and a huge positive ratio can easily be shown as the return-over-investment, measured in wars that did not happen, elections not overturned and human rights improvement in a few countries where the record was poor. Visitors are always welcome to view the training and meet the students, who have a close relationship with the city of Columbus. Several classes per year in resources management and logistics now get an all-day tour of the Albany Marine Corps Logistics Base, narrated in Spanish.

Latin America got a mere 2 percent of U.S. military assistance during the Cold War. The region has had the fewest wars, the smallest percentage of soldiers and the smallest military budgets (by percentage) in the world, measured since the year 1500. Today, only Communist Cuba is an excessively armed and brutally run dictatorship. Despite the mixture of leftist propaganda and anti- military falsehoods perpetuated by the highly paid press corps of the Andean drug dealers, Latin America has a far better human rights record than Africa, Asia, the Middle East or Eastern Europe. The region's armed forces have uniformed contingents serving, by request, in 12 of the world's 26 multinational peacekeeping forces.

School of the Americas can rightly claim a small role in helping to bring about the present conditions, and closing the school because of the often exaggerated and functionally non- attributable sins of a few graduates would be a perfectly stupid signal to send out to our Latin American neighbors, just as the hemispheric future is so bright.

Why a School of the Americas in 2001?
The National Security Policy Process Model

The Americas, 2001

	POLITICAL	MILITARY	ECONOMIC
INTERESTS/ VALUES:	Freedom	Peace	Opportunity
	Law	Protection	Justice
OBJECTIVITIES:	Secure borders	Power balance	Employment
	Open seas and	Civilian control of	Free trade

	skies	the military	
	Rule of law	Professionalism	Development
	Democratic elections	Respect for human rights	Stable currency
	Stable institutions	No wars	Fair access to minerals
	National sovereignty	Protection from crime	Human safety nets
	Regional cooperation	World peacekeeping	Balance between private wealth and social justice
	Fairness to ethnic groups	Nuclear free zone	Access to education
POLICIES:	Help emerging democracies	Offer regional military and police training	Help emerging economies
	Support OAS and UN	Balance power	Support GATT principles

[Fight drug war cooperatively, working across the spectrum to reduce both supply and demand]

	Negotiate disputes	Sanction human rights violations	Support economic education
	Oppose non-democratic forces	Maintain military & police dialogue	Oppose environmental destruction
	Encourage regional democratic models	Discourage arms races	Measure inter regional impact of policies
REGIONAL POLICIES / STRATEGIES:			

[Operate a network of inter-American military and police education/training centers]

"Human Rights Instruction at the US Army School of the Americas," *Human Rights Review,* April-June, 2001.*

The United States Army has invested about 60 years in both conscious and vicarious forms of Human Rights training with the armed forces of Latin America. Though Latin American officers attend schools throughout the Department of Defense system, the US Army School of the Americas (USARSA), located at Ft. Benning, Georgia, since 1984, has been the focal point of this conscious instruction. Founded in the former Panama Canal Zone in 1946, the program there was partly explicit and partly a system of role modeling modern military behavior by Army personnel for their Latin American counterparts. The school has been the backbone of security assistance training for the controversial Latin American military and police forces since its inception, offering standard military doctrine courses in Spanish that would otherwise only reach out to English-speaking personnel, as occurs in the case of the other world regions. USARSA's students attend a variety of service school courses, using the standard curriculum offered by the proponent schools but taught in Spanish by a mix of US and Latin American instructors under supervision.

No task carried out by any operative of the government is more controversial than efforts by the US Army School of the Americas to influence Latin America's military and security forces to support universal concepts of human rights. This article presents the Latin American context in which the US Army became the primary tutor of the region's armed forces, challenges the oft-heard assumption that US military tutelage worsened an already poor human rights record, and opens lines of examination by which to measure and evaluate the performance of USARSA.

What is Meant by "Human Rights?"

Every proponent of human rights issues has defined the target audience, the abuses to be checked, and the operant morality system in the context of contemporary events. Thus, Augustine's five classic precepts on the just use of societal force, and Ambrose's assertion of Church authority over the temporal government's use of force are fourth-century expressions of surging Christian morality in the late Roman Empire. Thomas Aquinas' refinement of Augustinian precepts on Just War are part of a larger effort by Roman Catholic theologians to assert a Christian moral order within medieval Europe during a time when governmental institutions were often unable or unwilling to protect citizens. The twelfth century Order of St. John of Jerusalem (The Hospitalers) was a Christian effort to care for wounded soldiers, and to minimize violence against non-combatants during the Crusades. This concept of soldiers sworn under religious vows to a humanitarian cause was repeated in the Iberian Peninsula during the Reconquest when the Military Orders of Alcantara, Calatrava, and Santiago served both as shock troops to fight the Moors, and as internal security soldiers who protected civilians during the turbulent migrations that followed behind the conflict.

Bartolome de las Casas' celebrated efforts to protect the indigenous Americans from brutal slavery was part of the greater struggle by the Catholic religious orders to exert humane social control against the rising power of the Spanish crown's secular authority in the early sixteenth century. Hugo Grotius' exposition on international law combined earlier Christian concepts into juridical principles which would bind the newly important nation-state, a secular political concept, to a humane moral standard on human rights. The impetus was the sickening violence, both sanctioned and non-sanctioned, attending the Thirty Years' War of 1618-1648. John Locke's advocacy for a contract between citizen and government, and for a functional division of governmental powers between the executive, legislative, and judicial arms, strengthened the northern European drive towards government that was rational and secular, yet morally responsible to a higher authority.

The French Declaration of the Rights of Man and the Bill of Rights to the US Constitution are both late eighteenth-century efforts to codify human rights within secular, representative government, and both contain an inventory sufficiently broad to demonstrate specific political scenarios of the era. The Red Cross movement is a nineteenth-century resurrection of the medieval Hospitalers, triggered by the suffering of soldiers and noncombatants in the Crimean War and the US Civil War. The 1907 Hague Conventions are an effort to empower Grotius' humane juridical order upon nations that had built up armies and navies equipped with weapons of mass destruction, and the so-called Geneva Conventions of 1949 reflect the world's disgust with the revelation of state-sanctioned violence against selected religious and ethnic groups, most of this by Nazi Germany in World War II. Recent efforts to define human rights display the same mixture of temporal political issues and appeals to a transcendental order of morality. The United Nations thirty-point Charter on Human Rights contains, for example, language on guaranteed universal employment which advocates of neo-liberal economics within democratic societies hold to be principles of socialism, not human rights. And during the Cold War years of diplomatic wrangling over ratification of the UN Human Rights agenda, the Western democracies always affirmed that the Communist powers were police states which did not, in reality, honor human rights at all. This dispute is substantively comparable to that which occurred when Britain's Oliver Cromwell condemned Spanish men-at-arms, who were Catholics, as murderous cowards, yet sanctioned brutal military tactics and civil repression by his own reformed Protestant forces. Moral reformers act upon secular events highly colored by culture and contemporary interests, but lay claim to a transcendental order, producing endless disagreement. Economic philosophy and religious affiliation are merely two of the variables that divide perceptions of human rights.[1]

Advocates for human rights may be divided functionally into the purists and the inclusionists. This dyad is often seen in the field of national security studies, where those who emphasize armed forces first are the purists, and those who examine the political-military-economic triad in sum are the inclusionists. Human rights as a set of doctrines applying to the conduct of nations at war, and to the behavior of a nation's military and police personnel toward non-combatants and prisoners, may be termed the purist concept. Human rights that include a broader set of human behaviors and actions may be termed the inclusionist concept. In the era of post-Cold War and post-constructionist social analysis, human rights as a concept has come to embrace a highly inclusive range of values. The human rights battle cry is raised in the 1990s on behalf of ethnicity, religion, race, sexual orientation, physical condition, socio-economic position, and an inventory of political causes, some of them denying the existence of any transcendental moral order but claiming a secular humanist foundation based upon scientific logic and consistency.[2]

Throughout the Cold War, human rights under the purist concept were taught by members of the US armed forces to foreign military and police personnel throughout the Cold War, both in the classroom and by personal example. The classes were usually called "Geneva Convention Principles" or the "Law of Land Warfare." Most recipients of this training were military personnel from nations allied with the United States, although there were always some students from countries whose Cold War loyalties were in doubt.[3] The training was conducted through a variety of modes: within the host country via mobile training teams, and external training within the United States conducted in unit packages, or through individual attendance at service schools. The universality of the Spanish language in Latin America made it expedient, since 1946, for the armed forces to offer their standard service school courses to Spanish-speaking Latin Americans, including some Spanish-speaking Brazilians, on one campus. The Army's School of the Americas, located at Ft. Gulick in the former Panama Canal Zone (1947-1984) and afterwards at Ft. Benning, Georgia, is by far the largest of these three schools.

Attendance at the School of the Americas by Country

COUNTRY	No. to 1994	COUNTRY	No. to 1994
Argentina	660	Guatemala	1,552
Barbados	1	Haiti	49
Belize	4	Honduras	3,788
Bolivia	3,954	Mexico	1,934
Brazil	337	Nicaragua *	4,318
Chile	3,356	Panama **	3,665
Colombia	10,205	Paraguay	1,045
Costa Rica	2,425	Peru	4,710
Cuba* * *	237	USA	1,621
Dominican Rep.	2,573	Uruguay	1,011
Ecuador	3,419	Venezuela	3,405
El Salvador	6,765		
TOTAL			**61,034**

*Ended in 1979; **Ended in 1989; ***Ended in 1960

Table I is a historical representation of how many students have attended this training. Any measurement of human rights training for Latin American military personnel by the United States would have to include the School of the Americas because of its size and culturally-focused program. However, the numerical total of its graduates (61,000+ in 1999) plus those of the smaller Navy and Air Force Spanish-language schools is still less than the total of Latin American military personnel trained in-country by mobile training teams and at English-speaking military facilities in the same manner as foreign military personnel from Asia, the Middle East, Europe, or Africa are trained.

What are the moral and legal values underlying civil-military relations and citizen-police relations in the region? Political independence came to Latin America in 1830 following two decades of bloody independence wars. In many regions the armed forces were the only institution left intact at war's end that could perform the normal functions of government, a situation not unlike the role of the military orders of the priesthood in Spain following the Reconquest. These are known to history as the Orders of Alcantara, Calatrava, and Santiago. The roots of political democracy came to Latin America through the southern Mediterranean Enlightenment, the French Declaration of the Universal Rights of Man, and the Spanish Republican Constitution of 1806. The region was IndoMediterranean, respectful of independence, agricultural, and humane in ways that differ from the institutional forms of northern Europe and North America in 1830. Separation of church and state did not exist as a pre-condition for the guarantee of human rights, which were the legitimate moral domain of a ubiquitous church presence in life. Civilian control of the armed forces took root early only in Colombia; throughout Latin America there persisted the notion that soldiers guard the borders from without and within. In the region which produced the world's fewest foreign wars after 1830, it seemed perfectly normal that part of the deliberative political process would include soldiers.

The Three Spanish-language Military Schools Operated by the United States for the Latin American Armed Forces Graduates by 1993

SCHOOL	LOCATION	GRADUATES TO 1993
US Army School of the Americas (USARSA)	Panama Canal Zone 1946-84 Ft. Benning, Georgia 1984-present	61,034 (23 countries)
Inter-American Air Force Academy (IAAFA)	Panama Canal Zone 1946-89 Homestead AFB, Texas 1989-1992 Lackland AFB, Texas 1992-present	29,443 (25 countries)
Naval Small Craft Instruction and Training School (NAVSCIATTS)	Panama Canal Zone 1961-79 Republic of Panama 1979-1999	5,365 (28 countries)

Source: Russell W. Ramsey, "A Military Turn of Mind: Educating Latin American Officers," Military Review (Aug. 1993), p. 16.

Military professionalism, not to be misdefined as purely apoliticism, came to South America in the 1880s via the Prussian and French military training missions. Professionalism came to the small armed forces of Central America and the Caribbean in the early twentieth century, under tutelage, and was partially intermixed with a hegemonic foreign policy for the region. In World War II, the United States became the teacher and role model for the South American armed forces, minus Argentina, which clung to European models until the early 1980s.[4] Dictators in Central America and the Caribbean converted the armed forces into personnel mechanisms through which to maintain power, and with the unique exceptions of Costa Rica, Mexico, and non-Hispanic Barbados, most military forces in these two sub-regions resisted the move to full professionalism until the late 1980s.

To what extent have the forces of defense and law enforcement seen themselves as upholders of citizen rights? The results of an honest public opinion poll about this subject throughout Latin America, taken at ten-year intervals since 1830, would surprise most US academic analysts of the region. Individual factions during a given internal struggle for power would obviously dislike the soldiers who opposed them. Reformist and leftist elements alike during the Cold War would report hatred of the armed forces in most of the countries, although a majority of the citizenry would not sustain such a feeling. But if such public opinion polls had been taken and compared with similar polls taken in Africa, Asia, the Middle East, eastern and even central Europe, the Latin American armed forces would rank high as defenders of human rights in the public estimation.[5] The police would not fare so well, but then the police would probably be seen as more repressive in other world cultures as well. Consequently, US military training for Latin America's armed forces during the Cold War was not cast in terms of rendering brutes into humane soldiers. It had the specific task of trying to teach respect for human rights to several armed forces which were used with the full knowledge and support of major civilian sectors against internal leftist forces, which were supported from Cuba and the Soviet Union. Training statistics show that one of the most heavily engaged nations in the anti-communist crusades, namely Argentina, had a numerically small exposure of their military personnel to North American influence through the US-operated Spanish language facilities available to the region's armed forces.

To what extent have Latin America's armed forces viewed themselves as agents of social coercion? In the nineteenth century, the armies of the *caudillos*, defined as regional politicians temporarily in uniform to seize power, did not remain in existence for long. They toppled their opponents, and they returned to civilian life, leaving the *caudillo* in power. Few soldiers remained in uniform, frequently serving to maintain the regimes of their former military leaders. The military as the ultimate protector to the *"patria"* ("fatherland") became embedded in the constitutional and statutory instruments throughout the region. In the twentieth century, some of the Latin American armed forces saw the struggle against communism as a holy war similar to the Crusades and the Reconquest of Spain. Early in the Cold War, US military personnel operating within Latin America joined US diplomatic leadership in mistaking social reform movements for revolutionary communism, sponsored from the USSR. The counterinsurgency doctrine of the early 1960s was expounded as a legitimate defense of friendly governments with fledgling democratic institutions against armed subversion by Fidel Castro's Cuban regime. It was President John F. Kennedy's defensive arm of the Alliance for Progress. US counterinsurgency doctrine was distorted by Argentine and Chilean military leaders in the 1970s into the French Algerian concept of national security, meaning military praetorianism and the intentional repression and abuse of selected citizens.[6] US military influence, overall, in the larger South American countries during the ugly internal conflicts of the 1970s, was small.[7]

The Central American conflicts of the 1980s included military abuse against citizens in El Salvador, Guatemala, and Nicaragua, with lesser abuses in Honduras. While government forces were specifically guilty, so too were rebel forces, both Communist and anti-Communist.[8] Polls today and even in that stormy time show that many citizens did, however, support the use of their national armed forces in the fight against leftist guerrillas in El Salvador, Guatemala, and Honduras, and against anti-Communist guerrillas in the Nicaraguan case. The limited US in-country tutelage of the El Salvadoran and Honduran armed forces included human rights training, plus warnings about the penalties for human rights abuses. There was also a credible amount of international humanitarian law curriculum for the unit packet training performed at Ft. Benning's Infantry School, taught in English through interpreters, and taught at the School of the Americas to individuals, not to units, in Spanish. The Soviet-Cuban tutelage apparatus working with the Nicaraguan Sandinista forces advocated a deliberate policy of abuse against the non-Communist and anti-Communist populace, coupled with a huge media campaign about US-sponsored atrocities in El Salvador and Honduras; there was counter-fraud behind some of the policy explanations by the national security team managing the Reagan administration's Central America program.

At the Cold War's end, most Latin American countries were decreasing the size of their armies, modernizing their navies and air forces, and increasing the size of the national police and security forces. Some of this trend represented dislike of military abuses in the recent past, some reflected the budgetary impact of armed forces upon economies strained under privatization, and some was the gradual and belated acceptance of the North American and European *posse comitatus* principle, under which armies defend the borders and police defend the citizens who live within them. An instructive correlation can be made between US active military tutelage and human rights abuses in specific countries by using these charts. Guatemala was cut off from International Military Assistance Training (IMET) Programs in the late 1970s, following which human rights abuses soared, then tapered dramatically when US tutelage resumed under Congressional authority. In El Salvador, human rights abuses soared in 1980-1981 when US tutelage was minimal, and dived rapidly downward during the decade as US military training of all kinds increased. Part, but by no means all, of these US training influences was the US Army School of the Americas. The US Congress has never legislated funds with which to evaluate the effectiveness of IMET programs, and so solid regression analysis is impossible. Empirical observation suggests that the ratio between human rights abusers who took US military courses during the Cold War, and total foreign personnel trained by the US Armed Forces, would be substantively better in the Latin American region than in Africa, Asia, or the Middle East. This matter urgently needs to be funded for scientific study.

Latin American Soldiers by World Standards

Where do Latin American military professionals stand on any kind of worldwide comparative analysis? Most US historians of Latin America begin their analysis with the notion that Latin America is conducting a quest for democracy, and that the elimination of its own armed forces is a precondition to success. Most US political scientists begin the analysis of governmental institutions in Latin America with the notion that the armed forces are a pathological set of institutions, and that US foreign policy has made them worse instead of better.[9] Neither paradigm stands up to comparative world analysis.

SCHOOL Chart, Democracy v. USARSA Influence/Participation

Country	Date, Civilian Presidency Restored	Date, Human Rights Were Measurably Improved	Date, Drug War Became A Serious Threat	Number Of USARSA Graduates
Argentina	1982	1983	N/A	660
Bolivia	1982	1983	1981	3,954
Brazil	1985	1981	N/A	337
Chile	1990	1991	N/A	3,356
Colombia[1]	1958	1997	1990	10,205
Costa Rica	1903	1903	N/A	2,425
Cuba[2]	Still a dictatorship	Still a Violater	Gov't policy of selling drugs ended 1991	237
Dominican Republic	1966	1966	N/A	2,573
Ecuador	1979	1983	N/A	3,419
El Salvador	1984	1990	N/A	6,765
Guatemala	1986	1988	N/A	1,552
Honduras	1982	1990	1981	3,788
Mexico	1912	1994	Gov't policy of selling drugs ended 1991	1,934
Nicaragua[3]	1991	1991, but still occur at times		4,318

Panama[4]	1989	1989	Gov't policy of selling drugs ended 1989	3,665
Peru	1980	1979	1983	4,710
Paraguay	1989	1990	N/A	1,045
Uruguay	1985	1983	N/A	1,011
Venezuela	1958	1958	N/A	3,405

[1] Long history of democratic government
[2] Ceased sending students to USARSA in 1960
[3] Ceased sending students to USARSA in 1979
[4] Ceased sending students to USARSA in 1987

The rule of "two" says much about Latin American men-at-arms. The region produced only two wars in the nineteenth century and two in the twentieth century that did not involve the United States or a European power. Since 1830, Latin America has been the only world region that has limited its military expenditure to approximately two percent of the gross national (or domestic) product. Since 1830, Latin America has been the only world region which has limited men-at-arms to two soldiers or less per thousand citizens. There are two exceptions to this rule: Cuba, 1959 to the present, and Nicaragua, 1979-90, both regimes armed to the level of a European Communist country at the height of the Cold War. Two Latin American nations made significant military contributions in World War II. Brazil contributed an infantry brigade and a fighter squadron to fight the Germans in Italy. Mexico sent a squadron of fighters against Imperial Japan in the Philippines, and some 200,000 Mexican males served as volunteers in the US armed forces during World War II. US foreign military assistance programs to Latin America during the Cold War, often termed "enormous" and "politically destructive" in the academic literature, summed up to about two percent of the total US foreign military assistance effort. Incidentally, US military assistance to Latin America during the Cold War was dwarfed by direct developmental aid, a disparity that has increased in percentage since 1990. These and other pertinent facts are clearly presented in the 1987 study *Arms Transfers to the Third World, 1971-85*, prepared for the Stockholm International Peace Research Institute by Michael Brzoska and Thomas Ohlson.

Latin America has suffered the lowest percentage of deaths in war of any major world region since 1830. It is the only world region which has never had an inventory of nuclear, biological, or toxic gas agents in its weapons arsenal. The average Latin American military professional, since World War II, spends more of his or her career attending professional schools than any world counterpart. Facts of this sort are clearly presented in a number of descriptive studies and again raise the philosophical question about why so much academic ink is employed on the generic vilification of the Latin American armed forces, when the same forces in other world regions are virtually worse on all counts.

The Colombian Battalion and a Navy frigate served with distinction in the UN Command in Korea; other Latin American contingents were offered and were refused by General Douglas MacArthur. Latin American military and police professionals are represented in today's United Nations blue helmet forces at a higher level than the forces of any developing world region. Colombian soldiers were vital in the UN Sinai Command of 1956-58, and they have been peacekeepers in the Multi-National Force and Observers in the Sinai Desert since 1982. Southern cone nations have contributed repeatedly to United Nations peace observation and humanitarian efforts in the Middle East, Africa, the Balkans, and Southwest Asia. Latin America's armed forces have been decreasing their troop strength since a decade before Cold War's end, and police forces are increasing in size and professionalism. Brazil, Colombia, Ecuador, and Mexico all have national public opinion polls in their popular news magazines showing the armed forces to be the institution most trusted after the priesthood, with numerical rankings far higher than civilian politicians, journalists, business leaders, and academics.[10]

Why, then, is academic literature about Latin American military institutions so negative, revealing authors so willing to assume that Latin American military personnel are human rights violators? Oliver Cromwell's "Black Legend" is alive and well in journalism and academia within the United States and Britain. Scholars who regard themselves as absolutely above racial bias regularly editorialize about the supposed cruelty, dishonesty, contempt for civilians, and love of violence among the soldiers of the world's region with the lowest record of military human rights violations. Second, many US scholars on Latin America line up on the leftist side of the liberal-conservative spectrum; this idiosyncrasy is less pronounced among US scholars who specialize in Europe, Asia, Africa, or the Middle East. Third, the Latin American armed forces have submitted to close scrutiny of their budgets, arms, and troop strengths far more readily than is done in other developing regions, yet this accessibility has been turned around and used as a weapon to discredit them by frustrated North American Marxists in search of vindication and re-opening the wars of the 1980s.[11] Fourth, the Cuban government, during the Cold War, and the Andean narcotraffickers in the 1990s, devoted substantive resources to creating a myth that Latin America was forcibly occupied by its own armed forces. The narcotraffickers have large media resources with which to supply US journalists and academics who study Latin America with staged massacres on videotape, fake witnesses on US television, and a sophisticated panoply of deceits. It is now virtually impossible to sort out truth from fantasy, especially in the academic literature.[12] Fifth, the US news media limit their coverage of developing regions to a few repetitive themes that sell well: Islamic radicals performing terrorism, Japanese leaders hijacking US markets, African tribes engaged in ethnic extermination, and, to be sure, allegations of human rights abuses by Latin American soldiers.

Foreign Military Influence in Latin America

The *conquistadores* of Latin America were Spanish warriors of world renown, fresh from the Reconquest of Spain. Most were rapacious; only a few upheld the noble ideals of las Casas, and of the military priesthood orders, about the humane treatment of indigenous citizens. Spain's Empire in Latin America endured for two and one-half centuries with the lowest percentage of occupation soldiers of any major world empire. Most of the colonizing was done by the Catholic clergy: Franciscans, Dominicans, Augustinians, Benedictines, Jesuits, and lay clergy. The Creole militias of the colonial era helped lay the groundwork for independence, but did not take on the importance or the values of the colonial militias in British North America. Napoleonic war veterans helped Simon Bolivar and other liberation commanders train their armies to fight against Spanish royal troops.

Chile imported a Prussian military training mission in the early 1880s, and Peru, recently defeated by Chile in the War of the Pacific, countered with a French mission. Argentina brought in Prussian military trainers and British naval mission personnel. Most of the training was technical. Civilian control of the military and respect for human rights were not salient European military values in that era, and such concepts simply were not taught by these foreign military training missions.[13]

US maritime influence exploded in Panama and the Caribbean at the dawn of the twentieth century. US Marines set up pilot constabulary forces in Haiti, the Dominican Republic, and Nicaragua. Intended to be apolitical and efficient enough to prevent public disorder and European intervention in time of chaos, these constabularies became regime support machines for reasons having to do with local diplomatic and economic policies, not US military doctrine.

As World War II loomed on the horizon, the United States became the military tutor in the region. The objective was to block German espionage aimed at creating pro-Axis sympathy in Latin America, limit the effectiveness of German U-boats against Allied shipping, block any possible German invasion of Brazil across the Atlantic, and promote stability to guarantee access to strategic minerals. At war's end, moderate quantities of jeeps, armored cars, trucks, and small arms, and light artillery were made inexpensively available to Latin American armies under Secretary of State John Foster Dulles' misguided notion that Latin American social protest in the early Cold War era was Soviet-sponsored. He thought that military modernization in Latin America would create a "mini-NATO" south of the border. US military leaders in this era saw the Soviet threat in Europe, and next the rim of Asia, as the Cold War's main theaters and did not press for the militarization of Latin America via aggressive training or arming of indigenous forces.[14]

Coincident with the formation of the Inter-American System after World War II, the US Army School of the Americas, in the former Panama Canal Zone, and later the Air Force and Navy counterpart schools, were established to give technical training only, but conveniently in Spanish for the participating countries. There was no sophisticated geostrategic scheme behind the schools' existence, and no conscious awareness at that time that military instruction in the region's primary language, by a multinational faculty, would yield benefits. In early 1961, President John F. Kennedy directed the Department of Defense to prepare Latin America's armed forces on a limited basis to fight Communist-inspired insurgent forces more effectively than the largely useless Cuban Army of Fulgencio Batista's regime had done. The new counterinsurgency course, like all doctrine at the School of the

Americas, came from the appropriate US service school, in this case the US Army Special Warfare Center at Ft. Bragg, North Carolina. It was based on a strategy of Defense and Development, and it included specific units on the Geneva Convention, the Law of Land Warfare, and the humane care of the wounded, prisoners, and non-combatants.

The war in El Salvador between the government and the FMLN communist guerrillas in the 1980s is the challenge which focused post-Cold War attention on human rights issues in Latin America. The El Salvadoran Army had never subscribed to modern US military doctrine about human rights, basking in the concept of the *fuero militar* ("soldiers are outside the law"), a custom dating from the era of the European medieval guilds.[15] It had dealt ruthlessly with a Marxist uprising in the 1930s without any US tutelage and applied the same methods at the beginning of the 1980s. In 1984, in conjunction with the return of US bases to Panama under the Carter-Torrijos Treaties, the United States moved the school to Ft. Benning, Georgia. The placement of the US Army School of the Americas at the former Infantry School (now Ridgway Hall) followed, unfortunately, an initiative to train Salvadoran infantry units via translators at the US Army Infantry School, a short distance away on the same military installation. By failing to articulate clearly that the US Army School of the Americas was a permanent institution for teaching military professionalism to individuals, and that the Salvadoran training contingents coincidentally located at the same military base were an emergency wartime measure, the US Army gave the FMLN Communist guerrillas and their US allies a free propaganda platform. In the l980s, FMLN spokespersons proclaimed through the news media that the US Army School of the Americas was put at Ft. Benning to train thousands of Salvadoran human rights abusers on the finer points of torture and murder, a fantasy continued in the 1990s by a US group called "SOA Watch."

Although human rights concepts were taught to the Salvadoran battalions that were crash trained at the Infantry School, Salvadoran officers who believed themselves to be engaged in a holy anti-Communist crusade remained in command throughout the training cycle, and these units returned to El Salvador in a high state of combat readiness and militant belief in their cause. Their battlefield impact in the late 1980s, along with steady improvement under US pressure, in their human rights record, broke the FMLN guerrillas as a military force and decided the war in favor of a negotiated settlement, supported by all parties except the North American neo-Marxists because it did not fit their ideological vision of a total victory.[16] However, some of the US-trained units committed human rights abuses, and some of their personnel were coincidentally graduates of various courses at the School of the Americas. Largely unknown is the fact that it was School of the Americas graduates in the Salvadoran Army who, at risk of their careers and lives, blew the whistle on those military colleagues who ordered the cowardly killing of six Jesuit priests who were believed to be collaborating with the FMLN in 1990. The FMLN propaganda arm invented the theme of School of the Americas as the "School for Assassins" and still markets this shibboleth in the 1990s through useful front organizations under the guise of Catholic social activism.[17] It is also vital to note here that most FMLN leaders are now members of the democratic political system of El Salvador, and the Vatican officially condemned in 1991 and again in 1993 the doctrine propounded by a splinter element from the Maryknoll Missionary Order to the effect that Jesus of Nazareth would be a guerrilla fighter like Ernesto "Che" Guevara in the present context. Leaders of the Maryknoll Order have recently discussed plans to shift operational focus to the Asian arena, where the Order served and often died heroically during the Communist takeover of 1950-51.

Affective v. Cognitive Education

Cognitive education deals with facts. In military terms, it deals with teaching a soldier to disassemble his rifle and clean it, reassemble it, fire it, and hit the target. Affective education deals with values and behavior. It tries, with less measurable effectiveness than in the case of cognitive education, to teach the soldier about the impact of firing the rifle. It deals with values about who is the enemy, about who is not the enemy, and about the public trust that has been placed in him to use his weapon under legally acceptable circumstances.

US Army School of the Americas (SOA, now called USARSA since 1996), the US Air Force's Inter-American Air Force Academy (IAAFA), and the US Navy's Small Craft School (NAVSCIATTS) all teach standard, on-the-shelf U.S. military courses, in a setting that includes military personnel from culturally homogenous countries, through a highly selective and rotating guest faculty that also represents several of the American Republics. But the doctrines are from the United States service schools in all cases, save for a new course on the role of the military officer in a democratic society ("Democratic Sustainment") developed in 1995 at the School of the Americas. Any criminologist will report that measuring *affect* (values orientation) among prisoners is virtually impossible, thereby explaining why parole boards worry about each criminal turned loose before the completion of sentence. How shall we measure *affect* among soldiers who are distinctly not criminals, but among whose ranks have occurred in the recent past some ugly human rights abuses in the name of duty, as perceived by their institutions?

The El Salvador case looks good, on the surface. In 1981 perhaps 20,000 persons per year were being killed, many of them by the armed forces. By war's end, the inexcusable murder of six Jesuit clergy by an Army unit was politically explosive, but statistically idiosyncratic, for legalized murder by Army personnel was generally stopped. Former School of the Americas guest faculty and students from the Salvadoran Army had even put their lives on the line to blow the whistle about the killing of the Jesuits, submitting the accused personnel to the "Commission of Honor," since a standard military court would simply vindicate them under the doctrine of fuero *militar*. US influence here was direct: 66 US military personnel on site in the country throughout the decade-long war, several hundred students per year at School of the Americas, and several thousand unit package trainees in the mid-1980s at Ft. Benning. As US influence increased longitudinally and numerically, human rights violations decreased dramatically.[18]

But a comparison of this case with events in Argentina ruins an apparently scientific analysis. In the "Dirty War" of 1976-1982, Argentine military personnel were formed into special counterintelligence units that are alleged to have summarily executed several thousand civilian prisoners. Military commanders justified this under the French "national security doctrines" of the 1960s, viewing themselves to be engaged in a holy war. The generals also invoked the *fuero militar* whenever civilians asked for accountability on military behavior, just as Salvadoran generals would do a decade later. Unlike the El Salvador case, there was very little US military influence operant in the Argentine "Dirty War," as military assistance was suspended under the Carter Administration. Argentina usually sent one or two guest faculty members to serve at the School of the Americas, and a few Argentine students attended the higher level officer and noncommissioned officer courses. Argentine generals made it clear that their cooperation with US military training programs for Latin America was not that they, the Argentines, had any need for US training and doctrines, but that they were a regional power simply keeping their hand in the game.

Yet Argentine military abusiveness, both human rights violations and the flaunting of the French national security doctrines, ended dramatically following the South Atlantic Conflict of 1982. Since no foreign power's military training apparatus played a visible role, one must conclude that the affective dimension is greatly influenced by a single external event, in this case, humiliation over a stinging defeat in the Malvinas / Falklands Islands. While Argentines still quarrel over punishing the guilty military personnel for their role in the "Dirty War," the loss of public confidence in the Argentine armed forces over their defeat now causes the military to accept civilian control, and the quality of the forces seems improved. It is no coincidence that Argentina's Navy performed well in the Persian Gulf during Desert Shield/Desert Storm, 1990-91; an Argentine battalion plays a vital role in UN operations within the former Yugoslavia; and an Argentine general commanded the highly successful peacekeeping force in Croatia in 1992. All of this is part of Argentina's own national commitment to operating a political democracy without abusive military interference in governmental deliberations.[19]

US security assistance programs for Latin American dictatorships played into the hands of critics in the early 1960s, a fact well documented by the late Edwin Lieuwen in his influential 1960 book *Arms and Politics in Latin America*. The fall of the Berlin Wall would seem to have ushered in a world wide rejection of the political and economic doctrines of the far left. However, there grew up within academia in the United States a school of "post-Lieuwenists" with sympathy for the romantic neo-Marxist left. The recent unfolding of events concerning privatization and democratization have demonstrated that neo-Marxist revolution was never a serious, indigenous force within Latin America, and Professor Timothy P. Wickham-Crowley's study *Guerrillas and Revolution in Latin America* (1992) demonstrates this point with convincing methodology. Yet most US academics completely missed the onset of privatization and democratization in the late 1970s, mistook liberation theology for a genuine political vehicle to revolution, and misread Raul Prebisch's concept of statist economics - essentially a democratic variant of 1920s Mussolini Fascism - as a preference for economic collectivism in Latin America.[20] Some of these same academics now insist upon breaking the relationship between the US and Latin American military institutions in the name of "truly" ending the Cold War and downsizing the armed forces. They tend to exaggerate the human rights abuse issue, sometimes attribute it wrongfully to conscious US training influence, and utterly reject the need for competent armed forces in the Americas to deal with contemporary challenges to peace.[21]

The collective damage of misperception was forcefully illustrated in August 1994, as the School of the Americas held its 6th Latin American Conference on the topic "The Armed Forces and Human Rights." Non-governmental organizations (NGOs) specializing on human rights lobbying within the Western Hemisphere refused to participate, even when the school offered to pay their expenses. Excellent lectures by military officers and diplomats who attended should have been paired with comparable discourses by knowledgeable NGO leaders.[22] Others who criticize the School of the Americas believe that its existence is acceptable as long as there are constant demands to "audit the curriculum on human rights."[23]

The Human Rights Curriculum of the 1990s

The United States Army School of the Americas (USARSA) has developed a Human Rights Curriculum that is in the vanguard of similar training currently being conducted in other US Department of Defense institutions. This curriculum has been developed over the course of several years through the creative efforts of Army officers and civilians of different branches and disciplines both within and without USARSA.

The Human Rights Curriculum at USARSA consists of three key components: Ethical Foundations, Legal Considerations, and Operational Imperatives. Every student that attends one or more of the approximately fifty different courses offered at USARSA receives Human Rights instruction consisting of these three parts. At a minimum, each USARSA student receives an eight-hour block of instruction on Human Rights and international humanitarian law. The length of Human Rights instruction received is proportionate to the duration of the course he or she is attending. Students in the year-long Command & General Staff College Course receive a forty-hour block of instruction on Human Rights. Current USARSA policy mandates that students attending those courses that are four weeks or less in duration must receive eight hours of Human Rights instruction. Those students participating in courses that are longer than four weeks but less than six months must receive twelve hours of Human Rights instruction. There are several exceptions to this policy, but these exceptions work only to increase the hours of Human Rights instruction. For example, the Peace Operations Course, which is five weeks in duration and therefore should receive only twelve hours of Human Rights instruction, actually receives twenty-four hours; and the Democratic Sustainment Course, which lasts six weeks and therefore should also only receive twelve hours of Human Rights instruction, actually gets twenty hours.

There are two reasons why ethics plays a crucial role in the study of Human Rights. First and foremost, Ethics is the underlying or foundational limit on individual action. Although most people are law abiding persons, they are law abiding not because of the legal consequences resulting from violating the law, although that is certainly a consideration, but rather because the law protects an ethical or moral precept to which they subscribe. Or to the contrary, the law often proscribes unethical or immoral behavior. By way of example, most persons normally articulate their refusal to commit an unlawful murder because it is morally wrong, and not because it is illegal. So in this regard, ethics, which encompasses morals, along with personal and institutional values, is the first barrier to inappropriate or unacceptable conduct or behavior by an individual. Examples of institutional values that are part of ethics would be the official statement of seven core values of the United States Army: loyalty, duty, respect, selfless service, honor, integrity, and personal courage. Morals and values are part of the Ethical Foundations portion of USARSA's Human Rights instruction.

The U.S. Army Chaplain at USARSA, who teaches this block of instruction, covers values in detail. He makes effective use of a video entitled "Joseph Schultz," which depicts the moral dilemma of a German soldier who, at the conclusion of a battle, is ordered to take part in a firing squad that is about to execute a number of civilians. Schultz's dilemma is apparent when the viewer sees blindfolded civilians docilely lined up against bundles of hay. Except for a brief recital in German, directed by the sergeant-in-charge at the non-compliant Schultz, whereby the former attempts to be persuasive through appeasement and then suddenly turns angry, the video is free of dialogue; the drama directs the students' focus towards this one display of moral courage. The video, which portrays a true account, ends with Schultz's own execution.

The second reason why ethics is taught is that soldiers are members of a profession; and what distinguishes a profession from any other vocation is not only the existence of, and the will to abide by a Code of Ethics, but a disciplinary system to castigate those members of the profession who fail to do so, in other words, a disciplinary Code of Ethics. When a soldier dons a uniform, he/she is representing to his civilian co-nationals that, not only does he know Human Rights Law and International Humanitarian Law, but additionally that he is capable of carrying out military missions in accordance thereunto. The same holds true for ethics. In many ways, the military's code of ethics provides a stricter disciplinary regimen than that of other professions because many of its provisions are judicially enforced. Certain moral values and behavior are legislated through the Codes of Military Justice. For example, certain types of adultery, sexual acts, and language, which may present only a moral dilemma for nonservice members, and members of other professions, violate the US Uniform Code of Military Justice and are judicially sanctioned. It is therefore essential, given that many ethical provisions are enforceable through the military justice system, for service members to know and abide by ethics. Cases where this applies differently in countries governed by different laws are regularly discussed and compared to US standards in the classroom at USARSA.

As part of Ethical Foundations, the U.S. Army Chaplain at USARSA concludes his class with the Just War Doctrine, or the *Jus ad Bellum,* which lists criteria for a justified war. The criteria consist of the following: authority to order participation in the armed conflict must have the legal power to do so; just cause (as for example self-defense, defense of others, or enforcing a U.N. Security Council Resolution); just intent, which is defined as a prohibition to exceed the purpose of the just cause (if the just cause is self-defense, then just intent would prohibit the conquest of enemy territory after a power has restored its borders); proportionality in the use of armed force; exhausting all peaceful means available to resolve the dispute; and a reasonable expectation to succeed in the armed conflict. Legal Considerations, or the *Jus in Bello,* comprise the second part of USARSA's Human Rights Curriculum. Legal Considerations entail Human Rights and International Humanitarian Law. Except for an initial comparison of the similarities and differences between the two, as authenticated in the Geneva and Hague Conventions, with protocols, these two topics are introduced and discussed separately.

Both the Universal Declaration of Human Rights, and the American Convention of Human Rights or, as it is more commonly referred to, the Pact of San Jose, are presented in detail. Many of the human rights delineated in the Universal Declaration of Human Rights are singled out for discussion and covered in depth. The conference method of instruction is used, and students are continuously engaged in directed and meaningful discussions on the subject of Human Rights and International Humanitarian Law. Comparisons are made with American Constitutional Law, especially those Supreme Court holdings dealing with legal issues such as freedom of expression and the burning of the flag, the right to life, and the death penalty. The greatest threat to a democracy is tyranny of the majority, and students come to learn that human rights not only limit the authority of government, but also protect the rights of the minority against the oppression of the majority. The rights of gays and women, as well as the non-derogable prohibition of torture, and the Chilean Pinochet Case are also discussed in earnest.

USARSA recently expanded its curriculum to include coverage of the Pact of San Jose, important for several reasons. First of all, it is a treaty rather than merely a declaration; and as a treaty it is enforceable. Whereas the Universal Declaration of Human Rights is aspirational and perhaps even authoritative, it is not enforceable as an instrument of international jurisprudence. Second, it surpasses the Universal Declaration of Human Rights in the number and scope of human rights covered. Third, it contains enforcement mechanisms specifically outlined within the treaty: the Inter-American Commission of Human Rights, and the Inter-American Court of Human Rights. We may dispute the effectiveness of these bodies in certain cases, but there is no denying that they are in place, available, and utilized. And finally, it is a regional document and therefore of particular interest to USARSA students.

International Humanitarian Law covers The Hague and Geneva Conventions, as well as the two Protocols (additional to the Geneva Conventions). USARSA includes the two Protocols in its curriculum even though the United States Senate has not ratified them, because for the most part they reflect International Customary Law. Additionally, the vast majority of South and Central American countries have ratified them.

The last phase of the Human Rights Program consists of an operational Case Study. Although the massacre in the hamlet of Tu Cung (My Lai is the name given to several hamlets falling within a certain proximity of each other) occurred on March 16, 1968, the issues and causes surrounding this unlawful mass killing are extremely relevant today, and will continue to be in the future. Military operations today, much more than in the Cold War, require a deep interaction between armed forces and the civilian populace. Current military operations span the full gamut from war to peacekeeping. United States Army doctrine (Field Manual 100-5) lists thirteen separate operations other than war. These operations often, if not always, necessitate a close involvement, or entanglement even, with civilians in general and noncombatants in particular. Therefore, it is absolutely crucial for today's military professional to know the difference between noncombatants and combatants, or between unlawful and lawful targets. In Vietnam, the distinction between the two groups became blurred; in My Lai, the distinction was rendered nonexistent.

USARSA has institutionalized two committees that act as watchdogs to assure quality instruction in this and other areas: the Human Rights Committee, and the Board of Visitors. The former has representation from the US Department of State, United States Southern Command (more commonly known by its acronym SOUTHCOM), and a prominent attorney in the field of human rights. The latter was created by the United States Army Training and Doctrine Command (TRADOC). Both of these committees scrutinize the Human Rights Program and provide essential quality control.

The Human Rights Committee helped create a video that is approximately one hour in length entitled "Basic Training in Human Rights." This video supplements and reinforces the classroom instruction. It reinforces classroom instruction on the importance and advantages from abiding by human rights and international humanitarian law, such as reducing enemy resistance, winning domestic support, helping to restore the peace, maintaining discipline among the troops, and focusing the troops on their military mission. This video details General William T. Sherman's burning of Atlanta as an example of the catastrophic consequences of unrestricted warfare on the future relationship between the warring factions, and of military operations that do not abide by legal limitations. Additionally, the International Committee of the Red Cross participates in USARSA's Human Rights training by sending its delegate from Guatemala City, Guatemala, as a guest instructor to two of the courses: the Command and General Staff Course, and the Peace Operations Course. This overall program is the most extensive of any presented in the Department of Defense school system, and is required of every student and instructor at the school.

It should be understood that USARSA's Human Rights curriculum is a living process, subject to continuous revision and strengthened each year by the participation of a growing number of regional and world authorities who come to participate. The process is major proof that the US Army School of the Americas, far from being some kind of pariah entity out of control by the US Department of Defense, is actually the cutting edge of regional military teaching in the applied Human Rights process for the armed forces and the police in the applied Human Rights process.

Conclusions

It is well to show how USARSA touches all the US regional policy goals for Latin America in the post-Cold War world before stating the conclusions which emerge from this discussion. US foreign policy since the early 1990s has prioritized the advancement of prosperity, democracy, and peace. The following national security process model hypothesizes that defending a democracy occurs at four levels: values, objectives, policies, and applied regional policies/strategies. It further hypothesizes that the content items in the model can be rationally categorized into political, military, and economic actors and actions, and that challenges and stresses penetrate the model on any level from both internal and external sources.

The National Security Policy Process Model
The Americas, 2001

	POLITICAL	MILITARY	ECONOMIC
INTERESTS / VALUES	Freedom Law	Peace Protection	Opportunity Justice
OBJECTIVES:	Secure borders	Power balance	Employment
	Open seas and skies	Civilian control of the military	Development Stable currency
	Rule of law	Professionalism	Free Trade
	Democratic elections	Respect for human rights	Fair access to minerals
	Stable institutions	No wars	Human safety nets
	National sovereignty	Protection from crime	Balance between private wealth and social justice
	Regional cooperation	World peacekeeping	WTO principles
	Fairness to ethnic groups	Nuclear free zone	Access to education
POLICIES	Help emerging democracies	Offer regional military and police training	Help emerging economies
	Support OAS and UN	Provide peacekeepers	Support UN PKO finance

[Fight drug war cooperatively, working across the spectrum to reduce both supply and demand.]

	Negotiate disputes	Balance power	Support economic education
	Oppose non-democratic forces	Sanction human rights and violations	Oppose environmental destruction
	Encourage regional democratic models	Maintain military and police dialogue	Measure inter-regional impact of policies
	Support arms limits	Discourage arms race	Fund military professionalism
REGIONAL POLICIES AND STRATEGIES	[Operate a network of inter-American military and police education / training centers]		

The School of the Americas is statistically not the majority component in US military efforts to professionalize, standardize, and link the armed forces of the Western Hemisphere since World War II. But functionally it is the most visible and significant component, and its efforts to impart modern military concepts of human rights are contextually measurable as one piece in the dramatic shift towards democratization within Latin America since the late 1970s. Ironically, one of its best contributions to Hemispheric defense modernization - teaching human rights through affective educational means - is now tainted by a flood of negative, ignorant, and sensationalistic journalism, written material that will negatively influence academics until the liberal arts and the social sciences in the United States recapture the central importance of ideological neutrality that was abandoned in the late 1960s.

Non-Governmental Organizations in the human rights arena such as the Physicians for Human Rights are ideally suited to develop a close dialogue with the world's armed forces and police leaders. The dialogue must include policy and, to be sure, academic curriculum at professional schools. NGO leaders of the inclusionist tendency must come to grips with national sovereignty as an operant principle. Simply because it is a juridical concept of Western origin is not a valid basis for it to be discarded in the spirit of deconstructionism, for under its aegis most of the world's nations do, indeed, enforce human rights. The effectiveness of teaching human rights cannot be measured by any means beyond analysis of regional trends. Spooning out generic morality sermons to the developing world's best military professionals in the human rights arena is an exercise in US political hypocrisy. It uses Latin American officers as shills for a show in which the United States caters to a noisy, leftist element within its own political spectrum. Latin

American leaders will eventually refuse to send their military professionals to be scolded ceremonially over the sins of the Salvadoran Army and the South American "Dirty Wars."

Empirical analysis suggests that democratic values come in a package, that they are learned longitudinally, that human rights is a slippery concept to define, and that respect for democracy and its institutions is learned at home. The US Army School of the Americas can and should share institutional structure and functional concepts about civil-military relations with Latin American military professionals. All military and police schools throughout the world should teach human rights, not as a palliative against negative publicity but as a vital component of sustaining democracy. US policy pressure against human rights offenders should be applied through the spectrum of economic and political tools, not by using school classrooms as an ideological battleground. No other armed forces school in the world has devoted so intense an effort to human rights instruction as the US Army School of the Americas, a remarkable conclusion when one recalls that the school began as nothing more ambitious than a friendly gesture in 1946 to help Colombia and Ecuador train some soldiers in vehicular and electronic maintenance.

As new inter-American defense arrangements for the twenty-first century are designed within the Organization of the American States, military education and training must also become truly inter-American in structure. It would be self-defeating to close the doors precipitously on the School of the Americas simply because its name is identified with sensationalistic press releases trumpeting false causal linkage to human rights violators. Any newly configured inter-American military college or academy serving army, navy, air force, and police personnel should begin operations with the School of the Americas' teaching modalities and legacy. A gradual transition into a truly inter-American military networking system is thereby facilitated, with full attention to the vital dimension of a human rights curriculum in all course offerings, and in all military policy deliberations. Latin America's military and police professionals have already made important strides in the human rights arena, long unperceived in the United States, and in any event such institutional mechanisms will only work when both military professionals and elected civilian politicians in Latin America and in North America desire to have cordial civil-military relationships with responsible, informed civilians at the helm.

NOTES

* Editor's note: The US Army School of the Americas officially closed in December 2000.
1. Russell W. Ramsey, "Warriors and the Moral Codes of Battle," *Military Review* Hispanic Edition (May-June 1994), *passim*.
2. Stephen Shute and Susan Hurley (eds.), *On Human Rights: The Oxford Amnesty Lectures*. 1993 (New York: Harper Collins Publishers, 1 993). These lectures, billed as the apex of intellectual attainment on the topics show the clear inability of secular scholars to come to consistent principles terms with transcendental moral principles.

3. Edwin Lieuwen, "The Changing Role of the Military in Latin America," *Journal of Inter-American Studies* 9 July 1961), p. 780.
4. Robert N. Potash, "The Changing Role of the Military in Argentina," *Journal of Inter-American Studies* (July 1961), pp. 790-3.
5. Russell W. Ramsey, "U.S. Strategy for Latin America," *Parameters* (Autumn 1994), pp. 77-80.
6. Julio César Carasales, *National Security Concepts of States: Argentina* (New York: United Nations, 1992), pp. 20-7.
7. Roger Miranda and William Ratliff, *The Civil War in Nicaragua: Inside the Sandinistas* (New Brunswick: Transaction Publisher, 1993), pp. 271-9.
8. Brian Loveman, "Protected Democracies" and "Military Guardianship: Political Transitions in Latin America, 1978-1993," *Journal of Inter-American Studies and World Affairs,* Vol 36, No. 2 (Summer 1994). Professor Loveman is skeptical, however, that reforms will last under political or economic stress.
9. Lyle N. McAlister, "Recent Research and Writings on the Role of the Military in Latin America," *Latin American Research Review* Vol.11, No. I (Fall 1966), pp. 5-10.
10. General Barry R. McCaffrey, "Testimony of the Commander-in-Chief, U.S. Southern Command, to the Committee on National Security of the U.S. House of Representatives, March 8,1995" (Washington, D.C.: U.S. Government Printing Office, 1995), pp. 7-11; Claude C. Sturgill, *The Military History of the Third World Since 1945* (Westport, Connecticut: Greenwood Press, 1994), pp. 131-94, *passim;* and Russell W. Ramsey, *Civil-Military Relations in Colombia. 1946-1965* (Gainesville: Regents' Press, 1978), p. 64.
11. Robert A. Packenham,: *The Dependency Movement: Scholarship and Politics in Development Studies* (Cambridge: Harvard University Press, 1992); and Robert Toplin, "Many Latin Americanists Continue to Wear Ideological Blinders," *Chronicle of Higher Education* (30 March 1994), p. A4.
12. Russell W. Ramsey, "US Narcotics Addiction Wrecks Colombian Democracy, The Facts About Her Army and Her Allies," (British) *Army Quarterly & Defence Journal* (January 1990); and Russell W. Ramsey. "Reading Up on the Drug War," *Parameters* (Autumn 1995), *passim.*
13. Robert Wesson (ed.), *The Latin American Military Institution* (New York: Praeger Publisher, 1986), pp. 71-103.
14. Stephen O. Rabe, *Eisenhower and Latin America: The Foreign Policy of Anticomumnunism* Chapel Hill, University of North Carolina Press, 1988), pp.40-1.
15. Susan L. Clark, *The U.S. Army in a Civil-Military Support Role in Latin America* P-2703 (Carlisle Barracks, PA: Institute for Defense Analysis, 1992), pp.11-14.
16. Max O. Manwaring and Court Prisk (eds.), *El Salvador at War: An Oral History of Conflict from the 1979 Insurrection to the Present* (Washington,

D.C.: The National Defense University Press, 1988), pp. 234-7.
17. Tim McCarthy, "School Aims at Military Control," *National Catholic Reporter* (8 April, 1994).
18. Manwaring, *op. cit.*, pp. 444-53.
19. Roberto F. Dominguez, "Amenazas a la Paz y Fuerzas Armadas en America," ["Threats to Peace and the Armed Forces in the Americas"] *Military Review* Hispanic Edition (July-August 1994), pp. 45-7; Virgilio Rafael Beltrán, "Seguridad Hemisférica ["Hemispheric Security"] *Military Review* (Sept.-Oct. 1 992), pp. 12-1 5.
20. Michale Radu and Vladimir Tismaneanu in their 1990 book *Latin American Revolutionaries: Groups, Goals, Methods* show convincingly that Marxism and neo-Marxism were first and always European intellectual imports lacking serious roots in Latin America. Also, see Robert B. Toplin, *op. cit.*, p. A4.
21. J. Samuel Fitch, "The Decline of U.S. Military Influence in Latin America," in Lars Schoultz, William C. Smith, and Augusto Varas (eds.), *Security, Democracy, amid Development in U.S.-Latin American Relations* (1994) opines that all US military influence south of the Rio Grande during the Cold War was either neutral or negative, and therefore he lauds and welcomes its demise. For the viewpoint that US military influence may be in decline but that a roundtable needs to exist among the force commanders of all the Americas, see Geoffrey B. Demarest, "Redefining the School of the Americas," *Military Review* (Oct. 1994); and L. Erik Kjonnerod, (ed.), *Evolving U.S. Strategy for Latin America and the Caribbean* (Carlisle Barracks, Pennsylvania: U.S. Army War College, 1992).
22. Manuel Sanmiguel Buenaventura, "Factores de Perturbación de los Derechos Humanos en Colombia y el Papel del Gobierno y las Fuerzas Armadas pare su Defensa" ["Problem Factors in the Human Rights Issue in Colombia and the Role of the Government and the Armed Forces in their Defense"]. Address to the 6th Latin American Conference, U.S. Army School of the Americas, Ft. Benning, Georgia, August 7, 1994, *Military Review* Hispanic Edition, Vol. LXXV, No.2 (May-June 1995).
23. Charles Coil and Rachel Neild, "Issues in Human Rights," Paper 3 (Washington, D.C.: Washington Office on Latin America (WOLA), 1992), pp. 28-34, and Jennifer M. Taw, "The Effectiveness of Training International Military Students in Internal Defense and Development," National Defense Research Institute (Santa Monica: RAND Corp., 1993), pp. 15-22. Human rights advocates whose views are morally genuine, and not motivated by resurrecting failed revolutions in Latin America, should concentrate their actions on Eastern Europe, the Middle East, Asia, and Africa, areas in which huge sums of US security assistance money have bolstered uniformed human rights violators steadily or intermittently for half a century.

"Military Leaders and the Warrior's Code," *Military Review (Hispanic Edition)*, May – June, 1994.

Since the Age of the Enlightenment, human rights may be viewed as a concept meaning "basic standards of treatment and existence to which people are naturally entitled." Jean Jacques Rousseau believed that these spring from a transcendental natural order. John Locke emphasized that the contract was between the governed and those who govern. Thomas Jefferson expanded human rights beyond the government's guarantee of life and liberty to include the pursuit of happiness.

But long before the Enlightenment, human rights were expressed both philosophically and theologically. Sun Tsu thought that the wise and honorable warrior would treat the fallen, the weak, and the prisoner kindly. Confucius opined that the humane ruler honored himself and the kingdom. Jesus of Nazareth brought human rights to the moral peak by commanding the love of God, the love of one's fellow human being, and the application of the Golden Rule. St. Paul harmonized Greek philosophy with Christian faith, and his teachings included the role of soldiers and government in the use of force. Ambrose of Milan made the Roman Emperor Theodosius subject to Christian moral authority in the 4th century. His mentor Augustine expressed the five bases for the official use of force known as the doctrine of Just War. These statements remain today the basis for all human rights doctrine now recognized by the world's other major faiths.

In the Middle Ages, Averroes found common ground between Christian and Islamic theology. Thomas Aquinas codified Augustine's principles for the use of force in an era when political authority was in flux. Atrocities committed in God's name during the Wars of the Crusades, produced the institutionalized expression of battlefield humanitarianism, the Knights of St. John, commonly called the Hospitalers. Queen Isabella of Spain commanded humane treatment of the Moors during the Reconquest. The Spanish military orders of Alcantara, Calatrava, and Santiago often put these mandates into practice during the late Middle Ages. Charles I of Spain ordered a more humane treatment of Native Americans, following attacks against royal policy by Father Bartolomeo de las Casas.

The Dutch lawyer Hugo Grotius delineated the legal responsibilities of the government in the wake of the bloody wars of the Reformation. The Treaty of Westphalia in 1648 gave the human race its modern fundamental unit for the conduct of human affairs, the nation-state. The rise of the nation-state as a political unit having sovereignty, a bonding set of values, government, and a defined area and population opened the way for the marriage of Augustine's doctrine on the moral use of force with Rousseau's concept of natural law and Locke's contract between the nation-state and the individual. Armies and police would have exclusive control of force, but under charter and public scrutiny.

The architects of independence in Latin America were products of two great moral traditions: Catholic theology and Enlightenment philosophy. It is no accident that Manuel Hidalgo, Simon Bolivar, Jose Francisco de San Martin, Andres Bello, and Fransice de Paula Santander all stated that the duty of soldiers, acting in the name of the state, was to protect human rights.

The battlefield suffering in the US Civil War and the Crimean War produced modern military medical services and interest in human rights treaties. The contemporary expression of the medieval era's military mercy orders is the medical service branch of most armed forces, the Red Cross, and a network of humanitarian organizations. The destructive power of dynamite led scientist Charles Nobel to fund the Nobel Peace Prize when his invention was converted to weapons of mass destruction. The Geneva Conventions of 1907 were an effort by the industrialized nations to limit excessive battlefield violence as conceived long before by Augustine. Visibly useless slaughter in the trench warfare tactics employed during World War I sparked continuing international efforts to limit unnecessary violence. The Washington Naval Disarmament Conference of 1925 is an example, as is the League of Nations intervention in the 1931 Leticia dispute between Peru and Colombia.

World War II brought mass slaughter that was both technological and ideological, shocking the world once again. Among the results were the United Nations, with armed intervention mechanisms; the Geneva Conventions treaties of 1949; and the UN Charter of Human Rights. These documents are neither perfect nor universally accepted, but taken in sum they create a framework for a worldwide human rights initiative.

The Cold War brought human rights issues to a new level of international activity. Ideological justifications for violence, mass communication, new technologies, sophisticated deception, and worldwide growth of democratic participation all played big roles. As bipolar ideology fades, rabid ethnicism creates an arena for human rights violations that appears to exceed the world's mechanisms and resources for control.

Human rights as a current concept having application to the armed forces and police is really three umbrella concepts. These are: the Geneva and Hague Conventions, the UN Charter of Human Rights, and the laws and moral beliefs of nearly 200 nation-states. The agenda of rights and values in conflict produces tremendous challenges for armed forces and police commanders.

Nation-states are expected to enforce human rights as an exercise of their sovereign authority. Yet some nation-states are the origin of human rights violations, forcing the world to choose between ignoring human suffering or invading the same sovereignty that empowers nations as actors.

Human rights education and training are the obvious core of the world's quest for a moral, humane order. Yet no major world figure in the human rights arena has ever identified that cognitive learning, the realm of facts, is different from affective learning, the realm of emotions and behavior. Further, those who advocate strongly for human rights education and training of military and police professionals decline to acknowledge the obvious limitation imposed by the fact that military and police officers act under the sovereign authority of their nation-states, not as independent figures working out of an extra-national doctrine manual.

Human rights organizations and the news media play the role of Father

Bartolomeo de las Casas in our time. Yet they seldom behave with las Casas' stern commitment to evidence and written moral authority. Human rights organizations are called NGOs (Non-Governmental Organizations) in the literature, a reference to their private, non-governmental status. While some, like the Red Cross, present impartial data, others have ideological agendas and present data that are far out of proportion, or even deceitful. The news media of today are notorious for hyperbole, distortion, partisanship and sensationalism, error, and outright falsehood. Yet the armed forces and police must respond to genuine accusations of human rights, somehow accepting the damage to public confidence caused by the false accusations at the same time. And this situation works negatively upon the human rights agenda.

Armed forces in the western hemisphere today mostly follow the *posse comitatus* principle, in which armies are to be used only against foreign enemies. They therefore are subject during employment to the laws of international warfare. Police and security troops, by contrast, operate internally under the national, state, or municipal criminal codes. Differing laws, command structures, and missions create a sophisticated set of challenges in the application of human rights. Making this issue of jurisdiction and force structure ever more complicated is the frequent use of both armed forces and police troops under the flag of the United Nations, a regional organization such as the Organization of American States, or of an international coalition having UN sanction.

Armed forces and police employment squarely address the full spectrum of human rights issues. Their own actions as protectors or abusers of human beings are only one narrow sector of a wider agenda. Armed forces have installed land and sea mines during wars, removed them after wars, and acted with varying levels of responsibility about maintaining records on the location of mines. The US Army is currently involved in a constructive international dialogue about the elimination of land mines, since they are the largest single source of persistent civilian death and injury from a military weapon. Yet many nations ay they need land mines for an adequate defense against technologically superior enemies.

Another source of conflict is the question of human disasters as a major cause of suffering. Statistics suggest that these challenges are the greatest human rights issues of our era. Famine and mass migration in the African Sahel are problems so vast that only armed forces have the logistics and the security services to handle the challenge. Yet upon occasion, human disaster assistance is asked or needed from armed forces or police forces with bad human rights standards. Indeed, some of the uniformed helpers in human disasters relief are at least in part the cause of the problem. Clearly, military leaders from the responsible nations need to articulate this dilemma to legitimate civilian authorities.

Another source of conflict over human rights is the question of irregular forces. Rabid ethnic and religious militias, guerrilla and terrorist forces, and to be sure, the armed legions of the narcotics and smuggling industries are all major human rights abusers. They invent their own rules, flout international law, deceive the public with sophisticated news media manipulation, and defy both domestic and international armed authority. Often the news media give these forces apparent sympathy as a result of their own morally distorted efforts to create the aura of impartiality. NGOs sometimes even certify supposed human rights violations which are carefully staged fiction. Armed forces and police leaders must engage in strong dialogue with their political leadership and the news media to prevent loss of public confidence in the moral norms of legitimate uniformed forces.

Since proportionality is one of Augustine's five principles in the legitimate use of armed force, we can rightly question the great attention paid to human rights violations by Latin America's military and police. By rational standards of evidence, Latin America has been the world's least violent region since 1500. It has the fewest wars and the fewest deaths and collateral suffering attributable to war; the lowest percentage of money invested in arms and troops; and has recently disproved its supposed predisposition towards Marxist revolution as the Cold War fades away. It is the world's only region having no inventories of nuclear, biological, and chemical weapons. Its uniformed personnel serve by request in 12 of 23 multi-national peacekeeping operations worldwide; only one militarized dictatorship, Cuba, remains in existence. Why, then, is there more hostile literature about Latin American soldiers and police in the English language than the combined literature on all defense issues pertaining to Africa, East Asia, Eastern Europe, and the Middle East?

This question has three answers, one of them in Latin America, the other two found in North America and Western Europe. Conspicuous dictatorships in the recent Latin American experience committed human rights violations under the guise of national security in countries proclaiming constitutions that protect human rights. Since Africa, Asia, the Middle East, and Eastern Europe have little democratic history, the world holds their armed forces and police to less humane standards, a backhanded and largely unperceived compliment to Latin America. Today's Latin American military and police forces by world standards are small, professional, and useful in many roles.

The other two causes for distorted perception of human rights abuses in Latin America are external. US and Western European academics, moralists, and political leaders place the issue of Latin America and the Cold War on the liberal-conservative spectrum. Liberals refused to acknowledge the existence of armed Marxist revolutionary threats in the region, and conservatives advocated the indiscriminate arming of several dictatorships to stop the growth of communist power in the region. While a mere two percent of US military assistance programs worldwide was sent to Latin America between 1947 and 1989, both the ideological and the applied dimensions of this issue resulted in a huge body of controversial literature, much of it defamatory. Behind the liberal-conservative ideological war over Latin America and the Cold War lay the *leyenda negra* (black legend), the view in Protestant North America and Western Europe that Latin American soldiers and police are cowardly killers, not professionals. The British dictator Oliver Cromwell articulated this theory over three centuries ago for political convenience, namely to whip his country into a war sentiment against the Spanish Empire. Just as today's human rights literature is often used for exaggerated condemnation of all uniformed personnel and national security policy, so too were Father las Casas' brave reports distorted first by Spaniards and then by British enemies to create hostility against Spain's empire in America. The leftist and anti-military tendencies of many US scholars who study Latin America drive them quickly to this modern version of the Black Legend, for it affirmed as an historical process that which they wanted to affirm in the present. *Coups d'etat* in Argentina and abuse of civilians by El Salvadoran soldiers were specific criminal acts, not generalized cultural tendencies.

The Western Hemisphere has the world's most cordial military and police relationships of any large world region. The School of the Americas, first in Panama and since 1984 at Ft. Benning, Georgia, has fostered both the relationships and heightened professional standards for 47 years. The task now is clear. Armed forces and police are accorded the unique control of arms and the legal use of force in political democracies. The Cold War is over, and a new paradigm of cordiality and equality must be fostered between the armed forces and the police of the Americas. Canada is looking for a seat at the table; ways must be found for Cuba to have a seat. Panama and Nicaragua must rejoin the roundtable as soon as possible.

Human rights must be a major topic in the academic curriculum at all military and police schools in the Americas. The armed forces of Colombia, Ecuador, and Peru have model programs and procedures already in place. Civilians who can exercise public and private sector leadership in human rights must be educated in these same classrooms. Legislators and civilian executive officials must be brought into the arena. Doctrine on coalition operations, international peacekeeping, disaster relief, international law enforcement, and civil-military relations must be promulgated. Budgets must be made to support human rights training to both individuals and units; and to equip forces appropriately. Research must also be conducted on how human rights violations occur, how they can be averted, and on their financial cost. The press must be involved to a much greater extent. The NGOs must be made functional participants, not kept aside as hostile snipers. Religious leaders and educators must be regularly involved in the making and promulgation of armed forces and police training doctrine, and policy for operations having a potential for human rights problems.

By pursuing this agenda, by holding sessions like the "Armed Forces and Human Rights" conference a the School of the Americas in August of 1994, we give life to human rights as a functional set of doctrines. All who bear arms as soldiers or police are defenders of human rights because their countries have entrusted them with the means of force. The voice of Augustine calls from afar to make human rights an institutionalized reality in the Americas and throughout the world.

Russell W. Ramsey, Ph.D., D.Min.

"Assembly's Call to Close School of the Americas Challenged," *The Presbyterian Layman*, September-October, 1994.

A current myth maintains that Uncle Sam spends millions of tax dollars to train soldiers and police in Latin America for bad reasons, and that these 55,000 alumni then use this training to topple governments, murder spokesmen for the poor, and wreck the democratic process. The main instrument of this wickedness is purported to be the School of the Americas at Ft. Benning, GA. Deceived into believing this fantasy, the 1994 General Assembly of the Presbyterian Church (USA) voted 373-132 to call for the closure of the School of the Americas.

In my training for the Commissioned Lay Preacher Program of the Presbyterian Church, USA, I have been impressed with the scholarly methodology by which our denomination conducts God's work on earth. The *Book of Confessions* contains the doctrines of our Church and the *Book of Order* lays out in painstaking detail the procedures by which our beliefs may be formally changed. I was therefore disappointed to find our 1994 General Assembly conducting its business in regard to several overtures about the School of the Americas without benefit of facts, in a climate of emotionalistic piety suitable for secular political convention.

The Military in Latin America

Latin America, compared to Asia, Europe, Africa, and the Middle East, has been less warlike and less militarized since 1500 than any other world region. I have measured this in number of wars, number of people killed in wars, percent of public funds spent for arms, percent of men in military uniform, and military penetration into the civilian culture.

Latin American soldiers are negatively perceived because of the *leyenda negra*, a cruel British prejudice dating from Elizabethan times, strengthened by Oliver Cromwell, and perpetuated by intellectuals in the present under the guise of neo-Marxist thought. Under this concept, all Latin American military people are either vicious, cowardly killers, or ridiculous figures like the fat sergeant on the television series "Zorro." It is easier to say "I don't like Latin American military men" than it is to say, "I don't like Latin Americans." Most Latin American countries have public opinion polls showing support for their small, relatively benign military forces.

The Age of Gunboat Diplomacy (1890-1931) put the United States into northern Latin America as an armed peacemaker and power broker, but not into continental South America. The Cold War (1947-1989) projected the United States into Latin America militarily in two ways. Until Cuba chose sides with the Soviet Union in 1960, the United States wrongly and foolishly backed armed dictators in Guatemala, Cuba, Nicaragua, the Dominican Republic, Venezuela, and briefly Colombia, and to a lesser degree elsewhere. Once Fidel Castro developed an apparatus for projecting armed revolution, there really was an armed threat, a Cold War threat, in the region, and U.S. military assistance programs took on stronger moral validity.

From 1947-1989, about 2 percent of all U.S. military assistance worldwide, and 4 percent of foreign arms sales worldwide, went to Latin America. And throughout it all the U.S. Army was the main agent of contact with Latin American soldiers, walking a delicate line between military interference in government and needed steps to oppose armed Marxist revolutionaries. Much polarization took place, not just in Latin America but among U.S. Christians. Some tried to justify Marxist revolution as part of Jesus' compact with the poor, and some tried to justify right-wing dictators as biblically necessary. Both were wrong, and the U.S. Army walked this tightrope with skill and sensitivity.

Ideological Opposition
The little group of Maryknoll activists advocating closure of the School of the Americas is seeking vengeance for past abuses by the El Salvadoran military. These Maryknolls prey upon ignorance, myths, and the good intentions of U.S. Christians, while others serve faithfully as ordained priests. They support armed Marxist revolution by the FMLN. But the scene has changed. El Salvador is an emerging democracy, at peace; and we do not design our policies for just one country in Latin American but rather for the whole region.
The Western Hemisphere is the world's model of emerging democracy under free enterprise economics, with small, apolitical armed forces doing mostly humanitarian and public order jobs. These forces both need and benefit from the U.S. Army School of the Americas, more so now than during the Cold War. They have to fight the druglords, and all nations have a right to maintain armed forces to express their sovereignty. Many are converting their armies to national police, on the model of the Costa Rican Civil Guards. The school's annual budget is less than that of a small junior college. In return, it averts wars that cost half a billion dollars a day.

Deceived and Inconsistent
I believe that commissioners in Wichita were deceived by persons who still think Karl Marx's revolutionary tenets and Jesus' love for the poor are reconcilable. Yet if we were to close the School of the Americas for the few bad apples among it graduates, we would have to close several other institutions first. For example, Heidelberg University produced Joseph Goebbels, spiritual architect of the anti-Jewish Holocaust. Edinburgh University, that bastion of Presbyterianism, produced Lord Pamerston, architect of the Opium War against China. And Harvard graduated Admiral Yamamoto, who planned the Japanese attack on Pearl Harbor.
Heidelberg, Edinburgh, and Harvard each had several years to train their infamous graduates. By contrast, General Galtieri, who misgoverned Argentina badly and led them into the Malvinas / Falklands war, only had four weeks in a technical course at the School of the Americas, four decades before seizing power. Shall we shut down the brilliantly successful U.S. Job Corps because a few graduates became criminals? Should we label Colombian Army officers, known as world leaders in human rights circles, as moral offenders in need of sermons from

Russell W. Ramsey, Ph.D., D.Min.

U.S. Christians? They, after all, are fighting the horrible drug war created in their land by the cash from U.S. narcotics addicts.

An Invitation

The School of the Americas invites all Presbyterians to visit, to view the curriculum, to meet the students, and, most important, to witness the work done by the graduates in their own countries. I see them as professionals who try to follow God's mandates carefully; they honor us by coming here for a brief schooling experience. Other countries far less moral on military and police matters are offering them free courses. They come here precisely because we care about human rights as well as technical excellence. They sometimes ask me why U.S. Christians, who oppose prejudice, are so prejudiced against them as a class. (Currently, 10 majors and lieutenant colonels from the Command and General Staff College class are devoting their Saturdays to helping flood victims in Albany, Ga., 90 miles away, repair their flood-damaged homes).

I doubt that Presbyterians, knowing all the facts, will want to send them away.

"The US Army School of the Americas & the Presbyterian Church," 1st Presbyterian Church, Americus, Georgia, Wednesday Night Supper, September 29, 1999.

Mission Clarification
1. Teaches standard US military professional courses offered to all friendly foreign countries at US schools, but in the native Spanish language, to Latin American military and police personnel.
2. Is an executive agent of the US Department of the Army, totally under Army policy and control.
3. Is supervised on diplomatic issues by the US Department of State through its network of Ambassadors and their staffs.
4. Has carried out these policies using a mix of US and invited Latin American personnel under the knowing approval of every President and Congress since 1946.

Two Factors to Consider
1. No course was ever taught unless it had total approval of the US Department of Defense.
2. No student was ever taught, nor any policy ever supported, that did not have approval of the US Department of State.
3. Six Presidentially-approved review boards have analyzed a great detail the question of whether the school ever taught murder, torture, disappearance of political enemies, and overthrow of the civilians governments.
4. Only one former faculty member out of over 8,000 US military and 2,000 LATAM military/policy) claims that these felonious things were taught. and he has refused to name am details for federal prosecutorial agencies seeking to bring charges if warranted. He made the allegation, unsubstantiated, on national television.
5. For the allegation of teaching murder to be true, there would have to be dozens of US military personnel who came on one assignment in their lives, taught murder and torture to the Latin American students, and then went on to complete their military careers in other tasks. There would have to be a universal conspiracy of silence among some 10,000 persons from many different backgrounds, in addition to some 66,000 graduates of nearly a hundred different courses across a period of 53 years.
6. The law prohibits, rightly, that US military personnel should enter into a political fray. In this case, seven members of the US House of Representatives have made disproven felonious allegations against 8,000 US military officers and non-commissioned officers, on national television in a record that will never be expunged. There has never been a universalized attack against the integrity of the US armed forces so falsified in the 20th century, nor against the police even where guilt has been shown to exist.

Russell W. Ramsey, Ph.D., D.Min.

Why Is It Going On?
1. The Latin American military forces are universally unpopular the United States, part of the Black Legend tradition.
2. Marxist groups I the United States are generally accorded a good press because they' are exciting even if as in this case, their allegation is totally false
3. Liberation theology, based upon Luke 4:18-23 is a mainstream doctrine of the Presbyterian Church. Politicized liberation theology which pretends to canonize Marxist revolutionary doctrines with the Gospel, has been formally condemned by Pope John Paul II. It re-opens the Arian Heresy, which divides Jesus from the Trinity (homo-ousios v. hetero-ousios. sometimes written as homo-iousous v. homo-ousous the second Greek word in both cases meaning Jesus apart from God and the Holy Spirit), disapproved by the Council of Nicea in 325 and many times thereafter.
4. Democratization and privatization are the hallmarks of Latin America since 1989, but many US citizens live in the past when militaries toppled governments and economies floundered. Latin America presents accounts for 35% of all US commerce, and external commerce accounts for 30% of the dollar's value, so Latin America comprises 10% of the US dollar's value.

Conclusion

The US Army School of the Americas is and has always been a loyal component of US regional policy and is responsible for considerable improvement in governmental stability and democratic activity.

"Affective Education and Values Transference, the US Army School of the Americas," *Journal of Resources Management,* Spring, 1997.

In 1993 the School of the Americas directed me to install the Resources Management Course taught in Monterey, California at the Naval Postgraduate School. There were three cognitive challenges to be overcome, but the success of the course was found in the affective dimension that opened doors for further success in the transfer of institutional values.

The U.S. Department of Defense Resources Management Institute offers a sophisticated curriculum that is heavy on calculus, probability theory, and specialized vocabulary. The case studies deal with the selection, acquisition, and life cycle management of the multi-billion dollar technology: Navy aircraft carriers, the Air Force's F-16 fighter plane, and the Army's M-1 Abrams tank. At the applied level, contractor personnel do the creativity part and the number crunching, under the auditing, budgetary, and contract supervision of Department of Defense officers and civilians.

Students in resources management at the U.S. Army School of the Americas are majors and lieutenant colonels, plus a few colonels and career civilians, in the armed forces and police of Latin America. The armies are downsizing, the police and internal security forces are stable or increasing, the navies mostly do coast guard missions, and the air forces specialize in transportation and border surveillance missions. The School of the Americas was founded in Panama back in 1946 to provide Spanish language military courses in technical and professional subjects for the region's armies. All courses presented to the 56,000 graduates by 1993 were Spanish translations of the equivalent U.S Army service school course. Cognitive translation for the new Resources Management Course was challenging and transcended the purely linguistic dimension in order to be useful to the school's clients in the post Cold War era.

Cognitive content was built around five areas: microeconomic analysis, decision science, comparative management theory, operations analysis, and cyclical budget preparation. Second, post-graduate mathematics were reduced to algebra and probability calculation useful to professional officers who will manage contractors and engineers. Third, case studies were reduced to believable dimensions. For example, instead of measuring cost v. effects for three supersonic aircraft platforms, School of the Americas students do the same for three possible control systems to protect a border prone to crossing by narco-traffickers: a police battalion, a cavalry squadron, or a helicopter surveillance unit.

Resources management entered the U.S. military culture in the Kennedy-McNamara era and matured in the post-Vietnam era. Today, its universal application has been the salvation of U.S. defense capabilities during post-Cold War budget slashing coupled with the identification of costly new international missions. The Latin American region, with the prominent exception of Cuba since 1960, has never devoted more than an average of 2% of its gross domestic product (GPD) to military expenditures, nor averaged more than two soldiers per thousand citizens.

Russell W. Ramsey, Ph.D., D.Min.

But neither have its armed forces and police been required, save in exceptional cases like Colombia and Costa Rica, to integrate and justify their budgets publicly.

The School of the Americas wanted to transfer the values and concepts that underlie resources management, not merely teach cognitive facts. And so the affective dimension of the new Resources Management Course was to design a group budget preparation exercise and an individual student research paper. Skeptics in the military training field said it would not work. In 1961, I was an Army Captain at the U.S. Army Caribbean School in Panama, as School of the Americas was then known I was told by a Panamanian National Guard captain named Omar Torrijos that the new Kennedy-era counterinsurgency doctrines I was charged with installing at the school would not work unless the Latin American armies and police could fit the concepts into their own thinking and apply them to their own social systems. At the time, I suspected that Torrijos was arguing for breathing space within which *latino* officers could engage in a little good old fashioned *golpismo* (overthrowing of democratically elected governments). In time, I came to see that he was talking about one of the tenderest of items on the international relations menu, the transfer of values among socially powerful institutions. I remember well how thoroughly the (then) Attorney General Robert F. Kennedy discussed this point when he came down for a personal inspection of the administration's counterinsurgency teaching effort. My wife, Dr. Roberta S. Ramsey, is a special education professor and textbook author, specializing in behavioral management. From her I learned about the impressive affective methodology within special education. Affective education is the process by which society best transfers behavioral values.

Affective education in resources management may be perceived as an odd marriage of concepts by academics at the advanced centers of research, but that is exactly what was set up at the School of the Americas in 1993. Students are given governmental roles in *Patria* (fatherland), a hypothetical Latin American country, and in the governments of four neighboring countries with a lower order of democratic and economic development. Each country identifies its military and police challenges for the coming fiscal year, using artificial intelligence. This information is converted to threats; an answering strategy is then delineated for each threat. Force structures are designed to fit the strategies, always under the resources management battle cry: Distribute scarce resources among abundant alternatives; minimize costs, maximize effects.

The final goal is a statement of costs v. effects, the costs being troops, equipment, structures, and contracts, and the effects being dissuasive border defense strategies and law enforcement programs, especially anti-narcotics efforts. Built into the scenario is a human rights exercise in which a trigger happy naval officer shoots up an oil platform believed to be hiding armed terrorists. The student role players calculate a full statement of costs v. means to prevent repetition of the incident. Throughout the intensive four week course, each student researches and writes a 3,000 word paper on one of the five fields within resources management as it applies to some problem within his or her force.

In July 1993, the first Resources Management Course brought only six students from four countries. In 1994, twelve students arrived, from six countries. In 1995, there were 28 students from eight countries; in 1996, extra faculty had to found in a hurry as 52 students showed up from ten countries. Equally encouraging is the quality of these officers. One was the Auditor General of the Ecuadorian Defense Ministry. A female Lieutenant Colonel from the Colombian Air Force prepares the personnel budget for the Colombian Defense Ministry and holds her master's degree in Business Administration from the National University of Mexico. A Peruvian National Police Lieutenant Colonel is now the Chief Budget Officer in his force. Equally fruitful in support of the regional trend towards democratization, privatization, and military apoliticism are the research paper topics. "Factors in Down-sizing the Army," "Civilian Contractor Alternatives to Armed Forces Production," and "Comparative Success in Anti-Narcotics Operations Between the Army and the National Police" are three titles with interesting implications for the region's future.

In 1995, it was my new task to design a course to be called Democratic Sustainment, actually a master's level college course on civil-military relations. Selling the *posse comitatus* concept, wherein armies are prohibited from internal employment, over the *fuero militar*, under which armies are corporate institutions, is a task for affective education. It meant overcoming a five hundred year institutional history in all the regional countries save Colombia, Mexico, Costa Rica, plus a few more that were in flux during the Cold War. Wisely, U.S. State Department and Defense Department officials concurred with School of the Americas faculty that bringing some career governmental civilians from the defense ministries into the course would help anchor the *posse comitatus* concept.

The Democratic Sustainment Course, first offered in September of 1996, attracted 28 students from ten countries. The four components for this six week course are historical case studies, theological and moral foundations of democracy, juridical fundamentals of democracy, and survey of contemporary ideology and democratic governmental structure. I, a Latin American history professor, teach the case studies. An Army chaplain and an Army lawyer teach the theological and legal blocks, and Dr. Harvey Kline, Professor of Political Science at the University of Alabama, teaches the political block. Students in the pioneer 1996 course were a fascinating mixture: civilian advisors within defense ministries, war college faculty officers, unit commanders, and police academy faculty.

But solidifying values in a period of historical flux calls for affective education. Here, the lessons learned from the Resources Management Course were valuable, and authorship of the course was completely vested in School of the Americas faculty for the first time.

The four topical blocks are each presented in one week, during which the students have extensive outside reading plus their research for a 3,000 word paper. During their final two weeks, the students prepare and submit their individual research papers, also giving an oral summary to the class. But the main all-day menu calls for role playing, again in *Patria* and its regional neighbors, this time in scenarios that have produced actual regional neighbors, this time in scenarios that have produced actual regional *coups d'etat* in years past. The principal faculty serve as umpires. Decisions are weighted so that student solutions that lean toward democracy receive the go-ahead, while solutions leaning toward the arbitrary use of armed force produce some combination of internal or regional disaster.

It is premature to proclaim success or failure with the institutional transference of such complicated abstractions as division of powers, freedom of the press, economic privatization, *posse comitatus*, and observance of human rights by means of one focused course. After all, the summative political and economic structures of the region have to validate these things; they cannot be artificially imposed by the armed forces and police in what would amount to a gross distortion of roles. And the School of the Americas is merely one small, focused player in the overall Western Hemispheric movement towards fully functional democracies. Student feedback validated two important parameters. First, the teaching materials and requirements invite the student to seek innovative solutions to old problems in a safe, free environment. Second, the course comes across as a shared series of learning opportunities, not as yet another moral sermon from Uncle Sam about how to run the ship of the state.

It is my own historical thesis that Latin America's armed forces were in the process of abandoning their outdated roles brought across from Spain during the colonial era when Fidel Castro mounted a serious challenge to their governments. President John F. Kennedy proclaimed the Castro route a wrong step in the general march of the body politic towards full democracy. Colombia and Costa Rica were already advanced democracies at the time; El Salvador and Paraguay slumbered politically in the late Middle Ages; and Argentina and Chile were partially enamored, at least, with Mussolini's jack-booted corporate state. The U.S. Army, principal military tutor to the Latin American armies since 1939, was caught up in a mixed transference agenda during Castro's adventuristic era: regime defense as a strategy, and civilian control of the military as an operating policy. With the former U.S.S.R. no longer feeding the Cuban revolution's dreams of exportation, the time is right for the transference of a full panoply of democratic institutions, and for that transference to find legitimacy in cultures that for too long have been accused *a priori* by U.S. regional scholars of lacking respect for human freedom. But selling democracy or human rights as a moral sermon is just as inappropriate as the excessive arm-twisting that was done to make the Latin Americans hate or fear communism. Cultural imperialism by any other name is still arrogance, and many Latin Americans are unimpressed with North American abuse of their abundantly guaranteed freedom: credit card junkydom, pornography, and narcotics use, to name a few.

The Resources Management Course and the Democratic Sustainment Course at the U.S. Army School of the Americas are two modest, inexpensive but useful steps in helping the Latin American armed forces to find humane and accountable roles in maturing democratic structures. As the civilian scholar leading this task, I invite any scholar to write or call, hopefully to schedule a visit. The School of the Americas John B. Amos Library contains a valuable and largely unmined collection. It is a time when affective education can affect a transference of operational values, and scholars are invited to share in it.

"Military & Police Roles in Latin American Sustainable Development," *Dialogo, The Forum of the Americas*, April-June, 1999.

Sustainable development calls for the knowledgeable and integrated commitment of all social and economic sectors. [Henderson, Rockefeller] In this context, the armed forces and police of Latin America are making a moderate contribution, thus becoming a part of the reason that this region does better at sustainability than other developing regions. [Gerry]

The term "grass roots" is more than a play on words when applied to sustainable development. At La Cruz, Costa Rica, Don German Brenes Vargas operates a multi-product organic farm and serves as ex oficio mayor. For him, sustainable development has three pillars; his "3 Ps" are proteccion, progreso, and pueblo. "Protection" means caring for the earth; "progress" means that the earth's resources must be used sustainably; and "people" means that the well-being of the citizens is the ultimate objective. [Author's Field Notes]

There are six over-arching processes at work within Latin America, all of them connected to global trends. Each of them interacts with the sustainable development movement. To appraise meaningfully the role of Latin America's security forces in sustainable development, these related megatrends need to be stated, defined, and evaluated.

Most influential is the privatization movement which has ended the three decades of statist economies based on the model prescribed by Argentine economist Raul Prebisch. [Brockeft, 1 et. al.] The sustainable development model acknowledges zones of conflict between public policy and corporate profit, and between local ecological communities and the central government. The security forces are public institutions as they play out their roles. [Millett and Gold-Biss]

Another transcendental process in Latin America is the movement towards the implementation of World Trade Organization principles. [Ramsey, "Role"] Again, negotiated tariff reduction pits public against private interests, and ecological against financial interests. The security forces function in this context, too, as public institutions carrying out public policy.

Private sector financial power in weak or changing political economies tends to distort public policy decisions, and security forces are certainly not immune from these influences. [Rodriguez]

Democratic pluralization is another transcendental process in Latin America. This tends to put more voices into the political arena on such complex issues as sustainable development. [Brockett, et. al.] It also embraces a fundamental shift in regional civil-military relations, with more competing interest groups. [Millett and Gold-Biss, Rodriguez] At Cold War's zenith, over half of Latin America's armed forces operated on the *fuero militar* concept of civil-military relations, making them deliberative organs in the traditional governance concept at work in the Luso-Hispanic world. [McAlister]

A significant few, such as Colombia and Mexico, functioned on the *posse comitatus* model of civil military relations, wherein police guarantee internal order and the armed forces defend the national sovereignty, both under civilian authority. With the departure of external Cold War pressures nine years ago, Latin America's armed forces and police are constitutionally obedient and able to discharge their functions in sustainable development as policy implementers rather than as policy makers.

[Ramsey, "Role"] Latin America's force ratios and costs have hovered at 2.2 uniformed individuals per thousand and 2.3% of the Gross Domestic Product since 1945. These figures average 1.7 per thousand and 1.9% respectively since 1989, with substantial transfers of manpower, budgetary resources, and roles from the armed forces to the police. [Ramsey, "U.S. Strategy"]

Two other movements strongly influence any discussion of armed forces and police in Latin American affairs. The universal impact of human rights awareness and the implementing role of Non-Governmental Organizations are strongly tied to both sustainable development and to changing civil-military relations. [Ramsey, "Affective"] Costa Rica's Peace University offers teaching resources in human rights curriculum to public and private sectors, including contact with regional military and police leaders through U.S. security assistance channels. Ecuador's model program for human rights enforcement within the armed forces also speaks to environmental protection. [Ramsey, "U. S. Strategy"] The other trend seen throughout the region is the willingness to provide blue helmet forces for international peacekeeping. More units have been requested than the region can provide. Again, with Latin American units projected into 12 of 26 recent peacekeeper forces, issues of human rights enforcement and environmental protection co-exist.

So privatization, W.T.O. implementation, democratic pluralization, restructuring of civil-military relations, human rights awareness, and blue helmet participation all interact strongly as the Latin American security forces address sustainable development. The concept has strong historical roots in the Iberian Peninsula and in Latin America. [Barber and Ronning, Glick]

The use of soldiers in economic roles predates Christopher Columbus, stemming from Ancient Greece, the Roman Empire, and the Medieval orders of the military priesthood in Spain. These are Alcantara, Calatrava, and Santiago, organizations of friars who defended pilgrims, superintended the agricultural re-population of Spain during the Reconquest, and sometimes fought as shock troops. [Ramsey, "Spanish;" and Van Wees]

Soldier-builders were common in the armies of Louis XIV of France. President Thomas Jefferson initiated the use of soldiers as economic infrastructure pioneers in the expanding U.S. West. [Glick] Latin Americans modernized the concept of soldiers as builders in the late 1940s under the term "civic action," first fielded by Colombia. [Barber and Ronning] Civic action is not military industry, a concept mostly abandoned now in Latin America as Raul Prebisch's nationalistic economic structures wither and fade. Civic action, properly done, means the use of soldiers under civilian authorization to do a useful economic task that civilian companies or agencies cannot do, either because of danger, remoteness, or because the armed forces are the only institutions that have the right equipment and trained personnel.

[Ramsey, "Role"]

Chile's National Environmental Council, since 1995, is composed of 14 Cabinet-level officers, only one of whom is military, and all civic-action projects with an environmental orientation require majority approval plus legislative funding approval.

With this foundation, we can identify six current military and police roles which allow activities in sustainable development. These are: many civic action projects, most disaster relief missions, all policing of resources, some policing of the population, education of military and police personnel, and good environmental practice by the forces. In some years these activities add up to a third or more of the total military and police budgetary expenditures.

An example or two of each function will illustrate. Roads built in the altiplano of Peru by Army engineers linked the indigenous population to markets, medical care, and police protection for the first time. Ecuadorian soldiers in 1994 extinguished a rash of underground fires in the Galapagos Islands, thus saving the green migratory sea turtle population.

Colombian and Mexican soldiers have rescued citizens from massive earthquakes recently, while simultaneously helping them erect safe structures. Brazilian soldiers have saved hundreds of indigenous people from death at the hands of plundering loggers who kill the rain forest dwellers and steal the logs. As a by-product, many trees were also saved. All five Central American countries have developed small forest ranger units within the police to cut down on poaching, illegal timber harvesting, and forest fires. Environmental education programs for soldiers, sailors, airmen, and police are in operation from northern Mexico to Patagonia. An interesting variant on this trend was agribusiness and bio-technology training for both ex-guerrillas of the FMLN and for demobilized soldiers in El Salvador under the 1990 peace accords. Some functions fulfill multiple roles. When the Colombian Army eliminates a rural cocaine processing center, they protect the people from murder and extortion by the narco-thugs, they end the river polluting caused by dumping toxic wastes during the refinement process, and they help the *campesinos* to resume legitimate agriculture.

Saving the environment while simultaneously expanding the economy is a compromise of goals called sustainable development. Costa Rica builds much of its Gross Domestic Product on this concept. [Author's Field Notes] With Cold War external tensions removed and greatly restructured civil-military relations now in place, Latin America's armed forces and police, acting under civilian authority, are making a quiet contribution to sustainable development in six of their functional areas. Don German Brenes Vargas of Costa Rica sees the security forces in this context as protecting the earth, facilitating the sustainable exploitation of resources, and ensuring the well-being of the people. His "3 Ps" proteccion, progreso, and pueblo thus unite the operant paradigms for constructive civil-military relations and for sustainable development in the region.

Russell W. Ramsey, Ph.D., D.Min.

"The Democratic Sustainment Course at the US Army School of the Americas," *Dialogo, The Forum of the Americas,* Fall, 2000.

Most US citizens know that their armed forces are governed by elected civilians, whose overall policies are accepted and carried out loyally by the senior military hierarchy. Intuitively, if not cognitively, most citizens know that the Armed Forces defend the nation against its foreign enemies, while the police protect the domestic population against crime, a concept in civil-military relations known historically as *posse comitatus*.[1] Latin America, colonized by Spain and Portugal over a century before the British colonized North America, inherited a medieval concept of civil-military relations known as corporatism. It featured the armed forces and police as independent, deliberative bodies. The legal structure behind this arrangement came to be called the *fuero militar*, which translates loosely as "the military institution making its own laws and governing itself from within." This system was structurally the same as the artisans' guilds in Europe but politically more sensitive because the legitimate means of violence were lodged monopolistically within one corporate institution.[2]

A few Latin American countries adopted the North American civil-military relations structure early in their national existence; Colombia, Uruguay, and Costa Rica are three. But the majority of Latin American countries abandoned the corporatist model of civil-military relations in favor of the North American civil-military relations model during the 1970s and 1908s, the very time when several Latin American countries engaged their small armed forces against leftist insurgents who were armed, supplied and trained by Cuban guerrilla cadres, who were in turn supported by the Soviet Union.[3]

Modest but continuous quantities of US Security Assistance Program money were allocated to the professional development of these same armed forces engaged in combating armed domestic subversion. US policy was often criticized for its tendency to foster the continuation of the outmoded corporatist military structure, since fighting a communist-sponsored insurgency and simultaneously shifting to civilian control of the military became conflicting goals at times.[4]

In early 1961, President John F. Kennedy feared that Cuba's Premier Fidel Castro would sponsor a series of guerrilla wars in Latin America, putting at risk his imaginative, "Alliance for Progress" framework of US assistance for democratization and economic development. To this end, he dispatched then Attorney General Robert F. Kennedy to the US Army Caribbean (USARCARIB) School, in the Panama Canal Zone, where standard US military doctrine courses had been offered in Spanish for Latin American military and police personnel since 1946. The USARCARIB School then added the Counter Guerrilla Operations Course, developed at the US Army Special Warfare Center in Ft. Bragg, North Carolina, to its course offerings, placing the US Security Assistance Program in support of armies and paramilitary forces engaged in domestic combat operations, against revolutionary sectors of their own populations who enjoyed Cuban subversive support.[5]

As the pilot project officer for this Counter-insurgency endeavor, I saw quickly that some, not all, of the Latin American military officers could not effectively apply the US Army doctrines because they were answering to a civil-military command relationship that made the Armed Forces politically deliberative in several sectors, sometimes connected directly to an authoritarian chief of state who depended upon their loyalty in order to govern. As part of the overall course development process. I prepared a memorandum recommending that the Latin American officers be offered a structural and functional course in civil-military relations, showing them the difference in national command authority.

The purely political aspect of this issue, however, was taken on by the US Department of State as an overall part of the Alliance for Progress reforms. In that era, several Latin American constitutional regimes were only partial democracies, and were at the same time fighting for their very existence against insurgents both domestic and foreign. So the USARCARIB School taught the Law of Land Warfare, a mandatory curriculum block that was presented to both US and foreign military students throughout the system in those days and commonly called "Geneva Convention" classes. In addition, the USARCARIB School sponsored extensive social programs for its Latin American students, activities designed to expose them to the US democratic way of life.[6]

In 1963, the USARCARIB School at Panama was renamed the US Army School of the Americas, and in 1984 it was moved to Ft. Benning, Georgia, as partial compliance under 1979 Carter Torrijos Treaties with Panama. The collapse of the Soviet Union in 1990 was accompanied by leaps forward into full political democracy in several Latin American countries, and the early 1990s saw the peace accord process succeed in war-torn Central America. A frustrated group of leftwing activists selected the US Army School of the Americas, by now totally engaged in the professional underwriting of democratization and privatization throughout the hemisphere, as the target of opportunity around which to salvage a leftist coalition in the United States by falsely accusing the School of the Americas of being the cradle for human rights abuses during the civil strife recently ended.[7]

In 1992, I returned to the School of the Americas as its new home in Ft. Benning. this time as Professor of Latin American Defense Studies and tasked to develop new professional courses that would support, within the military and police sectors, modernizing trends well under way in the political and economic sectors. In the fall of 1994, I proposed a curriculum of civil-military structural and functional studies, to be taught at the post graduate level via the seminar and case study mode. Since there is no single US Arms' course on this topic, the Western Hemisphere Affairs Bureau, US Department of State, agreed to act as mentor and approving authority for the course. First offered in 1996, the course has now completed four annual iterations with an average attendance of twenty-two students representing an average of nine different countries per iteration and thirteen countries, in total, which have sent students.

The Democratic Sustainment Course is conducted during a six week time block, in six phases that partially overlap.[8] Students are a mix of military officers and civilian officials representing the executive and legislative branches of their governments. I teach about one week of civil-military relations through the historical case study seminar method: Ancient Rome, medieval Spain, colonial New Granada, Spanish Civil War, modern Colombia, and the Philippines. Dr. Harvey Kline, Chairman of Political Science and Director of Latin American studies at the University of Alabama, teaches a week of seminars on current ideologies and governmental structures within the Latin American region. The US Army School of the Americas Staff Judge Advocate, a post graduate educated military lawyer, teaches a week of seminars on the juridical underpinnings of civilian control of the military, and the human rights issues which emerge from that structure. The US Army School of the Americas Chaplain, also holding post graduate credentials beyond seminary training, teaches a week of seminars on the moral functions of civil-military relations and human rights.

The final week of the course is dedicated to playing the "Patria" ("Fatherland") Game, an exercise in which the students pretend to be the leadership figures of five small countries in different stages of political and economic development. A series of events challenges their civil-military structure, and umpire decisions reward those choices which favor civilian control of the military and punish decisions which advocate more militaristically determinative solutions. Concurrent with these five phases, each student researches and writes an analytical paper on some aspect of emerging civil-military relations. Some prepare fascinating reports on structural changes within their own countries; others write about a different country or a topical theme of a specific country. At every possible step throughout the course, the seminar process and classroom discussion in small groups are employed in place of the large group lecture format.

Guest speakers for this course have included some of the most distinguished academic and governmental figures in the Western Hemisphere. Dr. Dan Papp, an international relations professor at the Georgia Institute of Technology ("Georgia Tech") in Atlanta, lectures on the strategic flash points that occur during the democratization and privatization process. Dr. Carlos Murillo, Dean of the Costa Rican EARTH University, a distinguished agribusiness institution, has lectured on educational foundations for democratic citizenship. Dr. Francisco Alves, a history professor at the Londrino University in Brazil, has lectured on civil-military relations in that South American giant. Diplomats representing the United Nations and the Organization of American States have discussed building exercises in the Western Hemisphere undertaken by their respective bodies.

Latin American priests with field experience in the region have discussed such sensitive themes as liberation theology and the movement in evangelical Protestantism. Care is taken to insure that students hear the case for the spiritual version of liberation theology, advocated by the Bishop Gustavo Gutierrez of Peru, as well as the political version of this concept, condemned by Pope John Paul II in 1991 and again in 1993. US Department of State speakers with high profile Hemispheric positions have discussed the US "democratization policy within the region." Professor William Banks, distinguished professor of international human rights at Syracuse University, has lectured on the United Nations Universal Declaration of Human Rights and its implications for civil-military relations.

Who are the students? The eighty-seven students who attended the first four course iterations between 1996 and 1999 include military and police officers in the middle and upper management sectors, plus civilians from the defense ministries and associated agencies. A sampling by position title includes the Argentine advisor on civil-military structure to the Minister of Defense, the Uruguayan Director of Agricultural Assistance, the Chilean Advisor to the Minister of Defense on Juridical Affairs, the Colombian Army's Chief Instructor on Human Rights, the Costa Rican Dean of Curriculum at the Civil Guard Cadet Academy, and the Human Rights Violations Monitor for the Archbishop of Guatemala.

A sample of the course research paper titles produced to date is instructive, especially since several have been published or are under translation prior to publication. A Colombian officer wrote on the structural impact of the drug war and its corrupting influences on the civil-military relations structure. A Peruvian Officer wrote on the Army's human rights training program and its implications for civil-military relations. An Argentine officer wrote on the 1988 reform laws which create the current civil-military context there. Several Costa Rican Civil Guards officers and civilians have written on the elimination of the Army in favor of one centralized national security force, and the ensuing civil-Civil Guard relations.

What ultimate national US objective does this course serve? It provides a small pool of highly educated persons in critical military and civilian defense positions who can speak across the previous yawning chasm to legislators, church officials, leaders of the private economic sector, and diplomats. There probably is little measurable, short-term payoff from the course. But on a long-range basis, these personnel are planting the seeds of modern civil-military relations that were long ago nourished within the United States by George Washington, Thomas Jefferson, Joel R. Poinsett, Abraham Lincoln, Theodore Roosevelt, Leonard Wood, Franklin D. Roosevelt, and Harry S. Truman. The ultimate civil-military mix across the greatly democratized and economically developed Latin American region in the coming century, however, will display a variety of possibilities, some of them not currently in existence anywhere. There will be traces of great Latin American civil-military visionaries, such as liberators Simon Bolivar and Jose de San Martin, Manuel Belgrano (Argentina), Diego Portales (Chile), Jose "Pepe" Figueres (Costa Rica), and Alberto Lleras Camargo (Colombia).

There will exist a functional engagement between those who make, administer, and adjudicate the laws, and those who defend the national sovereignty, from Canada to Patagonia.[9] The Democratic Sustainment Course at the US Army School of the Americas is part of the human machinery by which the US policy of engagement for democracy and economic development is helping to create a Western Hemisphere free of wars and poised for social advancement in the coming century.

NOTES

1. Russell F. Weigley, *The American Way of War*, 1977, p. 40-42.
2. Lyle N. McAlister, "Recent Researching and Writings on the Role of the Military in Latin America." *Latin American Research Review*, Fall, 1966, pp. 25-28..

3. Timothy P. Wickham-Crowley, *Guerrillas and Revolution in Latin America*, 1992, pp. 5-8.
4. Lars Schoultz, *National Security and United States Policy Toward Latin America*, 1987, pp.324-330.
5. Russell W. Ramsey, "A Military Turn of Mind: Educating Latin American Officers," *Military Review,* August 1993, pp. 12-13.
6. "Catalogue of Courses," USARCARIB School, Ft. Gulick (Panama) Canal Zone, 1960-1963.
7. John T. and Kimbra L. Fishel, "The Impact of an Educational Institution on Host Nation Militaries," *passim*, 1997.
8. "Catalogue of Courses," US Army School of the Americas, Ft. Benning. Georgia, 1996-1999.
9. William J. Clinton, *A National Security Strategy for a New Century,* 1997, pp. 8-9, 25-26.

Review of: *Security Cooperation in the Western Hemisphere: Resolving the Ecuador-Peru Conflict*, **by Gabriel Marcella and Richard Downes, Boulder, CO: Lynne Rienner, 1999. Reviewed in: Parameters,** *Journal of the US Army War College*, **Winter, 1999-2000.**

Professors Gabriel Marcella of the US Army War College and Richard Downes at the University of Miami North-South Center combine efforts here as editors and partial authors of a classic in the literature of conflict resolution. The preface by Ambassador Luigi R. Einaudi, US Special Envoy for the Ecuador-Peru Conflict, 1995-1998, certifies the precision of the diplomatic issues and traces the excellent military diplomacy described in the book. The introduction, by Marcella and Downes, is arguably the most complete and objective short summary yet written on the Ecuador-Peru border dispute.

David Scott Palmer, professor of international relations at Boston University, surveys the search for conflict resolution in Chapter 1. Under the Rio Protocol of 1942, following Peru's 1941 armed foray into the disputed zone, the United States, Argentina, Brazil, and Chile sponsored the overall peace process, but Ecuador and Peru were named guarantors of the eventual boundary determination process. Palmer concludes that the Organization of American States (OAS) was willing to broker a peace, but that Ecuador and Peru felt that the four overall guarantors named in 1942 could move faster to resolve the crisis. He further opines that without the military diplomacy achieved under the Military Observer Mission to Ecuador and Peru (MOMEP), the January-February 1995 crisis might never have been resolved.

Colonel Glenn R. Weidner, US Army, was US Contingent Commander of MOMEP, working under General Barry McCaffrey, Commander-in-Chief, US Southern Command. In Chapter 2, Weidner describes the incredibly complex command structure, with a Brazilian general as overall coordinator. The four-point work plan created and carried out seems simple and logical: preparatory work, supervision of cease-fire, separation of forces, and demilitarization/demobilization. But as Weidner lays out the competing forces and actors, the reader comes to see that bringing this plan to fruition was a miracle in military diplomacy. One example of this was US Southern Command's insistence on the immediate creation of a demilitarized zone as a precondition for operations, possibly driven by the Clinton Administration's Somalian disaster just weeks before. The Brazilian coordinator, Lieutenant General Candido Vargas de Freire, and MOMEP both thought that a demilitarized zone should be the sought-for end state, with MOMEP in the meanwhile moving directly to separate forces in the conflict zone.

In Chapter 3, Adrian Bonilla, Deputy Director, Latin American Faculty of Social Studies, Ecuador, evaluates the conflict resolution process from the Ecuadorian viewpoint. His overall conclusion is optimistic. In Chapter 4, Enrique Obando, a Peruvian professor of national security studies, evaluates the conflict resolution process from the Peruvian side. He details the huge military cost to Peru of the conflict, just under $100 million (US), and blames Ecuador for the January 1995 attack.

Russell W. Ramsey, Ph.D., D.Min.

Patrice Franko teaches economics and international studies at Colby College in Waterville, Maine. Her Chapter 5 presents a strategic survey of military downsizing on the South American continent. She reaches the conclusion that the downward trend in the regional arms race is better served by citizen appeal to each country's legislative body, rather than by arbitrary denials of US security assistance. Eliezer Rizzo de Oliveira is professor of political science at the University of Campinas in Sao Paulo, Brazil. His Chapter 6 surveys Brazilian diplomatic leadership in the 1995 Ecuador-Peru crisis, concluding that it led Brazil and the OAS into stronger roles in conflict prevention.

Edgardo Mercado Jarrin, former Prime Minister, Foreign Minister, War Minister, and army commander in Peru, argues in Chapter 7 that Ecuador was responsible for the "War in the Cenepa." While he considers the post-1995 era the most hopeful for conflict solution negotiations, he warns that Peru can resume an armed posture or even invade Ecuadorian military bases if negotiations fail. David Mares, who teaches political science at the University of California in San Diego, presents in Chapter 8 the results of public opinion polls taken after the 1995 conflict. He concludes that Ecuador must concede more than Peru if the long-standing border conflict is to be solved. Bertha Garcia Gallegos, Director of InterAmerican Studies at the Catholic Pontifical University in Quito, Ecuador, repeats in Chapter 9 an old Ecuadorian theme that the 1942 Protocol was unjust to Ecuador and "inexecutable," but she holds out future regional social and economic development as the way to end the "culture of conflict" between both countries.

Finally, Marcella and Downes conclude with an insightful analysis of Latin American military diplomacy in the context of the 1995 MOMEP effort. They bravely venture a long-term solution for the Ecuador-Peru border conflict.

Four conclusions emerge here. First, the total MOMEP process was a diplomatic event of universal importance that would have been, were the major US news media more attuned to strategic analysis and genuine mechanisms for peace, a "top ten" event of 1995. The MOMEP process, with coordinated civilian and military diplomacy, is a paradigm for successful peace operations. Building hemispheric military-to-military contacts pays off in conflict resolution. Second, this book joins an elite body of diplomatic literature with such works as Manley O. Hudson's *Verdict of the League* (Boston: World Peace Foundation, 1932), an account of the League of Nations peace process in 1932 for the Leticia border conflict between Peru and Colombia. Third, the valiant shuttle diplomacy of Luigi R. Einaudi in this matter places him in a league with Joel R. Poinsett, US Minister to Mexico, in the tumultuous years before the US-Mexican War, and with William Walker, US Ambassador to El Salvador in the early 1990s when the civil war was winding down. Fourth, the military diplomacy both performed and then witnessed in this book by Colonel Glenn R. Weidner places him in an elite group with the stalwart life-saving action of (then) Lieutenant Colonel Douglas MacArthur at Veracruz, Mexico, in 1914; US Navy Captain Edward L. Beach, Sr., at Port-au-Prince, Haiti, in 1915; and General Matthew B. Ridgway at Bogotá, Colombia, in April 1948.

This book and its protagonists should be part of any foreign relations discussion in the United States addressing where conflict is likely to occur.

ABOUT THE AUTHOR

Russell W. Ramsey, Ph.D., D. Min. is Graduate Professor of Hemispheric Security Studies for Norwich University and Troy State University. He is the nation's longest-standing and most published scholar who analyzes the Latin American military and police forces, plus regional security issues. His philosophical outlook differs with standard ideological interpretations; he has military and national security service against which to measure his academic analysis of the Hemisphere; and his writings are offered here in their original published form, unedited, so that the reader can evaluate them against the events occurring at the date of original publication. Ramsey lectures at academic conferences frequently and directs his own Conference series at the Western Hemisphere Institute for Security Cooperation, Ft. Benning, Georgia.

CPSIA information can be obtained at www.ICGtesting.com
Printed in the USA
LVOW06s1922071213

364249LV00003B/251/A